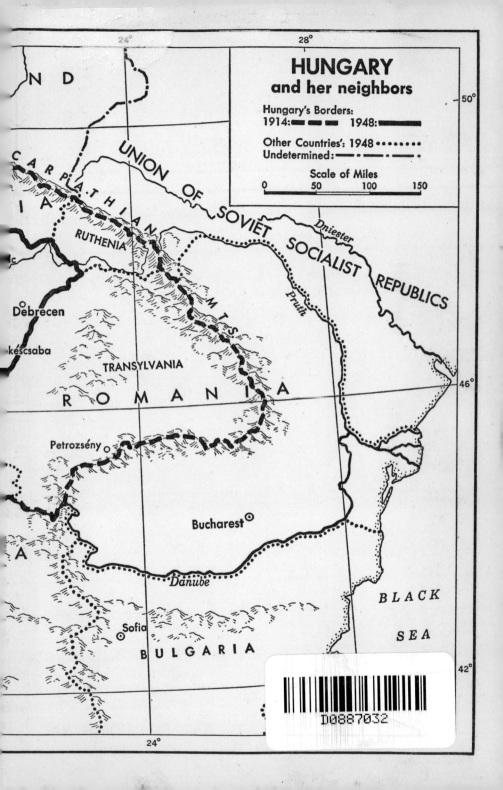

HUNGARY
and her neighbors

Hungary's Borders:
1914: ▰▰▰ 1948: ▰▰▰▰

Other Countries': 1948 ••••••••
Undetermined: ▰•▰•▰•▰•

Scale of Miles
0   50   100   150

N D

24°

28°

50°

UNION OF SOVIET SOCIALIST REPUBLICS

CARPATHIAN

IA

RUTHENIA

Dniester

Debrecen

késcsaba

MTS.

Pruth

TRANSYLVANIA

R O M A N I A

46°

Petrozsény

Bucharest

A

Danube

BLACK

SEA

Sofia

BULGARIA

42°

24°

The Struggle Behind the Iron Curtain

THE MACMILLAN COMPANY
NEW YORK · BOSTON · CHICAGO · DALLAS
ATLANTA · SAN FRANCISCO
MACMILLAN AND CO., Limited
LONDON · BOMBAY · CALCUTTA · MADRAS
MELBOURNE
THE MACMILLAN COMPANY
OF CANADA, Limited
TORONTO

THE STRUGGLE

BEHIND

THE IRON CURTAIN

By FERENC NAGY
FORMER PRIME MINISTER OF HUNGARY

Translated from the Hungarian by
STEPHEN K. SWIFT

NEW YORK

THE MACMILLAN COMPANY

1 9 4 8

I am a man of peace.
God knows how I love peace. But I hope I shall never
be such a coward as to mistake oppression for peace.

—Louis Kossuth

Preface

TO THE COURAGE AND DEVOTION OF THOSE VAST MULTITUDES OF COMMON people the world over, who live in the shadow of fear, these pages are dedicated.

Their substance is living history—events cruelly chiseled into the hearts of mankind. The course of a nation is reflected by the life of an epochal generation; its social symptoms evince the philosophy behind the major political issues.

The fate of the countries bordering on the Soviet Union weighs heavily on the mind of everyone, everywhere, and affords reason for caution. These pages cast light on the process by which, after the defeat of one peace-shattering tyrant, a new tyranny arose, using similar tools and methods to further its insidious growth in our civilized society by first subjugating the small nations of the world. The Communist determination ·to conquer has a deadly analogy in the recent past.

The defeated dictatorship uprooted the concord and peace of the human race, sowing tears and anguish for millions and bringing ruin to the monuments to man's creative genius. The danger to humanity from the rising dictatorship is no less.

By birth and breeding I am a peasant. My family's means did not prepare me to rise above the level of our tradition; without the benefits of formal education and that preparatory concourse with great statesmen which fits the leader for his tasks, the hand of destiny fell upon my shoulder.

Forever I remained in spirit and in thought with the peasantry, to which I am proud to belong. My life was their life, my battles were their battles; my victories, theirs. Imbued with the perennial desire to strike against tyranny, the people of Hungary are the protagonists of this book, represented in my personal history to the extent that I was chosen to represent them in actuality.

By his occupation and mode of life, the Hungarian peasant is deeply

vii

committed to the cause of peace. For generations, he has been called from his quiet pursuits to defend Western civilization; again and again he has returned, however decimated, to his native soil to beat his sword into a ploughshare.

My political thought was never apart from his. I did as an individual what my people would have done had they been one man. From early youth I struggled to raise the level of a people to whom progress had been denied. I wanted them to grow in culture, in prosperity, and in bodily health. No healthier spirit lives than that in the rough frame of the peasant, branded by the burdens of his arduous tasks to provide the necessities for human survival.

The peasants represent the spiritual and material force behind man's democracy; my inspiration has been the dream to see them free and independent.

In pursuing this goal I had to face powers of might; battle against the lords of the manor, against the strangling tentacles of despotic capital, and against the whole muster of bureaucracy from village elder to head of government.

Had this goal been realized, Hungary could not have been rushed into war; even as the victim of a dictatorship it could have resisted becoming its accomplice.

At the unvoiced command of my people, I fought the National Socialist ideology and its political onslaught which upset the peace of mankind. Persecution and prison became my lot.

That great part of humanity to which the Hungarian people belong, both spiritually and politically, became the victor. Upon the complete defeat of Nazi tyranny I hoped that, in the resurrection of the world, my people would not be suppressed. I hoped the peasant would reap the fruits of his thousand-year-long struggle and eternal valor. History placed me, shouldering a heavier burden than I desired in defense of my people's interest, where I had to bear the brunt of opposing forces by leading the silent struggle for the social concept and economic order of the Hungarian against the alien ideology fostered by one of the world's greatest powers, the Soviet Union.

Although my people and I stood firm by those rights to which we became heir, it was an uneven fight. After two and one-half years of unbearable pressure, being undermined from within and strangled from without, we broke. The first wave of the deluge of the new tyrany engulfed us; singlehanded, no small nation could stem the tide.

The peasant remains because he cannot leave his soil. But the wave swept over me, casting me, spent, on the shore of that country to which all humanity looks for resurrection.

In 1944–1945 two conquerors came successively to Hungary. First the Nazi scourge of occupation overran us in the dark of night, subduing the government and the unwilling citizens at point of gun, pressing the last drops of blood from Hungarian life to further its sinister war aims in a desperate hour. After it came the Soviet armies. The Hungarian nation welcomed them as liberators, and suffered them as conquerors.

The simple loyalty of the Hungarian reaped no reward. Amidst hunger and pestilence, terror and brutality, discomfort and poverty, and with the cries for mercy of their wives and daughters in their ears, the people of Hungary began to build a new state.

Upon the Hungarian, abandoned by his spiritual kin, an unnatural alliance was forced—a partnership with Communism, the greatest enemy of his traditional form of life. Beginning reconstruction of national life in concert with the Communists, Hungary at the same time had to defend herself against the new "partners." The slogans of a year before were exchanged for new ones; the new Soviet terror replaced that of National Socialism.

The independence of the Hungarian nation was proclaimed by the Soviet Union; the citizen took this seriously and in good faith while the Comintern actually began undermining it. And when the Hungarian people wanted to live with this independence and exercise it, the Soviet regarded these acts as aggression.

With the armistice agreement, Hungary was enslaved by an occupation force which brought in its wake the Communist party, an allpowerful political force and the dictator of progress. It eliminated from the administration every worth-while, upstanding man of experience. It prevented Hungary from pursuing the war against the Nazis. It piled revolutionary institutions upon the breaking back of Hungary, and forced its people to laud the Soviet continuously. It placed an armed Communist police by the side of the citizen to watch his every move; it increased the concentration camps, forcing jurisdiction from the hands of courts respected for integrity and placing it with elements intent on revenge. It forced into Communist-dominated bodies all classes of society except the peasantry. It branded any democratic manifestation as reactionary. It barred the nation from realizing its peace aims and diverted the people from its natural and normal stream of life.

More base, even, than the terror of the Communist party were the open and clandestine acts of the Soviet government itself. And thus the political constellation of the world wrote the most tragic chapter in Hungarian history, the costly experience in appeasing Soviet Russia.

Soviet generals ordered the first so-called Parliament convened according to their own design, and all but appointed the first cabinet. Their troops gorged themselves at the expense of a starving people. The Soviet Union turned the Allied Control Commission into its own agency, denying a voice to the two great Western powers sharing control.

It swallowed blameless leaders, statesmen and officers in dead of night, never to be heard from again. Its trained agents barnacled the nation as leaders of the Communist party. It interfered constantly with the creation of national defense and forced the army to become a Communist unit. It forged the Potsdam agreement into chains for our economic slavery; and forced Hungary, by this stranglehold, into unequal economic collaboration. It coerced the democratic parties, through these economic claims, to yield to the Communists. It tried to force a common ticket on the chosen political parties, to still the voice of democracy. It ordered the all-powerful portfolio of the Minister of the Interior granted to the Communists. It interfered with tranquil government within the cabinet by giving secret support to the Communist ministers. It decided who could be appointed in the cabinet and who must be dismissed. Its armed terror dictated the direction and pace of agrarian reform. It ordered hundreds of thousands of citizens uprooted and expelled because of their ancestry. It barred us from establishing desirable diplomatic relations. It prevented Hungary from giving insight into its economic affairs to the great Western powers which were desirous of helping. Its insistence resulted in the dissolution of the religious organizations. It always forced through the desires of the Communist party during political crises. It prevented humane laws from going into effect. Its direct inspiration and support prevented the so-called conspiracy from having a fair day in court. It abducted the revered Béla Kovács. It at last perpetrated the putsch which eliminated me from the premiership of my country and forced me into exile.

Thus events themselves indict the Union of Soviet Socialist Republics; the world must pass judgment. Penetration completed, today there is no breath, no motion, no life, in Hungary without Soviet direction or approval.

These appearances have been duplicated in all of Eastern Europe, a part of the world has become dark, impenetrable; where, behind the outward quiescence, a bitter ideological struggle rages against the new tyranny.

Were this the end of the black story, there would be no need to spotlight it. But Communist imperialism is an advancing process of penetration, not content with constricting the countries nearest its borders; shrouded in a pseudo ideology, the red snake inches from its pit in the east in a deadly attempt to poison the emotions of the civilized world.

By its very nature, it cannot stop. It has been said that a dictator is like a bicyclist; he may only move forward, if he stops, he falls. The course of dictatorship is irreversible—it must continue on the road of conquest paved by its agents in every country.

Only those who have fled before lava, prairie fire, and flood can convey their terror. I too have had to seek shelter from a dynamic force which threatens the concord of humanity and its highly developed form of life; threatens that political structure which, through the struggles and vicissitudes of thousands of years of human society, has developed into the highest form of social expression—democracy.

I stand on free soil. But unless I voice the warning that weighs on the hearts of people everywhere I shall not regard my obligation to those less fortunate than I, as discharged.

By the grace of destiny, democracy shall yet embrace the world.

Contents

Part III: Coalition: Its Life and Crises

Part IV: "Conspiracy"

CHAPTER 1

My Childhood

FEW PEOPLE HAVE EVER HEARD OF MY BIRTHPLACE, BISSE. A VILLAGE
of barely six hundred souls in southern Hungary, nestling in the low
hills of Baranya County near where the Drava meets the Danube, its
families are mighty proud of the fact that some of the ancient yellowed
parchments of the thirteenth century make mention of it. Always its
people have been poor peasants, most of whom worked on the neighboring baronial estates. Nevertheless, the village elders speak proudly of
its enlightened past. The records show that in 1848, when liberalism
swept over Europe and bondage was abolished, the lord of the hereditary
estate was a Count Batthyány; his ancestors were undoubtedly progressive, for centuries earlier they permitted the villagers to join the Protestant communion and freely exercise the reformed faith.

The history of the village is the history of its families. The Balogs,
Nagys, Szabos, Szekereses, Vastags, and Vajdas reach back as far as
the Middle Ages, and when the first birth-and-death register of the local
Presbyterian church was begun, two hundred years ago, it started with
their extensive family trees. Every one of these families lives where
its ancestors did and tills the soil its ancestors did hundreds of years ago.

In Bisse, every one is a peasant. The two learned men, the preacher
and the schoolteacher, are not regarded as exceptions for they receive
part of their income from the small acreage deeded to their positions
centuries ago. Even this small income forms a vital part of their subsistence.

The only two craftsmen in the village are a blacksmith who repairs
the tools and a shoemaker who mends and sews the footwear. More
craftsmen could not make a living. Even these two consider themselves
as peasants, for when harvest time arrives they close their shacks and
hire themselves out to work in the fields of the more well-to-do. Thus,
they insure their maintenance during the winter months.

Over the hills and valleys surrounding the village spread the fields and the meadows of the peasants. The golden wheat meets the maize, and the barley field borders on sugar beets. From the meadows comes the fodder. Although the steep hillsides are full of vineyards, little of the wine is grown for sale.

Small buildings dot the hillside. These are the wine houses where everybody vies with his neighbor to age a better-tasting wine. But the cellars, as they are called, also serve for get-togethers where the owners keep open house for sampling. Such a gathering generally begins with a discussion of local political questions. Then they joke, laugh, and finally settle down to sing old Hungarian peasant songs, and the valley echoes with the beautiful melodies till the wee hours. Since there is no theater, movie, or club in the village, these evenings are the highest form of social expression.

The single village saloon is dark and empty except on Sunday afternoon, when the men meet and sit around, playing cards; for, just to drink, they prefer the vineyards, where no one takes money for wine.

The work of tilling the soil from dawn until sunset weighs heavily on the people. No one tells them how much to work, but they toil until their aching muscles call the time. The relentless labor silences the joyous voice; heavy, plaintive gloom clouds good humor except when good friends gather in the vineyards for a glass of wine.

Trained by tradition, the peasant of Bisse is master of many skills. He is in sharp contrast to the American farmer, who is able to devote himself to a single crop. The man of Bisse must know how to breed cattle, how to raise crops, how to tend the dairy, how to treat the wine, how to nurse fruit trees, how to care for a vegetable garden, and how to fell trees. Having mastered all these tasks, he must also know how to turn the products to use for the family and the community. The peasant of Bisse sours cabbage in the fall so that his family will have a vegetable during the winter; when the heavy snow blankets the countryside the time to slaughter the pigs comes around, and he finds himself a butcher well versed in the smokehouse, for it is important to conserve the meat for the rest of the year. In midwinter he becomes a viniculturist watching to see that his wines do not spoil; in the spring he sets hens to increase his fowl family and attends to all of the little chores around the grounds.

These many-sided activities are forced upon him by a lack of acreage. There was very little land to be had, and no large holdings could ever develop. In my village the holdings range from one acre to thirty, and I can remember how, as a child, I felt that the estate of the landlord surrounded the small patches of my people like a wall of rock. No land was ever for sale because the aristocrats kept their property inviolate throughout the generations, just as the peasants did.

Superhuman efforts are necessary to accomplish all of the work that needs to be done. Only by the heavy sweat of his face can the peasant eke out even the most basic subsistence. So small are his patches that he cannot afford any modern equipment; and until very recently there was not a single peasant who owned a tractor. The plows were pulled by horses, and the only power used for hoeing and mowing was the muscles in the peasant's two arms. As a child, I watched my elders sowing the wheat seed by hand into the freshly plowed furrows. Seeding machines came into use many years later.

Despite the hard labor and the poverty, the peasant of the village never endangered the root of his existence, the land. Bailiffs were a rare sight, for if the man of Bisse was unable to meet his debts he chose privation, tightening his belt rather than give up a square foot of land.

Bisse is no different from other villages; life is the same in all of them: burdensome and poor. About fifty years ago a new thought invaded the peasants' mind: "If we cannot increase our land we should not increase the population it must feed." They began to practice birth control. Slowly the child richness of the families disappeared, and there developed the "singles." One child was born in every family. Until it grew old enough to assume the burdens of everyday existence it was spoiled with the best possible rearing and care.

Just as Bisse resembled all the other villages, my family resembled the other peasant families. My grandfather was still head of the household when I was born in 1903. The few acres which he owned were barely enough to give us a living, to say nothing of paying our debts. He also owned the house in which we all lived. The only other ancestor of whom I know, my great-grandfather, János Nagy, was a local celebrity with two claims to fame—his ten years of army service with General Radetzky in Italy, and his unique character.

In his day soldiering was different. By edict of the King the village had to furnish one soldier every ten years. The elders selected a youth of about twenty, and naturally they did not surrender the gentlest and most peace-loving youngster; instead the village sent a young man it could well do without. My great-grandfather, in youth, had that unenviable reputation. The army of that time was not an educational institution which released men mellowed and with improved morals; they emerged as harder and more determined fighters. Returning after ten years, my great-grandfather found that all of the men of his age were married and there were no available spinsters; nor did any of the white-laced maidens want to marry a toughened, thirty-year-old soldier. Nevertheless, the brave veteran found a spouse: eventually the young widow of an outlaw became my great-grandmother. Her first husband had traveled with the infamous bandit, Bandi Patkó, who spread terror throughout the primeval forests of western Hungary. Her husband was finally captured, and the hands of the law ended his life in the fortress of Siklós.

Life with my great-grandfather could not have been much easier for the poor widow. The ex-soldier came home overbearing and fearfully unsociable. He gave vent to his arrogance by avoiding communication even with his family unless it was absolutely necessary. His son, my grandfather, grew to the age of fifteen under his hand, without, as he said himself, much opportunity for conversation with his taciturn parent. The elders still tell a typical story about great-grandfather's farming habits:

There were no threshing machines in his time: the harvested wheat was spread out on the ground, and the horses driven over it until the grain parted from the stalk. One summer he was threshing like this, and his horses were trampling the spread wheat. At sunrise a great many children gathered from the neighborhood and stood steadily watching my great-grandfather at work. He could not bear it, and for half an hour his anger rose; but he would not descend to the level of using his very own voice to chase them away. Then a mongrel dog appeared and sat down a few feet in front of the children. My great-grandfather picked up a pitchfork and speared the animal with a lightning thrust. In seconds the children disappeared. The tale of this fearsome action spread, and from that time no child dared go near him.

But he was tough with the landlords, too. The fact that he had to render socage service annoyed him deeply. Once, when he was loading grain on his oxcart, the overseer appeared. The proud ex-warrior was heaping the huge cornstalks while his younger brother, the gentle Stephen, tossed the wheat sheaves with a pitchfork.

"Hey, peasant! One more whole cart must go in tonight, because the sun has not set yet," yelled the overseer.

My great-grandfather silently continued to stack the corn.

"Are we going to take in another cart, Brother János?" asked the intimidated Stephen.

"No!" answered my great-grandfather in a voice that could be heard in half the county.

"You dog-bred peasant, you! I'll have you strapped to the whipping post on Sunday morning," cursed the overseer.

The stack was pretty high. Great-grandfather jumped down its side like a cat; from the hand of his astonished brother he grabbed the pitchfork, and started for the despot. Quickly forgetting his dignity, the overseer took to his fancy coach; the horses jumped, the pitchfork missed its target and smashed the back of the carriage.

Another story went the rounds of the village. Great-grandfather in returning from the campaign in Italy wore his uniform, because his family could not ship his peasant clothes to the foreign land, and brought back a dilapidated army carbine. In his day a peasant was not permitted to own a gun; but, not bothering about the law, he hunted unconcernedly in the forests of the lord. The game wardens dared not tackle him openly. However, when the warrior was in the vineyards, the master forester broke into the house with his men and seized the gun. Thus the servants of the law had to steal to keep the law alive.

His son was a tough, hot-tempered man, but intelligent and able to read and write. From his early youth, grandfather was a member of the village council; and his debates kept the Sunday afternoon meetings pretty vociferous. He was a just man, and fought corruption. For years he was the treasurer of the village, and not a penny was lost. Once the preacher used church money to pay for his wife's extravagances. My grandfather made him give a final accounting, brought him before the church judicatory, and finally ran him out of the village.

Grandfather respected the accomplishments of his ancestors. An anemic young man, newly hatched from a city preparatory school, got the teacher's job in the village. He offered to teach me some high-school subjects in the evenings. Coming to our house for dinner to talk this over, the teacher favored us with a dogmatic lecture on the poor way in which the peasants of Bisse had built the manse.

"How could these peasants have been stupid enough to build a corridor through the middle of the manse, thus wasting the most valuable part of the building?"

My grandfather's ears perked up, and his eyes flashed.

"What did you say? How were these old peasants?" he asked the teacher.

"Stupid, because they did not know how to build the manse," replied the young man arrogantly.

Turning to me, grandfather yelled, "Open the door!" To the teacher: "Get out of my house. I'll have no one sit at my table who considers stupid the hard-laboring, diligent peasants who built this village."

The teacher edged away, and I had a premonition that with my six years of elementary school my formal education had definitely ended.

Father diligently devoted himself to hard labor and was little concerned with community affairs. While my grandfather loved to drive the horses, my father was more interested in producing good wine. There were years when we had the best vintage of the village.

My mother was the outstanding member of our family, always eager to learn, eternally in quest of culture. Although we had few books and could not afford to buy more, she read during every leisure moment. On weekdays she went to the fields with my father to share the day's labor on the estate of the landlord, but on Sundays she walked as far as the third village if she heard that the preacher, the schoolteacher or the miller had a book she could borrow. Miraculously, everything she read remained with her. She expressed herself simply but with unusual intelligence. We rarely heard her beautiful singing voice because the ever present specter of need had stolen its joy. None of the usual advantages of the only child were mine, but I had the mother's love and good teachings entirely to myself.

Mother tried to transplant in me as much of her character as she could. Not wanting to trust my spiritual development to chance, she did everything possible to lead me along the ways of religion, honesty, and love of country. In the works of history which she read, the story of the struggle of liberty-loving peoples most fascinated her. She enjoyed telling me of the lives and ideas of Hungary's two historic fighters for freedom, Ferenc Rákóczy and Louis Kossuth. She was awed especially by the personality of Kossuth because her father was a great devotee of this hero of the common people. She told me a characteristic episode which illustrated his admiration.

In 1894 news reached the village where my mother lived that Louis Kossuth had died in exile in Turin, Italy. Mother's father immediately went to the bell ringer and demanded that he ring the bells continuously until news of Kossuth's funeral arrived. When the bell ringer refused, grandfather thrashed him and himself rang the bells for days until it was learned that Louis Kossuth had been laid to rest.

Despite my mother's desire to be a cultured person, she had none of the advantages of education. She labored in the fields, and when I was twenty-five, stronger and more powerful than she, I could not equal the speed and quality of her work.

Such was my background. I was a good pupil, the best in the school. My mother had great plans for my higher education and even persuaded my father to send me to a city school. But this plan was checked by history.

When the First World War broke out my father, an old reservist, was immediately conscripted. My grandfather was already an old man, and so at the age of eleven I became, not a student as my mother wished, but the farmer. In my father's stead I was man of the house and, together with my mother, took over the additional work. When still a child I had to learn to plow, seed, hoe, mow, drive horses, spray the vines, and do all the other odd jobs in the fields. In the morning I went to the compulsory school; but every afternoon I joined my mother at the backbreaking field labor. If we encountered work that needed the full strength of a man, we called on the swineherd and I watched the pigs in his place.

Between working hard in the field and going to school it wasn't easy to find time for books, but reading had become an emotional necessity. I read constantly: at night by the glow of the kerosene lamp in the stables; by day grasping the book with the handle of the plow as I drove the horses; at mealtimes with the book lying open on the table.

With my physical labor I made my way, but with learning I hoped to build a better road. I cannot complain about results; in the first year of the war we had paid off all our debts. By this time my horizon was no longer bound by the village.

My earliest conclusion was that the peasant's two traditional millstones, the banks and the baronial estates, were grinding his life to wretchedness. How often had I felt the stones against my own skin! There arose in me a burning desire to improve the lot of the peasants everywhere, and the only road I saw open was education.

When mother went to the city to sell some vegetables and a few chickens at the public market, she always brought back a book or two. To satisfy my interest in the current progress of the world, she subscribed to newspapers and periodicals. I searched for the deeper causes of war and studied any article that dealt with international relations and the science of warfare.

My father returned for a furlough sick from two years in the trenches. The winter came, and he took work in the woods. But cutting down trees in our forests was not a one-man job and as he could not find a helper I went with him to fell the giant oaks. So at the age of thirteen, and for the thirteen following winters, I was a woodsman for the landlord. The tormenting cold hardened me to the realization that man must work to live.

The first political upheaval confronted me at the age of fifteen, when the World War ended. Revolution broke out when bands of returning soldiers joined forces with the leftist parties and overthrew the government, killed the iron-fisted Prime Minister of the war cabinet, Count Stephen Tisza, and severed all ties with Austria. They tried to create a government in the spirit of a wedding feast. Socialists and left-wing liberals formed one government after another, only to see it fall by the wayside in the mad race for power. As a result a small group of Communists took over and began to govern with methods alien and shocking to the Hungarian people. They blocked a new law to distribute land among the peasants, disclaimed tradition, and hurled slogans against church and God. Under the thin shroud of counterrevolutionary accusations, they executed first hundreds and then thousands. People in all walks of life were disgusted by these actions and dreaded them.

Before the Communists took control, the greater part of my county, including my village, was occupied by the Serbs. Although at first the occupation did not impose much hardship on the life of the village, bitter pain arose in the hearts of the peasants when they realized they might never again be part of Hungary. The occupation only served to intensify the peasant's flaming love for his country.

In unoccupied Hungary the Communists' regime soon destroyed itself. They debased their power and all strata of society, especially the peasants, united as one man to overthrow them. Some of the Communists took the road for Russia, which was still aflame with the fierce fires of the revolution. Another group escaped toward the south while some took refuge in Serbian-occupied Hungarian territory. My county and its villages also became the stage for Communist agitators. In Bisse two Red soldiers began to organize the Communist party, attracting some of the peasants with promises of land distribution. These good people did not know that in Hungary proper it was the Communists who prevented this much-prayed-for measure.

Resistance to this new political intrusion was strong in the village, and naturally I joined it. While my father and the other leading peasants tried to halt the spread of Communism among the people of their generation, I helped found a cultural society with the young people who believed in God and country.

Now I became more active in community life. My eagerness to learn and my thirst for knowledge did not segregate me from the youth of the village. I took part in their plays and games, and vied with the other young men in athletics. Since the village teacher was unable to give vocal instruction, I learned the elements of music and, before I knew it, led the singing society. None of the villagers of the county could compete with the youth of Bisse in singing beautiful songs. At weddings I was one of the groomsmen, and at funerals I helped dig the grave.

After three years the Serbians left us for their recently created country of Yugoslavia. About that time I had my first clash with the ruling class of Hungary. The new Hungary, cut to pieces by the Treaty of Trianon, was recruiting a small voluntary army restricted in size and with conscription abolished. Only volunteers were permitted to serve. The new law provided that one could offer himself for military service and after six months' training he could go home or remain a soldier for ten years. I induced a group of my village chums to join me in volunteering.

We had to appear before the sheriff to get a medical examination and to sign up. The sheriff commended us with a flowery speech and told us to sign the recruiting blanks. I read the declaration and there it said in simple terms that I was signing up for ten years.

"Sheriff, we understand that we are permitted to join for six months and we do not have to stay in the army for ten years. We are peasants and want to remain peasants, but we would like to get some military training," said I courteously.

"Where did you get that idea?" yelled the sheriff.

"From paragraph fourteen of the new law for the defense of the country," I replied firmly, and, turning to the others: "You want to be soldiers for ten years?"

"No! Only six months," they replied in unison. The sheriff got red in the face.

"You inciting Communist, you!" he screamed at me in the traditional voice of the ruling class.

"Don't you say that. Everybody in my village knows I am not a Communist," I answered.

"If you say one more word I'll smack you so hard you'll fly out of the window!" he yelled.

"That's possible, but you cannot stop me from slapping you back," I answered hotly.

The sheriff chased us out, but after a week we were summoned to his office. He declared that because we behaved outrageously he was sentencing us to eight days in jail or a fine of one thousand crowns.

The group exchanged glances.

"But we did not behave outrageously the other day, we left without a word," said I, speaking for all of us.

"Hold your tongue," said the sheriff. "Here is my witness." And he pointed to the meek, subservient clerk.

Such injustice wounded me deeply. I never forgot this incident, and all of my life remained wary of government administrators.

The fate of the subjugated peasants began to interest me intensely. I compared my mother's stories of present-day life with the reading I had done about Louis Kossuth's era, and concluded that the peasants had advanced very little on the road to political and economic freedom since the liberation of the serfs in 1848.

Before 1848, the peasants were the slaves of the landlords, in whose will lay the power of life and death. In my youth we still lived under the shadow of the feudal lords, and next to it loomed the shadows of the banks and mammoth corporations which exploited the peasants even as the barons had done. All this, it seemed to me, was typified by the unforgettable injustice and show of might of the sheriff who jailed me for asking a question.

In 1923, amid great festivities, a monument to the war dead was unveiled in Bisse. The Regent's personal envoy arrived from the capital, we had an army band and an honor company in attendance, and from all parts of the county young and old assembled for the occasion.

There were a great number of speeches, and I was asked to talk on behalf of the youth. As we were dispersing, a man introduced himself to me as the editor of the newspaper which was published at the county seat of Pécs.

"I listened to your speech at the unveiling," he said. "It is my feeling that anyone who can speak so concisely and poetically can write also. Write something for my paper."

"Pardon me, sir. I have never written anything for the public, nor dreamed of writing for a newspaper. I do not believe I would be successful," I answered.

"Try it," he urged. "I am certain that your writings will have hand and foot."

The newspaperman's offer stuck in my mind. In the earthy atmosphere of the stable, where I slept like the other young men, I thought a lot about his invitation. One night I lit the kerosene lamp and sat down next to the feedbox; using it as a table I started to write. Amid the heavy-breathing animals and the freshly stacked hay, my first literary piece took form, a short story drawn from the life of the common peasant. Its appearance in the paper encouraged me to try my pen at political and economic aspects of the peasant's life. My comments were printed in the county publication of the old Smallholders party.

These articles aroused the interest of the county leaders, and I was invited to take an active role in party life. Accepting the challenge, I spent my Sundays going from village to village, helping to organize the Smallholders party and telling the peasants my ideas about their problems. I drew their attention to their unjust treatment, and told them that they would be stronger if they would unite. The peasants believed me. I was a new man, but they felt the sincerity of my words and understood that I had not come to put something over on them. When the Smallholders party of the county was reorganized, I was elected vice chairman.

This is not the same as the historic, independent Smallholders born later, of which I became general secretary and finally national chairman. Stephen Nagyatádi Szabó, a simple peasant from the neighboring county of Somogy, founded the old party before the First World War. He was the first peasant who rose from rural simplicity to a position of national influence. During one period of his distinguished political career, he held the fate of the entire nation in his palm.

Stephen Nagyatádi Szabó was a wise, clear-sighted Hungarian peasant who recognized at an early age the yearnings of his people.

He knew that the political, economic, and cultural backwardness was not to be laid to the peasants, but to those who stifled their self-assertion. The two great political parties which existed before World War I, the pro-Habsburg government party and the anti-Habsburg

Independence party, ignored the interests of the Hungarian peasants. While in Denmark, Holland, and Sweden the peasants had been advancing on the road to prosperity, culture, and social recognition, in Hungary the ruling class did not care about the political position of the majority of the population.

Stephen Nagyatádi Szabó wrote the secret ballot, agrarian reform, and progressive taxation on the banner of the old Smallholders party. Before 1914 the party advanced slowly; but as the war neared its end, and both the Habsburg and Independence parties proved ineffectual, Stephen Nagyatádi Szabó and his Smallholders gained prominence in the political arena. At the end of the war, when everyone was losing faith, people turned to him and his followers, trusting their steadfast convictions.

Stephen Nagyatádi Szabó first headed the Ministry of Food and later Agriculture; with the reassuring support of the masses behind him, he controlled the entire political scene. After the fall of Communism in Hungary, the frame of the new political structure emerged on the foundations of the old Smallholders party, and its growth was phenomenal. After the horror of war and the revolutions following, this man and his party offered a new stability. Stephen Nagyatádi Szabó set up an organization to represent the economic interests of the peasantry, founded an agricultural chamber, and under his leadership, Parliament voted the agrarian reform. However, frightened by the responsibility of creating a new state, Stephen Nagyatádi Szabó shared his power with Count Stephen Bethlen—born, bred, and of conviction an aristocrat. Using the partnership to his own advantage, Bethlen chose to create an alliance with the gentry rather than with labor and the white-collar class. He permitted Stephen Nagyatádi Szabó to be slandered, and condoned the removal of loyal public servants. He withdrew the secret ballot, already given to the country, and narrowed the effectiveness of the agrarian reform. Stephen Nagyatádi Szabó watched with discouragement the slow collapse of his accomplishments, and in 1924, upon resigning as Minister of Agriculture, died suddenly.

With its guiding genius gone, party leadership floundered; at the time of my entry into its ranks, the withering Smallholders lived on the ruins of its former greatness.

The administration of the agrarian reform was taken out of the hands of the Smallholders, and although about one and one-half million acres were distributed, most of the peasants could not meet the severe

terms. Stephen Nagyatádi Szabó's idealistic conception never material-
ized. A partial success was achieved by the distribution of many
thousands of lots on the outskirts of the village, where the majority of
the peasants were able to erect their homes.

The postwar upheavals brought little change in the life of my village; none of the peasants received more than four acres as a result of
the redistribution. The authorities made a fatal mistake by refusing to
grant one square foot of land to any peasant who had been involved or
identified with the Communist party during its short-lived reign. I have
always believed it to be unjust to punish the masses after the fall of a
political regime.

When I first joined in the political activities of the old Smallholders,
I had no personal ambitions; I only wished to see realized the ideals
of Stephen Nagyatádi Szabó before he compromised with Count Bethlen
and the gentry. I wanted true democracy through a government headed
by clear-minded representatives of the Hungarian people.

I believe that Stephen Nagyatádi Szabó wanted something other
than the result of his deal with Count Bethlen. Once during the war,
when I was fourteen, I heard that he was coming to campaign during
a special election; I went by foot all of the way to Siklos to hear the
famous peasant leader.

The handsome, impressive peasant idol held us spellbound with his
address. He spoke of the wretchedness of the peasant's life, of the economic inequality and unjust taxation; he pleaded for the secret ballot
and agrarian reform.

"Count Zelensky says that the life of the landed aristocracy in
Hungary is fancy misery. Well, we would be very happy to relieve the
Hungarian ruling class of this tragic condition if they permit us to
distribute part of their land among those who actually till the soil."
These were the words that remained in my mind during my endeavors
to improve the situation of the landless. I never forgot my long walk
home; step by step I became more imbued with the great hero's
ideology.

Forceful reforms were needed; I firmly believed in them when I
entered county politics, treading later my county's endless miles for
my party; words and slogans became secondary to the effort to deal
with basic issues as did Stephen Nagyatádi Szabó. I analyzed the situation of the peasant; he was alone and uncared for; his production
and his marketing were unorganized; he could no more set the price

of the fruits of his labor than he could control the prices of the goods he had to buy.

"The peasant is not selling his produce, it is being bought from him," I declared publicly. Probably that was the basis of his immediate economic problems. The taxation had become even more unjust than it was before World War I. The expenses of postwar reconstruction were overburdening the peasant even after the general economic decline further impoverished him. The open ballot took away his only chance to improve his political situation. The fifty-year-old edict restricted his schooling to six years of compulsory education and neither law nor society provided for his social security.

Many people laid political and economic conditions to the reduction of Hungary's centuries-old territory to a fragment after the war. I knew of Grundtvig, who said after Denmark lost its great war in the nineteenth century, "Denmark can be stronger than ever if we start new life within our small borders." I wished that all Hungarians would have understood this statement as well as the Danes did when they created a new life in their country.

Our feudalists chose a different road. Under the regency of the politically inexpert Admiral Nicholas Horthy and the very able but biased Count Stephen Bethlen, the country lived again under the dictates of the old ruling class. After the war, the revolutions, and the severance from Austria, they rebuilt Hungary on politically unsound foundations.

I was not twenty-one when I took a village girl for my wife. We had been dear to each other ever since early childhood. Together we shared the joys of youth, together went to pluck the grapes, together appeared in religious plays. Whatever free time we had, we spent with each other. Two recollections of our closeness remain with me still.

The equipment of the school we both attended was primitive; there was not a nail on which to hang our coats and hats, much less a cloakroom. During the long winter months we sat in our coats and threw our caps on the window ledge. One day I swung my heavy sheepskin cap with such energy that I broke the window. In came the teacher, and, discovering the damage immediately, demanded the name of the culprit. Up jumped little Julia Balog.

"Teacher, it was already broken when we got here." No one contradicted her, and I knew that Julia Balog was my best friend in life.

One day when we were older, the elders told us to gather hay in the meadows—community work generally performed by children. The supervising elder said that we need not take any lunch because we should finish by noon. Naturally, there was a full day's work. The elder finally permitted Julia, as the youngest child present, to go back to the village and bring lunches for us all. She brought mine tied up in a kerchief, and when I opened it I found, next to the bread and green pepper, a piece of sausage. I knew that in our house there was no more sausage; she must have slipped it from her lunch into mine. I felt that anyone who was ready to share with me in youth would be the ideal person to share the burdens of later life. Faithfully she worked next to me in the fields; at night she copied with a pen, in her beautiful script, what I wrote; she was beside me during my political battles; she shared my anxiety for the fate of our country when I headed the government, and she came with me into exile. Her loving care, I share today with our three children.

Bisse personifies to both of us the strong traditions of Hungarian peasant life; little gladness, much misery. The joys and heartaches of my youth tie me permanently to my birthplace. Whether in county politics, in parliament, in prison, or in power, memory of this little village was always before me. I saw the weather-beaten, one-room schoolhouse where six classes of children tried to get educated together. I saw my boyhood friends with whom I met the vicissitudes of life. In my mind there was a picture of the little church with its Sunday services. I never forgot the profiles of the sweating peasants who cut the wheat under the scorching Hungarian sun. My thoughts wandered to the cellars of the vineyards where sorrow entered only if the kegs were dry. In my imagination I sat with the other villagers broiling bacon in the forests, and I have never decided a question of government or of the fate of the people without asking myself, What would the peasants of Bisse think of this, and what would my mother say?

CHAPTER 2

Class Consciousness

LISTENING TO THE WOES OF THE THOUSANDS OF PEASANTS IN THE COUNTY spurred me to achievement on their behalf. The more I heard of their problems, the more I knew that I needed insight into the history of the common peoples of the world. Up to now, in my reading, I had devoured the works of the great; travel books followed the novels and histories succeeded the classics. As my eyes opened, study of the evolution of human freedom became my hobby. The migration and the causes of migration of the Anglo-Saxon people to the new world, later the Mecca for Hungarian peasants, absorbed me. So did the story of the fight for liberty of the American colonists under George Washington, and the uprisings of the people of France which resulted in the bloody revolution. I studied the traditions, the problems, and the resulting actions of the oppressed. Naturally I had a special interest in my own country. I spent nights reading Acsády's "History of Hungarian Serfdom" and through its pages glimpsed the thousands of years of suffering of the peasants. I read with less criticism than enthusiasm Márki's "History of the Peasant Revolution of 1514" and secretly studied Ágoston's suppressed book, "Hungarian Secular Land Ownership." These writings taught me to concentrate on action as much as thought.

Reading, writing, and working for the party occupied my entire spare time. I tried my pen at one subject after another. I wrote a monograph about my village which won the gold medal in a contest, and a play of peasant life which was produced for years by amateur theatrical groups throughout the country. To exist, I had to continue to labor in the fields. My expenses increased as I became absorbed in political work.

Personal problems mounted, too. Our old house was ready to fall apart, and we had to build a new home. After finishing it, we were again deeply in debt. From the income on our bits of land it was hard to provide for clothes, taxes, bank interest, and for my political expenses. Our crops were barley, oats, wheat, corn, potatoes, and fodder. We had two horses, two cows, a few pigs and chickens. With the horses I did contract work and plowed. The rest of the field work, I did by hand. As the prices of produce and of animals declined, my financial problems mounted. Nobody paid me for my writing until I made a fateful trip.

On a dreary winter morning I undertook to bring some supplies in for our village cooperative store, which had difficulty in getting them because of the heavy snow. In payment, I agreed to take a few shares of its stock. Lacking a cap, I drove my horses through the freezing wind in a hat all the way to Pécs, the county seat, and when I got there my ears were stiff. At Pécs, I delivered a manuscript to the editor of the peasant weekly.

"What happened to you?" queried the editor anxiously when he saw my frozen ears swell to huge proportions in the sudden warmth of his well heated office.

"If I am not wrong, sir, my ears have frozen," I answered.

"Well, why did you not pull down the muffs of your cap?"

"Because I do not own a cap, only a hat."

The editor immediately gave me money to buy not only a cap but a winter coat as well. This made a tremendous impression on me.

In January, 1929, I wrote an editorial on our form of government, and sent it to the largest Hungarian daily, the *Pesti Hirlap*. To my great surprise, the article appeared; and there was an even more astonishing sequel. Numerous peasants of the county walked many miles to congratulate me, and over a thousand letters and telegrams poured in from all parts of the nation. But the most pleasant surprise was a registered letter from the editor containing fifty pengöes in cash as payment for the article. This was a lot of money. The price of produce had dropped to such an extent that you could buy ten bushels of wheat for fifty pengöes, or an entire suit of clothing. What is more, the editor invited me to continue to write, and I happily accepted the invitation. From then on, not only was I able to meet my expenses in political life, but the articles brought me some national renown; and letters from the more intelligent peasants through the country offered further material for political essays of country-wide interest.

Humanity was in the midst of an economic depression and the Hungarian peasants, like other farmers throughout the world, were hit hardest. When agricultural prices were falling the world over, produce was overplentiful, and the operation of the law of supply and demand brought poverty and near-collapse to the economic structure of Hungary. The crisis emphasized the political problems of the peasants and brought them to the foreground. I distinctly remember some of the plaintive messages which reached me by the thousands, and which voiced so well the questions in the minds of the peasants.

"The prices of agricultural produce are declining constantly, and despite that we are unable to sell either grain or animals," wrote one.

"The prices of factory goods needed by the peasants are rising steadily. While before the war we could buy a pair of boots for one or two bushels of wheat, now the same pair of boots costs three or four bushels of wheat," wrote another.

Naturally few of them could comprehend the influence of world trade upon the economy of the country; they viewed the situation in terms of their immediate wants.

"The most unjust taxes are those on wine and communal work; both serve to save the large landowners from just taxation. We pay twelve fillérs for each liter of wine that we produce and drink ourselves, and they assess us twenty-four pengöes for 'communal work tax' just because we own a pair of horses."

"When we have to borrow money for taxes or to pay for vitally needed supplies, the banks charge us 8 to 10 per cent interest, and our goods are ruthlessly auctioned off if we cannot meet the payments."

"Our present situation is hopeless without the secret ballot. Bureaucracy forces us to vote for a regime we do not want, and which should have fallen long ago."

"We are unorganized. The industries have formed cartels to determine the prices of both the goods we buy and the produce we sell."

"Our agricultural organizations are headed by large landowners who prefer pushing the cart of merciless capitalism to fighting the battle of agriculture. Who does not know that the head of the agricultural chamber has accepted the chairmanship of the Association of Alcohol Industries at a princely salary; the president of the National Agricultural Society heads one of the largest banks? How can these men serve our interests? How can they be the spokesmen of the ever toiling peasant?"

"As our income declines, our expenses increase. Ruin faces us."

These voices proved that tremendous responsibility had to be shouldered by the man who became spokesman for the peasants; only one who could vow to serve them faithfully should be allowed to carry their torch.

The economic policy of the regime was disastrous because the large mass of the people worked without having a voice in the political or economic management of their affairs. After the World War the new government aspired to economic autarchy for Hungary, and steps were taken to create a large industry in a country mainly agricultural by geography, tradition, and resources. The postwar Hungary, small in size, suddenly sprouted a number of industries which soon proved unable to compete with their rivals across the frontier. These industries the government had to protect by restrictive tariffs if they were to stay in business. The result was that the industrial countries whose consumer goods were thus prevented from entering Hungary retaliated by boycotting our agricultural products. Although the dissatisfaction of the population mounted, representatives elected mostly by the open ballot sat in parliament and supported the regime which secured their election. Only once in a while did one or another of the small minority elected on the secret ballot of the cities give vent to a minor complaint; it was just a voice in the wilderness.

I thought, and waited for the opportunity to bring the complaints of the people dramatically into the open. The opportunity arrived in May of 1930, when the county organization of the old Smallholders party arranged a memorial in honor of the great peasant leader and cabinet member, Stephen Nagyatádi Szabó. A large group of members of parliament attended this mass meeting, and the Minister of Agriculture honored his great predecessor by heading the delegation. The committee selected me as one of the speakers. I prepared an address embodying all the complaints of my peasant brethren, employing the strongest words I could muster to picture the conditions of the men, women, and children who carried the entire economic weight of the country on their shoulders. In summation I demanded that the present government reply in sixty days with satisfactory actions. Otherwise the peasantry of my county would move into opposition and declare an open fight against the regime.

Originating from a county leadership of the party that was still officially supporting the government in power, the news of this unprecedented ultimatum spread like wildfire all over the land. The peasantry tensely awaited the result. When the cabinet gave no satisfactory promises after the sixty days, I resigned as vice chairman and withdrew from the old Smallholders party.

Before my article in the *Pesti Hirlap* I had never seen the capital, Budapest. The editor invited me to spend some time in the city, and we agreed that I would work three months in his editorial department to learn a bit of the technical phases of journalism.

During my stay in the capital I met for the first time Zoltán Tildy, a Presbyterian minister who headed a religious printing establishment, and we spent Christmas Eve together discussing the general conditions of the country. We shared the same views about practically all aspects of the situation, believing that Hungary should have pursued a democratic policy after the World War, and that the cornerstone of this democracy must be the peasant. We decided that, unless conditions improved, we would start a new Smallholders party to represent truly the interests of the peasants.

Tildy and I took a great liking to each other, and for seventeen years we trod together, shoulder to shoulder, the rocky road of Hungarian politics. Together we fought against feudalism, together we began to unite the peasants, trying to bring new life to Hungary between the world wars. Together we lost as candidates during elections. Together we battled the National Socialists. I believed that we should remain together until the end of our lives, but history decided differently.

In the spring of 1930 we gathered in Budapest all the peasant leaders with whom we had been in contact; after lengthy councils and discussions it was decided that a new party platform would be presented to the country in the fall. The signs pointed toward urgency, and all circumstances urged us onward. We saw that the peasant was perishing rapidly of economic strangulation. We discovered that we had the ideological backing of some of the leading writers of the country. Hungary's literary geniuses were pulling on the cord of the danger bell, and some of the most popular authors voiced the case of the peasant. Young students became enthusiastic missionaries of the movement, walking throughout the land and writing essays about the plight of the common man of the soil. There was born at that time a new type of literature: young writers became champions of the peasant and pounded on the closed doors of feudalism.

We became convinced that the sturdy, freedom-loving peasant would prove the best basis for the new opposition party.

CHAPTER 3

A New Party Rises

THE SUMMER OF 1930 WAS SPENT IN DRAWING UP A PROGRAM FOR THE new Independent Smallholders Party, containing the following basic points:

(1) Total suffrage must replace the degrading open ballot; the

citizen had the right to express his free will and exert his influence on the government of the country within the framework of the constitution.

(2) The old dream of agrarian reform must be realized, to secure an economic foothold for the hundreds of thousands of peasants and strengthen their ties to the land with ownership, and to end the exaggerated economic influence of the large holdings.

(3) The prices of consumer goods must be reduced and agricultural prices must be raised to save small peasant undertakings and put an end to the subjugation of the Hungarian people by greedy capital.

(4) Taxation must be made just and progressive, and a tax-free minimum established, distributing the burdens of the country proportionately to the ability to pay.

(5) The cultural standard of the people must be raised, and the villages educated from ignorance to enlightenment.

(6) Administration must be simplified and made popular, the bureaucrats, drunk with power being exchanged for administrators with an appreciation and understanding of the social problems of the people.

(7) Equal social security must be granted to all members of the working class.

A number of detailed demands, with the means toward realization, were also included in the program.

The date for the unfurling of the new party's flag was set for October 12. The scene was the largest peasant township of the great Hungarian plain, the heavily populated Békés.

The peasants came from all parts of the country. This waving mass of humanity was an inspiring sight and encouraged us greatly. Even the most distant corners of the country were represented by the delegates who had saved their scarce coppers to pay the fare to Békés. Innumerable peasant carts lined the field, but many districts had organized caravans of motor trucks for which we could hardly find parking room. Thousands had made the pilgrimage by foot from the near-by towns and countryside.

Zoltán Tildy and I spoke to the mass meeting. "A new chapter begins in the history of Hungary," I said. "The peasants are entrenching themselves in the strongholds of the constitution." The party platform was read. The meeting received it enthusiastically and proclaimed the founding of the Independent Smallholders party.

The meeting proceeded to elect party officers. Valentine Szijj, a Smallholder peasant, close collaborator of the late Stephen Nagyatádi Szabó, and lifetime peasant member of the upper chamber, was made president; Zoltán Tildy became executive vice president, and I was made national secretary.

It was clear to me that the creation of this new party would alter the political balance; that the regime would make some concessions to the peasants if only to make our aspirations less urgent. But then we did not know that our party, in addition to fighting the feudal regime that existed between the two great wars, would have to struggle against the two great imperialistic ideologies: Nazism emanating from Germany, and Communism invading from Soviet Russia. I looked forward to the hard battle ahead, but never imagined our lot would be imprisonment, hiding from assassination, and eventual exile.

The Smallholders party grew rapidly. In hundreds of villages the peasants themselves organized the local units. But the suppression began, too. First our weekly, *The Hungarian Soil,* was suspended by government order; next the person of Tildy was attacked. We were slandered and ridiculed, but, paying little attention, we continued on the appointed road and looked for influential supporters of our cause. We needed an outstanding political leader and representation in parliament.

In the political life of that era the figure of Gaston Gaál stood out as a man of stern principles, respected by everyone. He and a group of his friends sat in parliament without any party affiliation. We invited him to become the political leader of our party. We laid our plans and platform before him, and Gaston Gaál accepted.

In the election year 1931, the innumerable difficulties set before us by the regime prevented us from waging an effective national campaign. Nevertheless we won eleven seats in parliament, despite the reactionary open ballot.

I traveled by train, cart, and foot from one end of the country to the other, putting life into the new party organization; in more than a thousand localities I myself helped found the local unit. The peasants did not have to be convinced; their increasing difficulties drove them to the new party.

In the fall of 1932 Gaston Gaál died. The entire country mourned the noble statesman, the valiant political fighter. The National Committee elected its ablest and most cultured member, Tibor Eckhardt, to succeed him. Always well liked throughout the Smallholders electorate, Eckhardt's popularity mounted when he won an election, on an open ballot in the home district of the minister of agriculture against the minister himself.

In the fall of 1932 I finally assumed the office of national secretary of the party. My writings brought me sufficient income to maintain my family in Budapest, and my traveling expenses, which had been coming out of my own pocket, were now paid by the party.

On a visit to the Smallholders office in my home county of Baranya, I was talking to the peasants and listening to their familiar complaints and their reports on party progress when a young man stepped up to me. Not more than twenty years old, he was a strong, good-looking, thickly built blond peasant.

"Permit me, Mr. Secretary, to introduce myself. My name is Béla Kovács. I am a peasant from Mecsekalja." We shook hands, and I told him, "Stay here when the rest leave."

When we were alone I started to talk with him. Boundless enthusiasm and vigor emanated from this young peasant.

"I would like to serve in the party," he said.

"Sunday we are having meetings in three villages along the river. Come with me."

"I will be very happy if you permit me to; since you issued the ultimatum to the government, I have been anxious to hear you."

"Ah, no, brother!" I answered. "I did not invite you for audience, I want you to speak."

The blood rushed to his face. "Please understand, I have never spoken at a public meeting. I'll be ill at ease and shame you. What is more, I would not know what to say."

"You will tell the people in their language what you told me during this conversation. Shyness will be overcome by experience."

Sunday he came to the mass meeting. In the first village, I ended my speech with the announcement that Béla Kovács would address the people. Béla began to speak. The words rushed out of him like water over the falls; spontaneously he described the peasants' injuries. Without finishing the first sentence he began the next; his thoughts ran ahead of his words. Such a burst of power, I thought, could not stay behind the plow.

"Didn't I say that I am no speaker?" he asked plaintively, turning to me after the meeting and wiping the sweat from his forehead.

"Very well," I laughed. "I won't force you again if you don't want to come."

"You say this because you know that I shall never leave your side if I can help it," answered Béla Kovács.

And he never did, until Soviet despotism dragged him from me and threw him into the dungeon. Until then, he was one of the most beloved leaders of Hungary's peasants.

After the funeral of Gaston Gaál, Zoltán Tildy led me to a tall, husky young Catholic priest, who had not been able to stem his tears during the interment.

"This is Father Béla Varga, the parish priest of Balatonboglár, the closest friend of Gaston Gaál," was the introduction.

Béla Kovács was with us. We both embraced the priest and sat down for a chat.

"I am the son of a peasant from the county of Györ," began Béla Varga. "I was with Gaston Gaál every day. Through him I know your party, and with my heart and soul I identify myself with its aims. If you take me in I shall march with you and help you as much as I can. I have no other goal than to serve the people of Hungary."

That afternoon, when Varga became one of us, began a historic union; none of us knew that one would become president of the country, another prime minister, the third president of Parliament, and the fourth minister of agriculture. Nor did we imagine that after the long battles and struggles there would come a day of judgment when the punishment of one would be to "serve his country" although the lot of the other three became imprisonment and exile.

As the Independent Smallholders party grew, its activities were conducted on two political planes, the building of the party organization and campaigns during parliamentary elections. Frequently there were vacancies in the various districts and we always put up a candidate if for no other reason than to publicize the party and its platform.

An illustration of what we were up against during the feudal regime is the special election in the district of Mezökeresztes in 1933. As soon as the seat became vacant I conferred with the district leadership and selected Zoltán Tildy as candidate. The regime, represented by the party of National Unity headed by Prime Minister Julius Gömbös, put up a retired colonel named Szabó Papp, while the Social Democrats ran the present minister of commerce, Alexander Ronai.

The struggles in Tard, a village of two thousand souls, typified the state of affairs. The local head of the Smallholders party was Stephen

Spisák, a member of the county legislature. Enthusiastically he organized the campaign in the village for Tildy's election, going from house to house to get the signatures needed for nomination. A number gave their endorsement gladly, but others were reluctant.

"I am sorry. I would like to do it, but the tax collector was here and threatened to foreclose for overdue taxes if I endorse Tildy."

Although Stephen Spisák knew these tricks well, he was nevertheless shocked when he faced them.

"I cannot sign. The banker in the city will refuse to renew my crop loan if I help the opposition."

"With my heart and soul I am for the election of Zoltán Tildy; but my boy who goes to school in the city wrote that the principal will fail him if I support Tildy."

"God almighty should put this chimney sweep somewhere where the eternal fires need no chimneys. He came to my house today with the sheet for the National Unity party and threatened to have my chimney condemned and torn down if I do not sign up."

Spisák, no novice, was sufficiently annoyed to report these happenings. We in turn protested; obviously without avail. In the district 3,200 persons signed up despite the difficulties; only 1,000 were required, but men like Spisák and his co-workers had foresight. On the appointed day they delivered the endorsements to the election commissioner.

"Two-thirds of these signatures are invalid," declared the commissioner.

"What do you mean?" asked Spisák. "All of these men are registered voters, and signed up in their own handwriting to support Zoltán Tildy."

"Oh, yes, but 2,300 of these also signed the lists of the National Unity party, and according to law I have to invalidate all those on both lists. Therefore, Tildy is supported by nine hundred signatures and you have twenty-four hours to get the other hundred," was the ukase.

Well, the race began, and for twenty-four hours the party busily sought the needed signatures. Before the twenty-four hours were up, they were obtained and accepted.

Then came the active campaign. Naturally Spisák and his friends wanted Tildy to speak in Tard, as in the other villages. A petition signed by four voters was needed, and four of the most prominent peasants requested that Tildy be permitted to speak in the courtyard of the inn. Almost as soon as the petition was delivered, the rejection arrived:

"The request is denied because the fence around the courtyard is unsafe."

Spisák and his co-workers labored over the new petitions; his own courtyard was declared a fire hazard. Permission for a meeting in the smallest yard of the village was granted only after the intervention of the National Committee of the Smallholders party. Election day arrived, with the procedural difficulties involved in open balloting.

The chairman of the board of elections informed Spisák that he had selected as the point of assembly for the Smallholders the schoolhouse yard, far from the voting place and the peasants' homes. But law was law, and it provided that the voters must assemble before marching in groups to the polls. Spisák rebelled against the fact that the Smallholders had to assemble nearly half a mile away from the polling place, while the National Unity party assembled within sixty feet and the Social Democrats within one hundred and fifty feet.

"If they do not like it, they do not have to vote," declared the chairman.

Spisák realized that little could be done about it on the day before the election. As he started to make the last round, giving the party workers final instructions, he encountered the sergeant of the village gendarmes—right in front of his home.

"Mr. Spisák, don't you think that your feverish activities on behalf of the Smallholders candidate may cause you trouble?"

"Do you realize that, according to the law, you have no right to interfere with the election campaign?" answered Spisák sharply.

"Well, I just wanted to warn you," sneered the gendarme.

Spisák ordered his workers to see that all voters assembled peacefully, that there was no yelling, nervousness, or disturbance which would give the gendarmes cause to intervene. Sunday morning the polls opened, and Spisák joined the board as the representative of the Smallholders party.

"Now we are going to draw lots to see which party shall vote first," declared the chairman, dropping three folded papers into a hat.

As soon as Spisák had drawn, the chairman immediately put the other two papers into his pocket.

"Well, which party is going to start?" he asked with a smile.

Spisák unfolded the paper, and to nobody's surprise it read, "Party of the National Unity." Strangely, in all twenty villages of the district the party of the National Unity was selected to lead, in the same way.

"I fix the group of voters at fifty," declared the chairman. "The first fifty may come now."

"There are not fifty voters of the National Unity party assembled," the clerk whispered.

Spisák, overhearing this, said, "Then, Mr. Chairman, according to law that party proceeds which has the appointed number of voters ready to come to the polls. The Smallholders party is ready now."

"I reduce the number of the group of voters to ten!" exclaimed the chairman.

Under such terror of authority the voting began. The National Unity party soon ran out of voters, but the Smallholders group increased rapidly and lost patience by midafternoon. The chairman still had a few tricks up his sleeve; over Spisák's protests his party workers brought in gypsies. Although they were not registered, the chairman let them vote. Then the gendarmerie delivered cartloads of vagrants, who were permitted to vote under the names on all the tombstones in the cemetery and of many former residents who had moved away. The party of the National Unity still lacked a secure plurality when it discovered that it could produce no more voters; in the meantime the voters of the Smallholders party had been permitted to vote only at times when the party in power ran out of stooges. A mass of Smallholders had been waiting patiently all day when the chairman, after whispering with the clerk, declared:

"I set the time for the closing of the polls at half an hour from now."

"I protest," declared Spisák. "The Smallholders have enough voters for at least three more hours."

But the chairman stuck to his decision.

Outcries were heard a short while later; the gendarmes had attacked the assembled Smallholders with fixed bayonets and chased them home. Not a single man was permitted to remain.

Spisák ran to the telephone. "More than two hundred voters were not permitted to cast their ballots," he informed the party headquarters of the Smallholders.

Protest after protest followed, without avail. The administration stole, cheated, forged, and used force to gain its end. In the evening there was a surprising announcement; since none of the candidates had received an absolute majority, a run-off election between the government candidates and the Smallholders would be held the Sunday following.

Protesting sharply against the arbitrary actions at the election of Mezőkeresztes, Tibor Eckhardt went to see Prime Minister Gömbös. The latter cynically disposed of the subject by telling Eckhardt that the government party must win the election.

The day following the first election, the gendarmes rounded up all of the Smallholders leaders in the village and escorted them to the town hall. One was threatened, another slapped around, a third kicked by the boots of authority to soften them up for Sunday's run-off election.

Stephen Spisák was in front of his house, discussing the outrages of the previous day, with his son and a friend, when a gendarme passed, escorting Andreas Molnár, one of the most respected Smallholders leaders, to the town hall. Molnár yelled: "Hey, Steve, come on with us now. They'll get you later, anyway!"

The gendarme hit Molnár on the back with the butt of his carbine. Molnár jumped like a tiger and took away the gendarme's gun and saber. As the gendarme started to run away, four others approached and fired a volley of shots under which Molnár fell, as he ran into Spisák's courtyard.

Spisák was quickly surrounded and dragged to the town hall. "Why are you arresting us?" he asked. "We just stood in the yard."

The butt of a gendarme's gun fell heavily on his back. Silence again.

Someone excitedly telephoned to the county headquarters, while I was there, to say that Andreas Molnár was dead and Spisák and two others were in the custody of the gendarmerie. I called the capital and asked that the national committee induce some members of parliament to visit Tard and make a personal investigation under the protection of their parliamentary immunity. While I was at the telephone some gendarmes arrived, searching for me, to expel me from the district under the claim that I had contributed to a riot. My host hid me in a huge flower box, and the gendarmes never found me, although they came back every hour.

Meanwhile, Stephen Spisák, his son, and his friend were undergoing systematic torture at the hands of the gendarmerie. Four men took turns in kicking them and hitting them with the butts of their guns. When one gun broke, the captain ordered the men to use sticks, so that no more guns might be wasted; and when one victim seemed about to collapse the gendarmes thrust bayonets under him and snarled: "You want to rest? Lie on these."

Next day the Spisáks and their friend were taken to the district court; the judge found no guilt and set them free. Not daring to go home, they went to party headquarters, where the search for me had been given up. The heroes could not stand nor sit nor lie; their bodies were broken. Young Spisák was crying. The father put a hand on his shoulder and pointed to a picture of the thirteen Hungarian generals who, after losing the fight to liberate Hungary, were martyred in 1849 by the Austrians.

"Don't you cry, son. One must suffer for justice. Look at these men, Hungarians who were even ready to suffer death for their convictions."

Warmth flooded my heart. Here I was face to face with the real nobility and greatness of the Hungarian peasant.

I took them to a hospital at Miskolc, where the doctor found that all of Stephen Spisák's ribs were broken, his son's stomach was displaced, and the right thigh bone of their companion was split. The doctor, in terror of the administration, refused to give a diagnostic affidavit.

Some people cannot be stopped when they want to do something; next Saturday night all three escaped from the hospital, went home to Tard, and voted next day for Zoltán Tildy. Andreas Molnár was alive too; the gendarme's bullets had missed him. While they were shooting he had thrown himself down, and he had crawled along the vegetable patches to hide in a neighbor's attic.

The same methods were employed during run-off elections, and Zoltán Tildy lost.

These were the actions we had to contend with as we tried to get parliamentary representation. In terms of registered voters, the Independent Smallholders became the largest party by 1935. At the elections that year the Smallholders had candidates in eighty-five election districts. In the other one hundred sixty nomination remained impossible. Prime Minister Gömbös broke his promise to Tibor Eckhardt to submit a new law giving the secret ballot to the whole country, and the elections were held under the old law. Of Hungary's 2,200,000 voters, a half-million voted the Smallholders ticket in the eighty-five districts. Accordingly, if candidates had been permitted in the other districts, they would have received a majority of the total vote. Despite this, the

Smallholders received only twenty-three seats in Parliament. I was nominated in my home district and although my people fought vigorously, I was defeated in the open ballot. The published results placed me 117 votes behind the government candidate.

A new chapter in Hungarian politics began after these elections, with the appearance of the first signs of National Socialism. We expected the government to crush any moves toward a Nazi dictatorship but were disappointed. Among the leaders of the government party were a great number who sympathized with National Socialism, and the cabinet dared not attempt to suppress the movement. The Social Democrats, with four or five representatives in Parliament, were much too weak to lead the fight against National Socialism. Although publicly opposing it, they lacked strength for active battle.

The Independent Smallholders party had to shoulder the responsibility of being the only democratic party in Parliament ready to fight Nazism. The Smallholders, under the leadership of Tibor Eckhardt, flung its full strength against the spread of National Socialism; but the party's efforts were ground to nothing between the government party above and the National Socialists below.

A bitter political impasse followed; as had happened so often before in our history, Hungary became a pawn in the political game of the great powers.

Although the great majority of the population of Hungary opposed National Socialism and disapproved of any cooperation with Germany, it could not prevent the developments that came. The great democratic powers did not counteract or even recognize the danger which was engulfing the small countries of central and eastern Europe. Hungary, with a farm surplus, was forced by economic necessity to the side of Germany and Italy. When the Munich Pact practically pushed all the central European countries into Hitler's hand the ideological invasion began.

In 1939, when the continued parliamentary pressure of the Smallholders had effected the first secret ballot, war threatened our part of Europe. The government party and the National Socialists flirted with each other over the heads of the people. The Independent Smallholders won only fourteen seats in Parliament that year. We could not stop the political trend, having no great power behind us to give weight and strength to our singlehanded fight against Nazism; as the war fever mounted, our difficulties increased.

One can say responsibly that, until it was occupied by German forces on March 19, 1944, Hungary as a whole had not supported Germany to the extent that other countries did. The Smallholders and the Social Democrats were the last to battle against the tide of Nazism. We considered our resistance justified because for centuries the people of Hungary have shown their distaste for dictatorship and absolutism. The peasants, especially, resisted the National Socialists; an awakened Hungarian peasant told me at the time: "There are natural reasons why salaried people and even labor accept National Socialism and the peasant does not. A wage earner in modern bureaucracy is not an independent human being—he can work only when he is told what his work is; and it is the same in factories. These people can accept a system of dictatorship more easily than the Hungarian peasant, who relies upon his independent judgment, because for centuries no one cared about him or gave him orders. The Hungarian peasant is an independent person and does not need any form of dictatorship."

While the Smallholders party had very few opportunities to express openly the will of the majority of the Hungarian people who opposed war and the dictatorships, it did so whenever its voice would be heard. When a law by which Hungary would join the Tripartite Pact was suddenly introduced by the government, everyone except the three Smallholders representatives present voted in the affirmative. As the secretary of the parliament, sitting on the rostrum, I was informed by the president that my official capacity prevented me from voting against the Germans.

In 1941, when Austria was already incorporated into the German Reich, when Yugoslavia was occupied by the Nazis, when Rumania had been fighting on the side of the Germans, when Slovakia was standing by Hitler and we were completely surrounded by Hitler's troops and allies, Hungary was finally forced into war. All possibilities for democratic political action ceased. Our small parliamentary group could do little to counteract the Nazi propaganda machine which fired the emotions of our people and drove our government relentlessly into an unwanted war.

Even the section of the German population of Hungary which professed fealty to the Hungarian state tried to stem the tide by declaring an open fight against a subversive, Nazi-promoted federation known as the Volksbund. These good people were suppressed as were the Smallholders. Uselessly we lifted our hands for help; those nations toward which the Hungarian people felt ideological kinship were far away. The longing for Anglo-American friendship could express itself only by listening to the American and English short-wave broadcasts.

CHAPTER 4

The Peasant Alliance

BEFORE THE WAR, NEW GOVERNMENT DECREES AND THE NAZI PROPAGANDA machine made political activity practically impossible for the Smallholders. Under the terrifying pressure of both the government and the Nazis our contact with our constituents was endangered; a new organization, ostensibly free of politics, was needed to supplement the party organization.

By uniting the peasantry, we could not only further the interests of the largest segment of Hungary's population, but preserve its political strength for the future as well. The peasants, prevented from exerting even the slightest influence on economic policy, could not improve their living conditions. Since their own schooling was in political bondage and they had no means of achieving for themselves and their children more than a grade-school education, the peasants' cultural ascendancy was arrested.

True, a few steps in the right direction, taken between the two wars, placed the Hungarian peasantry far ahead of the peasants in other southeastern European countries. For example, Hungary had a program for the care of infants and children through an institution known as the Green Cross. Francis Keresztes-Fischer created a government foundation for the protection of the family, enabling the poorest peasant to establish and maintain a subsistence; but both organizations were in their infancy and were more successful in avoiding starvation than in improving the living standard of the mass of the population.

Through a new, strong peasant organization, I felt, an old dream might come true. It would not only serve the economic, cultural, and social interests of the peasantry, but enlighten, inform, and train it for the future task of reshaping society along democratic lines. One day while visiting my friend Béla Kovács, who had become deputy secretary general of the Smallholders party, at his home in Mecsekalja, I put my plan to a test. Although Béla at first felt that political radicalism with its stirring slogans would more effectively counterbalance the existing trends, he finally became convinced that the Hungarian peasant did not need such artificial stimulants to recognize the political basis of this organization.

A conference with the peasant leaders of the nation resulted in the formation of a National Peasant Alliance with membership and administration restricted to peasants to prevent its misuse; we agreed to ask the government for a charter. I went to see the Prime Minister, Count Paul Teleki, who in spite of his aristocratic breeding had a great love for the common man. His decision that the time was not opportune for starting such a peasant organization delayed us for two years.

This refusal made me restless. Again the insurmountable stone wall of government power blocked the way. While searching for a way around it I found that, although each trade and occupation had its own publication to further its interests, the peasantry lacked a press.

I laid careful plans for the publication of a newspaper designed to serve the common peasant. It was quite an undertaking in those times, for it is much easier to sell a paper loaded with political slogans than a medium of education. Beginning as the first farm journal in Hungary, the *Smallholder* eventually became the largest publication, and within the next two years it had 23,000 subscribers. Written in language the simplest peasant could understand, it brought its readers every improvement in farm work, every scientific discovery concerning the soil, and every new invention in mechanical farming. I was considered a good farmer behind my father's plow, but behind the editorial desk I became an expert.

Naturally the *Smallholder* later became a powerful tool in the resistance. To shorten the war, it was suggested between the lines that as much produce as possible be used at home and on the land, cutting down the amount that could be delivered to Germany.

In 1941, when the Germans forced the Hungarian government to break a recent treaty of friendship with Yugoslavia and permit the safe passage of German armies through Hungary for the invasion of that country, Count Teleki, an ethical statesman of strong convictions, committed suicide. The death of the Prime Minister caused a deep shock; everybody felt this tragedy to be a warning to all small nations. After the passing of the strongest, most outstanding human bastion against the upsurge of war, Hungary, under the premiership of Leslie Bárdossy, was forced into the conflict.

When Bárdossy became Prime Minister I knew that the strong hand of Minister of the Interior Francis Keresztes-Fischer guided the cabinet in matters of internal policy. This enlightened, intelligent man made it possible for the Social Democratic party to function during the war, although its abolishment was demanded violently by the National Socialists and a group in the government party. The Social Democrats supported the Smallholders' policy of resistance.

Francis Keresztes-Fischer made possible the protection of the refugee Poles who had escaped to Hungary, and he identified himself with every worth-while Hungarian enterprise. Before becoming Minister he was the Lord-Lieutenant of my county; and we knew and respected each other well. Considering Bárdossy's ascent to power an opportune time, I put my plans for the peasant alliance before him.

"As you know, I have been supporting your endeavors for a long time, but was unable to get the cabinet's agreement. Now I think the time is ripe," he said. And soon he issued our long-awaited charter.

With the road open and the Minister's acquiescence in our hands, I called a convention of all leading peasants of Hungary; and in September, 1941, the Peasant Alliance was formally founded. I was honored to be elected its first president, and Béla Kovács was made its national secretary.

What was to become the largest organization in Hungary grew by leaps and bounds. The peasantry, disregarding political boundaries, joined throughout the country and soon the alliance's program of democratic education was under way. The Hungarian National Socialists began to oppose the Peasant Alliance violently. When it declared that no member of their party could join, one of the leaders, Andor Jaross, minister without portfolio, attacked us in parliament, accusing the Peasant Alliance of pursuing left-wing political aims and charging that it would become a hiding place for Communists. Jaross openly demanded its prohibition, claiming that it endangered the war effort.

Actually this smear campaign helped the Peasant Alliance, and within one year it had opened offices in a thousand localities. That was the peasants' answer to the parliamentary attacks of the National Socialists.

One of the largest daily papers in Hungary, the *Kis Ujság*, whose editor, Count Julius Dessewffy, is now living in exile, joined our ranks. It became the official voice of the peasantry and the medium for my editorials.

CHAPTER 5

In the Depths of War

THE EARLY SUCCESSES OF THE GERMAN ARMIES DAZZLED SOME CLASSES OF Hungarian society. Part of the officer corps enthusiastically supported the war, and some members of the bourgeois intelligentsia, made giddy by Hungarian Nazi propaganda, glorified it. The country was full of German agents who used every psychological trick to stimulate war fever among the masses.

As the artificial war spirit spread, anti-Semitism spread with it. Two laws were passed which reduced the rights of Jewish citizens. The unnatural psychology within the country and the Nazi pressure from outside forced the government to serve the Germans increasingly. Hungarian economy fell more and more under German control; Nazi pressure bore down upon the press; Hungarian troops were sent to the Russian front.

Although it appeared that Hungary fought by the side of the Axis, the people's hatred of National Socialism increased, and the antiwar sentiment spread rapidly in Hungary.

The peasantry, forced to increase its produce deliveries to the government, had to account for each ounce of its production. Industry became a tool of the German war effort. Finally, censorship killed the comparative freedom of speech; even silence was dangerous, and one was permitted only to hail the war.

Whoever spoke of "democracy" was immediately stamped as a Jewish agent and was attacked by the National Socialist party. Whoever dared to doubt German victory was called "traitor"—a word applied today to those who do not praise the Soviet Union's "generosity" toward Hungary. Although there was no basic change in the constitution, the means and methods of dictatorship became the order of the day.

As a result, the Smallholders party was labeled "a hireling of the

Jews" because it would not condone the Jewish persecution. The once teeming office of the National Committee of the Smallholders party in Budapest was empty; a simple peasant or an ordinary citizen could not visit us without great personal danger.

The Hungarian Nazi party, known as the Arrow Cross, entered the circles of the industrial workers. Some of the large industrial enterprises, whose employees were formerly members of the Social Democratic party, fell into their hands. In the factories and in the mines Arrow Cross party commissioners watched to prevent the workers from engaging in any anti-Nazi or antiwar activity.

The only untouched class was the Hungarian peasantry, which resisted National Socialism of any color as one man. Of course one could find peasants who were forced to join the Arrow Cross, but the large majority despised them. Even at the peak of Nazi war successes, simple peasants told one another that the Germans would eventually fall and the war be won by the democracies.

The leaders of the Smallholders party and the Peasant Alliance felt that the time to unite the democratic forces had come. We decided to arrange for cooperation between the Smallholder peasants and the industrial laboring men still in the ranks of the Social Democratic party. This was no easy undertaking: the Hungarian peasants coupled the Social Democrats with the Communists. We had to find a common denominator before we could overcome peasant resistance and achieve such cooperation.

The leaders of the Social Democratic party, Charles Peyer, Francis Szeder, Anne Kéthly, and Árpád Szakasits, met with us to discuss how the parties would react to the unavoidable entry of the Communists into the postwar political arena. Social Democratic leaders, aspiring to a truly democratic state, promised to fight any thrust of Communism, and declared that their platform was general suffrage, private property, and self-government; and we believed that on this basis our efforts could be coordinated.

In the spring of 1943 we invited a hundred leaders of the Smallholders party to the capital for a conference. To them we sketched the national outlook, believing that after the war the political stage would be democratic, and that we in rebuilding our country could not afford to collaborate, like Stephen Nagyatádi Szabó, with the landed aristocracy and selfish capitalism. But we also could not oppose industrial labor, obviously one of the pillars of any postwar democratic structure.

Therefore we had to begin the cooperation with the Social Democrats immediately, and continue after the war's end.

I moved that the Hungarian peasantry declare, for the first time in the history of the country, in favor of cooperation with the party of industrial labor, the Social Democrats. After long, intelligent discussions the motion was adopted, and one of Hungary's most satisfying political partnerships was approved. Until the established leaders of the Social Democrats were pushed aside after the war by men servile to Moscow and the Communists, peasant and laborer marched hand in hand along the road toward true democracy.

In 1943 the German pressure became unbearable. But more unbearable was the thought that when the war ended Hungary would stand among the accused before the bar of world public opinion, in spite of the fact that the majority of its population was entering this war against its will and had not elected the government that delivered the country to Hitler on its own responsibility.

At this time Andrew Bajcsy-Zsilinsky rose from the ranks of the Smallholders deputies to become one of its outstanding leaders in the parliament. A man of great education and broad vision, but endowed with the hot blood of his peasant forefathers, he could not remain idle in the face of developments. He prepared a memorandum, signed by all the Smallholders deputies, to the new Prime Minister, Nicholas Kállay, setting forth several measures which the Smallholders felt were necessary to the preservation of the nation:

(1) Hungary should quit the war and declare its neutrality.

(2) The government should recall all Hungarian troops from the Russian front.

(3) All officers in sympathy with Germany and National Socialism should be removed from the army.

(4) The persecution of the Jews should cease immediately.

(5) All army and gendarmerie officers who encouraged or permitted abuses of the nationalities in the territory regained from Yugoslavia should be punished.

(6) A bill insuring equality before the law for all minorities living in Hungary after the war should be prepared.

Premier Nicholas Kállay, to whom the memorandum was delivered, was a descendant of an ancient Hungarian family. His ancestors were among the founders of our land, and it was said that Kállays had declined a peerage offered by the king because they considered themselves better than the barons and counts whose lines were only a few hundred years old. Kállay did not like the Germans and probably did not even believe in their victory. Undoubtedly that is why no proceedings were started against us; for under the wartime laws each signer could have been charged with treason.

One copy of the memorandum reached Switzerland, where a newspaper published the entire contents; afterward it became known all over the world. The memorandum of the Hungarian Smallholders followed a declaration of the Finnish opposition; it was the second time liberals of a territory under Nazi influence tried to induce its satellite government to break with Germany and quit the war.

After the memorandum was presented to the premier, the leaders of the Smallholders party held some clandestine meetings with the people in all parts of the country to prepare them for postwar events. We returned from our secret trip through the country with the happy conviction that the peasant was little infected with Nazism and was convinced of eventual Allied victory.

When leaders of Hungary's intellectual life joined in active party work a new cycle started for the Smallholders. Here they began the political activity which later led them to important achievements in the life of the country. There developed among the democratic forces a very healthy union of peasantry, labor, and progressive intellectualism.

We felt that a new history was in the making. The Hungarian government, we knew, would be judged among the satellites; but we were sure that freedom was in the offing—a freedom which would end the subjugation of peasants, workers, and citizens. There would be a new life for the nation, in which the downtrodden of all classes would build together the towering structure of democracy.

CHAPTER 6

German Occupation

HUNGARY COMMEMORATES THE FIGHT FOR LIBERTY IN 1848 BY A GREAT national holiday on March 15; in 1944 a group in the Smallholders party decided to observe the day by placing a wreath on the monument to Louis Kossuth. The plan was kept secret, but word evidently got around, for when our small group of deputies appeared at the monument on Parliament Square a mass of people rushed out from hiding in doorways and behind buildings and joined in the demonstration.

After the ceremony Julius Dessewffy, the editor of the *Kis Ujság*, pulled me aside and told me that German military forces were massing on Austrian soil near the Hungarian border. This must mean the occupation of Hungary.

Zoltán Tildy and Andrew Bajcsy-Zsilinszky agreed to call on Premier Kállay for an explanation while I saw Francis Keresztes-Fischer, the Minister of the Interior, for the same purpose. I was not able to reach the minister until the evening of March 18, after I spoke at a festival arranged by Poles who had escaped into Hungary.

I gave the minister the information, which by this time had reached me from several sources, and expressed fear that the Germans were planning to occupy Hungary. The minister was nervous but said that a request for information regarding troop movements had been transmitted to the Germans by the government. They had replied that they were increasing their troop reserves in Austria because it was easier to feed them there and they could be transported faster, in an emergency, to either the Italian or the Russian front.

Keresztes-Fischer's answer, and the government's weak acceptance of the dubious German explanation, shocked me. I told him that the Hungarian government, upon hearing the news, should have reenforced the frontier before asking the Germans what they were doing.

As we discussed the situation, I implored the minister to use his good influence in the cabinet to effect a last minute armed resistance against occupation. We could not hold out long against a German onslaught, but we must show that we would not complacently accept "subjugation."

That night my heart was full of anxiety for my people, for the nation which had for centuries stood so many trials and fought so valiantly for freedom and national independence all through its history. The minister's assurances left me with the feeling that we were on the brink of a new national catastrophe. That sleepless night was the first of many to come; questions of the future seemed to bear on my brain with an almost physical weight.

At daybreak the telephone rang. "What did the Minister of Interior say?" asked Tildy.

"He tried to quiet me," I answered, and gave him the Germans' explanation.

"Kállay said about the same, but the German troops are advancing toward the capital and have reached Györ," said Tildy.

I left instantly to join him.

As I reached the square I saw the yellow military cars of the German army in position, and German gunners lounging about; continuing on a streetcar to Buda, I encountered whole armored columns. I ran up to Tildy's home.

"The Germans are already in our streets," I reported.

"Yes, I know." A suspense filled the room; but we had to act.

"Zoltán, are you leaving your apartment?"

"Absolutely," he answered. "And I suggest that you do not return to your home either."

In the parting moment our fourteen years of shoulder-to-shoulder struggle passed before us on the screen of memory.

From a coffee shop near my home, I telephoned to my wife what had happened, asking her to take the family on the night train to the country if traveling was still possible. I also reached my friends, who told me that the Gestapo had already appeared at the home of Andrew Bajcsy-Zsilinszky. The hot-blooded, fearless man greeted them with revolver in hand, and was shot. Tears filled my eyes when I heard the news, for Andrew Bajcsy-Zsilinszky, one of the bravest and most progressive figures in Hungary's political life, meant much to all of us. An ardent believer in democracy, he was the most emphatic opponent of Nazism in parliament although, by an uproar, the National Socialists had prevented him from addressing the chamber. He loved his people, and was deeply convinced that an improvement in the standards of the peasant would elevate the whole country.

In the coffeehouse I started to look through the papers. Naturally one of the first was the *Kis Ujság*, the front page of which was occupied by my article "Louis Kossuth and the Peasantry," written for the anniversary of Louis Kossuth's death, March 20. I concluded bitterly that I would write no more articles until the end of the war.

I began to walk the streets, seeing everywhere downhearted people with bitter faces and eyes blazing hate for the invading Germans.

Later I learned that the regent of Hungary, Horthy, after having spent the critical days at Hitler's headquarters, had been on his way home during the early hours of March 19. His train was stopped between stations because the tracks were blown up, enabling the Germans to occupy the country in his absence. They need not have feared Horthy's resistance; although he had been anti-German in recent times, he was impotent to shake off the influences surrounding him. Much later I learned that in many cities the commanding officers were ready for armed resistance, but that the general staff had issued specific orders to all divisions not to resist.

That night I went home to Bisse, accompanied on the train by my mother who was recuperating from a major operation, my youngest child, and my wife. For a few days I lived furtively on the outskirts of the village, but since the Germans were not looking for me in Bisse I went home. From morning to night I labored in the fields, trying to work off my stormy and bitter emotions. While I was planting some grapevines with my father and my son Ferenc, home from law school, the first squadron of American bombers passed above us on their way to the capital. Although they were carrying destruction to the most beautiful city in the world, we felt that they brought something more valuable than things of brick and wood—the end of the war, peace, and justice.

Of my friends I could establish contact only with Béla Kovács and Béla Varga. Kovács visited me a few times; Varga wrote from his hiding place through one of our party secretaries.

I was pruning fruit trees in my mother-in-law's orchards when Aunt Eszti ran breathlessly toward me.

"German soldiers have come for you."

This news came as no surprise, for I expected them every day. Deciding to stall for time, I used the house of a neighbor as a retreat. The soldiers searched for me till night, then informed my family that if I did not appear at Gestapo headquarters at Pécs within three days, they would take them into custody. Therefore I had to suffer arrest and imprisonment for my political beliefs, because a man could not visit this suffering upon his wife and children.

I used the three days' grace to go to Budapest and call on Andrew Tasnády-Nagy, speaker of parliament.

"I have come," I told him, "because I shall be arrested by the Gestapo in two days. My parliamentary immunity is being infringed, and I also announce this on behalf of all the deputies who have been arrested and had no opportunity to inform you that their parliamentary immunity has been violated. I ask you to be good enough to read this announcement at the next open session of parliament."

On April 17 I became a prisoner of the Gestapo.

The Gestapo prison was the police jail in Pécs. Ten of the twenty cells were requisitioned by the Gestapo, and the others left in the hands of the Hungarian police. Thus the prisoners of the Gestapo and the Hungarian police were mixed in the overcrowded prison. There were only ten or twelve Christian political prisoners in the German cells; the rest were Jews who had been dragged from their homes. As the prison was underground and its entrance was barred by an iron grille, both the Germans and the Hungarian police left the cell doors open; we could at least walk around and mix with the others.

The Gestapo had no way of feeding us, so that everyone had to provide for his own meals—a great advantage for the prisoners. This gave us an opportunity to make arrangements with a near-by innkeeper to send us our meals, and through him we received packages from our families.

Meals were delivered three times a day by white-coated waiters whom the Gestapo did not know. My friends found this out, and one day Leslie Samu, the secretary of the Peasant Alliance, appeared in a white coat with my food. He whispered:

"We have opened a route for you all the way to Tito's troops. Try to escape—you can be out of the country in a few hours. I'll go and stick with you in Yugoslavia. But the question is, can you escape?"

"Escape would not be difficult," I answered. "I could find a way but after my escape my family would be arrested. I simply could not risk it."

Days later a huge waiter in a tremendous white coat entered the prison mess hall—none other than Béla Kovács.

"I wanted to see you," he hissed. "They are organizing armed resistance in Transylvania. In your opinion, shall we join?"

"Who is the leader?" I asked.

Béla Kovács whispered a name in my ear.

"Do not let anyone join," I said. "The man is unreliable, and until recently he flirted with the extreme right. One cannot prepare an uprising with him."

The Gestapo conducted its questioning outside the prison, in a building especially outfitted for the purpose. Most of the prisoners

returned from these inquisitions half dead, and I looked ahead to my
own session with some misgivings. A week after my arrest I was taken
to Gestapo headquarters for questioning, but was not harmed. I heard
that other lawmakers imprisoned by the Gestapo experienced no brutality in any of the prisons.

I met the leaders of the Gestapo only once after this short examination. Two weeks after my arrest a transport of Jewish people was prepared for deportation to Germany. One of the Hungarian guards informed me confidentially that he had overheard the Germans discussing
my inclusion in it.

Well, great activity began in the prison. I stayed back when we
were supposed to take our afternoon walk in the yard. After the German guard followed the rest of the prisoners for an hour's stroll in the
sunshine, I managed, with the help of a decent Hungarian policeman, to
telephone the Lord-Lieutenant of the county, Michael Nikolics, who at my
request had remained in office during the occupation. I told him that the
Gestapo was taking me to Germany at daybreak. This brave and intelligent friend called on the Gestapo commander and told him that ten
thousand peasants of Baranya had signed a demand for my immediate
release; he intimated that they should be prepared for a peasant uprising if I were taken from Pécs. No news arrived from the Gestapo.
Late in the evening, policemen smuggled my family into one of the
Hungarian cells. While my German guard was not looking, I slipped
over to them to say farewell. Little Lacika, one and a half years old,
could not grasp the situation; nor did I realize that a few years later
he would play an important role in politics.

In the cell opposite mine, there were two Jewish women and a
Swabian who was imprisoned because she opposed Nazism despite her
German ancestry. One of the women was very old and heavy. After she
was helped to lie down at night on the concrete cell floor, she was unable to rise until morning. As one of our self-imposed daily chores, my
cell partner, Baron Biederman, and I helped this poor crippled woman
get on her feet.

One cloudy, dark night we were awakened at three in the morning
and ordered to pack our things. They read our names and lined us up
in rows of four in the dark prison yard. When the old lady from the
opposite cell slipped in the darkness, Germans with machine guns in
hand dragged her by the hair to a wheelbarrow, threw her on it, and
ordered two Jewish prisoners to push her to the railroad station. The

soldiers pointed machine guns at us, counted us again, and ordered "Right face"—we knew we were on the road to deportation.

With flashlight in hand, a steel-helmeted German soldier neared our column, shouting my name. When I answered he ordered me to step out, and I was soon back in the cell block. I had a feeling that the intervention of the Lord-Lieutenant had been successful: I should remain at Pécs. The Hungarian policemen gladly helped me take off my rucksack, and amidst the joyous shouts of my prison mates, I threw myself on the plank that served as my bed and fell into deep slumber.

In the next weeks the peasants did not rest; they petitioned constantly in Baranya and throughout occupied Hungary for my release. The Gestapo had a hard time avoiding response to this peasant avalanche.

In the meantime the prison started to fill up again. A characteristic incident occurred one evening when the police arrested some people for disorderly conduct and brought them to the jail. The Hungarian head keeper yelled at the top of his voice to the arresting officers:

"Didn't I tell you a hundred times not to bring in any ordinary criminals? This jail is already too crowded with honest people."

Finally the Gestapo decided; not to release me but to transfer me to Budapest. At the end of May I was moved to the jail of the criminal court in the capital. A number of anti-Nazi leaders were there already; among them Leopold Baranyai, a member of the upper house and president of the national bank; Desider Laky, a deputy and former cabinet minister; John Makay, former deputy; young Zoltán Tildy who had been arrested in his father's stead; Aladár Szegedy-Maszák, the brave high official of the foreign ministry; Aladár Baráti-Huszár, chairman of the social security board; and Andor Szentmiklosy, the deputy foreign minister. I was happy to greet the many politicians, economists, and soldiers who were imprisoned there for their crime of refusing to bow to German rule; but, embracing Andrew Bajcsy-Zsilinszky, I was completely overwhelmed. Although reported dead, he actually was only seriously injured.

First I was put into a large collective cell; next to me lay Stephen Perényi, the splendid director-general of the Credit Bank. The rest of the cell was filled with unknown little people whom the Germans, for some reason, considered dangerous.

Every Wednesday packages could be sent into the prison, and once a German guard bit into an apple in my parcel. His tooth struck a small pencil which my friends had tried to smuggle in. He immediately reported the well deserved injury to his palate, and I was put into solitary, for a whole month.

Alone in the narrow cubicle with plenty of time to think about the political outlook, I already knew that Hungary was going to be liberated by the Russians and not by the Americans or British, when they landed in Normandy instead of the Balkans. In terms of the future political readjustment of southeastern Europe, I concluded, this decision by the Western powers would prove to be a tragic mistake. The Soviet army would bring along agitators to promote organizing of the Communists after the Germans had been kicked out. My inability to take part in the preparations for the period after liberation irked me terribly. My fears that the Smallholders party would be found unprepared were later justified; at the time of the readjustment it would lack strength to direct the re-forming of the political line-up.

The American and British air forces had not bombed Budapest before the occupation; this stand touched us and gave us hope. To make up for lost time, however, the attacks were intensive after the occupation. In the prison in Budapest I lived through twenty-two bombings; during the day it was the Americans; during the night, the British. We knew because, when the bombings began, the few American pilots in prison sang their national anthem, and at night the British, recognizing the sound of their planes, sang theirs.

Although the Hungarian jailers led their prisoners to the air-raid shelter, the prisoners of the Gestapo, housed on the upper floors, were left in their quarters by the Germans during the raids. When the sirens announced the approach of the bombers, the German guards double-locked all exits, went to the shelter, and left us to our fate. Fortunately our prison and the surrounding buildings were never hit by English or American fliers.

Following the onrush of the Germans through Poland, a mass of Polish statesmen, army officers, and intellectuals found refuge in Hungary. Its people received them with open arms.

Two men in particular did a great deal for the refugee Poles. They were Joseph Antall, a fellow prisoner and future cabinet minister, and Father Béla Varga.

Varga, as parish priest of Balatonboglár, received with warm friendship the Poles who had camped there. He had a large community center erected in the village, and, upon its completion, granted it to the Poles for a university; for a time it was the only institution of higher education the Polish people had anywhere in the world. A number of important Polish leaders owe their lives to Varga; the son of Mikolajczyk, Prime Minister of the London Polish government-in-exile, was one of his wards for a long time. Varga arranged for his escape to Switzerland, disguised with clerical robes. There was no end to his labors on behalf of the suffering Poles. Antall was, before the German occupation, chief of the department in the Ministry of Interior which cared for refugees. He bravely established, executed, and defended the policy under which the Poles could find temporary shelter in Hungary.

After my month in solitary, Henry Slavik, head of the relief society which cared for the Polish refugees in Hungary, was thrown into my cell. My new cell mate was one of the leaders of the Polish Socialist party and its fighting publicist. He knew no Hungarian and, like most of the world's peasants, I spoke only my native tongue. In the Gestapo prison I learned a few German words and Slavik acquired some Hungarian expressions; this was the basis for our communication with each other. Using bits of two languages and substituting signs for the missing word, we even discussed the political news reaching us by grapevine.

The Soviet troops had by this time reached the suburbs of Warsaw, where General Bor Komarowsky led a successful uprising. Upon awakening every morning, Slavik anxiously inquired if the Russians had broken into Warsaw and relieved General Bor and his valiant handful of followers. When it became obvious that the Russians delayed conquering the city until the Germans had butchered Bor's strong-hearted men, Slavik became hopelessly disheartened. We concluded that, because the uprising was not Communist-controlled, the Russians did not hurry to the relief of Warsaw; that was why they permitted the mass murders in that city.

"They are wrong," he noted bitterly. "Poland will never become a Communist state. The people despise Communism because they are religious and believe in traditions. Only democracy can shape Poland's future, no matter what the Russians want."

It was not long before Slavik and five of his associates, together with Fietovicz, the representative of the exiled Polish government, and Filipievicz, the famous painter, were dragged into the German deportation camp and brutally murdered.

My next cell mate was Aladár Baráti-Huszár, a member of the Upper House. This prominent Hungarian was one of the nobler leaders of feudal Hungary; love of country flamed constantly in his heart. It was interesting to see how the personality of this unusual man mirrored the conceptions of the anti-Nazi gentry. He talked at length about how he would chastise, at the first meeting, those members of the gentry casino who had served the Germans during the occupation. He was flabbergasted when I suggested that the splendid structure of the gentry casino might be used to house a union headquarters or a labor center after the war—while the members he intended to chastise swung from the gallows or served long sentences in the penitentiary.

Until September, 1944, Döme Sztojai, the former Hungarian minister to Berlin, was the puppet premier under German rule. In September he was succeeded by General Géza Lakatos, a man deeply conscious of his Hungarian ancestry. Lakatos' hot blood boiled at the injury to his country's sovereignty. He demanded that the German government set free all members of Parliament and the Upper House; he even announced this move in a speech in Parliament. When this news reached us in prison, we were overjoyed. Great hopes for the approaching day of liberation lighted our dark lives.

A few days later the names of six of the more prominent prisoners were listed by the Germans. Mine was not among them. I had become resigned to not being released with the others when, on October 10, the Germans ordered me to gather my things and get ready. Within an hour, Bajcsy-Zsilinszky, Baranyai, Laky, Makay, young Tildy and I were transferred into the custody of the Hungarian prosecutor. Poor Aladár Baráti-Huszár was not freed; since his term in the Upper House had expired in the meantime, he had ceased to be a lawmaker.

While we were waiting to be booked at the offices of the Hungarian prosecutor, a distinguished vistor, Gabriel Vladár, then Minister of Justice, arrived. He came to see us in person, he said, because, although the Hungarian government had succeeded in making an arrangement with the Germans, the Nazis had attached an obviously illegal and ticklish "rider." The Germans had agreed to return to Hungary all members of Parliament and the Upper House whom they had deported to Germany and Austria, but only on condition that the Hungarian government indict and prosecute us. He asked us if we were ready to submit. We signed a declaration saying that we were ready to undergo any sacrifice to help our comrades and friends suffering on foreign soil. We figured that, as soon as the deported legislators were returned, we should all leave custody together. There were other inklings of the

approaching day of liberation; on the way from the Gestapo prison
to the Hungarian prosecutor, we had heard the roar of the guns of the
advancing Russian army. Soon our vile treatment would reach an end.

These were the days when Regent Nicholas Horthy and Francis
Szálasi, the moronic leader of the Hungarian National Socialists, were
racing each other for time. In the early part of October, Horthy sent a
secret delegation to Moscow to ask the Soviet for an armistice. The
group included Count Géza Teleki, a college professor and son of the
suicide Prime Minister; Gabriel Faraghó, a gendarmerie general; and
Dominick Szentiványi, an envoy from the Foreign Ministry. On October 11, this delegation signed the temporary agreement for an armistice, and Horthy prepared to declare the armistice publicly.

At the same time, under the leadership of Szálasi, the Hungarian
Nazis were preparing a putsch. The Germans, grabbing at the last
straw, united with Szálasi whom they had despised up to now. On
October 15 Regent Horthy decided the time was ripe to announce on
the radio that he had asked the Russians for an armistice; but simultaneously the Hungarian Nazis and troops under their control began to
occupy all public buildings. In the forenoon, the beautiful illusion of
peace overjoyed the public; but by noon everybody knew that Szálasi
had executed the putsch and assumed executive power.

Naturally the Germans did not keep their bargain to release the
deported legislators to the Hungarian government. When Minister of
Justice Vladár, who had made the deal with us, saw that within a few
hours the followers of Szálasi would be in power everywhere, he immediately ordered the release of the political prisoners. He was afraid
that, if both the Germans and the Hungarian Nazis found us in the
prison, they would deport or execute us. So, around midday of the
Hungarian Nazi putsch, the doors of the prison swung open. The road
before us led, not to long awaited freedom, but into hiding.

CHAPTER 7

Underground

FRIENDS BROUGHT WORD TO MY FAMILY THAT I HAD LEFT THE GERMAN
prison on October 10. My wife and daughter immediately set out for
Budapest, but my son, Ferenc, could not come—he had been taken to

a punishment camp. They arrived just as I was leaving the prison, and so we were able to go on together. During our last five days in jail, Albert Bereczky, a Presbyterian pastor of Budapest who, after the liberation, was to become a state secretary in the Ministry of Education, and his assistant, Michael Högye, visited us daily. They told us that they had found hiding places for all of us; mine was to be Bethesda Hospital, an institution run by the Presbyterian Church. Arriving there with my wife and daughter, I heard Regent Horthy's address to the people over the radio, just a few minutes before it carried the voices of the Hungarian Nazis, the Arrow Crossists.

Our happy reunion was interrupted when the head of the hospital informed me that we should have to leave. The gateman was a Nazi and had recognized us.

Taking time only to shave off my prison-grown mustache, I went to look for a new hide-out. My wife and daughter found refuge in the home of the bell-ringer of the Calvin Square Presbyterian Church, while I spent the night at the house of Dr. Leslie Cseh-Szombati, formerly a Smallholders deputy.

Next day Michael Högye took me to a workers' settlement on the outskirts of Budapest, where a minister had offered shelter. But when we rang his doorbell late that night there was no one at home. He had apparently left town to avoid the danger of hiding me. Michael brought me instead to his father's home in the same suburb.

The elder Högye, an ironworker, was a forthright Social Democrat. That evening, after a long day's work, he told us of the terrorism of Arrow Cross leaders at his factory. Months later I mourned from the depths of my heart the death of this clear-sighted old man; he had been killed by a mine during the siege. His son Michael, a promising young Presbyterian pastor, had linguistic gifts and long ministerial experience among Hungarians in France that gained for him a diplomatic post in Paris during my premiership. Later, he, too, was declared a "conspirator" and deprived of his Hungarian citizenship.

As the Red army neared Budapest, the Germans began evacuating the workers' settlement; not to rescue the workers and their families but to plunder their abandoned homes.

I had to seek another hiding place and found haven in the Scottish Mission, in which several charitable institutions of the Presbyterian Church were located—among them a school for converted children. Therefore the building was under the protection of the Swiss and

Swedish Red Cross. Arrow Cross gangs armed with machine guns were combing the city for Jews and anti-Germans, who were herded into concentration camps or shot on the spot. Prospective victims sought to save their lives by moving to houses under such diplomatic protection. Later, Arrow Cross execution squads broke into these buildings, too.

At the Scottish Mission, Zoltán Tildy also had taken refuge with his family. He was terribly thin, and I hardly recognized him with his mustache shaved off, his hair strangely combed, and wearing over-sized glasses. Escaping imprisonment, he had been in a position to direct the resistance movement from constantly shifting hide-outs. From him I learned that the anti-German parties, functioning in secret, had founded together a joint organization called the Hungarian Front, including the Smallholders and Social Democrats (banned at the start of German occupation) and the underground Communist party. Their leaders met frequently and decided to form a coalition government after the war.

Tildy told me that on October 11 he and Árpád Szakasits, a Social Democratic leader also in hiding, had secretly visited Regent Horthy, who approved of the Hungarian Front and promised to support a coalition government after the armistice. It was a curious reflection of the policies maintained by Horthy that, recognizing that all gentry traditions were tottering, and even ready to admit Communists into the Cabinet, he still resisted land reform.

Those who arranged the meeting were amused by the great concern of Szakasits (a future leader of the far left) as to how he should procure a dress suit for the audience. They finally persuaded him to go in street clothes. Afterward Szakasits spoke with admiration of Horthy, saying that the meeting had been an unforgettable experience for him.

Tildy also informed me of the preparations, progressing under conditions of utmost peril, for military resistance under the leadership of Andrew Bajcsy-Zsilinszky and Lieutenant General John Kiss. A man who went under the name of Fekete and claimed to be a liaison agent of the Russians offered his services to the organizers. Later, after winning their confidence, he betrayed the movement. Bajcsy-Zsilinszky, Kiss, Lieutenant Colonel Eugene Nagy, and Captain William Tarcsay were seized by the Nazis and executed. Others, such as Joseph Kővágó, later mayor of Budapest, received long prison sentences. Thus ended the first military uprising since the War for Independence in 1848.

Meanwhile the Scottish Mission was becoming unsafe. Because a

Jewish forced labor brigade was quartered there, the building became suspect. There was danger that not only Tildy and I, but also Béla Varga, Zoltán Pfeiffer, and Julius Dessewffy who were often with us, would be captured. Desperately we sought patriots brave enough to hide us.

One day Simonfy-Tóth, a major on the general staff, visited us in civilian clothes. He was planning to fly to Moscow, and had come to ask if we wished to send someone to discuss post-armistice questions. Tildy was for sending me, but it seemed advisable that I stay to organize our party after the liberation. Finally we settled on Zoltán Tildy, Jr., who made preparations to leave next morning. Two of Simonfy-Tóth's men were to call for him at the Presbyterian Church on Pozsonyi Street and take him from there by auto to the airport.

The car was late. When it did show up, Tildy, suspicious of its occupants, sent a woman to tell them he did not live there. On this, the men in the car rushed at breakneck speed to the airport. Luckily the plane had left on schedule, and by the time they arrived it was gone. It soon became evident that the men in the car were Nazi agents; young Tildy's intuition had saved Simonfy-Tóths and his whole party from capture and execution.

The plane reached Moscow safely. Eventually, Simonfy-Tóth returned to Hungary with the armistice delegation and helped organize the army. In 1945, however, the Russians seized him, and no one has heard of the brave young soldier since.

During our last days at the Scottish Mission we learned that the Arrow Cross government had fled from Budapest together with those members of Parliament whom they had been able to organize into the rightist National Alliance. I was shocked to hear by radio the voice of opportunistic Archduke Joseph Habsburg, calling on members of Parliament to support Szálasi by joining the National Alliance. Veering with every wind, this spineless member of the ruling house, during the 1918 Communist upheaval, had renounced his name and title to curry favor with the extreme left. On the overthrow of the Communist regime in 1919, he reassumed his rank and even succeeded in winning election as president of the Academy of Science despite the fact that he did not know the difference between astrology and astronomy. In the era of National Socialism, here he was in the Arrow Cross camp.

While in hiding I had had no news of the peasants' welfare. Were they able to defend themselves against the plundering Germans and

Arrow Cross men? Did they have enough to eat? I was especially concerned over their leaders, who had incurred the wrath of the Nazis by systematically sabotaging all government measures.

One morning the fiancée of Tildy's eldest son said to me, "Uncle Feri, I know of a good hiding place."

"Where, Catherine?" I asked.

"A schoolmate of mine lives at the mint with her parents. Her mother is a wonderful woman. She goes out of her way to shelter anyone the Germans are after. The police who guard the building can be trusted. There are no soldiers or Arrow Crossists around, and the hugeness of the mint makes it a good hide-out."

That same night during the black-out, behind the Ministry of Justice, I met my new host. He was Leslie Solthy, an inspector of the National Bank. He had seen my name in the papers, but I had never heard of him before. Yet I stayed with his family from the middle of November until January 18, the day of our liberation. Always I shall remember their deep courage and warm kindness.

In the family circle was another fugitive, Solthy's son, an engineering student who had disobeyed orders to leave with his class for Germany.

Food was a great problem in those days, but Solthy's son-in-law, who was planning to desert the army in January, managed to smuggle in a butchered pig. The city family did not know what to do with the huge carcass, but I, as a peasant Jack-of-all-trades set to work carving it. The ham, bacon, and sausage turned out so well that the Solthys often reminisced about it later.

By this time news reached us of the brutal assaults on women by soldiers of the Red army. I was terribly worried about my wife and daughter, and wanted to return. Toward the end of November Béla Varga helped me get a letter to my family, asking if they knew of any quiet spot in the village or vicinity where it would be safe for me to hide; but when my son's reply arrived, in the middle of December, the Russians had encircled Budapest, and it was impossible to leave.

The siege of Budapest began on Christmas Eve. The Russian army had closed the ring of iron around the capital. That very night a shell hit the house opposite, smashing our windows. Solthy took the women of his family down to the air-raid shelter; but his son and I, having no desire to mingle with strangers, elected to stay in the apartment. There was always the chance of someone recognizing us and tipping off the Nazis.

Thus the siege and destruction of this beautiful city took place before our eyes, as did the Arrow Cross persecution of the Jews. We could hardly look out of the broken windows without seeing a weeping group of these unfortunates being led to the ghetto or to slaughter on the bank of the Danube.

On the radio we followed the advance of the Red army across Hungary; when I heard it had crossed the Danube in South Baranya, my heart grew anxious for the fate of my family.

"What will you do if you find that the Russians have assaulted your wife and daughter?" Solthy once asked.

"I shall love them as much as ever," I replied with a heavy heart.

On the 29th of December Mrs. Solthy rushed to us breathlessly from the air-raid shelter.

"Come right down to the shelter," she cried frenziedly.

"What's happened?" we asked together.

"It's an Arrow Cross raid. They're searching every room in the house!" she exclaimed despairingly. "I'll take you to a part of the cellar they've already examined. Maybe that way you can still escape."

She hustled us to a storage room in the cellar. Just as we reached it, a terrific explosion shook the building. As soon as the debris stopped falling the residents began collecting the dead and wounded, and Solthy led a group of fire-fighters to the roof. A bomb had struck the building, wrecking the upper part. In the Solthy's apartment, only the vestibule was left. Just that afternoon I had been sitting there in the armchair reading John Stuart Mill on liberty, while young Solthy attempted to paint my portrait. Now the armchair was littered with bricks and glass and sections of the bathroom door. Had Mrs. Solthy not summoned us, both of us would have perished.

Now we had to live in the cellar. My host had provided false papers well in advance, and I already knew the family tree of my alias, Ferenc Szentes, as well as I knew my own. Ready answers to embarrassing questions often meant the difference between life and death. In the air-raid shelter I appeared as an out-of-town employee of the National Bank.

In the shelter, we had every reason to bless Providence. Elsewhere apartment dwellers were jammed in basements like cattle, sleeping where and when they could—in chairs or on the floor. A single unlucky hit by a bomb would often wipe out hundreds of people. Our shelter, by contrast, was excellently equipped and even had a ventilator and stoves where the women cooked meals every day. Each of us had his own bed. To provide against a possible failure of the city water supply, Solthy had a well drilled in the courtyard. There was also a battery-fed lighting system, and when the batteries gave out oil lamps were available. Here we lived through the siege of Budapest, a hell only those who went through it can imagine.

Mines and shells rained on the city, successive explosions merging into one continuous thunder. In the sky, planes engaged in murderous dog-fights; and falling bombs punctuated the earsplitting racket. Anti-aircraft guns provided a furious counterpoint.

In the shelter, it was not easy to keep calm. Fear, nervousness, mistrust were written on every face. We knew that there were pro-Germans and anti-Germans among us; but no one showed his colors. Some feared the Arrow Cross gangs still running berserk in the city; others dreaded the Russian advance. No news was good news.

We heard that a temporary assembly had been set up in Debrecen and was later supplemented by a cabinet. As a politician, I felt uneasy, having no details and not knowing the attitude of the army of occupation.

As the Red army advanced house by house, street by street, the anxiety of the women grew. My feelings were mixed. As a refugee I could hardly wait to see the first Russian soldier; but family men with wives and daughters trembled to think what might happen. I shared their worries, knowing that if it came to the worst we men could not look on idly. I was afraid we would get involved in a fight with the Russians.

One night, during a momentary lull in the engagement, we heard a Russian broadcast in Hungarian over a loud-speaker, stationed near by. Through an open window its message could be clearly heard even in the shelter. The Red announcer sought to reassure the populace and incite resistance against the Germans.

The same night the watchman came into the shelter to report that Russian soldiers were in the building. He told us to be calm—the soldiers were friendly. A few minutes later a group of enlisted men and officers, with machine guns ready to fire, entered. They asked if there were any Germans in the shelter. After convincing themselves that we were all unarmed civilians, they settled down near the entrance.

Two officers joined them, bringing accordions and expensive liquor. It was strange how everyone in the shelter craved alcohol—even those who had never had a taste for wine or whisky. Drinks were passed around, and the atmosphere grew very friendly. Around noon, however, the drunken soldiers began demanding women, frightening all of us. A young husband and Solthy's son volunteered to go through shell fire to get some women from a brothel. They succeeded in locating several, offering them money and valuables to induce them to come with them to the mint; but the women were afraid and would not come. When the young men returned empty-handed the Russians were furious; only an order to advance, arriving at the critical moment, saved the day.

I remained a few days in the cellar, doing what I could to protect the families of those who had so selflessly sheltered me, but planned as soon as was practicable to rejoin my friends and begin reorganizing the Smallholders party.

CHAPTER 8

The Liberation

ON JANUARY 22 TWO YOUNG CIVILIANS, WEARING THE RED ARMBANDS OF the revolutionary, appeared in the cellar with word that Zoltán Tildy and his family awaited me at the Scottish Mission.

At the head of the stairs I faced a terrifying scene. Man-high rubble covered the streets. High blockades of concrete, steel girders, lumber, brick, and glass from the collapsed buildings jammed the thoroughfares. The wrecks of thousands of planes, tanks, and motor cars were everywhere. Some planes were hung precariously with their unexploded bombs in the crumbling masonry of the shattered houses. Merciful snow covered the uncounted dead; animal carcasses littered the streets, the stark outlines of their frozen bodies sharp against the murky snow. Shop windows were full of the dead, while the wraithlike living ransacked the abandoned stores. Twisted streetcar rails jutted skyward like thin fingers of an imploring hand.

Fires burned all over the city; smoke rose from most of the buildings, and in the clear, cold winter air a heavy cloud of brick dust and smoke hung over the capital. Hugging the crumbling walls, emaciated survivors, dragging stoves and pieces of furniture, sought dubious shelter from the shells. The sobs of children filled lulls in the earsplitting noise of the continued shelling of the city. We in Pest, on the left bank of the Danube, were bombarded by Nazis entrenched in the hills of Buda on the right bank, mortar shells alternating with heavy railroad guns. The Russian armies responded in kind, and fliers from both sides dropped their missiles like hail in the spring.

Starvation was rampant. People cried and begged for food. As the water supply had been destroyed, they melted snow in any available container by clenching it in their frozen hands or clutching it to their bodies. The terror-stricken, agonized faces mirrored an inconceivable horror.

Those courageous enough to venture along the streets passed the dead and climbed over the bodies with a terrifying lack of emotion. There was not a window left in the city; all had been broken by bombs and shells; everyone searched in the freezing weather for life-sustaining heat. The hollow eyes of the people reflected the ruthless battle for survival.

I finally reached the Scottish Mission and the embraces of Zoltán Tildy and his family; after exchanging experiences we had to think of reestablishing the Smallholders party. A room in the center of the building, with wrapping paper pasted over its empty window panes, became the first new headquarters of the Smallholders. No propaganda was needed; as soon as people learned that the parties acceptable to the Soviet had begun to reorganize they streamed in.

The greatest activity centered around the newly emerged Communist party. They selected the most acceptable building (formerly the seat of the Nazi Volksbund) put it in order, and were operating smoothly within a few days.

The mass gravitating toward the Smallholders party made it impossible to delve into the past of each applicant; we therefore decided to issue only temporary party identifications.

To people of democratic conviction, used to decent political activity, the means and methods of the Communists brought hourly surprises. While we broke our heads to find some spot that we could rent and restore adequately to serve as party headquarters, we heard that the Communist party had, in addition to occupying the least damaged building in the city, requisitioned huge structures in every district for use as party clubhouses. Our first reaction was that this was not decent, but after a few days we concluded that we could not operate long without a party headquarters ourselves. Not wishing to trespass on public interest or private property, we requisitioned the former gentry casino building in the best spot in the center of the downtown district. I knew that there would be no more gentry casino, and that we injured no one's interests. In selecting a headquarters we had to consider future accessibility; and its central location, between railroad stations, was ideal for peasants visiting the capital.

The next day we heard that the Communist party was taking over printing plants; knowing that party work could not be conducted without a press, we had to secure an available printing plant. We chose a small but well equipped plant, the *Pester Lloyd,* convinced that when normality returned we could come to an agreement with the corporation. The same day the director of the largest publishing house, the Atheneum, begged us frantically to occupy his plant, too, before the Communists requisitioned it. We agreed, and put out the sign, "Occupied by the Independent Smallholders Party." The next morning Red soldiers tore down the sign and took over the plant for the Red army newspaper, *Uj Szó.* This was the first time the Red army actually impaired our activities; but we did not yet recognize the political tendency.

A few days earlier, everyone had eagerly nailed on the protective signs of the Swiss and Swedish Red Cross; now these signs were suddenly being replaced by those of the various political parties. Encouraged by the actions of the Communists, the Social Democrats and the small Radical Peasant party plastered notices of occupation on any halfway decent building.

As the Smallholders party moved into the gentry casino building, our young members began a feverish activity, substituting wrapping paper for missing window panes, cleaning away rubble, and bringing iron stoves for heat from all parts of the city. Nevertheless we began the party administration wrapped in sheepskin coats and blankets.

Tens of thousands, all wanting a party membership card, lined up outside our offices. We soon discovered why.

A Communist party membership card gave the bearer safe conduct amidst the Red army. Soviet soldiers rounded up the male population of the city in a most peculiar fashion, patroling strategic thoroughfares to pick up every male and detain him in one of the huge courtyards. Everyone was told that the men would be ordered to do some short-term public works, but when groups of a few hundred were lined up in fours and, surrounded by the bayonets of the Red army, marched towards Gödöllö, people were flabbergasted. But when it was learned that the Russians had restored the railroad lines to Gödöllö, and witnesses reported that all these men were packed into railroad cars, people awoke to the fact that thousands of the best men were being deported to the Soviet Union.

The deportation was unsystematic: men who did not go to the streets, or avoided the Red army patrol, escaped. Only those taken who could produce the membership card of the Communist party were released. The little card with the red stamp had a miraculous influence upon even the most primitive Russian soldiers; their respect was proof of the fact that exceptions were made on orders from above.

The party leaders who were in the capital met for their first conference around the end of January. The Smallholders party was represented by Zoltán Tildy, Father Béla Varga (who had reappeared in the meantime), and myself; the Communist party, by Zoltán Vas, a Hungarian-born Muscovite, and Stephen Kossa, the streetcar conductor who had been trained for union leadership in Moscow; the Social Democrats, by Anthony Bán and Francis Szeder; and the Radical Peasant party, by Emery Kovács and Joseph Darvas.

Since there was no municipal government at this time, we decided to bring some order into affairs, by naming a national committee for the capital consisting of the membership of this meeting and other party representatives. As temporary head of the municipal executive department we chose Dr. John Csorba, a former Smallholders deputy. Because the Communists had the only available newsprint, we agreed to publish an interparty paper, *Freedom*, with an editorial board composed of one editor from each party.

I soon inserted a notice for my family, announcing that I was alive, busy rebuilding the party, and waiting for an opportunity to be with them again. This was easier to think about than accomplish, because there were no railroads operating west of the Danube and the Smallholders did not have a single automobile. It was impossible to get anywhere afoot because of the ungovernable looting, robbing, and murdering by wandering Russian soldiers. I prayed daily for the lucky break by which I could reach my family.

Political life was difficult in the paralyzed capital. Only the Communist party found sure footing, its leadership arrived from Moscow unweakened by the privations of war and siege and confident from the experience gained from other countries previously conquered and occupied by Soviet arms. Eager to begin their work in Budapest with quieting gestures, they first tried to reorganize food distribution. They were better able to do so than the newly created municipal executive department, for practically all food was in the hands of the Soviet army, after having been sequestered from the population. The Communist party received a large part, which it began to distribute at the district party clubs. When the people saw that the Communists were able to dispense food as well as save their membership from deportation to Soviet Russia, a great number joined to satisfy their momentary needs.

The Communists had a great advantage in the fact that they had close communication with the Red army and many of them spoke Russian. Their leadership, during the post-siege horrors, tried to convince the trembling population that the Red army bore no ill will—this in the face of boundless rape, pillaging, and murder by Soviet soldiers. They sought to erase the memory of the Hungarian Communist terror in 1919 and disprove the tales out of Russia about the brutality of Soviet rule. The long cherished ideal of liberation had become in reality a scourge of conquest.

CHAPTER 9

The Country in Turmoil

NEWS REACHED US IN THE EARLY DAYS THAT A TEMPORARY GOVERNMENT had been formed in Debrecen, a national council was in session, and political life had begun east of the Tisza River. The Communists, the only ones to bring any news to Budapest, painted a rosy picture of conditions in this territory. No word from our own leadership reached us.

I was still working in the Scottish Mission building when Tildy's son-in-law, Victor Chornoky, rushed joyously into my office, exclaiming: "Béla Kovács is here!"

I ran into the vestibule and tearfully embraced my old friend and co-worker. For many years we had seen each other every day, and I knew his every step and thought. Béla was still deputy secretary general of the Smallholders party and national secretary of the Peasant Alliance.

As Baranya County was liberated from German rule by the end of 1944, Béla Kovács took part in the political reorganization of the country at Debrecen. Called in as deputy from Baranya, he was appointed undersecretary of the interior in the temporary government.

I was overjoyed to see him for another reason; he brought news that my whole family was well and had come through the battle for the village safely. He had come to Budapest to take me to Debrecen and then home to Bisse and my family; we decided that I should leave with him next morning for Debrecen, take a look at the political situation there, confer with the government and, after visiting my family, return to Budapest.

Tildy and I talked till the early hours with Béla Kovács, who had had much more experience with the Communist party than we and more clearly recognized their aims.

"The Communists are well organized, well prepared, and of set desires," said he. "Their leader is Ernest Gerö; Mathias Rákosi hasn't yet arrived. They act haughtily and deliberately."

"Can we work with them?" we asked.

"As I see it, we can," answered Béla Kovács. "But naturally we have to prepare in the same fashion. Although their true goal is not known, they claim on every occasion that it is necessary to work together."

"And how does the Soviet feel?"

"They are cooperating with the temporary government," answered Béla. "But the real crux of the matter is that the cabinet, because of its composition, is impotent. Ferenc, come to Debrecen and try to appraise the situation. I can assure you that everybody will put themselves at your disposal."

As a member of the government, Kovács had a car, and the next morning we started on the road to Debrecen.

The sights of desolation that presented themselves defy description. As I passed through half the country, I could see that no foot of land had escaped the battle. The Germans made the foreign soil pay a dear price for every mile of their retreat; Arrow Crossists plundered everywhere. Not a single town, village, or farmhouse had been given up without a battle; not a church spire was saved. Along the road and in the ditches lay remnants of the conflict; dead animals, tank wrecks, unburied bodies bore silent witness to man's destructiveness. The sturdier buildings stood empty and roofless, ravished churches stood exposed to wind and weather. Nowhere was there a house which had escaped the war, and nowhere a window to protect the life that was slowly gathering strength.

I was dumfounded also by the thoroughness of the occupation. Mass units of the Red army were found not only in the cities and on the lines of communication, but even on the smallest farms and in the fields. The people were in constant dread. The women of the small cities and the villages lived in hiding to escape assault.

The life of the peasants in the vineyard districts was sheer hell, where Red soldiers found stores of wine. One could not speak of humanity, honor, decency, or the sanctity of the family to drunken Soviet soldiers. They raped half-grown girls and screaming grandmothers; they robbed the peasants of their animals, they stole the linen and in many places even the furniture.

Tens of thousands of women and children were carried off and inflicted with venereal diseases by ruthless Red soldiers. Lack of doctors and medicine, and the innate shyness of the countryfolk, prevented treatment.

The barbarism of the Soviet occupying forces can best be judged by the fact that many thousands of Hungarian men were raped or forced to unnatural excesses by Russian women soldiers. The Reds established a recreation camp near Kecskemét for more than thirty thousand sick and convalescent women members of the Soviet army and police forces. From this camp, for instance, the Russian women banded together at night and swooped down upon the surrounding hamlets, kidnaping the men and sometimes holding them captive for days.

Often these abductions led to the peculiar situation of women and girls hiding, not themselves, but their men in the forests and in haystacks to keep them from the disease-ridden Soviet women troops.

The facts were first reported to the Swiss Legation in Budapest; the results of its investigation were published by the Swiss Foreign Office in May, 1945, as a warning to the world.

The Soviet army seized men from all over the country and deported them en masse to Russia. "Malinka robot"—"A little work"—was the slogan with which the male population was taken to a foreign land and never returned.

My heart ached as I saw the situation of the peasantry.

Béla Kovács tried to soothe me by saying that conditions in Baranya were much better. The peasants had some food left, and a few even had saved their farm animals.

One of the bitterest aspects of the occupation was that the Germans had forcibly evacuated the population from some districts before the Red army's arrival. Flight to the west was obligatory, and the families could await liberation near their homes only by hiding or escaping from a transport.

The Jews trickled in from deportation and labor camps; we did not yet know that very few of their number were released from concentration camps by the Russians. The rest were forcibly taken to the Soviet Union, as were the Jewish labor battalions taken as prisoners of war. Innumerable families, torn apart, were looking hopelessly toward the future. In tens of thousands of Jewish families only one or two members survived; the rest had perished in death camps or gas chambers, or were lost to sight behind the iron curtain.

The Red army did not bring adequate food or supplies and so fell like locusts upon the scanty stores left by the Nazis. The soldiers, naturally not satisfied with the small amounts their commanders doled out, foraged for themselves. They shot cattle or pigs in the meadows, in the gardens, in the courtyards, in the fields. They ransacked the food cellars and carried away the last ounce of flour from even the simplest, poorest peasants. In the small villages where there was no commander stationed they usually appeared in a row of armored trucks, with a dozen machine guns, and marched from house to house punishing any resistance with death.

The people of Bisse had defended themselves against these Red thieves in a unique way: Whenever someone noticed Soviet soldiers in the village, he began to ring the bells. The entire population would gather around the endangered building, making it more difficult for the Russians to proceed. Many a Hungarian peasant was victimized when he tried alone to protect his small home, his food, or the honor of his wife or daughter.

Politicians and newspapermen made timely public comparisons between the Mongol invasion of the thirteenth century and the Soviet occupation in the twentieth century. But these remarks had to be silenced. It was the cruel irony of political necessity that we had to stand up before world public opinion and declare that the Red army came to the people of Hungary with kindliness and friendship. To create new life in our devastated country we had to bear with forced patience and humility sufferings and brutalities that we hoped might be transitory.

CHAPTER 10

Conditions in Debrecen

I LEARNED ABOUT THE POLITICAL SITUATION BEYOND THE RIVER TISZA from Béla Kovács and was able to deduce conditions in sections occupied by the Russians.

Life was easier in Debrecen than in Budapest, for the suburbs of this agricultural town provided food for the populace. But the political situation was bleak; the government, entirely out of touch with the rest of the country, was unable to govern. Local administration had fallen into chaos. Most officials had fled to the west, particularly if they had dealt with the Nazis. A large proportion of the reliable civil employees had been transferred forcibly to Germany. Here and there officials were on the job, although out of contact with the central government. Only the Hungarian peasants' respect for order and discipline forestalled utter chaos.

There was no telephone, no telegraph, no mail. Trains ran only on lines the Red army had ordered the people to rebuild in order to assure their own military replacements. Atop freight cars, "passengers" swarmed like ants, risking their lives in the freezing weather. Often the government, ignorant of conditions in the country districts, would issue impractical decrees and regulations which local authorities found illogical and refused to execute.

The seat of the "government" was in the former building of the collector of internal revenue. Each cabinet minister had one room, and had to house his entire staff in a tiny anteroom—an arrangement revealing that the Russians had only allowed the government to form in order to provide a pretext of legality for its future actions.

No Hungarian in the liberated districts possessed a usable automobile. During the war private cars had been requisitioned for military service, and the Germans had taken those left to physicians and clergymen. If any still remained, the Russians sequestered them. A few were hidden in haystacks, but their owners did not dare use them until Russian thievery had ceased. At first the temporary government had not a single car at its command; but when it was formally established the Russians allowed one car to each cabinet member. However, thirteen or fourteen cars evidently could not go far in a country-wide administration, especially since most of the ministers used the cars primarily to visit their families and go to party mass meetings.

Only the Communist party officers had enough cars; the Red army provided them in profusion. The Communists, enjoying Russian support, had more contact with the people than the central government and all the other parties combined.

At first members of the government resided at the Golden Bull, a hotel run by the Red army; then they were told to leave because the Russians needed the space. This was a severe blow, for it was tremendously difficult for the governing officials to find food for themselves and their families elsewhere. Certainly the gorging feasts of the Soviet general staff could not be duplicated.

There was no regular food distribution: the Russians had seized all grain and other supplies, and the only foodstuffs the Hungarian government could call upon were those previously hidden from both armies of occupation. This was mighty little—not nearly enough to provide for methodical rationing.

The temporary government had no money. To relieve the shortage, the Red army offered to lend the government some paper money it had printed, with the understanding that it would be reimbursed. The minister of finance wanted to issue currency; but there was no paper and no suitable presses.

Helpless, members of the cabinet gave up trying to run the country and turned feverishly to party organization work, to the limited extent permitted by the Communists and the Soviet.

The old police force, branded as the tool of the former reactionary government, was disbanded, and a new force hurriedly organized which soon became notorious throughout the country. It was an undisciplined horde, composed chiefly of former members of the forced-labor brigades, of Communists and "liberated" common criminals, more interested in looting than in maintaining order; its chief aim was the strengthening of the armed bands of the Communist party. In the absence of any central authority, the Communist leaders and their "police" took affairs into their own hands in town and country.

Looking around in Debrecen, I saw a new and, to me, utterly strange world. I realized that the peasant had a tough fight ahead to attain his rightful place in the new Hungary.

PART TWO

A Nation in Twilight

CHAPTER 11

Red Army and Communist Party

ONE COULD TRUTHFULLY SAY THAT THE COMMUNIST PARTY CONQUERED the country with the Red army. As the Russians advanced, Communists from Moscow arrived at once in the newly acquired territories; home-grown Communists often slipped through the lines to join leaders fresh from Russia. While the other parties were still in the dark about future events, the Communists went ahead, fully informed and with ready-made plans.

From March 19, 1944, the country had been under German occupation, which had banned the activities of the Smallholders, Social Democrats, and Peasant Alliance. Although the people received underground instruction for sabotage, they could not be adequately informed politically. Fear of the Germans changed, after the liberation, to fear of the Russians. Neither the Smallholders nor the Social Democrats could organize—only the Communists, backed by the Red army, were everywhere.

During their short rule in 1919, the Communists had been detested for their violent radicalism and derogation of God and country. They launched a frontal attack against church and priesthood and, in an open war on private property, murdered peasant and aristocrat alike. It was mainly the resistance of the Hungarian peasantry that brought about their downfall.

Taught by their failure in 1919, and briefed by Moscow, the Communists now sang a different tune to the people of the villages. First of all, they restrained their attacks on the church and posed as a patriotic organization ready to defend national interests and private property. There was not a word of Communism, or even socialism; they talked only of democracy—quite obviously under orders. Not only in Hungary, but in all Soviet-occupied territory, the Communists began their activity with similar assurances.

71

They sought to be encouraging about the future and vied with Russian military leaders in proclaiming Hungary's freedom and independence. While excoriating the reactionary past, they promised national resurrection and a life of individual opportunity. At the time, our people were guileless enough to believe that the Russians would live up to the provisions of the Yalta Agreement guaranteeing national integrity. They remembered, moreover, that Soviet Russia had announced the dissolution of the Comintern during the war, and they really believed she would be generous not only in word but in deed.

Everyone thought it natural that the Communist party should be more radical than other parties, but expected it would work shoulder to shoulder with the others in reviving the country. No one realized, then, that the Communists were merely affecting a show of loyalty and would soon resort to open terror; few suspected that the program of penetration for every Soviet-occupied country had long been in readiness. Few would have believed that, within a year or two, a handful of Moscow's agents would gain control of every country in southeastern Europe and destroy any illusions about Communist party aims held by the peoples. Nor did many imagine that, after Yalta, the great powers would sign two newer agreements surrendering this whole region to Soviet dictatorship, allowing it to become the base from which the Communists could penetrate the rest of Europe.

From the very first days of liberation, well trained leaders of the Communist party were active in carrying out their instructions; they knew exactly what they were after. The other parties had to accommodate themselves as best they could to any conditions established by the Communists and the Red army.

It was part of the tactics of the Communists to seem generous at first. When they started setting up the administration of the country, they pretended unselfishness, encouraging other parties to organize, too. They even went so far as to let Smallholders and Social Democrats have a few important posts here and there. They took the Peasant Alliance into the framework of the administration and praised to the skies members of other parties still in prison or hiding. But in the very first stages they gained decisive influence for themselves. Soon they had the backing of the Inter-Allied Control Commission through its chairman, as Russia had the deciding voice; that of Moscow was quick to follow openly.

Of one thing the Communists were especially careful. At every step they sought to clothe their acts in a show of constitutionality, in order to invest with a semblance of legality all their terroristic activities, until such time as absolute power should be theirs.

CHAPTER 12

Comedy of the First National Council

BÉLA KOVÁCS, STEPHEN VÁSÁRY, AND STEPHEN B. SZABÓ TOLD ME IN Debrecen how the temporary National Council and its temporary government were formed. It is worth while to deal with each separately, as their method of creation throws light on preliminary political tactics of the Soviet in the different occupied countries.

When the Russians had taken the region beyond the river Tisza, Red army and Communist leaders announced that the political reorganization of the country should begin. The Communists dashed about in Red army cars, looking for collaborators to represent the other parties. From the Peasant party they secured Francis Erdei, author of books on Hungarian social conditions with which they were very familiar. John Gyöngyösi was asked to represent the Smallholders party. They visited Stephen Balogh, priest of a country parish near Szeged. Father Balogh, until then an independent, decided to join the group under the Smallholders' colors. Francis Takács, stalwart Social Democratic leader in Hódmezövásárhely, and Austin Valentini, a lawyer of Szeged, were recruited to join the Social Democrats. This group became the political executive committee of the region beyond the Tisza. They were advised by the Soviet to organize some kind of national council, to pass new laws, and "elect" a temporary government. The group was supplemented by Béla Dálnoki Miklós, John Vörös, and Gabriel Faraghó, generals who had gone over to the Russians in the last weeks of the war, and by Count Géza Teleki, who had been in Moscow with Faraghó in October to sign the temporary armistice.

It was decided to call a national council. The more difficult the convocation of such a council appeared, the more willing the Communists were to concern themselves with it, since they would be bound by fewer procedural rules. Since it was impossible to elect representatives, because there was no way of registering the electorate within a reasonable length of time, they simplified the whole matter by making a list of the towns and villages of the liberated territories and arbitrarily fixing the number of representatives that each might send to the assembly. The Communists, being well informed as to the political leanings of each district, determined the number of representatives accordingly. Towns where large numbers of left-wing workers and landless peasants lived were assigned many representatives, while communities favoring liberal democracy received correspondingly fewer. For example, the leftist town of Orosháza, with its population of 30,000, was assigned fourteen representatives while Pécs with 80,000 and the surrounding county of Baranya with 300,000 were allowed only seven representatives between them.

As soon as the convocation of the council was decided upon, four Communist-driven cars set out from Debrecen to arrange the election. A single representative of some other party was permitted to go along in each car. Upon arriving in a community, they called together the party and trade union to nominate representatives. Just proportions were out of the question; the Communists said that since no one as yet knew the relative strength of the parties, an equal number of representatives should be chosen for the Communists, Social Democratic, and Smallholders parties. Only the Peasant party was given smaller representation. As soon as the flying squad of nominators agreed on the nominees, they announced mass meetings in the cinema, theater, or village square and told the people that a new political life was about to begin, calling upon them to elect by acclamation the candidates chosen. The unfortunate citizens, who had lived through the oppression of the German occupation and were now experiencing the terrors of Russian occupation, cheered the speakers and unanimously accepted the nominees in the hope that a national council would bring a desperately needed change for the better.

After staging this comedy throughout the liberated territories, the Communists at once convoked the National Council at Debrecen. Soviet trucks transported the "elected" representatives to the meeting, and during the few days that the assembly was in session the representatives were lodged and fed by the Russians.

The Communists wanted to elect as president of the council a certain Béla Szentpéteri-Kun. Someone, however, yelled, "Why, that's the same gentleman who was a Rightist during the war!" The Communists, caught short, were nonplused; they could hardly begin by saying that they would forget the past of any reactionary who joined the party. Their nominee was dropped.

During further consultations, the distinguished figure of Béla Zsedényi, old-time democrat and professor of law in Miskolc could be seen in the middle of the auditorium. Someone cried out, "Béla-Zsedényi will do!"

It was thus that Béla Zsedényi became president of the National Council. Later, he proved to be a man of courage and determination in the face of Communist terror.

Assuming that the Soviet had no selfish motives in helping to start Hungarian political life, we were moved by these signs of support. How often we praised the leaders of the army of occupation for their generosity, and how often did I state that the Red army had come, not as a victor, but as a friend ready to help! Under what an obligation this Soviet aid placed the later development of Hungarian politics! And how often the Soviet carried through its one-sided directives on the ground that, after all, it was Russia that had made new political life in Hungary possible!

CHAPTER 13

The Provisional Government

THE DESIRE TO REVITALIZE POLITICAL LIFE NECESSITATED THE CALLING of a national council to create a cabinet. In the declaration address to the population of the liberated parts of the country, it was emphasized that the governing cabinet, elected by the National Council, would unquestionably be the choice of the people.

While the National Council was called, negotiations were started on the personalities who would reform the government. Ostensibly the Soviet did not take part in these negotiations, but naturally controlled them through its tools. The ruling spirit was a General Susejkov who later became the chairman of a control commission in Rumania. Under these circumstances the conferees agreed that the Smallholders, the Communists, and the Social Democrats would get two cabinet posts each while the diminutive but radical National Peasant party had to be satisfied with one. Five men without obvious party affiliation would also be included. The Smallholders conferees, Mayor Stephen Vásáry of Debrecen, John Gyöngyösi, and Stephen Balogh argued that their party should get more representation because it had the largest following; but the Soviet contended again that, since relative party strength was not known, even distribution of the seats among the three major parties was justified.

They also selected the cabinet members, choosing as Prime Minister Béla Dálnoki-Miklós, the first general to join the Russians with his armies when they crossed the Hungarian border. The Russians, valuing this pro-Soviet gesture highly, used it relentlessly on the Moscow radio; thus the general's name became familiar among the Hungarian people. Although he had never been politically active nor able, he was considered right for the job that had to be done.

John Gyöngyösi was proposed for Foreign Minister. The leader of the Smallholders party in Békéscsaba, he began his career as a teacher but left it to open a bookshop. Gyöngyösi was a faithful, fighting member of the Smallholders party who had lost several elections under the terroristic open balloting of the feudal regime.

For the post of Finance Minister, the conference proposed Stephen Vásáry, mayor of Debrecen, and a Smallholder deputy during the war cycle of the Parliament. Vásáry was a brave man; the oldest male member of a large peasant family, he was equipped with an excellent brain and experience in public administration.

The important Ministry of the Interior was to be filled by Francis Erdei, a member of the "radical" peasants. This man became, during the months of liberation, the willing tool of Communist politics and could be depended upon to direct the police, which fell under the jurisdiction of the Ministry of the Interior, in a Communist-approved way.

The two Social Democrat posts, the Ministry of Justice and the Ministry of Industry, were given respectively to Austin Valentini and Francis Takács.

The Communists insisted upon getting the Ministry of Agriculture, to which post they nominated former Muscovite Emery Nagy. It was obvious why the Communists demanded this ministry on the eve of land reform; they could distribute the land according to their own radical concepts. Moscow agent Joseph Gábor, as Minister of Commerce, filled their other post.

The conference named Erik Molnár, a man without official party affiliation, to the Ministry of Welfare. We discovered later that he was an old party member; thus the Communists managed to get a third post in the cabinet.

General John Vörös was named Minister of Defense and another general, Gabriel Faraghó, Minister of Supplies. Count Géza Teleki was selected as Minister of Education, after being informed in Moscow that he must be in the new government because the name of his martyred father fell harmoniously on the ears of Hungarians and other peoples of Europe.

Stephen Balogh secured the undersecretaryship in the Prime Ministry, knowing that he would be second in importance only to General Miklós. All threads of political life converged in the Prime Ministry, and Balogh was quite able to hold these threads in his palm and weave them into a coherent pattern to keep himself well informed.

At first it seemed as if the temporary government would be elected by the National Council, but actually it was appointed by Moscow. The party conferees considered the Russian political viewpoint before they presented the list for approval to the Soviet plenipotentiaries. The National Council did not even see the list until it was approved by Moscow; then it went through the motions of a parliamentary election —the first of many farces to come.

Existing conditions restricted the temporary government; we were not surprised to learn that cabinet members received their lodging, their food, and even their clothing from the army of occupation. The temporary capital, Debrecen, like all the other "liberated" parts of Hungary, was full of Russian soldiers. Central administration was impossible in the face of chaotic conditions; economic life was nonexistent. The activities of the foreign ministry consisted of endless conferences, euphemistically called "negotiations," with the Soviet Army Command. The only two cabinet members who were able to work toward a definite goal were the Minister of Agriculture, who, having received his directives from Moscow, worked feverishly on agrarian reform, and the Minister of the Interior, who, by order of the Communists, organized and sheltered the activities of the gangsterlike agency which claimed to be reorganizing the police structure of the country.

The Minister of Defense was eagerly trying to create a new army, and everybody felt that at least a few divisions should be sent quickly into the battle to liberate the rest of the country and defeat the Germans. The people believed that any declaration of war by the temporary government against Germany should be backed with military action—partly to show that the Hungarian people have always sincerely desired the defeat of the Germans and partly to gain its rightful place at the peace negotiations.

It would have been very easy to put a Hungarian army into the field against the Germans; our soldiers would have fought more valiantly against Germany than against any other nation because of the curse the Nazis brought to the Hungarian soil. Technically it would have been simple to put the army into the field immediately, for most of the soldiers were still on Hungarian territory, concentrated in large prison camps; they could have been easily equipped and sent to march against the common enemy.

Although the Soviet did not openly veto the idea of Hungary's waging active war against the Axis, the familiar underhand tactics of the Russians prevented it. The Soviet let the question ride, not, as we had imagined, from inertia, but as part of a planned campaign. For one thing, the Russians wanted Hungary to be at a disadvantage at the peace conference; and they did not care to have an organized national military prevent pillaging by the Red army as was the case in Rumania and Bulgaria.

As it could not, because of its composition and lack of information, do otherwise the National Council unanimously "elected" the government. Then the parties proceeded to distribute the undersecretaryships, and Béla Kovács became Undersecretary of the Interior. The undersecretaryships were important weapons in the hands of the Communist party; into the ministries headed by weak representatives of other parties they put a strong Communist undersecretary. These men could direct, or rather misdirect, their principals and so enforce their will even in departments where power, nominally, did not rest in the hands of the Communists.

CHAPTER 14

A Country Divided

WHILE TECHNICALLY UNDER THE TEMPORARY GOVERNMENT, THE COUNTRY actually groaned under two different powers. The eastern part of Hungary, including the territory between the Danube and the Tisza, had been conquered by the Russians, who were busily chasing the Nazi armies westward and trying to dislodge the German soldiers who had fled into western Hungary. The Nazis had forcibly evacuated a large segment of the population of eastern Hungary, later under Russian rule, and even part of Budapest before the siege; western Hungary was thus congested with Nazis, Arrow Crossists, refugees, and forced evacuees.

Into western Hungary fled Szálasi's puppet government, and, while Debrecen was the capital of the "liberated" sections, they declared the city of Sopron to be the seat of their administration. Here the executive offices were established and even a parliament, composed of those deputies who had fled with Szálasi, was in session.

Most of the economic wealth of the country, carried by Szálasi from the liberated sections and Budapest, was in Nazi-controlled territory; heaped, next to the factories dismantled by the Russian onslaught, in stationary railroad cars. The new printing plant of the mint was established in an ancient cave. In these interim months, the people who fled west of the Danube suffered terribly; some were Arrow Crossists or National Socialists afraid of being called to account, some ran westward because they were afraid of the cruelty of the Red army. All were exposed to the horrors of a continuous war; every day they dragged themselves in front of the retreating army, desperately seeking refuge and rest. Those who remained in Red-controlled territories were tormented by another power, the pillaging armies of Russia.

The Hungarian troops in the western territory tried to quit the war and turn against the Nazis; but their supervision was so strict that escape was possible only for a few individuals, who dared cross no-man's-land. The Germans had devised a method by which all armed Hungarian military units were under the supervision and command of the Schutz-Staffel, and many a brave Hungarian soldier was killed by the Germans and the Arrow Crossists for refusing to continue to fight on the Nazi side. The male population of the country was forced to take up arms for the Germans, and the women and old people were put to work digging trenches and repairing fortifications.

Whenever transportation permitted, the Germans moved the looted wealth and the population into Germany. Rarely could a family remain together; usually some members stuck to the soil and stayed in Soviet-occupied territory. The uncertainty was indescribable. After the liberation of Budapest, the Red army pursued the retreating Germans to the fifty-mile Lake Balaton; hundreds of cities and villages along the lake shore became deadly battlegrounds. Practically all of the inhabitants and their homes in this sector were destroyed.

This condition recalled the times in Hungarian history when German armies subjugated the western part of the country while the Turk lorded over the eastern part. But there was no precedent for the destructiveness of modern warfare; no grass grew and no seed took hold while the motorized steel monsters vomited destruction and their terrible wheels violated the sanctity of the soil. Germans and Arrow Crossists herded countless Hungarians toward the west while the Russians deported hundreds of thousands of men to Russia as slave labor.

The situation of the Hungarian youth was especially tragic. The students, peasant boys, even school children were forced into military or semimilitary formations. The Nazis and Arrow Crossists dragged these units with them, at times even forcing them into combat. One of my neighbors in Budapest had a lively, shiny-eyed fifteen-year-old son, Charles Polyák, whom the Arrow Cross took in the spring. When the snow of the next winter melted, they found the body of this good-humored high-school boy in one of the trenches, his stiffened little fingers still clutching a hand grenade.

The chancellor of the Budapest Institute of Technology was ordered to transport his student body as a closed column to Germany. While some of the youth got wind and escaped before the transport was begun, several trainloads of them left for Germany. Hundreds of promising engineers perished when one of these trains was bombed and destroyed.

News reached us that more than fifty thousand hopeless young Hungarian men, herded together in the camps of the western zone of Allied occupation, left in droves to join the foreign legion.

The soil, lifeblood of Hungary, was perishing. The fields and tiny houses were full of mines and unexploded shells. In the wake of the battle, our valiant peasants tended the furrows torn by the iron hands of war. Sometimes the point of a plow awoke the sleeping explosives. Little children, playing with strange gadgets, set off new infernos of devastation.

No people of the world suffered in this war as much as the Hungarians. The miraculous grace of God spared their will to live; after so much misery it empowered my people to rebuild anew their lives and their homeland.

An ancient folk song, dating from the days of Ferenc Rákoczy's fight for liberty, refers to the time when the country was split under German and Turkish rules:

> Peasant blood is cheap blood—
> Twopence a day, it's worth;
> Between two heathens slaking thirst,
> Bleeding for his native earth,
> He cannot spend its worth.

This song was reborn in the soul of every citizen when half of the country was in German and the other half in Russian hands, when Hungarian life was perishing and Hungarian blood was flowing. How could one forgive the crimes of those Hungarian leaders who threw their nation into the abyss of despair?

CHAPTER 15

Reincarnation of Political Life

THE POLITICAL PARTIES IN THE LIBERATED REGION HAD ALREADY BEGUN to organize by the time I reached Debrecen. Everyone thought it only natural that the groups with National Socialist leanings should not be allowed to reorganize; such as the National Socialist (Arrow Cross) party led by Szálasi, the Rebirth party of Imrédy, and the former government-sponsored party of Hungarian Life. It was after all this last-mentioned party, with its crushing majority, that had made possible the organization of the National Socialist party. This party's votes also led the country into war under the premiership of Bárdossy. Of the other parties, only those which had proved themselves worthy of a future role during the war, or at least had not compromised themselves, could be permitted to reorganize.

As I have said, the Communist party, whose leaders the Red army had brought from Moscow, was the first party to come to life. They had not been able to organize openly in Hungary, because in the period between the two wars Communism had been outside the pale of the law. It had secret agents, however, in some of the other parties, particularly the Social Democratic but also to some extent the Smallholders. The Communist party had no roots in the Hungarian people, who always detested extremes. This was especially true of the peasantry, whom neither the Arrow Cross party of the far right nor the Communist party ever succeeded in winning over.

In Hungary as in other countries of southeastern Europe, the Red army's occupation created a boom for the Communists. If the great powers of the west had followed Churchill's plan in 1944, and launched their attack on Europe via the Balkans, Communism would not have been able to gather strength in a single country of southeastern Europe.

Communist leaders came, not only with ready-made plans, but with extensive experience secured in Poland, Rumania, Yugoslavia, and Bulgaria. With the help of the Red army, plus resolute and adroit execution of their plans and ruthless terror in dealing with their political opponents, they were soon able to outweigh their lack of previous organization.

The chief leader of the Communist party is Mathias Rákosi, the son of a village storekeeper. He attended school in Szeged and was graduated from the Academy of Commerce, where he was quick to join leftwing student organizations. For a while he worked for a firm in London. Then, in World War I, he became a soldier and prisoner of war in Russia. Returning, he took an active part in postwar revolutionary politics, becoming commander of a division of Communist troops and a commissar in the Red government. After the collapse of Communism in Hungary, Rákosi continued working as an agent of the Comintern in other countries of Europe, suffering arrest and imprisonment in most of these. Possessed of a great store of practical experience, he became expert on penology. After slinking into Hungary in the early twenties, he was arrested, put on trial, received a death sentence that was commuted to life imprisonment. He had served fifteen years of this when he was accepted by Moscow in an exchange for men imprisoned in Russia. From then on, he lived in Moscow until the "liberation," when he came back to Hungary as leader of the Communist party.

Rákosi is a well informed and cultured man with a tenacious memory. During his prison years he read much. Moscow training and work in the central Comintern developed his sense of political tactics. A professional politician and an absolutely dependable tool of Moscow, he has nothing in common, spiritually, with the Hungarian people. It is beyond question that among the Communist agents turned loose on southeastern Europe by Russia, Rákosi is of the greatest political caliber.

In the earlier stages of political development in Debrecen, it was not Rákosi, but Ernest Gerö, who led the Communists. Gerö, whose real name is Singer, had spent his childhood in Ujpest, a factory district on the outskirts of Budapest, and soon joined the Communist party. After spending some time in prison, he reached Russia and received several assignments from the Comintern, including work with the French Communists. He took part in the Spanish Civil War as a political observer and later returned to Moscow, where he continued to educate himself by working in the central offices of the Comintern. He is a man of great energy, a resolute and fanatical Communist willing to serve the cause even to the limits of asceticism.

Gerö's right hand in Debrecen was Josef Révai, the publicist and foreign policy leader of the Communist party. Révai had likewise lived for years in Moscow and returned with the Red army. In Debrecen, his biting pen took the lead in spreading Communist propaganda. He made full use of considerable talent to undermine, through his paper, the basis for a peaceful atmosphere.

Zoltán Vas is another leader whom the Red army brought along. He had been called Weinberger, and originally went to Russia, like Rákosi, as an exchange prisoner. Following his agile organizational work in the days after liberation, Vas became the economic and financial expert of the Communist party. For a time he was mayor of Budapest. He is known to be a high-ranking officer in the Russian army.

Among the arrivals from Moscow was Michael Farkas, who received a high organizational post in the party.

All these men issued orders to a varied crew of minor agitators who had accompanied them. These minor figures were joined by fellow travelers at home who had been disguised as members of the Social Democratic and Smallholders parties. In accordance with their leaders' instructions, they disclosed their real allegiance and began working openly as Communists.

The Social Democratic party was for a long time the party of the Hungarian worker. In past decades it had accomplished much in alleviating the sufferings of the working classes. Even before World War I, and also between the two wars, it possessed experienced, resolute, and well trained administrators. Heading them was Charles Peyer, one-time factory worker, who after World War I held a minister's portfolio and later was delegated to the League of Nations as a labor representative. Although Peyer led his party with a firm hand, he was a man of honor and moderation who always had the interests of the workers at heart. By his side was Francis Szeder, one-time field hand, and Anne Kéthly, a schoolteacher. All three had long been members of Parliament. Árpád Szakasits, former stonecutter who became editor of the party organ, *Népszava*, was also among the leaders, as were Géza Malasits, Elias Mónus, and Louis Kabók, members of Parliament. These last two were murdered by the National Socialists. The party also had many agile secretaries in industrial centers who attended executive meetings only in an advisory capacity.

The Social Democratic party had several hundred branch organizations in towns and in the larger communities of the region beyond the Tisza, with many staunch, faithful members of whom nearly a hundred thousand had remained in the party even in the days of fiercest National Socialist persecution. The Arrow Crossists had demanded the dissolution of the Social Democrats during the war, but the Minister of the Interior, Francis Keresztes-Fischer, the most level-headed and outstanding member of the war cabinet, would not permit this. He saw clearly that if the Social Democratic party were banned, the workers of the industrial districts would be sucked up by the National Socialists. As it was, although the great majority of workers did join the Right camp, a small democratic core remained, around which the party could be rebuilt after the liberation.

The Social Democratic party, which entered into formal alliance with the Smallholders party in 1943, could doubtless have influenced very favorably the development of democracy after the liberation, had it not hurried to make a pact with the Communist party which assigned it a very subordinate role. However, the party's most forceful personality, Charles Peyer, was imprisoned in a German concentration camp at Mauthausen, and Árpád Szakasits had seized power, relegating Francis Szeder and Anne Kéthly to very minor positions and allowing Malasits and the rest no voice at all. In their place, he called to his side Anthony Rosemeyer, a former assistant secretary who later changed his name to Anthony Bán; a lawyer named Stephen Ries, who was to become Minister of Justice, and a party member with a doubtful past called Zoltán Horváth. With them, he assumed autocratic power in the party. When Charles Peyer arrived from Mauthausen, they relegated him completely to the background and even tried to flatter him into accepting a diplomatic post of some sort in order to get him out of the country.

Everyone was astonished at the unrestrained friendship that the new leader, Árpád Szakasits, showed for the Communists. During the war, as editor of the *Népszava,* he had shown himself to be a loyal, socialist follower of Horthy; and as a newspaperman played very cautious politics.

I recollect that in 1943, before our parties allied, Szakasits and I met at the Simplon Coffeehouse with Béla Kovács and clarified a number of issues. After discussing the question of political convictions, I asked Árpád Szakasits a question:

"What will the Social Democrats do when the Red army crosses the Carpathians, bringing the Communist leaders living in Moscow and lending its support to the reorganization of the Communists?"

Szakasits, without a moment's hesitation, answered:

"If you organize the Smallholders party as well as we shall organize the Social Democratic party against penetration by the Communists, then we don't have to worry about Red expansion."

Szakasits's later actions showed that he had forgotten this pronouncement, and evidently believed that I had forgotten it also. I am afraid poor Béla Kovács would not be able to substantiate it in his present condition.

The National Peasant party, strictly speaking, did not come into existence until the "liberation." It is true, however, that the weekly *Szabad Szó* gathered together a few peasants in 1939 and announced the founding of the Peasant party. But they did nothing to organize it. For months they sought to persuade me to leave the Smallholders party and become the leader of the new party, but as I was not willing to shift my allegiance no further steps were taken to organize the Peasant party. During the war years, Emery Kovács was active in the intellectual division of our party; not until the German occupation, when the Hungarian Front had been formed, did he tell Zoltán Tildy that he would like to represent the Peasant party in the Hungarian Front. Tildy accepted his decision and that was how the non-existent Peasant party became part of the Hungarian Front.

Had Emery Kovács continued to lead it, the policies of the Peasant party would doubtless have been quite different. But in the fall of 1944, having slipped through the German and Russian lines in order to reach liberated territory, he was seized by the Germans and confined until a left-wing, Communist-dominated party leadership was established. On his release, Kovács had to deal with a *fait accompli*. Though he tried several times, his attempts to free the party from Communist domination proved unsuccessful.

This radical Peasant party was organized in two ways. While I was still hiding in Budapest, many village leaders were deceived by a rumor spread to the effect that the Peasant party was identical with the Peasant Alliance which I headed. But from the standpoint of organization it was of even greater significance that the Peasant party was organized by the Communist party. In hundreds of villages the Peasant party was formed without a single one of their executives present; the work was done by the local secretary of the Communist party.

Only the Smallholders possessed the facilities for mass organization. Even before the war, local branches of the party had been established in twenty-four hundred villages. Till 1941, Tibor Eckhardt headed the party; subsequently the leadership was vested in Zoltán Tildy, Béla Varga, Béla Kovács, and myself. Practically every party member in the whole country knew us personally. No one knew exactly how many members there were, for we collected no dues and kept no membership lists because we wished to protect our adherents from persecution by the reactionary administration.

The prewar election figures showed an overwhelming strength of the Smallholders party, compared to the other remaining parties. Yet we were forced to give in to the argument of the Communists, with their Red army backing, that German and Russian occupations had rendered uncertain the relative party strength.

It might be interesting to note what classes joined which parties after liberation. The small-fry Nazis rushed first of all to seek haven under the wing of the Communist party. Those who had not fled with the retreating German army sought to escape the consequences of their previous affiliations by thronging to the Communists, for they knew that there they could enjoy the protection of the Red army too. Opportunist officials who did not want to break completely with their social traditions sought safety with the Socialists. The Smallholders were approached mainly by peasant members of the old government party and by the braver and more resolute middle-class elements. There were naturally Arrow Crossists and members of the Volksbund who joined the Smallholders and Social Democrats, but only a fraction of the number who joined the Communists. Some of those who received land in the course of the agrarian reform became members of the Peasant party, which was loudest in its promises to uphold the rights of the new landowners.

It was easy to see by the attitude of the people that after the liberation the Smallholders party was foremost in representing those principles of pure democracy and autonomy which best fitted the spirit of the Hungarian people. Substantiation for this lies in the fact that religious, creatively minded free men were quick to join us.

A fifth party was also formed in Debrecen, the "Civic Democratic party," which enjoyed the support of only a very thin stratum of society, the city intellectuals. Its membership was drawn from the former Democratic party of Charles Rassay. Since it stood for the establishment of order, democracy, and consolidation, Smallholders approved its formation.

On my arrival in Debrecen, I had to confer not only with the members of the cabinet, but also with the representatives of the parties. Béla Kovács arranged for a meeting with Gerö, Révai, and Farkas, the three leading Communists. I was told that they looked forward to the meeting with particular interest; they were well acquainted with my anti-German activities and aware of the extent of my influence upon the peasantry. As for me, I knew that I should secure a number of very important first impressions at this meeting. It was plain that we should have to work with the Communists for a long time.

Révai, as their spokesman, said that they wished for a democratic, independent Hungary; that they did not wish to force their views on the country, but would fight against the return of fascism and reaction side by side with the other democratic parties. He also stated that the Soviet had no intention of interfering in our internal affairs, nor would it seek to force its own way of life on Hungary. It sought, he said, only friendship between the two countries.

In general Révai sought to calm me about future developments.

"These pronouncements are, of course, very reassuring," I said, "and, at the moment, our joy over our liberation allows no room for doubt about each other's intentions. But I may say that certain facts are in direct contradiction to what you have been saying. The Communist party, in many villages and towns in the region beyond the Tisza, makes it impossible for decent, democratic elements to prosper. This alarms and embitters the Smallholder peasantry. This must be changed," I said.

"Where did you experience this?" they asked.

"At Hajduhadháza, Hajduszoboszló, and in many villages and towns in that neighborhood. But those able to reach Debrecen bring similar news from Szabolcs, Zemplén, and Bihar counties."

"What is the nature of the Communist oppression?" asked Révai.

"Members of Communist labor brigades have taken over the direction of the newly organized police force; they have created what amounts to a reign of terror in many places. At Hajduhadháza a man by the name of Kaffler is confining former Smallholders leaders in cellars; and another Communist at Hajduszoboszló is doing the same thing. In Eger, John Danca, a former locksmith's assistant, now chief of police, has achieved notoriety. Do you know what this means? It means that the Hungarian peasant couldn't prosper between the two wars because the government was reactionary. A Smallholder could not become a village judge, because the chief magistrate wouldn't allow his election. Now after the war he creeps out of his cellar and, on looking about him, finds that this time he can't prosper because local Communist chiefs, for the most part men of no weight or authority, again suppress the will of the majority. The Hungarian peasant will be disappointed in democracy. After all, there can't be real democracy in Hungary until every peasant can regard the new system as his own achievement and way of life."

"These can be only local excesses," said Gerö. "In every concrete instance we shall take steps to stop them."

"It is important that every peasant should regard the new democracy as his own," echoed Révai.

"In our democracy we must carry through the principle of majority rule," I affirmed. "The peasants of the Smallholders party, after fifteen years of persecution, deserve the right to run their own affairs. We cannot stand by while the peasantry is shoved into the background, disillusioned and apathetic, with no voice in politics. If the peasants don't participate in the building of a democracy, then there will be none," I went on.

The Communist leaders resorted to tactical maneuvers; they began attacking Smallholder personalities.

"You were quick to notice the abuses of insignificant Communist leaders," said Révai, "but it seems you don't notice the destructive work of the Vásáry brothers and a representative in the assembly named Zoltán Lévai. They act as if nothing had happened, as if the old world were about to return unchanged."

"We shall deal with those who do not accept the spirit of democracy," I said. "After all, during these past fifteen years we were not fighting merely for a change of government, but for a change of regime —for a regime under which peasant, worker, and intellectual can prosper equally without fear of oppression. Democracy isn't endangered by those you mention, but by the excesses of Communists who follow a political policy diametrically opposed to that which you have been talking about."

"We shall consider what you have said about the principle of majority rule, and shall deal with the question publicly," said Révai.

In parting with the Communists I had the feeling that although we should probably often meet with injustices, which their leaders would characterize as "local abuses," we should nevertheless be able to work with them, provided their pronouncements regarding their own aims and those of the Russians were borne out by their actions. The fact that we believed the Communists, and thought cooperation possible, resulted in unending disappointments during the future course of Hungarian politics.

Foreign Minister Gyöngyösi informed me, during my stay in Debrecen, that Pushkin, the diplomatic representative assigned to the Red army, wished to have a talk with me. He lived sumptuously in a villa on the edge of the city, and we agreed that I would call upon him at seven o'clock in the evening. That was a very dangerous hour in Debrecen. There was a curfew at seven, and anyone on the streets, even with an official permit, was liable to return home in the wintry night minus his clothes and effects. If he did not like being robbed, he would be shot at by the pillaging Red soldiers.

The chauffeur assigned to me said he would be glad to take me to Pushkin's villa if I would let him go home before seven o'clock. A few days earlier, he had left for home a few minutes after seven and Red soldiers had taken from him the bread that was to have been his supper.

Pushkin was a short young man with a squint in one eye. At the time we did not yet know that his commission went far beyond that of an ordinary diplomat. Since I had arrived early and there was no translator, we tried with much difficulty to understand each other with the little German we both knew.

Soon Attaché Grigoriev, who spoke Hungarian perfectly, arrived. With his help our conference started.

"What is your opinion regarding friendship between Russia and Hungary?" asked Pushkin.

"The friendship depends upon the Soviet Union," I replied. "We can only accept such friendship if the Soviet makes it possible. Hungary's attitude must certainly reflect her gratitude to the Soviet for liberating her from Fascist oppression, and she must also take into account the fact that the Soviet has become Hungary's neighbor and friendship therefore is a matter of practical politics, too."

"The people of Russia had a sincere regard for the Hungarians before the war. Russian prisoners of the last war had many fine things to say about Hungary, and your prisoners of war in Russia also made a very good impression on the people. The emigrants who had been living for years in the Soviet Union increased the good feeling of Russians toward Hungarians. Unfortunately, during the war, the behavior of Hungarian soldiers was very disillusioning."

I smiled at the craftiness of the last sentence.

"As for me, I should hardly find it fitting on this occasion to discuss details of the behavior of the soldiers of the Red army of occupation, particularly with regard to their actions against our women. In the interest of mutual understanding, perhaps it would be best to consider that in wartime the behavior of soldiers never reflects the sentiments of the people at home, but is the consequence of the coarsening effect of prolonged hostilities. It is my sincere opinion that friendship between our countries can be lasting and real if it is supported by actual good relations between our peoples and not merely by statements of our leaders. I believe that friendship can be established between our countries, despite the behavior of their respective armies, if political conditions do not prevent it," I answered.

"The Soviet Union only wishes to have a voice in Hungarian affairs to the extent that it is necessary to destroy Fascism in the whole of Europe and to see to it that truly democratic regimes are formed everywhere. The Soviet Union regards Hungary as a soverign state and has no desire to force its way of life upon the country," said Pushkin.

This speech was reassuring, but I did not know by what authority and right this young man had made it. Pushkin continued to question.

"What is your opinion on agrarian reform?"

"I have long been in favor of it," I replied. "The breaking up of large estates and the granting of land to peasants has been a cornerstone of the policies of my party."

"Do you approve the extent of agrarian reform that Hungarian papers are writing about?" asked Pushkin. He referred to articles in Peasant party and Communist organs demanding that no large landowner should be permitted to retain more than a hundred and fifty acres, and that only those landowners whose ancestors were peasants and toiled on the land themselves should be allowed to retain three hundred.

"Yes, I am in favor of agrarian reform even to that extent," I replied. "But I would urge greater forethought in its execution than these Peasant party and Communist articles show. It is my opinion that those to whom we give land should be carefully selected, and in dividing the properties we should keep in mind the possibility of providing them in time with the necessary public utilities. And we should be especially careful to retain under state administration a number of middle-sized estates for stud raising and seed culture. Hungary's stock of cattle has diminished not only in quantity but in quality. The same is true of seed farms; these must be replaced by government-controlled estates."

I concluded from Pushkin's attitude that the Soviet wished to know to what degree Hungary was willing to introduce democratic measures.

Frankly, at that time I had no idea that Russia wished to determine the extent and tempo of the execution of agrarian reform.

"What is your opinion of Tibor Eckhardt?" asked Pushkin.

"I consider him one of the most gifted of our democratic statesmen and sincerely regret the divergence of views between him and the Soviet Union."

"It was he who caused them," announced Pushkin, "by unwarrantably attacking the Soviet Union. Incidentally, what do you think of Horthy?"

"He is a poor politician, but it is beyond doubt that he has merits; during the war he took a very decided stand against the Germans and in September, 1944, decided to ask for a separate armistice. Though it is certain that he cannot resume his position, it would not be a good thing to attack and pillory him."

"The Regent committed a serious mistake in October, of which the Russian army and the city of Budapest reaped the fruits. When Horthy asked for an armistice late in September, 1944, it was joyously accepted in Moscow. On October 11, the Hungarian delegation had already signed the armistice. At this time the Red army was in the midst of a great drive. Within a matter of days it had advanced from Szeged to Szolnok; in fact, between those cities it had crossed the Tisza at all points. We were well on our way to occupying weakly defended Budapest; in fact, our forces were in Nagykáta, 50 kilometers away, when Horthy suggested that the Red army halt its advance for a few days because he wished to bring to Budapest the Hungarian army corps at Debrecen which could take the city without occasioning much damage. So the Red army halted. The Germans meanwhile reenforced Budapest to such an extent that they were even strong enough to attack and force back the Red army from Szolnok to Mezötur. Horthy was unable to bring the Debrecen forces to the capital, and the result of his thoughtless request was that Budapest was destroyed and the siege cost us the lives of ten thousand Red soldiers."

(It would be worth while determining from authoritative military documents the extent to which Pushkin's story is true.)

It was near midnight when we concluded our conversation. Pushkin offered his car and Grigoriev's escort home. In parting, he turned to me, saying,

"Marshal Voroshilov, who is to be president of the Allied Control Commission in Hungary, has arrived. In a few days there will be a reception at the Golden Bull, to allow the Marshal to meet the democratic leaders of Hungary. We have already sent you a formal invitation, but I use this opportunity to invite you personally for that evening."

"If you please, I have come from prison and from hiding. I'm wearing the suit I had on when I left my home in Bisse months ago. I can hardly wear it to an evening reception," I replied.

"That makes no difference," said Pushkin. "Any clothes will do. It would be difficult to explain to the Marshal that you stayed away for reasons of raiment."

I said goodbye, promising to come. At the door another question occurred to me, and I turned back.

"The government and the people complain much because of the Russian army's immoderate requisitioning of food supplies. The people are starving, and the government is unable to calculate the needs of the Red army because it doesn't know how much food is due it. This question ought to be settled."

"Of course," answered Pushkin. "The question can be settled the moment your government is in a position to ascertain the amount of supplies at its disposal."

I thought bitterly that, by the time the government collected the supplies the Germans had not taken, it could easily do that because the Russians would carry away everything. When Grigoriev and I stopped in front of the Bius Dormitory where I lived, I turned to him:

"Minister Pushkin mentioned the behavior of Hungarian soldiers in Russia. I couldn't bring up all the things that Red soldiers in Hungary are guilty of. But I should like to tell you that last night on this spot Red soldiers robbed the brother of our finance minister, Vásáry, just as he was about to step inside."

"My dear sir, we are quite aware of the actions of the Red army; but in this respect it is extremely difficult to keep order among the soldiers despite the fact that the chief of staff punishes pillaging severely. Just the other day, at an open trial in the Debrecen Theater, the authorities sentenced a Red soldier to death for robbery. But we can't deal with every single case."

The following night, on the streets of Debrecen, Red soldiers tried to strangle the famous Hungarian writer, Lajos Zilahy, with his muffler. They stole his valuables, and only the quick intervention of people who answered his cries saved his life.

The reception for Voroshilov took place at the Golden Bull. The great chorus of the Red army's camp theater, as well as richly decked tables (the result of Russian requisitioning) awaited the hundreds of guests. Only the caviar, vodka, and salmon were Russian products. The Hungarian guests who had been starving for months did full justice to the regal banquet.

Straightforward in conversing with members of the government, Marshal Voroshilov made a very good impression on those assembled. At the table set apart for the political leaders he offered seventeen toasts. He questioned me at length about my arrest and hiding; then, when I told him that I had not been home since my arrest, and that only the lack of gasoline kept me in Debrecen, he ordered that twenty-five gallons be supplied so that I might go home.

Next day I set out for Baranya in the company of Béla Kovács to visit my loved ones, who until now had only known through messages that I was alive. My heart grew warmer from hour to hour as we neared my home county. All along the way we heard the ominous sounds of the battle beyond the Danube; but I was happy that I was at last to embrace my family. On the main street of the little village it was not the ruins I saw first, but my wife at the gate holding in her arms our two-and-a-half-year-old son, Lacika. My daughter Juliette and my son Ferenc, my old, bent father and my dear blessed mother, ran out one after another to greet me. While in prison and in hide-outs I had often pictured to myself the many possible circumstances of our meeting, but I had not been able to imagine the emotions that now gripped me. I thought how wonderful it would be if one could relinquish public life to others and stay at home to rebuild the little house, plow the fields, drink wine in the vineyards with old friends, and at night tell stories to little Lacika about good fairies and a happy future, not letting him see the adults' bitter struggle among the ruins to re-create life in our beloved Hungary.

With one glance I took in the village. Through a curious irony of fate, artillery fire during the battle for the village had struck only two houses, and these were our two. A mortar shell had smashed the front of our home and another shell had blown to bits the little thatched-roof house behind it.

There was no end to our exchange of experiences. My wife told me that the battle for the village had lasted two days, during which they found shelter in the cellar and escaped harm. The Red soldiers took only a few bits of jewelry. Our clothes were saved; even before the Germans arrived we had buried them in various parts of the garden. This was especially good news for me: before my arrest I had had two suits made which I counted on wearing until better times came and I could again think of buying one. Alas, those two suits served me even during my premiership.

Father said that, although many of the farmers' horses had been taken, he still possessed his huge Belgians, because, when the Russians wanted to take them, he went along and in the desperately cold winter carried the wounded from the battlefields of Yugoslavia. When the fighting was over, they gave him back his horses and wagon. He told me that, despite the fact that Red soldiers had robbed every wine cellar, he still had wine because he had had the forethought to bring home a few barrels and bury them in the garden.

A week later, when I was again in Budapest, Bulgarian soldiers of the occupying forces broke into my father's barn and drove off those same jealously guarded horses.

Despite the trials sustained, my heart was full of thanks to God for sparing my family.

CHAPTER 16

Penetration Through Democratic Institutions

THE DISINTEGRATION OF THE GOVERNMENT OF THE COUNTRY OPENED the way for Communist penetration. None of the old town councils or municipal assemblies remained; the new political order substituted for them transitory administrative bodies called "national committees," with unlimited power. Assuming control of the municipalities, townships, and even cities, they appointed their own men as elders, councilors, and committeemen to pass judgment upon the political past and present of each citizen. The national committees managed the scant food supply; few aspects of daily life escaped their control.

This situation was not peculiar to Hungary; the Communists acted similarly in Rumania, Poland, Bulgaria, and Czechoslovakia.

These committees were not elected by the people but were formed by the delegates of the political parties. The Communists repeated the dubious argument they had used during the formation of the National Council: because the strength of the parties was unknown each party would have equal representation on the committees.

Thus, for example, a town with a thousand Smallholders and possibly half a dozen members of other parties sent four delegates from each party to the national committees. Naturally the Communists and the Peasant party were in no position to select outstanding, respected citizens; they had to delegate anyone available. While the Smallholders party was able to select respectable citizens, the Communists and the Peasant party were often forced to pluck vagrants, radicals, ex-convicts, and drunks off the streets to represent them.

The standards of these national committees were dismally low. The leftist parties naturally voted *en bloc*, preventing the Smallholders representatives from promulgating or enforcing any worth-while decision.

The people of the village were horrified at the ineptitude of the men who managed their affairs. It was not unusual for a one-time convict to find himself police captain of an entire district.

It was lucky that only Smallholders could be found in many of the hamlets; the party appointed its best men to the national committees. Admittedly, the committees accomplished some good. There was leadership of a sort, and something like a communal assembly. If the national committees had been elected by the local citizenry, they could have served adequately as a revolutionary body during the transition. The committees, blamed for every crisis and every crime, had many enemies among the people.

If, for instance, the policemen pillaged, the people of the village immediately blamed the national committee. Frequently stolen goods were found in the homes of the policemen; art treasures belonging to Jews who had returned from deportation were often seen on the living-room walls of police officers. The reputation of law enforcement officers, and indirectly of the national committees, suffered.

Later, agricultural production committees were formed in exactly the same fashion. No one could expect increased production from leftist members who hated work; in some villages the worst farmer, who neglected both his fields and his animals, became chairman of the committee.

The stewardship of the village wealth was in the hands of its least competent citizen—generally the first to offer himself for public service. Many circumstances prevented the return of peace of mind and a stable economy; one was the denunciations. Malfeasants with the right party affiliations started to denounce any who stood in their way, particularly the former respected and sure-handed leaders of the community. The new police force needed no proof; without warning they arrested and tortured anybody marked by a Communist party member. Many of these high-principled men were interned by police authorities who were on a moral level with the denouncer, and spent months in detention camps for the offense of performing their duties well in the past.

It was a sorry state of affairs when former Gestapo quislings switched their allegiance to the Communist-controlled police. In most cases the victims were respected, responsible members of the community.

We made efforts to advance consolidation, but increasing abuses forced us to complain to the Soviet authorities and the leaders of the

Communist party. Since in those days it was still impossible to check on the execution of any orders, it frequently took us months to find out that no directives had been issued which would have helped correct injustices. Thus consolidation seemed to march steadily backward, but we blamed the revolutionary conditions for everything; later we realized that all these excesses had been part of a set plan, for it was essential to Communist and Soviet aims that scourging hordes should make respectable people tremble with fear.

We saw the necessity for an informed public opinion; the people of Hungary had awaited democracy for a long time but had to be taught its application. For this we needed a press. As there was little newsprint in the country and both manufacturing and importing had stopped, the Communists proposed that all parties should unite in publishing a single newspaper in each of the cities. Conditions forced us to agree. Suddenly we awoke to the fact that our joint newspapers were attacking us, and the Communists were maligning the leadership of the Smallholders in the press in which we owned an equal share. Paying no heed to the paper shortage, we requested publishing permits and put out our own newspaper. We learned from our nonpartisan publishing effort that anyone allied in any Communist enterprise will be pushed out sooner or later. It happened, too, when we tried to govern with them.

CHAPTER 17

Unions Become a Political Tool

AS SOON AS THE OLD LEADERS OF THE SMALLHOLDERS PARTY EMERGED from their prisons and hide-outs and began to work for the party and exert their influence on national politics, the political scale approached a balance. Against the original advantages of the Communist party, the importance of the Smallholders party continually increased. The Smallholders actions moved us further along on the road to consolidation, its strength growing not only on the national political stage but in the hamlets and cities. As the well-meaning Social Democratic and other liberty-loving representatives in the national committees began to accept the opinions of the wise and experienced Smallholders, order began to evolve.

Naturally the Soviet wished to offset the influence of the Small-holders party, using as a tool the promotion of an organization to which, because of its honest and blameless past, no one could object. This was the Federation of Hungarian Labor. These workers' groups were for decades under the leadership of the Social Democratic party. They were respected institutions of the laboring class, credited with many advances against selfish capitalism and responsible for welfare institutions for the workingman.

This determinedly socialistic organization of the working class came, soon after the liberation, under the influence of Communist laborers who had exchanged their Arrow Cross membership cards for the current variety of absolutism. Naturally the Communist party did not neglect the Federation; to lead it, they brought along from Moscow a well trained former streetcar conductor of Budapest, Stephen Kossa. This terroristic, uncouth, and one-sided individual became a prisoner of the Russians in the early stages of the war. They discovered a good Communist in him, and put him through the political education mill. Returned as a star union leader, he became a blind tool of Russia and the Communists.

Kossa worked fast. He reorganized the Federation of Hungarian Labor and appointed himself executive secretary. Next to the weak president, Edwin Kisházi, he became practically dictator of union life. Seizing its leading positions from the hands of the Social Democrats, he soon divided the leadership within the unions equally between the Communists and the Social Democrats—which is to say that the Communists planned the orders while the Socialists obediently executed them.

This union organization was sent by the Communists to dam the rising Smallholders tide. First they demanded that unions get the same rights as political parties, then asked for membership in the national committees, and city and municipal governments.

The union member regarded these demands as the rightful aims of labor and, in the beginning, backed up the moves of the leaders with mass demonstrations. Later, naturally, the leaders never troubled to ask the workers to approve their actions, but meanwhile the Socialists backed Kossa. Either they did not recognize the machinations of the Communists, or they dared not oppose them.

There was not even a debate about giving the unions equal status with the political parties; Zoltán Tildy, who was at Debrecen at the time, granted the demands of the unions but argued that Rákosi promised the same status and rights to our Peasant Alliance. The net result was that, while the unions achieved political equality, the promise regarding the Peasant Alliance was forgotten. Openly the Communists agreed to equalize the status of the Peasant Alliance; actually they sent out confidential instructions to their local leaders to refuse admittance of representatives of the Peasant Alliance to the national or production committees. In some villages, where a few sensible men represented the non-Communist parties, the Peasant Alliance was seated, but in most instances the secret orders were followed. The Peasant Alliance could not offset the advantage gained by the Communists through political representation of the unions.

A handy political tool for the labor unions developed with the establishment of "political clearance" committees. In all Soviet-controlled countries, every public servant, professional worker, clerk, and laborer had his political past scrutinized by these clearance committees, on which, next to the representatives of the political parties, sat a union man with equal voice. They usually voted the straight Communist line, and a great number of persons lost their livelihood through the rulings promulgated. The clearance committees urged the public to report on anyone who appeared before them, and a flood of accusations engulfed all who were not members of the Communist party.

These clearance committees used great pressure against government employees: any mistake would be reprimanded, and a man with a tainted past could be transferred or forcibly retired. Against the decision of the clearance committees an appeal could be made to the Peoples' Court, which was the only recourse for old-time, reliable public servants with no unsavory political past. Thus a few were saved from dismissal despite the radical methods of these clearance committees.

As every individual appearing before these panels knew that the Communist party had the majority vote, many accepted the hint that clearance would proceed smoothly for party members.

Thus the respected, long-standing institutions of labor became tools of the Communists, halting the advancing consolidation and serving as springboards for the onsurge of the united forces of the Soviet and local Communists.

CHAPTER 18

The Soviet Construes the Armistice

THE GREAT POWERS DECIDED THAT AN ARMISTICE WITH ALL LIBERATED countries except Germany had to be signed. The conditions were to be agreed upon by all; the conquered nations, including Hungary, had no voice in their framing but had to sign them none the less. It is now obvious that the armistice agreement was not carefully thought through by any of the great powers, except the Soviet Union. The Russians knew that, as no armistice would be signed with Germany, Italy was the only conquered country that would be occupied by the Western powers; all the other countries would drop into the palm of Moscow.

There were many valid reasons why Hungary could not demand the right to negotiate an armistice with the great powers; first of all, she was hardly a free agent when all her cities, villages, and hamlets, and every foot of walkable land, was occupied by Soviet troops; also, other countries had already signed armistice agreements before the Russians got to Hungary without even trying to impose any difficulties or claim the right to negotiate.

Hungary had to be content with an armistice which at least officially ended the state of hostilities, thus arriving at a nebulous halfway point between war and peace. From the very first, it could be seen that the pact would impose heavy burdens; but we believed that only the letter of the pact would be demanded and hardly thought that the life of the people of Hungary would be littered with obstacles on the road to its healthy revitalization.

At that time it was impossible to comprehend the economic conditions; even the government did not know how much, exactly, the Germans and the Arrow Cross had carried with them, how much of the wealth was destroyed by the war, and what the Russian army had removed as spoils of the victor.

Later a rough survey showed that the Germans and the Arrow Cross had robbed Hungary of two hundred complete factories and stolen, in addition, the most valuable machinery of another three hundred industrial enterprises. They had moved all of Hungary's Danube shipping to Upper Austria; they had driven away approximately a third of all the livestock, and taken with them the entire gold and silver bullion of the National Bank. Priceless art from museums and public collections was stolen; vaults were looted; historical documents and relics were removed to Germany. They had robbed our hospitals of their equipment and stolen the nation's entire store of medical and pharmaceutical supplies. One would not believe it, but they had carried with them all of Budapest's ambulances and her entire fire-fighting equipment.

On the other hand, we could not ascertain how much of the industrial equipment would be left by the Soviet because every day more and more trainloads of dismantled Hungarian machinery left for Russia without being controlled or accounted for. One could not estimate how much the remaining livestock would be reduced by the endless columns of cattle, horses, and pigs driven by Red soldiers toward the Soviet Union.

It would be hard to describe the impact of the three-hundred-million-dollar reparation on the economic life of the country; nor could one foresee how the political "rights" secured by the armistice agreement would limit the independence of Hungary and the political freedom of its people; and to what extent the country would be forced to follow a one-sided, Soviet-dictated, political direction.

And no one, least of all the great Western powers which signed the agreement, thought that the Soviet would take every advantage of its position to overstep the terms.

Despite its fears, and in the face of insecurity, Hungary signed the armistice dictated to it in January, 1945, because it saw one encouraging aspect: the agreement specified a tripartite control commission composed of the United States, the United Kingdom, and Soviet Russia, and both the government and the public believed that the great Western powers would exercise their supposedly equal authority. We thought that the Western powers would not only control Hungary's fulfillment of her obligations under the armistice agreement, but also prevent Soviet occupation authorities from abusing the rights granted by the pact.

The bitter awakening came when we discovered that the Soviet used the armistice agreement to influence Hungarian political life and to strengthen the Communist party. During the temporary conditions, before the elections, the Soviet sank deep roots into Hungarian political soil which even the subsequent elections could not tear up completely.

The Hungarian government discovered soon that the control commission was a one-sided Soviet institution, in which the great Western powers participated only to the extent of shielding Soviet force from world public opinion and removing responsibility for the high-handed actions of Russia.

Up to the middle of 1945 no direct intercourse could be established between leading Hungarian statesmen and the representatives of the Western powers. Some of these representatives sought clandestine meetings with democratic Hungarian leaders—a fact which scarcely encouraged the leaders of the Smallholders party. We heard remarks like, "See, the Americans and the British follow Soviet orders, so why shouldn't the poor, conquered Hungarians?"

The Soviet first used the armistice agreement to strangle the Hungarian economy. It controlled the organization of the political parties to such an extent that even those it recognized, like the Smallholders, had to get a permit for each meeting or assembly. The Russians set limits on the countries with which we could establish diplomatic relations; continuously preventing us, for example, from reestablishing diplomatic intercourse with the Holy See. Claiming the right under the armistice, it censored the newspapers and interfered in Army appointments and transfers. It demanded that the Prime Minister report in advance any changes in the cabinet.

The armistice agreement did not empower the Soviet to do these things, but when we saw that it was able to enforce its one-sided conception of the armistice upon the representatives of the great Western powers, too, we could hardly question or complain.

The armistice was one of the greatest mistakes of world politics, leading to the Soviet political action which was to line up the countries of southeastern Europe on its side, hermetically sealed off from contact with the west and from resumption of normal international relations. The armistice enabled them to exploit the countries of southeastern Europe both politically and economically, and use them as a spearhead for the further political penetration of the world.

In these days, the United Nations looked upon these small countries, which had been liberated after being forced into the war by the Nazis, as defeated nations that had to be punished—not realizing that if the Soviet took them in hand it would use them to achieve its own political goals.

Any endeavor to reconstruct democratic society throughout the civilized world will prove to be superficial unless it considers the political and economic wounds inflicted by the armistice agreement.

The first step toward putting the world political scene in order is to investigate the trespasses committed by the Soviet on the basis of the armistice, and restore the economic and political liberties of the countries thus enslaved by the Soviet.

CHAPTER 19

A Starving Country Feeds the Red Army

THE ARMISTICE AGREEMENT COMPELLED HUNGARY, LIKE ALL THE OTHER "liberated" countries of southeastern Europe, to "supply the army of occupation with food." If the Red army's occupation had been confined to military necessity, like the American occupation of Japan— and a few battalions would have sufficed in Hungary—the country would have fulfilled her obligations easily despite her stripped and weakened condition. But the occupation was totalitarian, and the Russian armies in Hungary, like the scriptural locusts, covered every inhabited acre.

"It seems no man has been left in Russia," Béla Kovács said to me once when we were traveling together. And in truth, we saw more Red soldiers than natives.

While the strength of the occupation forces and their equipment was, naturally, a military secret, it was whispered: "Every five Hungarians have to feed a sixth, a guest who has overstayed his welcome. Five human beings must starve so an unproductive sixth may feast well."

If our army could have taken part in the military action on its own soil, and could have prevented the Russians from seizing all the supplies left by the Germans, it would have been easier for the country to "feed the liberators." If the administration had not disintegrated completely the existing supplies could have been ascertained, and the feeding of the hordes of Russian soldiers might have been coordinated. As it was, no order could be brought into the chaos of the first months. When the Russians wanted food they simply sequestered everything they could lay hands on, taking away the stores, the supplies of the mills, and even seed reserves. In the village they forced the elders, at the points of guns, to assist in requisitioning, and thus peasant families lost their scanty supplies and sometimes the livestock vitally needed to work the farms.

The condition of the peasant, in these days, was tragic. Not only must he look on helplessly as the Red soldiers carried away his livelihood, but he was exposed to daily torment. When they arrived (and in the early months Russian army trucks stood every day in the village square) the women ran to hide. Anything valuable in sight was immediately lost.

The columns of livestock driven eastward along the roads of the country made a dramatic sight. The weaker cattle were used to feed the occupation forces; the rest continued on to Russia.

Naturally the peasant tried to save what he could. Where there were forests, he drove the cattle into them; but soon this became known, and Russian soldiers "hunted" the hidden animals with machine guns. Next he tried to dig caves into straw ricks and hide his cattle there; but if the rick caught fire the animals were burned alive. Indeed, it was only with the blessed help of God that the peasant saved enough animals to begin breeding a new stock.

Not until later, when the reorganized Hungarian administration coordinated requisitioning and production and managed to enforce some justice, was order brought into the feeding of the Red army. But by that time starvation was rampant and tens of thousands of infants and young mothers in the cities had perished from malnutrition. Also, the conditions under which the government had to plan for the feeding of the "liberators" were extremely difficult, because the Russians never informed it of the exact amount of food needed or the numbers of soldiers to be cared for, and nobody could ever ascertain the food ration of the individual soldier.

A great number of injustices occurred after the Hungarian government took over the gathering of supplies for the Red army. The local committees were ordered to requisition food and livestock; wherever Communists controlled the majority on these committees, they naturally ignored the supplies of Communist party members and enthusiastically requisitioned from the Smallholders. They also would requisition more than was necessary, and divide the extra cattle among themselves. Often a Communist policeman, who had never had even a piglet to his name, suddenly had milch cows in his barn.

They lived up to the letter of the established Communist axiom: "What's yours is ours. What's mine is none of your business."

CHAPTER 20

The Allied Control Commission: A Very Expensive Guest

THE ALLIED CONTROL COMMISSION, ESTABLISHED ON THE BASIS OF THE armistice pact, not only failed to fulfill any of its promises but was a very expensive guest. It became a huge organization with an unknown total membership. Naturally the Soviet swamped us with "Controllers" of all ranks, in addition to a much smaller number of Americans and British; but later there were added, "to control the fulfillment of reparations," a large number of representatives of Czechoslovakia and Yugoslavia.

The commission became a mammoth institution. The Hungarian government was compelled to provide for its housing and food, pay its transportation costs, and give its members cash for expenses. At a time when the government was hardly able to secure the absolute necessities for an unavoidable reception or official dinner, it was hard-pressed to meet the commission's requirements.

First of all, housing had to be provided, which meant that hundreds of private palaces, villas, and homes, had to be put in order; most of these had been damaged by the siege, and required rebuilding or restoration. The members of the commission selected the homes, which naturally had to be furnished, too, and not always according to the taste of the Hungarian government. The members of the Allied Control Commission went to the remaining furniture dealers, selected the most beautiful furniture (which might be priceless antiques) and the most expensive oriental rugs—and the Hungarian government had to pay the bills. The commission also told the government what kind of food supplies must be delivered to it.

The complaint of the mayor of Szekszárd, who was ordered to provide for the Soviet subcommission stationed at that city, comes to mind. The major who headed the subcommission had the mayor report every morning to his office, where he issued the daily supply orders. One morning he ordered,

"Mayor, deliver today one ton of coffee and a tenth of a ton of tea!"

The mayor was horrified. "But, honorable major, in all of Hungary today there is not a ton of coffee or a tenth of a ton of tea to be had."

The astonished Soviet major said, "Well, then bring me as much as you can."

The next morning the major issued another order. "Mayor, today you must deliver twenty chickens and one hundred eggs."

"It shall be," answered the mayor.

Another morning the Russian made the queerest demand for an army officer, the head of a subcommission.

"Mayor, my present cook is clumsy and old. By tonight I want a young cook in my kitchen, and she must be beautiful."

Nonsense! thought the mayor. I am certainly not forced to procure kitchen help. He thought of refusing, but concluded that it was better to satisfy all the demands as well as he could than to have the Russian troops execute them by force. But he had to come to the capital and report it to us.

Subcommissions were stationed in all of the cities and had to be supplied by the local authorities; the first demand was always to furnish the best house or palace and maintain it in style. This, never easy, kept the local administration busy day and night.

The greatest problem was caused by the Control Commission and its headquarters in Budapest. Aside from the homes, we had to provide exclusive social casinos and maintain garages and automobile repair shops. Every detail of the food requests had to be executed. The demands exceeded all bounds of decency; in one month the Czechoslovakian delegation attached to the Control Commission requested 13,000 bottles of liquor in addition to tremendous amounts of food. This delegation consisted of ninety people—which meant that each individual had to imbibe 140 to 150 bottles of alcohol during the month. Hearsay had it that this liquor was not all for the members of the commission; the greater part was sent to families and friends in Czechoslovakia. But the claim was "for use in Budapest."

The ninety persons in the Czechoslovakian delegation were not all needed to control the fulfillment of the reparations obligation; they were stationed in Hungary to increase the propaganda facilities of the Czechs, who sought to induce the Slovakian population to leave Hungary.

When I was Prime Minister I invited the three heads of the Allied

Control Commission for a conference to discuss this ticklish problem—because the Commission's excesses were undermining the financial stability of the country. They defended unequivocally the luxurious style of living. In the end we reached an agreement: each of the foreign missions stationed in Budapest would express its requirements in monetary amounts, and the Hungarian government would put the cash at their disposal, and would establish special shops where members of the Commission could buy with the money given. Later we had to face difficulties with this simplified method, as the restricted currency in circulation at times made it impossible for the government to deliver these sizable amounts of actual cash on time.

But credit should be given where it belongs; some members of the Allied Control Commission made gratifying gestures, some helped to alleviate suffering. The acts of these few but true humanitarians will be remembered forever by the people of Hungary.

CHAPTER 21

Birth of Agrarian Reform

AMONG NATIONAL PROBLEMS AWAITING SOLUTION, AGRARIAN REFORM had been the most urgent. The liberation of the serfs in 1848 had given them political freedom and equality before the law, but it did not help the landless peasants.

For an agricultural worker there were only two roads toward advancement. After completing his compulsory military service he could go into government employ as a policeman, gendarme, tax collector, or railwayman; or else, by great privation and sacrifice and decades of work, he could secure for himself a little house and possibly one or two acres of land.

The economic progress of a hundred years brought no improvement in the life of the agricultural worker. During the premiership of Gömbös, at the time of the world crisis in the thirties, the average earnings of an agricultural worker were less than forty dollars a year—an amount barely sufficient to keep his family alive.

There were about half a million such landless peasant families in Hungary. The only way to help them was to give them each a piece of land, but the large landowners objected. A considerable number of the large holdings could not be broken up even if the owner wished to sell portions of them, because they had been declared subject to the laws of entail, which meant that only the eldest son in the family could inherit the land; even the other children could have no share in the holdings.

Another group of large estates which could not be distributed was in the hands of the bishoprics. The Roman and Greek Catholic churches owning large estates saw to it that they remained in perpetual possession of acquired lands.

Although the third group of large landholdings could be broken up by sale or inheritance, they seldom came into the hands of agricultural workers. Such "free" land was generally bought up by wealthy lessees or by owners of smaller properties who were able to secure credit to expand their holdings.

The land question in Hungary could be solved only by agrarian reform, which could give land from the six million acres belonging to the large and middle-sized estates to the poorest class of peasants.

The upper classes had always been able to block agrarian reform. The big landowners, the church, state officialdom, and capital generally joined hands to defend the large estates. It was as if they felt that, once the large estates were broken up, not only would their influence be weakened, but reforms might easily be introduced in other fields. On no other question was the opposition to social progress so unified as on the defense of the large estates.

At the end of the nineteenth century, when Darányi was Minister of Agriculture, a small-scale distribution of land had been carried out, in the course of which the state settled the families of several thousand agrarian workers on former large estates. But this was far from being a solution to the land question. After the First World War, Stephen Nagyatádi Szabó's Smallholders party forced through an agrarian reform bill, of which only the section dealing with the distribution of house plots was ever successfully executed. The land given to the peasants was not enough to insure a living, but it prevented them from expending their full efforts on labor as farm hands. In addition, the price of the land was so high that many, unable to pay it, gave up their portion.

Agrarian reform was of course a natural consequence of political change; for decades the opposition parties had demanded it. The Social Democrats supported it, as the Smallholders were its chief propagators.

They drafted several plans which were as radical as the times permitted.

In the middle thirties, Tibor Eckhardt, the leader of the party, announced a large-scale plan for agrarian reform which sought to distribute four and one-half million acres among the peasantry, and provide for the compensation of large landowners.

In 1940 we forced the government to bring before Parliament a bill dividing up large holdings and leasing them at low rents. The measure did not satisfy the peasantry, but we got it voted, thinking that it would be better than nothing. The government, however, never carried out the provisions of this law, either.

The Ministry of Agriculture was run, in the prewar years, by the large landowners. After I had requested many times in Parliament that the bill be carried out, the government began applying the portion of the bill dealing with the distribution of plots for homes. A state secretary in the Ministry of Agriculture, himself a large landowner, directed that only this section of the bill should be acted upon, since it called for the allocation of land in the village limits, most of which was in the peasants' possession.

Naturally every party was feverishly planning agrarian reform in the days following "liberation"; I, too, worked with my experts on a detailed and large-scale plan.

At this time it was far from easy to do thorough work in a field demanding facts and records. The capital lay in ruins. The records of the government offices had for the most part been used as fuel by the occupying armies. None the less it proved possible to secure the necessary data, on the basis of which we drew up a detailed plan.

In the first days of March, 1945, just as I was putting on the finishing touches, a car stopped before my temporary home. Out stepped a Russian colonel who asked me to leave with him at once for Debrecen. He told me to pack my things because he had received orders to bring me to Debrecen that same night.

"What do they want with us?" I asked.

"The agrarian reform decree must be prepared," answered the colonel through an interpreter.

I was taken aback. Was it the Soviet that decided when we should draw up an agrarian reform law? I had imagined that such an important measure would be initiated, not by decree, but by a bill in Parliament.

"Couldn't we start in the morning?" I asked. "The road is bad, and it is dangerous to travel by night."

"It is urgent that you and your associates come to Debrecen now, because the discussions are already in progress," answered the colonel.

Taking with us Koloman Saláta (a chief suspect in the later "conspiracy"), we left in two cars for Debrecen. On the way the Russian chauffeur told me in sign language that he had not slept for two nights. I wanted to take the wheel, but he would not let me. It was plain that he had orders not to allow anyone else to drive.

Near Kisujszállás the chauffeur fell asleep and our car ran into a ditch. With the help of the passengers in both cars, it was pushed onto the road again and we continued our journey.

By morning we arrived in Debrecen, where discussions had already begun. We saw Zoltán Tildy seated at the conference table.

Emery Nagy, the Communist Minister of Agriculture, read the temporary government's plan for agrarian reform, characterized by radicalism and superficiality.

I stated my attitude, stressing three points: (1) Everyone should be allowed to retain 150 acres, no matter how large his estate had been. (2) Landholders with children should be permitted to retain correspondingly more. (3) The price to be paid for the distributed land should be at least equal to the foreign debts with which they were encumbered. The interparty conference voted down all three proposals.

I turned, aghast, to Tildy. "What's going on here? Why is it impossible to get a single reasonable proposal accepted?"

"Yesterday Marshal Voroshilov called us in and settled the extent of agrarian reform and the time within which it could be carried out," whispered Zoltán.

I at once concluded that there was no point in my sitting at the conference table, because I should share the responsibility for the decree without having had a chance to carry through my convictions. But I determined to try to force one or two points. My proposal that the land distributed to the peasants be measured out in plots, and that each owner receive a deed of title, was accepted. My aim here was to forestall attempts to form kolkhozes on the Russian pattern. I also suggested that the law should state precisely the amount of compensation the state would give for land taken from churches, so they could continue their schools and institutions. This was voted down. Ever since, it has depended on the pleasure of the government what sums churches, schools, and charitable institutions shall receive in compensation for their expropriated properties.

Another idea which I advocated was that the land-requisitioning committees, which determined what lands were to be distributed, and which drew up the list of poorer peasants to whom these should be given, should not consist solely of landless applicants. They should include experienced peasants of good standing, whose holdings would not be altered—men without partiality in choosing applicants and in supervising equitable distribution. This was also voted down, and thus the distribution of the land was entrusted exclusively to the claimants. Generally they performed their epochal task with the utmost irresponsibility at a time when a Hungary composed of great estates had to be changed into a peasant state in the course of a few days.

As soon as the agrarian reform decree was published, it began to be executed feverishly in all parts of the country. In some localities the big estates were parceled out in a few hours without benefit of surveyors or experts. In some places the committees sought to do the job more carefully and weighed the merits of the applicants; but then armed Russian soldiers appeared, ordering the committee to distribute the land within three or four days. Of course there was no possibility of planning future roads, or choosing sites for settlements. The applicants did not trouble to consider how the plots would be connected later by roads, or how they could be reached by public utilities. In a word, my whole plan, which I had elucidated before Pushkin when we first met, collapsed. I do not think it is libelous to infer that the radical tempo of land distribution was directly caused by my earlier discussion with Pushkin.

The execution of agrarian reform was seized upon by the Communist party as an opportunity for expansion. On tremendous posters it proclaimed that the Communist party was giving the land. In many districts applicants joined the party *en masse* in order not to be overlooked. It was true, the Communist-dominated land distribution committees were generally less interested in the applicant's ability and experience as a farmer, than in whether or not he was a party member. Thus men with no farming experience whatsoever—tradesmen, newfledged policemen, and party officials—suddenly became owners of farms.

A police sergeant of the old school told me that soon after the land had been distributed one of the new Communist landowners appeared before him.

"Sergeant," he said, "I want you to bring me four Nazi internees."

"What for?"

"I want them to plant my corn," said the new owner.

"But the land was distributed so that it should belong to those who work it," said the sergeant.

"I've worked on other people's land long enough. Now let other people work on mine," was the reply.

A paragraph in the decree which stated that anyone who was a traitor or who had committed antisocial acts could be deprived of his land was the excuse for a great many injustices. A prosperous peasant would be accused of having mistreated or struck farm hands, and thereupon the land-requisitioning committee would confiscate his land.

Nearly three years have passed since the agrarian reform in Hungary, and despite many injustices and excesses it must be admitted that its swift and radical execution was the surest course to follow. While in peacetime the argument that radical agrarian reform would cause serious disturbance in the continuity of production was valid, war and the occupying forces had now so disrupted the economic life of Hungary that the only way to cultivate the land was to put it into the hands of the toiling farmers. The large estates would not have been able to find workers, but the peasants did cultivate their own land.

It was moving to see the peasant, lacking technical equipment and farm animals, use hoe and spade and his own two hands to put his land again at the service of his nation. In many places men harnessed themselves before the plows, replacing tractors or animals. Often women and children broke up the clods to plant the seeds. The miraculous power in the peasant eternal produced the will to harvest: 93 per cent of all arable land was under cultivation by 1946. The Hungarian peasant, through his creative energy, brought life to the neglected and ruined fields and secured the minimum food requirements of the long-suffering nation.

CHAPTER 22

The Government Moves to the Capital

AFTER THE LIBERATION OF BUDAPEST, THE DIFFICULTIES IN GOVERNING the country from Debrecen became even more evident. The heart is Budapest, the administrative center of the country; railway lines start from it, and all highways lead to it. Debrecen can be governed from Budapest, but not Budapest from Debrecen. The people, especially those living in the capital, demanded that the government move there.

Prime Minister Béla Miklós sent Béla Kovács, Undersecretary of the Interior, to Budapest to prepare for the transfer: no easy task. Previously the offices of the Prime Minister, the Ministries of Defense, Foreign Affairs, Interior, and Finance had been on the hill of Buda near the royal palace. That district was wiped out by the siege, along with the Ministries of Commerce and Industry in Buda on the shore of the Danube. When the Germans and Arrow Crossists were forced to surrender Pest, they blew up the beautiful Danube bridges and retreated to the hills of Buda, where they held out for yet another month. Thus not a single usable building remained on the Buda side.

Public buildings on the Pest side were also badly damaged and were not adequate for the apparatus of government. The difficulties were aggravated by the fact that all buildings of this type which had withstood the siege had been requisitioned by the Red army. Its main and subsidiary headquarters occupied separate buildings; many were occupied by the Control Commission and its various missions and divisions; the NKVD (formerly GPU) moved into several large structures. In addition it was necessary to secure quarters for the various legations. There was little space left for the government.

Nevertheless, by April, 1945, the transfer was possible. In addition to the repaired public buildings it was necessary to use the buildings of several large corporations; thus the Prime Minister at first occupied two floors of the Commercial Bank.

In shifting the government to Budapest, we also wished to attain a higher standard of achievement; and for this reason the reinstatement of experienced officials was begun. Party leaders as well as public opinion were demanding greater efficiency from the government, and the number of its duties was continually increasing.

The local autonomies were beginning to take shape. The municipal and county governments, through which the country was administered, had to be reorganized. The city and county councils had a noble past; often they had forced back to the correct path governments that deviated from the traditions and spirit of the Hungarian people. Thus it was up to the central administration to reestablish the autonomous local governing bodies and start them off on a proper road.

The people of the country districts had become aware of the arbitrary violence of the Communists, and there was great dissatisfaction in those towns and counties where it had not been possible to set up the local committees in relation to the actual strength of the parties. Disputes among the parties began, with the dictatorship of Red army commandants and Control Commission representatives adding to the difficulties of the situation. Not only the party leaders, but the government too, had their hands full trying to smooth the rocky road and silence the many just complaints.

CHAPTER 23

"Everyone, Join a Party!"

IN HUNGARY AND OTHER SOVIET-OCCUPIED COUNTRIES, THE COMMUNIST party did not follow the Russian policy of admitting only proven and selected men to its ranks. Except in Yugoslavia, they initiated a country-wide drive for membership. There, Communist adherence was kept secret, and the other parties did not organize openly either, with the result that in Yugoslavia no one dares deny that he is a Communist.

In Hungary the Reds were not finicky as to whom they admitted to membership, knowing that they could keep members in line by strict party discipline and, if necessary, with the help of the NKVD. Their motto was, "Everyone should join a party"—those who do not are not real democrats, but only waiting for an opportune time to support some antidemocratic movement.

We of the Smallholders party believed that it was proper for free men to join whatever party they pleased, but that it was not fitting for men in state employ to do so. It would be best if the soldier, policeman, and government official were nonpartisan, because it was their duty to serve the citizenry without discrimination.

But the leftist parties launched a great membership drive among civil servants, who then demanded that the Smallholders do likewise. Naturally here, as everywhere except among industrial workers, the Smallholders party attracted the greatest number of members. The leftist bloc could achieve significant results only in ministries headed by their members. The Communists were particularly active in organizing the police force.

Their work here was easy, because most of the leading positions were already filled by Communists, who could exert pressure on subordinate officers and members of the rank and file who had belonged to the former force. None the less, the Smallholders also started active organization and gained a number of members within a short time.

The left bloc began exerting pressure on government employees, promising security and promotion to those who joined them. Many officials who had done favors for National Socialist members of Parliament, associating themselves with German aims and attacking the Reds, sought to atone for their sins by joining the Communist party. The Communist ministers hurried to put reliable men in charge of departments where they could exert pressure on non-Communist subordinates and show favor to their own party members. The Smallholders were able to enroll in their ranks only men of moral conviction and courage, but even at that attained a sizable majority in the ministries.

We, as leaders of the Smallholders party, were well aware of the many unhealthy developments in the situation; but during the life of the temporary government Soviet influence was so one-sided and dictatorial that we only hoped for some degree of improvement after the elections.

As the months passed, we realized how empty were Russian declarations about state sovereignty, as long as the interpretation of the armistice devolved on the Soviet alone.

CHAPTER 24

The Police Uproot Democracy

THE ORGANIZATION OF THE NEW POLICE FORCE WAS THE GREAT AND enduring crime of Francis Erdei, radical Minister of the Interior. This gifted writer, entirely unversed in administration and inspired by an innate, long-standing radicalism, paved the way for the introduction of the most drastic changes. He detested the former administration, preferring even the most obscure figures to the experienced men who had served in the past. In country towns he often appointed former field hands and radical friends to the post of chief of police. It did not disturb him to see the police rob and murder; in everything they did he saw the fulfillment of his own lust for vengeance. Whether it was right for the whole police force to be subservient to the aims of the Communist party never occurred to him. In any case he could not or did not dare oppose the extension of Communist control over the force.

In every larger community and town a political section of the police was organized, unbound by any rules or restrictions and with rights and duties undefined. Free in every respect to do as it pleased, it favored in every way the members of the Communist party and hunted down those opposed to the extremes of the far left. From all parts of the country came reports of its terrorist activities.

Soon after its formation, the new police force rounded up at Gyömrö, not far from Budapest, those opposed to Communism and secretly tortured to death or shot down twenty-six men, including the parish priest. This aroused tremendous indignation throughout the country, with demands for the punishment of the guilty; but the Minister of the Interior, backed by the Communist party, refused to take any action.

Reports reached Budapest that the police chief at Eger had filled the dungeons of the old castle with outstanding leaders of the district, and spent the nights robbing wine cellars. There were reports that at Kaposvár the police made a specialty of pouncing on leaders of the Smallholders party, often employing an *agent provocateur* and then arresting them on the basis of anti-Communist or anti-Russian assertions. We learned that at Kecskemét the chief of police was employing bloody torture to force damaging confessions from suspects.

But this man, a Captain Báno, exercised his power in other ways. Through his subordinates, he had wives and daughters of respected citizens brought in for "questioning." These questionings, which were sometimes "celebrated" with liquor, generally took place at night. All were assaulted and raped, except those who, because of their "fake bashfulness," were killed. The women of the city and surrounding countries lived in unceasing terror, because wherever a husband, father, or fiancé was caught resisting Báno's men, he was either arrested for deportation to Russia as a "prisoner of war" or murdered. At best, he was interned or sentenced to jail.

The case of Báno is not isolated except in one respect—he did not have a natural end. One night, while he was motorcycling back from one of his little excursions to a country inn, a wire strung across the road between two trees sliced off his head.

The depraved "police force" ran riot through the country, intent on only one thing: to force as many people as possible to join the Communist party.

A group of political police had a rendezvous at a wine cellar in the suburbs of Budapest. After a long session of drinking they began to talk freely. They were complaining.

"I have twenty-three notches on my gun and still haven't gotten the evacuated German house I applied for," said one.

"That's nothing," replied another. "I have seventy-two liquidations to my credit, and all I got was a little three-room house in a suburb."

Possibly both men were just stupidly boasting; but their attitude was characteristic of the new police.

Austin Valentini, the Social Democratic Minister of Justice, found the atrocities committed by the police force insupportable. In the summer of 1945 he proposed at a cabinet meeting that, in cases of crime by policemen in which the force itself failed to take adequate action, he as Minister of Justice should be empowered to conduct a separate investigation with the aid of policemen of proven experience. After a long and violent discussion, his proposal was accepted by the cabinet. We felt that now at last there would be order. The powers voted to Valentini were never used, however. The leader of his party, Árpád Szakasits, in response to Communist pressure, forced him to resign the following week, and the killers at Gyömrö were at liberty to commit further murders.

Inasmuch as the crimes committed by the police had become a constant topic of discussion at cabinet meetings, the government issued a decree which provided that only such men as had been nominated by autonomous local councils could be appointed by the Minister of the Interior to leading positions on the police force. The local councils made their nominations. Where the Smallholders' influence was strong, responsible men were nominated; but where the Communists had the deciding voice, the bitterly detested officials were confirmed in their posts.

In the Ministry of the Interior, a Communist law clerk named Szebenyi, (who, I hear, has since become undersecretary) was put in charge of the police department. This man's Jewish relatives had been murdered by the Germans in deportation camps, and he breathed revenge not only against all Germans and Nazis but against everyone who was not a Marxist. This spirit of vengeance inspired him in police affairs, too. When the nominations of the towns and countries arrived, he quickly had the Communist nominees installed by Minister Erdei, but delayed the appointment of the rest indefinitely so that, despite the nominations of the local councils, there were many districts in which no changes took place.

The autonomous council of my own county of Baranya asked the Minister of the Interior to discharge a certain Vörös, who was chief of police even though he was not a Hungarian citizen. Vörös had lived for twenty years in Yugoslavia as a Communist émigré. He was charged with seeking to Communize the police force, spying on behalf of Yugoslavia, and collaborating with the Yugoslav partisans who were raiding the frontier towns of Baranya. The Minister of the Interior paid not the slightest attention to the council's request; only after a personal struggle, lasting a year and a half, did I succeed in getting the man removed.

It was reported from Szolnok that Herpai, the chief of the county police, inflicted ghastly tortures on innocent men and winked at robberies and corruption of the county police. It was only when I became Prime Minister that I was able to have him displaced. More and more men were being interned; the number of objects of police and Communist vengeance was constantly increasing. We sought information about the activities of the police in other countries under Soviet occupation and were shocked to learn that the situation in Rumania, Yugoslavia, and Bulgaria was the same. Police there, too, prosecuted all those who were not Communists and terrorized the populace. In each country they were particularly ruthless in dealing with anyone who uttered anti-Soviet opinions. We concluded that the police in all southeastern Europe must be under unified direction; later we had proof of this when, at the time of the putsch in Hungary, we learned that the head of the political police, Gabriel Peter, was head in name only. The real leader was Zabersky, a general in the Red army.

The people, craving a peaceful life and security for their community as respite from the horrors of war and its aftermath, and experiencing such terror from their own public servants charged with their safety, were wondering if the roots of true democracy would ever take hold.

CHAPTER 25

The Ministry of Reconstruction

IN THE SPRING OF 1945 I WAS FORCED TO TAKE ON MANY DUTIES IN addition to my work in the Smallholders party. I was appointed vice chairman of the Supreme Executive Council of the Cooperatives. I was elected to the Budapest Municipal Assembly and chosen a member of its governing body; aside from these responsibilities I represented, with Zoltán Tildy, the Smallholders in all of the interparty conferences. Devoting all my spare moments to strengthening my party, I had little time to myself.

In these days it was still difficult to have a heart-to-heart talk with a friend, for the outrageous behavior of the Red soldiers made the streets unsafe after dark, and if you had dinner or spent an evening at his house you had to stay overnight. After one such night at a friend's house I dropped in at Tildy's apartment in the morning to discuss a few pending questions.

"I've been trying to find you," he greeted me. "Last night Rákosi and Szakasits came to see me, and we discussed at length the reconstruction of the country. We concluded that this utterly devastated land can be made to live again only if we coordinate all efforts in a Ministry of Reconstruction and put a strong man at the head of it. The work of this new ministry would be to unify all national resources and direct the work of the economic ministries. We agreed to invite you to become the new minister."

I listened with surprise, and answered:

"Sorry, I can't accept."

Tildy asked why.

"First of all, I do not want to take part in the cabinet as it is now organized; but this is the lesser consideration. The other is that I do not wish to discontinue party work under any circumstances, because that is the most important part of my life and that is where I am most needed, right now. You are constantly occupied with political activities. The entire time of Béla Varga is taken up with party organization in Budapest. Béla Kovács is Undersecretary of the Interior and has no time for party activity. I am alone right now in the active national leadership and will not leave until we can find the right man to succeed me."

"Think it over, Ferenc. You can do a great deal for the people, and thus the party, as Minister of Reconstruction," continued Tildy. "The villages and cities will get help and loans from your hand. This is a great opportunity to popularize the party."

"Don't you believe it, Zoltán!" I interjected. "They want to put me in the Reconstruction Minister's chair in order to eliminate me from party work. The Smallholders are in the ascendancy, and it looks as if we shall be, despite all pressure, the strongest political force in the country by election time. They want to retard the party by making a minister out of me."

Tildy's words astounded me for other reasons. I never wanted to become a member of the cabinet. In 1930 I accepted the general secretaryship of the Smallholders party to serve the peasants, the most forlorn class of society. When I became spokesman for my people in Parliament my ambition was satisfied.

The ghosts of the period following the First World War flitted before me, reminding me that there was the same kind of chaos. A peasant was needed to order and unify the national life. Stephen Nagyatádi-Szabó was pushed aside after he finished his great task. How much more he could have accomplished in the political emancipation of Hungary if he had remained the Peasant party leader, instead of accepting a post in the cabinet!

I was also reminded of another aspect; it was the foolhardiness of former leaders who had flirted with the Germans that had led the country along the road of destruction. Was I, a peasant, to rebuild my land? No, I would not abandon the peasantry for any post of honor.

"Let us ask Béla Varga's opinion," I suggested.

"Varga is not in the capital, but Béla Kovács will arrive in a few minutes," answered Tildy. "Whatever Kovács's opinion is, and despite all your arguments, I think it most advisable for you to take on the great task of helping the country to live again."

When Béla Kovács arrived I tried to paint in lurid colors the cunning plans of the leftist politicians.

"Undoubtedly the organizational work of the party will suffer if your hand is withdrawn; but one can't dispose of the question so easily. We are weak in the cabinet. Not only will we be stronger numerically, but they respect you; and your authority will increase the influence of the Smallholders," was Kovács's first reaction.

Further arguments were futile. In the end I turned to the time-proven test which I used before every great decision: "What would my village say? What would the peasants want me to do?" I saw before me the picture of the five villages of Baranya, which were completely destroyed by the retreating armies of General Weichs; I envisaged the more than a hundred towns and villages which had been destroyed during the operations west of the Danube.

The talks continued, and in the afternoon Béla Kovács finally turned the scale by undertaking, as my permanent deputy, the active direction of the party organization and later resigning his post as Undersecretary of the Interior. With his pledge I yielded to the wish of the party and accepted the post of Minister of Reconstruction.

It was very easy for the party leaders to decide to create a new cabinet post; but they were unable to supply an administrative background, complete with functionaries, nor to make any suggestions for a program. I had never had any experience as an official, and with my peasant background I had to start from scratch; I had to find a home for the new ministry and assistance in the great task. I took as under-secretary Joseph Antall, the efficient executive of the Interior, who had been imprisoned with me. I made Dr. Francis Kapócs, who had distinguished himself during the war by his independence and forthrightness, my personal secretary. With these two men I started to organize the ministry which, within a month, was operating smoothly.

The administrative structure of this ministry was unique; it resembled an inverted pyramid. After all available experts had been appointed to the top positions, there were, for instance, three times as many division chiefs as secretaries. Brains and initiative were needed in this ministry—not bureaucracy.

But both the Communists and the Social Democrats used this opportunity to strengthen their own positions within the cabinet. The Communists exchanged for Joseph Gábor as Minister of Commerce one of the most powerful men in the party, Ernest Gerö. The Socialists put in place of Austin Valentini as Minister of Justice the chief legal counsel of the party, Stephen Ries; and in place of the very worthy Francis Takács as Minister of Industry the assistant general secretary of the party, Anthony Bán. In this grouping the Smallholders and the Communists had three cabinet seats each, and the Socialists tried to gain a third; they campaigned publicly against the Minister of Supplies Gabriel Faraghó until he became discouraged, quit, and was replaced by Socialist Alexander Ronai.

Soon another change took place. The Smallholder Minister of Finance, Stephen Vásáry, sharply criticized the economic inroads of the Soviet in Hungary and fearlessly attacked the activities of the Communist party. This stand gave the Soviet and the Communists an opportunity to unite in a campaign of personal attacks against Vásáry; in the summer of 1945 we were forced to let him resign and put in his stead Emery Oltványi, then president of the National Bank.

Strengthened by the ambitions of the new men, the government tried to give further impetus to consolidation; and this endeavor, together with the exemplary attitude of the Hungarian people, produced fruits. Hungarian democracy, trying to surmount obstacles, advanced on the road to healthy development, striding far ahead of all the rest of southeastern Europe.

CHAPTER 26

Budapest Rises from the Ashes

BUDAPEST PLAYS AN UNUSUALLY IMPORTANT PART IN THE LIFE OF Hungary, not only because of being the capital and the source of all government functions, but because of the unique character of its physical development. In other countries some of the lesser cities develop into cultural or economic centers; but in Hungary all cultural, economic, industrial, and commercial enterprises are concentrated in the capital. The economic development of the country and its commercial achievements fall under its influence. Budapest is the true heart of the country; its population pumps the blood that keeps the outlying cells alive.

After the siege the people of Budapest continued to live in the cellars for a long time. Practically every home was more or less in ruins; there was not a single window in any apartment, and street traffic consisted of pedestrians and pushcarts. The men on the streets wore beards, and the women wore pants. It was not hard to get shaved, but the men tried to look older than their age in order to escape deportation to Russia. The women wore pants belonging to their husbands, fathers, or brothers for protection from the freezing cold and on the assumption that Red soldiers liked women in pants less than those in skirts.

Koloman Latabár, one of the great comic actors of Hungary, gave the best characterization of the Budapest scene after the siege in a recent operetta:

"And along the ruins came my dream girl. She wore her father's baggy pants, her back was bending under a heavy rucksack, and under her arm she carried a stovepipe."

The pushcart and the rucksack represented the ordinary transportation facilities. The homes, slowly being put into order by people living meanwhile in the shelters, were restored with lumber transported on human backs. Whoever caught an injured army horse that could still walk and secured a cart earned its weight in gold.

Those visitors from abroad who raved about Budapest's beauty, remembering its castle on the hill, its row of modern hotels along the Quay, its Opera, its health-giving springs, its gypsy violinists pouring out the romance of Hungary, would never have recognized the capital devastated by the siege.

The scarcity of food in Budapest was unimaginable. A wave of pilgrims swamped the near-by countryside; on the main roads masses of people, walking the uncounted miles, carried rucksacks with clothing or other valuables to exchange for food. Many fathers made a hundred-mile round trip to bring food to their starving families.

All political parties started a strong propaganda campaign in the villages, trying to induce them to feed the capital. The hearts of the villagers responded, and truckloads of gifts started to arrive. But there also developed the black market; people who had no work, who had to leave their jobs, men with a shady political past, and all who were out for easy money at the expense of the starving people began to trade in misery. These leeches trafficked in food, carrying it in every conceivable fashion—bribing Russian soldiers to help them transport by truck, or using pushcarts or rucksacks and at times even human load carriers to swell their profits. They sold the food to people ready to sacrifice anything to secure their life-sustaining needs; only gold, jewelry, silver, and other valuables were accepted as payment.

As a result of the ruthless requisitioning of the stores and livestock, the only considerable food supplies were held by the Red army. The Communists and the Russians brewed a brilliant political idea—the city of Budapest should turn to the Red army and beg for a food loan. Using the critical conditions, they attacked John Csorba, brave mayor of Budapest, who, recognizing the reasons behind the attacks, resigned. The Communists and Socialists immediately united behind the appointment of the Communist leader Zoltán Vas, a half-baked intellectual.

The day the terroristic Vas became mayor of the city, he turned to the Red army for help. From the sequestered Hungarian stores he was granted a food loan of 180 carloads of grain, a few thousand animals, and a few carloads of sugar. This loan, which only a Communist mayor could secure for the starving city, later was used by the Communists to exert pressure on the national government.

The food, the gracious gesture of the Red army, was used to strengthen the political stand of the party and enable them to claim that the Communists had been the first to feed the city. The food, "loaned" to a starving population from which it had originally been taken by force, was only one link in the chain of collusion between the Red army and the Hungarian Communists.

CHAPTER 27

Reparations Enslave the Economy

ONE OF THE MOST GRIEVOUS PROVISIONS OF THE ARMISTICE WAS THAT concerning reparations. Of the $300,000,000 that Hungary had to pay, Russia received $200,000,000 and Yugoslavia and Czechoslovakia $100,-

000,000. The Soviet, careful to keep up appearances, invited the Hungarian government in June, 1945, to discuss the agreement.

It was only when they sat down in conference that the delegates realized what a burden was to be imposed upon their country. The Russians demanded reparations in goods. Inasmuch as Hungary had neither agricultural nor industrial goods with which to pay, the Soviet Union designated machinery of factories and power plants which should be dismantled and shipped to Russia along with whatever basic materials were on hand, to meet the reparations payments.

Consternation was general when it turned out that a great portion of the plants which the Nazis had not succeeded in carrying off would have to be dismantled and handed over. Our government tried to reason with the Russians, asking them to wait until we were in a position to send goods, and pointing out that if they took our factories we should never be able to pay future reparations installments.

But the Russians were adamant. Later, we often saw Soviet-bound trains stand for weeks on sidings; the expensive factory machinery with which they were loaded was exposed to rain and snow and rust. By the time it arrived in Russia, it could probably be used only for scrap metal.

It was also at the reparations conference that the worth of the goods to be sent to Russia by Hungary was to be determined. The Russians set the prices. The Hungarian delegation protested vainly that the goods could not be produced at the rates dictated but, with no one to turn to, they had to accept the terms.

In consequence the Soviet Union received goods at one-third to one-fifth their value, and sometimes for even less. The $300,000,000 in reparations that Hungary had to pay amounted actually to more than a billion dollars. For as soon as the Yugoslavs and the Czechs learned of the rates Russia was getting, they insisted on a similar fictitious accounting.

We now see that reparations absorb 60 to 70 per cent of Hungarian industrial production and place the economic life of the country under a far greater strain than in Finland, Bulgaria, or Rumania, where economic life has been far less seriously disrupted.

The most tragic and immoral aspect of the matter, however, is that the Soviet dictated a clause in the reparations agreement to the effect that if Hungary fell behind on payments she would have to pay a fine of 5 per cent monthly—that is, 60 per cent a year—on the unpaid balance. In the second half of 1945 Hungary was able to pay only by dismantling her factories and sending a certain number of cattle. Even so, this made up less than a third of the required amount. The period of reparations indebtedness and economic slavery was beginning.

We had to consider liquidating valuable interests abroad at infinitesimal prices, so as to catch up with our reparations payments and free ourselves of the weight of exorbitant interest. Thus we were forced to sell to Russia a coal mine at Petrozsény in the Transylvanian territory, adjudged to Rumania, for a price far below its real value. Expert opinion appraised it at a minimum of $40,000,000, and we gave it to the Soviet for $12,500,000, to be rid of our reparations balance. It is true that the coal mine was accounted for in reparations dollars, which meant that it was the equivalent of about $40,000,000 in goods that we should have had to send to Russia.

It was on the peasantry that the reparations payments had the most disturbing effect. The reparations agreement also required Hungary to deliver large numbers of cattle, horses, and pigs. The government could not buy these animals because, for one thing, the peasants did not want to sell their depleted stock and, for another, the government had no means of paying for them. Inflated money naturally meant nothing to the peasant. Thus it became necessary to requisition and take by force from the peasant a portion of the few animals that he had left, so that they might in part be sent off as reparations and in part used to feed the Red army. If local officials were tardy in their requisitioning, the Red soldiers themselves went plundering with the help of local Communist leaders, who were only too glad to lead them to the farms of non-Communists.

The reparations thumbscrew, painful to the Hungarian people and troublesome to the government, meant long years of economic slavery for the whole nation.

CHAPTER 28

Balance Sheet of Destruction

DESPITE GREAT HARDSHIP, LIFE BEGAN ANEW IN HUNGARY. THE PEOPLE felt that although they had to endure much suffering and humiliation, they were leaving chaos and the cruel early days of the occupation behind. They believed that the day of freedom had dawned; after overcoming temporary difficulties, it would be possible to live a free, democratic life. At that time the Hungarian peasant, laborer, and white-collar worker did not yet know that we were only falling from the frying pan into the fire, and that the Soviet dictatorship and Communist terror would quickly replace the Nazi oppression. The people sorrowed for the many deportees and prisoners of war who were not present to share in reconstruction, but themselves worked all the harder.

First to begin was the peasantry. Although left entirely to their own resources, the first breath of spring found the Hungarian peasants attending to their everlasting duties. Their livestock was depleted, and the greater part of their farm equipment was destroyed; but what they lacked in supplies, they made good with sweat. To make up for requisitioned draft animals, many had found injured and abandoned army horses that they nursed back to usefulness by spring. Others converted idle ammunition wagons into carts. The fields were often dug by hand; sometimes the peasants themselves would draw the plows. If they had no grain they planted corn or beets or potatoes. If they had no cattle or pigs they turned to chickens.

The resourceful peasants set to repairing their homes with their own hands. They replaced tile roofs which had been shot to pieces with roofs of straw, rushes, or cornstalks. They pasted the broken windows with paper, easily obtainable by tearing down a few of the innumerable Communist posters that continually decorated public walls. Agrarian reconstruction cost the state practically nothing because of the industry and sacrifice of the peasants.

The reconversion of industry was a difficult problem. Much of our large plant machinery had been carried off by the Nazis; what remained was taken by the Russians as reparations or booty; and many factories had been destroyed by bombing. By ordinary methods of reconstruction it would have taken decades to bring all our factories back into operation. But the workingmen pitched in. It was moving to see the sense of responsibility with which simple workmen, who for many years had been at odds with the owners and the management, set about rebuilding the plants—first laboriously digging out the machinery from the ruins and clearing away the rubble. Then they began repairing the machines. After months of effort they would produce usable equipment from a ruin of tangled steel. Thus one factory after another was set in operation.

Propaganda was a factor in reconstruction. "Storm brigades" were organized on the Russian model to repair, by overtime work, a tooling machine or railroad car in advance of the required schedule. The results would then be heralded in the newspapers or on posters.

Here, too, the cooperation between the Communist party and the Soviet was evident. The Red army often helped in work done under the leadership of a Communist minister. When the building of a bridge was undertaken by Minister Gerö, for example, Soviet pioneers would at once appear and help him complete it at least a few days in advance of the scheduled time, so that the Communist press could then proclaim to the country: "That's how a Communist minister works."

Office workers did not lag behind, either, often digging their desks out of the ruins and clearing their offices of rubble, so that they could begin working.

Resourceful tradesmen, who in the weeks after liberation sold mostly personal belongings in front of their burned-out stores, now set about clearing out premises that had been used as stables by the armies. They put up their counters, and gradually the public found itself able to buy urgent necessities.

Here and there restaurants, where meatless meals could be bought by those who had no food at home, began to function.

As Minister of Reconstruction I observed the principle that the productive parts of the nation's economy should be restored first, to start economic life functioning. Then we could think about rebuilding homes and public edifices. I arranged loans for such repairs of public and private structures as were needed to save them from further damage by the autumn rains.

We began clearing away debris from the streets of Budapest and other cities; thus, by 1945 all ruins which interfered with traffic were cleared from the streets of Pest and all houses which threatened to collapse had been torn down, although in Vienna, which had suffered so much less, rubble still encumbered the streets in the spring of 1947.

I tried to coordinate the activities of the economic ministries, ordering damage statistics compiled. As president of the Economic Council, I asked my fellow ministers to draw up budget estimates. This work, however, only progressed with difficulty since quick and accurate determination of the extent of damages was impossible. It was even more difficult to compute the amount of basic materials at our disposal, because the data we received were incomplete and slow to arrive.

Nevertheless, I tried to learn the facts about the damages sustained by the country, for the sake of thorough planning.

During the following months, when the statistics were compiled, we had to face the most disheartening balance sheet of destruction.

The basic economic loss of the country, exclusive of individual and personal property damages, was more than $8,000,000,000.

In Budapest alone, of 333,358 households, 180,705 suffered losses while of 35,677 buildings, 29,987 were damaged or destroyed.

This was the picture that faced us amidst economic chaos; the population was in dire need of the necessities of life, and starvation was rampant in many parts of the country.

Many bridges had to be crossed on the road to recovery.

I issued the Public Works Decree, one provision of which was that men of means should bear a proportionately larger share of the responsibility. This decree is still a cornerstone of the reconstruction program.

The costs of reconstruction could not, of course, be covered by state funds. Taxes could not have been collected from the ruined populace even had there been collectors to do the work. The government could produce money only by printing it, and the circulation of bank notes grew; but, since there was no supply of goods to match it, inflation, which brought much suffering to everyone, began. It was impossible for wages to keep pace, and the money received was almost worthless.

A great inflation has terrible effects on economic life and society. Everything had been destroyed, and life had to start somehow even if it meant temporary suffering to the people. Gold and the dollar were the gods of inflation, but they gave comfort to only a few. The people traded what valuables they had left, in order to bridge, somehow, the interim until stabilization. Only the industry and self-sacrifice of the Hungarian people made reconstruction possible.

CHAPTER 29

The Potsdam Decision

STRUGGLING TO RISE FROM THE DEPTHS, HUNGARY RECEIVED ONE BLOW after another; and one of the heaviest was the Potsdam decision. Here, too, it was the Soviet Union that most thoroughly analyzed the terms of the agreement and derived the greatest profit from it. The Potsdam decision made it possible for the great powers to exploit completely the countries that fell within their spheres of influence. Conscience alone determined the extent to which each power took advantage of its provisions. Events have proved that the Soviet has a very flexible conscience.

At Potsdam the leaders of the great powers did not wish to take time to clarify the details of the agreement; and it seems that the experts, who should have defined the rights of the Allies and the extent to which the small vanquished nations might be exploited, took their task casually and did not consider future effects.

There was an unconfirmable rumor that the great powers had only intended to define matters relating to Germany at Potsdam. Toward the end of the meetings a third-rank Russian expert was said to have asked if the agreements relating to Germany were not also to be applied to the satellite states. Since there were no objections, Russia had this inserted into the agreement.

Soviet economic experts in Hungary at first only demanded the property belonging to German citizens. But, as the proverb has it, eating develops an appetite. Russia soon made other demands.

There was already trouble about the delivery of German properties. When the Soviet representatives designated objects and interests which the Hungarian government, in accordance with the terms of the Potsdam agreement, was required to surrender, we often pointed out that citizens of other nations had vested interests in many of these. The Russians insisted that the ownership of the properties designated was purely German and suggested that it would be better for the Hungarian government to cease concerning itself about the rights of other nationals. Thereupon our government was forced to issue a memorandum directing nationals concerned to turn to the Soviet for settlement of their claims.

Later the Russians made more serious demands based on the Potsdam decision. They announced that they would take over the German properties, but not the debts with which they were encumbered. Then, with another variation on an overworked theme, they laid claims not only to all German property in Hungary but also to all sums owed to Germany by Hungarians. If such debts were in German marks, the Russians reserved the right to determine arbitrarily their value in dollars or other currency.

The sum involved in what was labeled German property in Hungary amounted to more than $200,000,000. Negotiations about payment were held with the Hungarian government in Moscow after I had been eliminated from the scene.

In Potsdam the leaders of the great powers had held discussions regarding the resettlement in Germany of German minorities in neighboring states. They authorized these states to resettle such minorities if they so desired.

Not long after the Potsdam decision an official communication from Marshal Voroshilov required Hungary to expel to Germany a half-million of her German-speaking citizens.

The Hungarian people were undoubtedly anxious about the behavior of a portion of the German-speaking population, which glorified Hitler. Officers and officials of German descent had actively disseminated National Socialist propaganda and had organized among the German-speaking population the anti-Hungarian Volksbund, which terrorized citizens of German descent who had the interests of their adopted country at heart. In short, a good number had acted against the interests of the state.

At the same time there were many who had strongly opposed Hitlerism, and carried on an open struggle against the Volksbund, encouraging their fellow citizens of German descent to be patriots.

When Voroshilov's directive arrived, the cabinet held a meeting to which Prime Minister Miklós invited Zoltán Tildy, Mathias Rákosi, Árpád Szakasits and Peter Veres, party leaders who at that time were not yet members of the government. At this session the Communist and Peasant party members insisted on the expulsion of all Germans and tried by sheer force to carry through Voroshilov's desires. At best they were willing to exempt only preëminent men whose exceptional services to the cause of democracy were generally known.

In the course of the meeting I pointed out that in the whole country there were not enough Germans to make up the number Voroshilov wanted us to expel. The statistics of 1940 showed that there were 477,000 inhabitants whose mother tongue was German. I also stated that under no circumstances should the Germans be expelled on the basis of collective responsibility. Such an act could not be justified before history or humanity. On the other hand, all Germans who were guilty as individuals should be expelled.

I proposed that the cabinet set up four categories of resettlement. The first would comprise those whose mother tongue and nationality were German according to the census of 1940. To have claimed German nationality at that time was equivalent to taking a stand, since, as everyone knew, Hitler regarded Germans all over the world as tools of his aims. The second category should comprise those who had joined the anti-Hungarian Volksbund. The third should include those who had volunteered in German military units such as the S.S. during the war. In the last category would be those who had changed from German to Hungarian and then, during the Hitler era, had re-Germanized their names.

I informed the cabinet council that somewhat more than 300,000 Germans belonged in these categories, but with regard to the rest there was no reason why we should persecute honest, patriotic Hungarians of German descent. The cabinet accepted my proposal and instructed the Minister of the Interior to draw up the resettlement plans accordingly.

It was only later, when the expulsion of the Germans had actually begun, that I learned that the Potsdam decision had not required Hungary to expel them, but had merely given her authority to do so. Voroshilov had imposed upon the Hungarian government by saying that this course of action was required.

In dealing with the results of the Potsdam decision, facts will show how the Soviet used it to undermine Hungary's political and economic independence.

CHAPTER 30

Why the Smallholders Could Not Resist Encroachment

FOR AN ANSWER WE SHALL HAVE TO GO BACK TO THE STATE OF AFFAIRS in July, 1945.

The war was over. As economic conditions improved, so did the self-respect of the people. They soon realized that Russia's pronouncements regarding Hungary's freedom and independence were not to be taken literally. It also became evident that the Communists were by no means sincere in their protestations of patriotism and their alleged desire to work in constructive collaboration with other parties. Their violent methods and despotic aims were everywhere in evidence. Most significant was the fact that the peasants had hardly more say than at the time of reactionary oppression.

The Communists' attitude caused Smallholder leaders much anxiety. We shared the dissatisfaction that filled the hearts of our followers and sought to free the country from its difficult and humiliating position. Sometimes we were able to right grievances through conferences; sometimes one or another official agency was able to aid the peasants in the face of the Communists. But the general political situation was already grave.

The question came up often as to whether it would not be best for the party to withdraw from the coalition, despite its decisive majority, and disclaim responsibility for further developments.

There were many reasons why this could not be done. For one thing, without a share of political power our leaders and masses would have been at the mercy of tyrannical leftist agencies. There would have been no check on the persecution of Smallholders who had no part in the government.

It would have been difficult to convince world opinion that *we* were the democrats and unable to cooperate with the leftist parties because of our principles. Why would this have been difficult? First, because our party was not the only one representing the peasants in the coalition; there was also the radical Peasant party, which the Communists kept in the coalition so that if at any time they should have difficulties with the Smallholders they could point to the Peasant party and say that this was a democratic party that *could* cooperate with the extreme left.

It would also have been hard to justify our withdrawal, because at that time each party possessed one daily paper and the single organ of the Smallholders would have been faced with three opposition papers, all actively trying to pin the label of reaction on our party.

The most serious obstacle, however, was the fact that the Soviet Union and the Red army stood behind the parties of the left. Withdrawal would have been regarded by them as a provocation, thus bringing forth a wave of political persecution and additional terror. In the end the Smallholders would have had to bear all blame.

The obvious question also arises as to why our party could not have brought its complaints and the sufferings of its people before the bar of public opinion. It should not be forgotten that there was still censorship in Hungary at this time. A Hungarian-speaking Russian officer, himself a member of the Communist party, was in charge. But even apart from this an open stand was impossible because of the presence of the Red army with its absolute control over Hungarian affairs.

We had no defense against the influence of the Soviet Union. The western powers did not concern themselves particularly with Hungary's internal affairs, and the parties of the left vied with one another for Soviet favor.

The most important consideration was that the West, too, was undivided in urging us to cultivate, at all costs, the friendship of Russia. Politicians, diplomats, and newspapermen kept saying Hungary must not provoke the disfavor of Russia, because she could have "no stronger protector" than the Soviet Union.

There was no one to whom we could turn. In the face of the Yalta agreement, the armistice, and the Potsdam decision, and in view of the high respect with which Russia's allies treated her, we knew that there would be no point in airing our grievances before the court of world opinion. We should only have had to shoulder responsibility for the deterioration of the country's relations with a neighboring great power which was in a position to exert constant pressure. We had to be satisfied with maintaining an easily visible difference in Hungarian internal affairs as compared with those of neighboring countries, where Communist influence became absolute. In Hungary we held, as well as we could, to the principles of democracy. We were successful for two whole years.

Three phases of Hungary's future development became clear to me, and I often discussed them with my friends in confidence.

I felt, first of all, that it was essential that we arrive at a parliamentary election without passing through revolution and civil war. We must strive to enable the Hungarian people to express its will in free and peaceful elections. But I at once added that, even if the Smallholders were victorious in the elections, there would be no radical change. Russia would not allow our majority to rule but would insist on a coalition government. After the elections we should gain in influence on policies, but should not be permitted to govern.

The second phase, in my opinion, would be initiated by the peace treaty. It was absolutely essential to bid for time during the armistice period, so that the country might attain without inner upheaval the status of a free and independent state to be guaranteed by the peace treaty. But even then our party would not have the power to govern.

The third phase, as I conceived it, would come when the peace treaty was ratified and the occupying forces removed. Then we could gradually proceed toward constitutional consolidation, avoiding all violence and vengeance. Until then, and afterwards, too, we must do our best to maintain friendly relations with the Soviet Union, although without allowing this to influence adversely the seeking of good relations with the West.

I maintained this policy from the very first moment of liberation. Later, as Prime Minister, I followed it in a practical way. Often I faced the criticism of my own party and the violence of the Communists. My policy gave the leftist parties an opportunity for peaceful cooperation and, in so far as they did not find it satisfactory, they provided evidence of the fact that their aims were not peaceful cooperation, but the extension of the unconstitutional rule of the minority.

The Smallholders party could only be patient and pray. We wished to follow a more ethical policy than our neighbors, where men murdered each other without finding a solution. We sought to lead our people to freedom and independence without bloodshed.

At that time we still hoped that the spirit of the Atlantic Charter and the conception of the United Nations would finally prove victorious, and that the little nations would find peace and freedom from fear. We trusted that there would be consolidation in Hungarian affairs as in world affairs, and that the western powers could carry through the great moral principles laid down in the various international agreements.

CHAPTER 31

The Soviet "Trades" with Hungary

IT WAS DIFFICULT TO START INDUSTRIAL PRODUCTION EVEN AFTER workers had rebuilt a great part of the destroyed factories, because the necessary fuel and raw materials were lacking. Our heavy industries needed iron ore, coal, and coke; our textile factories needed cotton and wool. Yet it was important to put all our strength into organizing production. The threat of unemployment hovered over us, and there was also the pressure to fulfill the reparations schedule. Every country turned away from us, a defeated land in the throes of inflation. Hungary was not regarded as a good business partner.

During the summer of 1945 the economic development of southeastern Europe could still have been influenced to a very great degree, if the western powers had concerned themselves seriously. The Soviet Union could not have exerted such an overwhelming political influence on this region if the West had lent support to its economic rehabilitation. But there was no hint of such a program. Only UNRRA aid was offered to the ruined countries, and even this was faultily conceived. Effective and significant aid was planned for non-Axis countries during the war, but to the so-called enemy countries sums were allotted which, even as alms, were petty.

In July, 1945, the Soviet government proposed a trade agreement. The democratic elements of our government, as well as the great majority of the Hungarian people, would have welcomed such a proposal from the western powers or from neutral states, but there was no choice —the only offer received was from Russia. The proposal offered us iron ore, coke, cotton, and various metals in exchange for goods.

Prime Minister Miklós called a cabinet council in which we decided to draw up a $30,000,000 trade agreement covering the importation of the raw materials offered by Russia. We appointed a trade delegation with Ernest Gerö, Minister of Commerce, as chairman to go to Moscow to discuss and conclude the agreement. Anthony Bán, Minister of Industry, went along as vice chairman.

After its departure, the delegation kept in contact with the government by telephone and, from time to time, intimated that the discussions were making rapid progress and a $33,000,000 trade agreement was in prospect. Of course we could not deal with the Soviet Union as equals on this occasion either. Inasmuch as we had received no offer from any other country, we had no opportunity to compare prices, and not until later did we realize what a poor bargain had been forced upon us.

On August 19, the national committee of the Smallholders party held its session at which it customarily appointed new officers, listened to the proposals of county representatives, and settled party policies.

At that time our party had been without a leader since the resignation of Tibor Eckhardt in 1939. In view of the astounding revival of political activity, in which the Smallholders played an important role, the party wished to appoint suitable leaders. The executive session chose Zoltán Tildy as political leader and myself as president of the party. Béla Varga became executive vice president, while Béla Kovács took my place as general secretary.

I was delivering my inaugural address as president, when my secretary handed me a note saying that the Prime Minister wished to see me immediately about an urgent matter.

I hurried to his office, where he awaited me with Finance Minister Oltványi and Undersecretary Stephen Balogh.

"Anthony Bán," began the Prime Minister, "has flown back from Moscow to report that the Soviet Union wishes to conclude a general economic agreement with Hungary in addition to the trade agreement. Here is the proposal." He handed me a number of mimeographed sheets.

I read the proposal, for far-reaching and permanent collaboration in industry, mining, aviation, shipping, trade, and agriculture. Soviet-Hungarian joint stock companies were to be set up for promoting Hungarian economic development and increasing economic relations between the two countries. There was a hint that the Soviet Union wished to utilize in Hungary the factories and equipment awarded to it by the great powers in the Potsdam decision and these would be the basis of the Russian share in the joint companies.

This Russian proposal caused great consternation among us all.

"Has any action been taken on this in Moscow?" I asked the Prime Minister.

"No," replied Béla Miklós. "That was the reason for Bán's return. He came to discuss the matter with the government and to secure authorization to sign."

"We musn't give such authorization under any circumstances. We should answer that Hungary, at this very moment, has no idea of its assets and it will take time to determine them. In view of the fact that we are approaching national elections, it should be left to the newly elected Parliament to decide an issue of such magnitude."

The others agreed with me.

When Minister Gerö came back with the delegation from Moscow he was plainly piqued at his failure to receive the requested authorization. To our great surprise he announced at the cabinet council that he had "signed" a preliminary agreement.

"How could you do that without authorization?" I asked.

"I was duly authorized," replied Gerö. "My authorization from the Prime Minister provides for signing of accords beyond the trade agreement."

I glanced at Prime Minister Miklós. Red in the face and flustered, he stated that he had delegated no such power.

Gerö pulled the Moscow authorization from his brief case. The paper which Miklós, in his ignorance of administrative affairs, had signed, really did convey wide powers. It was on this basis that Gerö had signed the preliminary agreement.

Naturally the agreement did not take effect with Gerö's signature, but the public soon learned of the Moscow proposal. I visited Minister Schoenfeld, head of the United States Mission to Hungary, as well as the British Political Representative, A. D. F. Gascoigne. They, too, were surprised by the Russian proposal, which they knew meant the complete economic penetration of Hungary. I suggested that England and the United States make similar proposals to Hungary and so neutralize the Soviet offer. Unfortunately, we did not receive such proposals—only a memorandum from the United States to the effect that it regarded the trade agreement concluded in 1925 as valid and would insist on its remaining in force.

From then on, the Soviet government kept urging us daily to conclude the agreement, saying that in the event of an unfavorable decision it would transport to Russia the industrial equipment in Hungary awarded to the U.S.S.R. by the terms of the Potsdam decision. Discussions, lasting three months, began in Budapest. Because the western powers showed no inclination to intervene, Hungary had to accept the proposal. We announced, however, that the agreement was not exclusive and reserved the right to conclude similar agreements with other countries.

That was how the Soviet-Hungarian agreement for economic collaboration came into being. Later on, my forebodings were justified.

I should like to refer here to an interesting phase of internal politics. The peasant members of the executive session of the Smallholders party were also on the executive committee of the Peasant Alliance and met at my call in their second capacity on the same days.

I prepared a proposal designed to have a significant effect on the political, social, and economic position of the peasantry. One of its provisions stated that the peasants should have the same right to strike as other classes of workers. Every Hungarian peasant understood the implications of this proposal; there was no need for long discussions. All knew that if the peasants—who comprised the majority of the population—could secure the right to strike, it might prove to be a decisive factor in Hungarian politics and a weapon of many uses. It could force capital to alter credit and price policies; force officialdom to adopt more reasonable attitudes.

The labor parties realized the significance of the proposal at once, and it caused a sensation among them. Until then, they had always spoken of me as a standard-bearer of democracy; but from then on they began to attack me as the underminer of reconstruction, the inciter of the peasants, and, in general, as one who was attempting to throw a monkey wrench into the smooth-working machinery of the government. I was constantly pilloried by the Communist press. The leaders of the leftist parties were startled by the prospect that the peasants might be in a position to exert pressure on them.

The attacks proved that the peasants had secured a degree of influence on public affairs such as they had not had for a thousand years.

CHAPTER 32

The Death of My Mother

IN THE NATURAL ORDER OF THINGS, A MAN MUST FACE THE LOSS OF those who brought him into the world, guided his first steps, and loved him most unselfishly. Throughout the years, my parents have been the living representations of the ideals of steadfastness, loyalty, and perseverance. My mother was a strong force for good, she was at once friend, guardian, and tutor, imbuing in me her spiritual consciousness and yearning for knowledge. There could be no greater monument set to her life than the tragic circumstances of her death.

Until that black day in September, 1945, my parents' life alternated between great sorrows and great joys. The war's destruction brought much worry and nervous strain as their economic problems mounted because of the lack of animals, man power, and tools. But their worries were lessened by the knowledge that we all had survived the horrors of war. I returned from imprisonment, and my son, Ferenc, whom the

Nazis had put into a punitive forced-labor camp, came home in comparatively good health.

My good father, a splendid steward of our land, had the shell holes in our buildings repaired and even succeeded in getting a team so that farm work could be resumed. The vines were flowering; all the peasants of Bisse awaited a good vintage to make life more bearable during these times of strain. Slowly food started to be more plentiful in the little community.

The latter helped me a great deal, because even I had to rely on my father to feed my family. Every week I sent my official car to Bisse to bring some fresh food. Once when I was home helping mother store some provisions in the car, my father remarked jokingly:

"Son, we love you and we are happy to feed you and your family because there is harvest enough for all of us. But I cannot undertake to provide the clothes of a cabinet minister."

His remark was not without foundation, because during these inflationary days the salary of a minister amounted to about three or four dollars a month.

In fact, one could not get any clothes or shoes in the village. My parents had a young driver whom they liked for his diligence and loyalty; they wanted to buy a suit of clothes and a decent pair of shoes for him if these could be had. In the first days of September, my mother, having had some excess produce, decided to drive into Pécs and barter it for a pair of shoes for him. The deal was concluded successfully. After dinner at my uncle's home in Pécs they climbed into the cart, a woman from the neighborhood accompanying them in the back.

The women talked pleasantly as they rode through the country; my mother spoke of me. They had gone about four miles when the neighbor exclaimed:

"Look out, Joe. Stop the horses. A huge tank is following us!"

The driver drove to the side to let the tank pass. A few seconds later, the woman shrieked:

"God Almighty, the tank is going to run us over!"

Indeed, the tank did not use the wide space left for it but headed straight for the peasant cart. The driver, trying to escape, pulled his horses so far to the right that the wheels on that side dug deep into the soft shoulder, practically skirting the ditch.

The huge Russian tank made no effort to avoid the cart; it crashed into it, crushing the back under its steel tread. The protruding gun hit my mother on the head, pushing her off the cart and under the speeding tank which killed her instantly. The neighbor and the driver fell to the right into the ditch, thus escaping with slight bruises.

After this brutal murder, as if to signify a job well done, the tank made a large semicircle through the bordering field and took the road back to Pécs. Despite the fact that Red soldiers were sitting on the outside of the tank, it did not bother to stop.

On the evening of September 14th, the telephone rang in my home. John Keserü, Lord Lieutenant of Baranya, an old friend of mine and a great admirer of my mother, reported in a shaking voice the death of my mother under the wheels of the Martian monster.

As I was going home to Bisse, we had to pass the spot where the white gravel of the road was stained a deep crimson by my dear mother's blood. For a fitting monument to her death, not far from the spot, a tank destroyed during the war was deeply embedded in the fruitful earth.

I have always tried to make myself believe that this dreadful tragedy had no political intent against me behind it; that it was the impulsive act of a group of drunken Russian soldiers who had lost all human feeling and instinct.

Our home county of Baranya, where my mother's character was so well known, proclaimed her its own and buried her with official honors. On her grave lay wreaths from the government, from all the political parties, and from every outstanding organization in Hungary.

My loss was shared by the people of Bisse, who loved my mother dearly. She had always read to the village women during their meetings, selecting the stories and poems that most interested them during the long winter evenings. They had turned to her with their problems and sorrows, and no one ever left without some counsel or help. The village conducted a funeral for my poor mother such as had not been seen in Bisse before.

As a man who had been practically led by his mother's guiding hand from the rough wood stools of the poorest peasant to the velvet chair of the cabinet minister, I was deeply wounded. My human loss was felt throughout the land, where practically every one kindly tried to lessen my pain.

Leaving my mother's grave, I reexamined my thoughts about the policy I had followed. My soul, still aching from the irreparable wound, told me that I should continue doing what my mother would have wanted—work for my people and try to guide them to a better to-morrow.

While the news shocked the entire country I have never drawn any political conclusions from the tragedy; it did not change my decision to follow the appointed road. I knew that we Hungarians must use every possible means to maintain friendly relations with the Soviet government and, despite this tragedy, I tried to put the interest of my people ahead of my own feelings.

CHAPTER 33

Factors in Hungarian Politics

THE HISTORY OF THE FIRST YEAR AFTER THE GERMAN DEFEAT IN Hungary, and the political events of the next eighteen months, make it necessary to pose the question whether the political leaders of Hungary planned for a democratic future, or allowed the Communists to march unhindered on their appointed road, while people of liberal convictions stood by impotent.

In answer, I must say that while the ranks of democratic leadership could claim no extensive government experience, there was no lack of ideological conceptions about the foundation of true democracy. Without constant Soviet interference, bringing planned promotion and support to the Communist party, democracy in Hungary would have been stronger than in any of the surrounding countries.

To arrive at a just analysis of the internal political situation of Hungary one has to consider first the handicaps imposed by the necessity for restoring basic subsistence to a ravaged population, reestablishing a disintegrated administration, and laying the foundations for a new economy. Also, we had to govern, under these circumstances, by a coalition of political parties with diametrically opposed ideologies. Only by evaluating all these factors can one realize how much energy and self-sacrifice was needed to work, and build, and bide time until the three aims of the immediate future were accomplished: the elections, the peace treaty, and, most important, the ratification of the treaty and with it the end of the Russian occupation.

Under these conditions, the maximum we could expect was that we should reach the third phase without the Communists' usurping the government and people completely. Perhaps then consolidation could peacefully develop a truly democratic life.

From the point of view of the internal situation, the general elections were most important, and each political party had its own ideas. The Smallholders believed that if orderly and unfettered elections were held, and the people allowed to express their will freely, the Smallholders would receive a majority of votes. If the Smallholders by taking part could enable an undisturbed government to run affairs and lay the groundwork for the period following the end of occupation, consolidation would gain in momentum and the future of a truly democratic state be insured.

The Social Democrats relied on close cooperation with the Communists, and while the latter would lean exclusively on the Soviet they would try to strengthen their ties in the West and thus insure existence in both directions. At the same time the more liberal Socialists nourished the secret hope that labor would sooner or later be disappointed by the methods of the Communists and, looking toward theoretical Marxism, turn to the Social Democrats.

The aim of the small, radical Peasant party was, by skillful jockeying, always to add to the weight of one or the other political factions interested in strengthening their own position in such a way as to insure its own survival in the arena. At this time the Communist party proved to be most dynamic, and so the Peasant party played along with it.

No sane, constructive politician of that day imagined in his darkest dreams that soon the Soviet Union would openly and brutally inject itself into the internal political life of Hungary and, with this intrusion, nullify all human efforts toward constitutional solutions of the political future of the country.

Besides these internal questions we had to face constantly threatening problems across the borders. While the heart of every decent political figure of Hungary burned with the eternal quest for conclusion of the peace treaty, there were immediate and vital problems of relations with our neighbors.

In Czechoslovakia a new idea took hold; to change the republic from a state of nationalities to a national state. In accomplishing this by force, the governing parties did not lay foundations for a higher ideology but sought to rid the country of all foreign-speaking residents, particularly such as were of German and Hungarian origin. It did not occur to them that nothing permanent could be accomplished except by self-sacrifice—they justified the expulsion of Germans and Hungarians by the Potsdam decision. The disorganized relationship between the countries was used as a basis to begin to throw masses from annexations of Hungarian territory across the new border.

The situation of Hungarians in Transylvanian territory, given to Rumania, appeared much better to the world because Premier Groza often made statements friendly to Hungary and repeatedly emphasized that full protection of the rights of Hungarians in Rumania would be maintained. In reality their situation was anything but rosy, because powers other than Groza controlled the administration, stripping all civil rights from Hungarians. We had to stand by while the Hungarian minority in Rumania lost houses, wealth, trade and land—and while Groza manicured these acts for the eyes of the world.

In Yugoslavia, the Tito regime was too much interested in making Communism absolute to trouble about the interests and rights of individuals, particularly minorities. Undoubtedly, after the massacre of Hungarians which followed the German retreat, the fewest complaints came from our people under Yugoslav rule.

Naturally, in conceiving our foreign policy, we could not forget for one instant our own humiliated and oppressed situation. Besides retaining the benevolence of the great powers, we had to establish a basis for friendly relations with our neighbors, while avoiding inclusion in an exclusively Communist set-up.

In June of 1945, more or less as the National Assembly had been convened at Debrecen, delegates from the newly liberated western territories were summoned. As these conferences were now attended by the leadership of the Smallholders, we were able to prevent recurrence of some of the earlier injustices. More Smallholder delegates were called in from the western territories, and thus the relative strength of the Smallholders in the temporary assembly increased. Actually, this correction had little effect, for in September, 1945, the negotiations resulted in a new electoral law, which was good, except that the Smallholders erred in one respect.

From the beginning we had been trying to give the population the widest possible franchise. Only later did we discover that it would have been wiser to emulate the Austrian law and disfranchise all who had held membership in Fascist organizations. The new electoral law could not have been regarded as reactionary in that case, even though it would have disfranchised the large masses of laborers who had held membership in the National Socialist parties. Instead we were satisfied, with the quiet approval of the Communists, to disfranchise the active National Socialists, the leaders in all phases of National Socialist life, and party officials. As a result, the rank and file of former National Socialist labor rushed to the Communist party for protection, swelling the Communist vote in the elections of November to 17 per cent of the total.

The new electoral law made the population politically conscious, and in September all parties began an active campaign.

In traveling through the land, I met countless hopeful faces but could not promise a straight route or quiet after the elections, because I knew that the country would remain in armistice status until the peace treaty was signed. My only plea to the people was to be steadfast and patient, even in the face of constant provocation.

The hopes of the people slowly began to crystallize. One could sense that the majority were enthusiastically attempting to lay the foundations for a political structure in which Hungarian traditions and progressive democracy could harmoniously unite.

CHAPTER 34

Budapest Municipal Elections

BY THE END OF THE SUMMER OF 1945, THERE WAS A DECIDED ELECTION-day atmosphere in Hungary. Constant discussions at public meetings and in the press, and franchise debates, kept the election in the foreground of public attention. In such an atmosphere it would not have been advisable to defer the popular vote beyond 1945.

At the end of the summer, the Communists and Social Democrats illogically requested that the Budapest municipal elections be held in advance of the parliamentary elections. It would have been natural to expect that the parties would decide to hold *all* municipal elections either before or after the elections for parliament.

We saw at once that these parties counted on a majority for the labor parties in the Budapest ballot, which they hoped would have an effect on the national election. It was a challenge which we accepted with good grace. We made the condition that the parliamentary elections would be held not more than a month later. It was clearly evident that the Soviet representatives in Budapest greatly favored the move.

In the Budapest election the Communists meant to put not only the Smallholders, but also the Social Democrats, in a tight spot. Using the motto, "Workers, Unite," they forced upon the Social Democrats a common ticket of nominees. The rank and file of the Social Democratic party opposed it, but Árpád Szakasits and his clique made a deal with the Communists which they forced on the rest of their own party. The worker-members of the party knew that in the event of a common list, their votes would elect the Communists. They were afraid not only that the common ticket would be unpopular because of the inclusion of the Communist nominees, but that they would lose their identity as Social Democrats. Later a remark by Szakasits gave ground for the inference that Voroshilov had forced them to accept the common list, on which Communists alternated with Social Democrats.

A famous gypsy fiddler once played in Gödöllö at a court dinner given by King Francis Joseph in honor of guests from abroad. Later he was asked what the dinner was like. He replied:

"It was wonderful. At the dinner they seated us alternately: a gypsy and a king; another gypsy and another king. That was the way it was, all the way down the table."

The workers' common list was compiled on that principle.

A young diplomat, representing one of the western powers, did all he could to dissuade us from accepting the challenge of the left. He wanted the Smallholders to block the Budapest election on some pretext, so that the weakness of our party should not be revealed. A poor showing, he thought, would influence the West unfavorably and also have a bad effect on the outcome of the general election.

However, we went ahead with the election campaign, which was led by the widely respected Béla Varga. Great crowds took part in daily meetings, at which he movingly reminded the people of their duties to God, country, and Hungarian traditions:

"The people of Hungary are determined to stand by the Smallholders party in the national elections. Let the people of Budapest show that they, too, have the interest of their country at heart. We must win in Budapest to prove to the world that we insist on keeping our independence."

The long-suffering inhabitants of Budapest prepared enthusiastically for election day. Everyone had a good word to say about the Small-holders party.

We, the leaders, felt that if we won 30 to 35 per cent of the votes in Budapest, we could enter the national election with confidence.

The Communists, perceiving that our adherents were constantly increasing, launched a tremendous counter-propaganda campaign. This had no effect, however, on the better elements of the Social Democratic party, who had not the slightest desire to vote the Communist ticket. The workers recalled the faithful collaboration between the Small-holders and the Social Democrats during German oppression, and in the policies of the Smallholders they saw a guarantee of the preservation of the principles of democracy. Many of them openly affirmed support for the Smallholders.

On the morning of the municipal election the Communist mayor of Budapest, Zoltán Vas, appeared at our party headquarters.

"I came to ask whether the Smallholders have any complaints against authorities or election boards," he began, with a condescending air of generosity.

"In two districts the chairman of the election board refuses to recognize the Smallholders delegates," declared Leslie Jékely, who was campaign manager.

"In that case, let someone come along with me in my car, and we'll set things right," said Vas. "We can afford to give the Smallholders an advantage to the extent of attending to their complaints," he answered sarcastically.

"Are you so sure of the victory of the workers' parties?" someone asked.

"There can be no doubt as to the result. The workers' parties will get the majority," Vas answered.

My wife and I went to vote in our district. The voters cheered when they recognized us and politely offered to let us vote ahead of turn, but we waited in line so as to observe their reactions. Down the long queue passed the words: "Vote for list number four," (our list of nominees). In a corner, a young woman coached her white-haired mother: "List number four!" The old lady nodded vigorously.

That night the members of each party assembled to await the returns, and I was waiting at our party headquarters. Men were continually betting on the outcome; the general opinion being that our party would poll about 40 per cent of the votes.

The first telephone call came at eight o'clock. The votes of the smallest election district had been counted. Out of a total of 103, 94 had voted. The Smallholders had received 48 votes; the workers' parties, 43; the National Peasants, 2; the Civic Democrats, 1. The voters were mainly factory workers and railway employees.

I told Zoltán Tildy, and ventured the opinion that we had won the election in Budapest.

By midnight we knew that the Smallholders had won by a majority of 51 per cent the very election designed to show up its weakness.

The results were received by the Communists with long faces and by the Social Democrats with bitterness. The Communists realized that they had been able to attain even this low result only through the aid of the Social Democrats; if they had run on a separate list they could not have polled half the workers' votes.

The people of Budapest stood by the principles of democracy and set an example for the rest of the country.

It was murmured throughout the town that Mathias Rákosi, leader of the Communist party, had a most unpleasant session with Marshal Voroshilov next day.

CHAPTER 35

The Soviet Higgles for a Common Ticket

AFTER THE BUDAPEST MUNICIPAL ELECTION OF OCTOBER 2, WE IMMEDI-ately began organizing the campaign for the parliamentary election to be held four weeks later.

Béla Kovács resigned as Undersecretary of the Interior to attend to organizational work. We could only put eight automobiles and very little money at his disposal. The provisions of the new electoral law demanded much additional work on the part of the central office and country branches of our party; fortunately we had many experienced leaders who had conducted any number of difficult campaigns and had a knack for mobilizing men.

The leaders of each district set up a list of nominees, after which the central directorate of the party decided on their order of precedence. The law created sixteen large election districts. The nominees were to receive one mandate for each 12,000 votes polled. Every person over twenty was entitled to vote unless he had held office in a fascist party or organization.

When the election campaign had started and the parties were drawing up their lists of nominees, Zoltán Tildy informed me that Marshal Voroshilov wished to see us to discuss a "common ticket."

Voroshilov received us with his usual suave cordiality.

"Elections are at hand. We ought to try to prevent too much friction among the parties, and so I should be glad to lend my support to some plan which would eliminate the battles. It would be well if the four parties who have a share in the government could agree on a common ticket, which might possibly also give a few mandates to the Civic Democratic party. In this way the election struggle could be settled in an interparty conference and the election race not excite the people."

"The joint ticket would not provide for democratic elections because the voters would not be able to indicate the real proportionate strength of the parties," I remarked.

"We know by now that the Smallholders are the largest party," answered Voroshilov. "And for this very reason the lists could be set up so as to give them most of the places on the ballot."

I began to protest against the principle, but Voroshilov kept talking of the practical details of the common list and of its advantages.

"In your opinion, what percentage would be granted to the Smallholders?" asked Tildy.

"That depends on the agreement between the parties," replied Voroshilov, "but I should suppose that the Smallholders would be granted at least 40 per cent."

Hereupon we pointed to the result of the Budapest election, which portended an even more decisive victory in a national election.

"We must not attempt to produce a situation in which the workers' parties would feel that they were entering the contest as a disproportionately small minority, and thus one must not strive to secure an absolute majority for the Smallholders party," counseled Voroshilov. "But we might discuss the possibility of the Smallholders getting 45 per cent of the nominees on the list."

The bargaining and attempts at persuasion went on for hour after hour. We agreed to try to hold some sort of interparty conference, after consulting with our membership.

I departed, deeply shocked, knowing that if the Soviet insisted on a common ticket, our opposition would provoke an even more intransigeant attitude.

Public opinion and the western powers learned of the plan surprisingly soon. It was received by Smallholders leaders with intense indignation; rebellious meetings of leaders and deputies gathered from hour to hour, and discussed means of combating the danger of a common ticket; and the American and English radios spoke very sharply of the antidemocratic election plan. Marshal Voroshilov continued higgling, bidding finally as high as 47.5 per cent.

Indignation was rife in the country districts, too. The Smallholders party received stern admonitions to refuse the common ticket proposal. Our chauffeurs, for example, unanimously announced that they would not drive our cars if we accepted the common list. Public opinion realized that it was a Russian plan, and protested against it forcibly.

One morning a large group of Smallholder deputies appeared at my home and asked me to go to party headquarters, where a party caucus was meeting. On arriving, I listened to the complaints and announced that I would not approve of having the party leaders make a decision in this matter alone, but would call the national executive committee into session.

The caucus cheered and rushed to shake hands because of this decision. Everyone knew that the national executive committee would under no circumstances accept a common ticket.

The afternoon papers carried my announcement, and by nightfall the Communist party, with the consent of the Russians, stated that it would not insist on a common list—the elections could be held on the basis of individual nominations. That was how the devilish plan fell through; it was used later to smash democracy in every southeastern European country.

Our party held a number of mass meetings at the start of the election campaign. Communist terror brigades appeared at Smallholder meetings in the factory and suburban districts of Budapest starting some bloody fights. We called an interparty conference at which the Communists denied that these groups were acting on official instructions and agreed to curb them.

Since the "liberation," the parties had joined in an organization called the Independence Front. The interparty conferences were really meetings of the Independence Front. At this session the Communists suggested that we issue a declaration defining as our policy the accepted basic principles of democracy. We assented, and thus was born the declaration in which the parties promised to pursue pure democracy and join forces in the struggle against reaction. They also agreed that in state ownership they would not go beyond nationalizing natural wealth and sources of energy. Thereafter the Communists ceased provoking fights, and we were able to hold our mass meetings in peace.

This important conference arrived at another decision which was not included in the declaration: We would continue the coalition after the election, but would not determine our proportion of governmental power until after we knew the outcome.

I called the national committee of the Smallholders party into session and it approved the declaration of the Independence Front and continued maintenance of the coalition.

The Social Democratic party, and even the little Peasant party, were much better prepared for an election campaign than the Smallholders, who abhorred every sort of property grabbing and were not involved in commercial ventures. Our party's very modest campaign expenses were covered by contributions from the members and supporters. But Béla Kovács did a magnificent job of setting in motion our nation-wide party organization. The voluntary activity of the masses kept adding to our cohorts.

Naturally the Communist party was most thoroughly prepared for the campaign. With many cars at its disposal it easily carried out its dynamic program of publicity. It could reach the smallest villages, and everywhere found one or two men willing to do the work of organization. With Russian aid it had amassed enormous stocks of paper, so that it could print limitless quantities of posters and publications. It had money aplenty, which surprised no one; everybody expected that the Soviet Union would finance the Communist party's election campaign.

CHAPTER 36

The Only Unfettered Elections

GREAT MASS MEETINGS AND FEVERISH CAMPAIGN ACTIVITY PRECEDED THE elections of November 4th. The posters of the Communist party, "Land, Bread, Freedom," glared at one constantly. "The Peasant Party is the

Party of the Poor Peasants" proclaimed another. One could see nothing but slogans and posters. The Smallholders had two posters. One, in firm, black, block letters, read "Law, Order, Security." The other, in lovely pastel shades, portrayed a cluster of grapes, a loaf of white bread, and a prayerbook. Below, stood the text: "Wine, Wheat, Peace."

On election day the poll watchers had taken the oath and were ready for their duties when, at eight in the morning, the voting began in orderly fashion throughout the nation. On the ballots were the names and symbols of every party and the names of the first four nominees.

Late that night the telephone reports from the various election districts began to arrive. It could be seen that the Smallholders were leading in the western part of the country. Hungary is small, but it seemed as if, within such limited space, the conflicting trends of East and West could be discerned.

By dawn the results were in; the Smallholders had received 57.5 per cent of the votes, the Communists and Social Democrats 17 per cent each, the Peasant party, 7 per cent. The remaining 1.5 per cent was divided between the Civic Democratic and the Radical parties. Accordingly, the Smallholders received 243 mandates; the Communists, 70; the Social Democrats, 69; the National Peasants, 23; and the Civic Democratic party, 2.

The fairness and legality of the Hungarian elections was justly recognized abroad; but even those who were close to the scene and in a position to observe minor flaws could not but hold the same opinion. The Hungarian people had met the challenge of extremely difficult times; the election returns attested to the sober judgment which had made possible their existence as a state for a thousand years. How refreshing the sight of this election was to those who had witnessed the prewar balloting which had trampled the rights of the people!

Hungarians thoroughly refuted the assertions of their former rulers that they were not sufficiently mature for the secret ballot. It was awe-inspiring to see them stand massed behind the interests of their country when given the opportunity and not obstructed in the exercise of their rights. It was not the desperate economic situation nor emotions inflamed by political wrongs that influenced their judgment, but pure principles and the best interests of the nation.

Our party and the friends of true democracy received the news with boundless enthusiasm, expecting better results from the elections than the situation warranted. They thought Soviet influence would diminish and the Red army's occupation be less onerous. They thought Russia would stand by her pronouncements that she would respect Hungary's national sovereignty and not interfere with internal affairs. They thought that the Soviet Union would be satisfied if the country maintained friendly relations with Russia, and would not demand that Hungary be obligated only to her.

Our people expected that justice would prevail in all aspects of life. Thinking that municipal elections would quickly be held, they assumed that men chosen by the people would be in charge of administration and hoped for radical improvement of police personnel so that the public security could be entrusted to honest men. After the election, they thought, the violence of the Communist party would cease, and the Reds be content with that share of governmental power which the voters had apportioned to them. Our people expected that economic reconstruction and internal harmony would not be disturbed by any sort of political struggle, and that they would all be allowed to work and live in peace.

Under normal conditions these expectations would have been completely justified. After all, a people cannot live under constant political stress, because *a nation strives by work and not by politics.* Unfortunately the world situation was as yet far from stable, and Russia and the Communist party had enough time to wreck the hopes of the Hungarian people.

Smallholders are not in the habit of staging parades and have always disapproved of street demonstrations; but the day after the election a tremendous crowd gathered before party headquarters and enthusiastically demanded speeches from the leaders. We spoke briefly, expressing our pleasure at the election results and urging the people to patience, hard work, and perseverance.

The crowd, marching through the streets, grew to tremendous proportions. There were cheers for our party and its leaders and some boos for the Communists. But this single demonstration by our party adherents came off in orderly fashion and without friction.

The workers' parties took their defeat ungraciously and were not able to sincerely congratulate the Smallholders on the victory. We were hardly surprised, for it was evident that Rákosi, for example, must be quite a bit annoyed by the fact that he barely won election in his own district of Zala. It was only with the greatest difficulty that enough votes could be scraped together to obtain a single Communist mandate. The overwhelming result in the election, however, prevented them from making disparaging remarks. Rákosi, Szakasits, and Peter Veres all stated that the election had been completely fair and legal, and that through it the Hungarian people had given proof of their faith in democracy. Before the election they had declared that democracy would be victorious—which they often denied later, hoping to weaken the value of the Smallholders' victory.

The attitude of the Soviet Union after elections was also interesting; soon Tildy and I met Voroshilov and Pushkin. Though Voroshilov was visibly piqued by the failure to carry through his plan for a common ticket, he congratulated us nevertheless. It is impossible to end a conference with Soviet leaders quickly. Now, too, a long, involved conversation began, at the end of which Voroshilov said that they were satisfied with the decision of the voters, but would be pleased to have a deeper understanding evolve between Russia and the Smallholders which represented the majority of the people, because the Soviet Union wished to base its friendship with Hungary on its relations with the Smallholders party.

Tildy and I saw great significance in this statement. We had long worried over the Soviet feeling that the Communist party was the only political group Russia could cooperate with, lest this cause it to give the Communists such strong support that we should be subjected to intolerable pressure. We felt that, if Russia backed Voroshilov's statement, then the victory of the Smallholders would greatly contribute to achieving independence. If Russia regarded our party as friendly we need not fear the extremist influence of the Communists and should be in a position to broaden our contacts with the other great powers.

Whether or not Voroshilov was sincere at the time, it soon became apparent that the statement was aimed to lighten temporarily the suspicions of the Smallholders. When the moment arrived to ruthlessly carry through the plans emanating from Moscow, it was conveniently forgotten.

Of course the Communist party soon got wind of this pronouncement and did everything in its power to prevent realization. First of all, Rákosi had Szakasits call on Voroshilov to protest against the extension of relations with the Smallholders and explain that Russia could not trust our party.

Later, Szakasits admitted that Voroshilov's statement had inspired much jealousy on the part of the left-wing parties. Rákosi really had great need of spokesmen whom he could send to Voroshilov, because after the elections he had been taken to task severely by the Soviet representatives for failing in his mission, since he had not been able to create a political situation similar to that fostered in the other countries of southeastern Europe by Soviet agents such as Dimitrov in Bulgaria, Gottwald in Czechoslovakia, Tito in Yugoslavia, and Bodnaras in Rumania.

It was patent infamy to state afterward that the majority had favored reaction. The people voted for democracy. The Smallholders party had no ties to the political systems of the past and did not desire the return of the bygone oppressive administrative machine. In the elections our party stood for pure democracy and fundamental progress, and it was for these that the great majority of citizens voted.

But there was another consideration. In addition to a constructive program, the people looked to see which party was the best guardian of Hungarian traditions, and which was closest to their religious ideals. And the people were not indifferent to the fact that the men who had led our party had stood by their principles even in the shadow of exile, prison, and the gallows.

PART THREE

Coalition—Its Life and Crises

CHAPTER 37

Communist Connivance for Police Power

THE ELECTIONS INITIATED A NEW CHAPTER IN POST-LIBERATION POLITICS. After the elections, the temporary government naturally resigned. After heading the government for ten and a half months, Prime Minister Béla Miklós handed his resignation to the National Council of Three. It should be stated that the temporary government, despite its inexperience, had accomplished worthy results in a chaotic situation. With honesty and good will it had laid the foundations for the constitutional government which was to follow.

Party leaders assembled to discuss the formation of a new cabinet. We could not dream of running the government on the basis of majority rule; one-party administration could not have carried the burden of so many difficult tasks in the face of the minority opposition by the leftist parties. Besides, Voroshilov had told us, in a way not to be misunderstood, that the Allied Control Commission would not approve of such a government. A coalition was the only solution.

Many of our newly elected deputies were in favor of our requesting a 57.5 per cent share of governmental power, in accordance with the election returns. Tildy's opinion was that we should not accept more than 50 per cent; if we did, we should be held responsible for every single step forced upon us by the occupying power. Moreover, according to his information, the Communist party would refuse to join a government in which we had an absolute majority. I too leaned toward this solution, and finally it was decided that the Smallholders should ask for 50 per cent and the rest should be divided among the other three parties. This proposition was accepted by all parties of the coalition.

Next came the choice of a prime minister. All agreed that he should be a Smallholder, and the choice quickly fell on Zoltán Tildy. In Hungary, tradition has it that the leader of the party in power shall hold the post of premier. I then urged that Rákosi and Szakasits, Communist

159

and Social Democrat leaders, be given posts in the cabinet. It would have been most unfortunate to leave these two leaders free to play politics without shouldering responsibility, and to allow them to bring pressure to bear on the government from the outside. Because neither was willing to accept a portfolio under any circumstances, we agreed to let them join the cabinet as vice premiers.

Until now the Smallholders had had the Ministries of Finance, Foreign Affairs, and Reconstruction; the Communists had had the Ministries of Commerce, Agriculture, and Social Welfare; the Social Democrats, the Ministries of Industry, Justice, and Supply; and the Ministry of the Interior had been in the hands of the Peasant party.

At the opening of the interparty discussions, it was found only natural that the Smallholders should have the Ministry of Agriculture in the new government. Nor were there any objections to its having the Ministries of Foreign Affairs and Finance. But beyond this the other parties would have liked us to satisfy ourselves with unimportant portfolios.

Tildy had presided at the discussions until he was appointed Prime Minister. Then I took over, and found it extremely difficult to harmonize the divergent viewpoints. There were days when it seemed as though the conference would be profitless and either the parties of the left or the Smallholders would have to be left out.

The great struggle was for the Ministry of the Interior. In Hungary as in most European countries, the Minister of the Interior is responsible for the administration and for the public security, and internments are decided at his discretion. His office has exceptional significance in times of turbulence when the police and other authorities are greatly concerned with political issues. He has power to favor certain parties and interfere with others. Even in normal times, when the country has a regular army, the police are a strong armed force. After the collapse, the Hungarian army was weakened by Russian obstruction and by the lack of funds and equipment. In consequence, the police were stronger than the army.

Naturally every party sought the Ministry of the Interior, so that it might control the police. First the Peasant party wanted it, because it had already held it during the temporary government. Then the Social Democrats claimed it, asserting that they alone, in the middle ground between Smallholders and Communists, could keep the Interior portfolio neutral. The real struggle, however, developed between the

Smallholders and Communists. Both were aware that, despite the tendency toward coalition, they polarized Hungary's political life.

All sorts of arguments were brought up by both sides, and the talks were without results for days at a time. Party leaders would leave the discussion table daily to consult with their directorate. The Smallholders would not yield. We had already decided to name to this post Béla Kovács, the hard-fisted peasant who, until recently, had been Undersecretary of the Interior.

After resisting stubbornly for days, the Communists finally agreed to let the Smallholders name the Minister of the Interior. The leftist parties were to have the undersecretaryships.

That night I invited our parliamentary deputies to dinner and announced that the Ministry of the Interior was ours. There was an ovation for the success in the discussions and for Béla Kovács, the minister elect.

The discussions continued on the next day, and it was then that the incident occurred which showed that the Soviet Union meant to have a hand in determining the composition of the coalition government.

The leftist parties insisted that in the interests of arithmetical distribution, the number of portfolios should be set at eighteen. Of these, nine belonged to the Smallholders, four each to the Communists and Social Democrats, and one to the Peasant party. In the temporary cabinet there had been twelve, and so six new portfolios had to be created. The parties had received three portfolios which went under the title of Minister of State—including Rákosi's and Szakasits' posts of vice premier and a state ministership of the Smallholders. Three additional portfolios had to be created, either by dividing up the functions of existing ones, or by creating new departments. The Smallholders also had to accept one of these newly created portfolios, and I thought we should set up a portfolio for cooperatives, to be headed by a Smallholder minister.

I recognized that Hungarian agriculture, which had been broken up into small units, could prosper only by founding strong cooperatives. I also knew that a federated peasantry, supplemented by a ministry for cooperatives, would have a great influence upon economic life.

Marshal Voroshilov, president of the Allied Control Commission, asked to be continually informed about our discussions. That afternoon I went to him and told him that, inasmuch as it was necessary to create a new portfolio, I wished to set up a ministry for cooperatives headed by a Smallholder. It seems that Voroshilov had received, by then, the Communists' report on my intention.

"I don't approve of setting up such a ministry. The cooperatives should remain independent," said Voroshilov with a hypocritical regard for constitutionality.

"They will remain independent, even if a ministry is established. We want a ministry to represent cooperatives in the government, not to oppress them," I replied.

"But the cooperatives must not be organized by a ministry. They must organize independently," said Voroshilov, as though in Russia the cooperatives were free of governmental control.

"Yes, the cooperatives are to organize themselves; but their activity will be more widespread than in the past. The distribution of the goods produced by those who have received land must be organized. The joint use of the machines of former large estates can only be arranged for on cooperative lines. Only through cooperatives is it possible to convert Hungarian agriculture to small-farm production. Cooperatives must be prepared to overcome marketing difficulties in the years to come. In short, they will have many tasks to fulfill, and it is only fair that they should be represented in the cabinet."

"No," countered Voroshilov. "This decision is not justifiable. The affairs of the cooperatives fit well into the Ministry of Commerce. You people have greater need for a ministry of propaganda to aid the growth of democracy and publicize its achievements. You must drop the idea of a ministry for cooperatives and set up a ministry for propaganda."

Obviously Voroshilov, in order to give support to the Communists, infringed the armistice terms with this obdurate request.

I argued for a while, pointing out that the public relations division of the Prime Ministry would suffice for the popularization of democracy. But Voroshilov remained adamant and I returned empty-handed to the interparty discussions.

The conference between the parties lasted another few days. The distribution of all the portfolios was decided upon, and we set the day for the official appointment of the cabinet.

The day before the official appointment, the Communists requested an immediate interparty conference. When it assembled, Rákosi asked to be heard.

"The Communist party," announced Rákosi, "must insist on the modification of the interparty agreement. Our party must receive the post of the Minister of Interior. Otherwise, it can take no share in the government."

I reproached the Communists sharply for creating this sudden break. It was quite evident that if the Communists withdrew from the government, the Social Democrats and the Peasant party would follow, leaving the Smallholders to form the cabinet. Our party membership would have favored such a solution, but we, who knew that Voroshilov would only approve a coalition, realized that it was unwise. I asked Rákosi to explain this unwarranted demand.

"The Communist party must lead the fight against reaction," said Rákosi. "For this reason it needs the Ministry of the Interior. Besides, after the elections, crowds of Smallholders began to terrorize the Communist party. We need protection. Though we regret to disturb the discussions with this request, we must nevertheless insist on getting the Interior."

"The Smallholders have proven themselves in the fight against reaction," said I. "Terrorization of Communists by Smallholders is an entirely sporadic phenomenon, by no means to be compared with the terrorism of the Communist party up to now. We guarantee that Smallholders will not harm Communists, and must insist on retaining the portfolio."

"You don't seem to realize! Look around in southeastern Europe, and see if you can find a country where the Ministry of Interior isn't in the hands of the Communist party," said Rákosi.

We were to understand from this pronouncement that the Communists made this sudden demand in accordance with Soviet instructions.

Smallholder leaders were assembled for a special meeting, where Béla Kovács said:

"If, with the Ministry of the Interior in its possession, our party were to seek to right every wrong suffered until now, it would be impossible to uphold the coalition. In a practical sense the Ministry of the Interior would not represent the power it symbolically holds. Let us not disrupt the formation of a government by demanding the Ministry of the Interior, but let us give this portfolio to the Communists and appoint a strong undersecretary to head the police."

We had no choice but to surrender the Ministry of the Interior.

Critics have an easy task. Even today they ask why the Smallholders relinquished this portfolio. They do not know, of course, of the many ways in which the Russians interfered. They do not know, either, that the other members of the Allied Control Commission adopted a hands-off policy on the praiseworthy ground that the formation of a cabinet was an "internal affair" in which they "could not intervene." The pressure brought to bear on us was great and could not be disregarded, yet there was no means of bringing it to the attention of the public.

After this the cabinet was formed. The composition was as follows: Prime Minister, Zoltán Tildy; Minister without Portfolio, Stephen Dobi, a former field hand; Minister of Agriculture, Béla Kovács. John Gyöngyösi continued as Minister of Foreign Affairs; Francis Gordon, director of a large department store in Budapest, became Minister of Finance; Eugene Tombor, soldier and military writer, became Minister of Defense; Joseph Antall, my former undersecretary, became Minister of Reconstruction; Anthony Balla, writer and journalist, became Minister of Propaganda; Charles Bárányos, an expert in agriculture and food, became Minister of Supply.

Communist members of the cabinet were: Vice Premier Rákosi; Minister of Transportation Ernest Gerö; Minister of the Interior Emery Nagy (until now, Minister of Agriculture); Minister of Social Welfare Erik Molnár (succeeding himself). Árpád Szakasits was Vice Premier; Anthony Bán, Minister of Industry; Stephen Ries, Minister of Justice; and Alexander Ronai, Minister of Trade. The Peasant party was given the Ministry of Education, and Desider Keresztury, teacher and writer, was appointed to head it.

I had decided not to accept a post in the new cabinet, and was elected president of the parliament. Because there was as yet no decision as to the constitutional form of the state, the powers delegated to the head of state were vested in a Supreme Council of Three presided over by the president of the parliament. Thus, for three months I was president of parliament and exercised the powers of the head of state with Béla Varga and the Communist, Leslie Rajk.

The United States was first to recognize the new cabinet, with the Soviet Union following an hour later. It was the expressed "wish" of the Russians, however, that the press announcements should state that the Soviet Union had been first to grant recognition.

CHAPTER 38

Struggle Instead of Reconciliation

ON THE LAST DAY OF THE INTERPARTY DISCUSSIONS I STATED THAT THEY must continue until all government posts had been distributed fairly among the parties of the coalition. Rákosi said that he regarded this as a most natural request from the Smallholders; Szakasits and Veres nodded their approval.

The Tildy government had hardly begun functioning, when, in the middle of November, I called the party leaders together for this purpose. Again the negotiations made hardly any progress; Tildy was more concerned with accomplishments related directly to his premiership. The parties of the left, showing practically no interest, handled the apportionment of posts lackadaisically. This seeming indifference was, however, a well planned tactical move to prevent the Smallholders from gaining strength commensurate with their victory at the polls.

Nevertheless, we held several conferences, discussing first the apportionment of the undersecretaryships. There are two in each ministry; one is a political appointee, the other, a career official for whom this is the highest post attainable.

First we settled the appointments of political undersecretaries, deciding that each party should have as many undersecretaries as it had ministers. Each party was to place its appointee in a ministry headed by a member of another party. I succeeded in securing an exception in our favor. The Smallholders were allowed to retain their man, Joseph Vásáry, in his post as Undersecretary of Agriculture, despite the fact that the minister was also a Smallholder.

Then I forced through the distribution of other posts. We came to the lord lieutenants, who are delegated by the national government to head the city and county autonomies. Of twenty-nine such posts, our party had so far received five. I demanded fifteen, but accepted fourteen, on condition that the Smallholders receive the one in the county of Pest, four times as large as any of the others.

In general, while the Smallholders party was under my leadership, naturally the proportion of peasants in public service increased notably. They first held two portfolios in the cabinet, and then, under my premiership, three. There were peasants among the undersecretaries. Five of the prefects were peasants without schooling but versed in administration. Of 243 members of Parliament, 120 were simple farm workers, representing an advance in public life which, for the Hungarian peasant, had no precedent. Now that Béla Kovács and I have fallen from power, it is doubtful whether the Hungarian peasant will ever again possess such influence.

Unfortunately, this was as far as we got in proportional representation. The direction of political affairs is naturally in the hands of the Prime Minister. I did not want to interfere with Tildy's plans through my insistent demands, and so I left him to continue with the proportionate distribution of the remaining posts as he saw fit. Tildy, however, was too busy governing and could not find time to attend to the just claims of the Smallholders. During his premiership I forced another interparty conference to redistribute judicial posts and the top positions in public security.

I proposed that wherever the prefect was not a Smallholder, the chief of police should be one. I then demanded that, of the 240 district captaincies, 120 should be filled by Smallholders; and that, wherever the chief was not a Smallholder, his assistant should be one. With regard to administration, I demanded that we similarly divide up the posts of lord lieutenant and mayor, so that half should be Smallholders; and that, where such posts were not filled by Smallholders, the deputies should be. This arrangement would have satisfied the members of our party and would have corresponded to our share of the coalition government.

We should have been able to oppose the aims of the Communists and Russians much more effectively if Smallholders had filled half of all positions. It would have been easier for democratic consolidation and reconciliation to come into existence if the leadership in all fields had been proportionately distributed.

During the negotiations, when I brought up these questions, it was impossible to reach an agreement. Though strongly supported by Béla Kovács and Béla Varga, I was unable to call any further conferences.

In December, a month after the formation of the new government, every one began to feel that the elections and the coalition had not ironed out all differences, and that the struggle between the parties would go on. Through the elections Hungary had obtained a position more advantageous than any of the other states of southeastern Europe; but the Smallholders could not capitalize on their position because the leaders of the party were not agreed on the necessity of using the psychological situation after elections and strengthening the party by any lawful means at our disposal.

But we also saw that the Soviet Union did not concern itself seriously with Voroshilov's and Pushkin's announcement that they wished to base Russo-Hungarian friendship on the Smallholders party. Russia and the Communists continued their game and turned again to more violent tactics.

The Smallholders, seeking to deepen personal contacts with Russia's representatives, arranged a concert in honor of Marshal Voroshilov and his staff. On this occasion, Professor Eugene Adam directed a fascinating program of Hungarian folk music.

After the concert, I greeted Voroshilov, who replied with a toast and a speech in which he warned Hungary not to hope for any sort of dollar assistance from abroad—the country would have to depend on its own resources and should cultivate the friendship of Russia. Subtly he made us feel his disapproval of the Smallholders' friendly feelers toward the United States.

At the end of December there was surface peace under Tildy's government; but a sharp observer could perceive the resolute preparations of the Communist party. His premiership gave the Communists no ground for open dissatisfaction, but they prepared for battle, drawing up plans which were to be executed systematically with Russian aid.

Before Christmas, the government made a very unpopular move. As a curb on inflation, it ordered all money turned in to be overstamped. For every four pengös, people received one stamped pengö; which meant that they lost three-fourths of whatever cash they had on hand. Yet, despite the drastic cut in circulation, prices remained the same.

The spiraling inflation inspired the Communists to a proposal that, instead of having the cabinet deal from day to day with matters of an economic nature, a separate Supreme Economic Council should be set up. The chairman of the new body would be the Prime Minister, while Zoltán Vas, the Communist mayor of Budapest who had been defeated in the election, would be its executive secretary.

Zoltán Tildy agreed to the proposal, and the body governing economic life was created. It became a state within a state, and the continual target of complaints and curses. Through it the Communists were able to exert an irresistible influence on the life and economy of Hungary, just as in the other countries of southeastern Europe.

CHAPTER 39

The Russians Have Their Versions

WHILE TILDY WAS PRIME MINISTER, VOROSHILOV AGAIN BROUGHT UP THE question of expelling the German-speaking minority. Tildy called a cabinet meeting to discuss the matter.

Since I knew that Voroshilov's directive would recommend a radical solution, I called together the political committee of our party beforehand and summarized the conditions under which we might accept the resettlement decree. We must make sure that members of the German-speaking minority were not expelled on the basis of collective responsibility. As grounds for expulsion, we must insist on the four categories of guilt decided upon the previous summer.

The cabinet meeting was distinctly under the influence of the new Voroshilov directive. It repeated that Hungary was "obliged" to expel the Germans from her territory, and neglected to mention that the Potsdam decision left it to Hungary's discretion. That decision, superficially drawn up, did not determine any categories of guilt, but simply referred to those whose mother tongue was German. Voroshilov's communication used the same terms.

On the only occasion of a vote in the Tildy cabinet, a majority acceded to Russia's request to expel the whole minority with a minimum of exceptions for persons of outstanding merit. A few Smallholder ministers voted against the decree drawn up by Tildy in accordance with Soviet dictates.

Tildy did receive the majority of the votes, but in pressing this issue he utterly disregarded resolutions passed by the Smallholders party.

Throughout the nation, the decree caused dissatisfaction. Every one knew at least a few persons of German origin who had proved their character and patriotism, and whom it would be unjust to expel. But every one knew, too, that the decree would give the Communist Minister of the Interior a chance to play his party's politics, and feared that he would deport worthy Germans and exempt those affiliated with the Communist party even if their records proved that they had been Nazis or members of the Volksbund. This anxiety later proved justified.

The Minister of the Interior's first step was to grant blanket exemption to all miners and skilled industrial workers on the ground that they were indispensable to the industry. Thus Nazis and Volkbundists in these categories immediately escaped the effect of the decree. Most of them had already joined the Communist party, while a few were Social Democrats.

In the villages, the leaders of the leftist parties were exempted on the basis of rather dubious documents purporting to prove that they had fought for democracy as members of labor organizations. On the other hand, practically every member of the Smallholders party was black-listed, even if it were known that he had fought pan-Germanism tooth and nail in the heyday of National Socialism. These men had to apply for exemption individually and prove in a most complicated fashion that they had been active members of the Smallholders party, or how they had opposed the Nazis. Their applications were reviewed by the Minister of the Interior, who more often than not refused approval. Our party headquarters was swamped by requests for intervention in these cases.

A wave of indignation swept through our party, whose members were not willing to stand for such highhanded procedure a month or two after the election victory. Besides, Hungarians by nature take sides with the underdog; thus even those who had never liked the Germans and had been loudest in demanding their expulsion, were indignant. I had to make a strenuous fight to save worthy men from deportation.

Dissatisfaction was rampant for many reasons. A currency measure, hitting the public just before Christmas, was very unpopular. The interruption of the conferences to distribute civil service posts proportionately contributed to dissatisfaction. And now, the resettlement decree, which had embittered the rank and file of the Smallholders. Tildy's popularity had seriously waned during the first ten weeks of his premiership.

In many respects I understood the difficulties of his position; and I conspicuously supported him at every possible opportunity. Béla Kovács and Béla Varga did the same, and sought to explain Tildy's attitude to the people as best they could. Tildy himself hinted quite frequently at the causes for his compliance, affirming that he often had to struggle against things which he could not discuss even with our own party in Parliament. He was referring, I knew, to the concerted Soviet-Communist pressure. This, the people could not discern. They only knew that Tildy, during his administration, had been laying the foundation for appeasement so strongly that now it was no longer possible to correct it.

Queerly enough, another factor added to the unrest. Under Tildy's premiership the People's Courts began to try the war criminals delivered to Hungary by English and American military authorities. Since the end of the war, public opinion was unanimous in demanding that justice be meted out to men who had so lightly gambled with the blood and welfare of the nation.

The People's Court began with the trial of Leslie Bárdossy. On the basis of his self-confident defense, which served to emphasize the parallel between the former German and the present Russian pressure on the government, people thought he would receive a relatively mild sentence.

Bárdossy's death sentence did not increase the popularity of the government and the new "democracy." It was a mistake on the part of the Ministry of Justice not to begin with the trial of Szálasi and his Arrow Cross confederates, to whose execution no one would have the slightest objection.

The Russian insistence on the unqualified expulsion of Germans and the Russian persecution of them is strangely similar to the previous German persecution of Jews in satellite countries, and it is an axiom of dictatorship that satellites should be made partners in cowardly crimes against humanity.

CHAPTER 40

Hungary Becomes a Republic

SINCE DECEMBER, 1945, THERE WAS CONSTANT TALK ABOUT A NEW FORM of government. Rákosi and Szakasits had dropped hints from time to time. Tildy now brought the matter squarely before me, pointing out that the state could not remain in the supposed constitutional uncertainty it had maintained between the two world wars. Hungary had retained its status as a kingdom; while official circles rejected the idea of a monarch, a regent acted as head of state. Tildy expressed the opinion that Hungary should become a republic.

I agreed that we could not go on without creating a stable, democratic form of government, and told him I would cooperate in the change.

Tildy broached the matter to party leaders, who decided they would consult with their respective parties. I discussed the question with Béla Kovács and Béla Varga, both of whom were receptive to a republic under the circumstances but said they could pledge their wholehearted support only on condition that I become president.

I at once said that, if we supported the move, it should be without regard for personalities.

The great majority of our representatives in Parliament favored a republic in principle, yet there were a great many who thought the proclamation of a republic inopportune. Some said we had much more important questions to settle. Others thought that, though the idea was sound, we ought to wait until the end of the Russian occupation, when the nation could exercise its will in full possession of its sovereign rights. There were also a few deputies who said that, since constitutional questions had not been mentioned before the elections, it was not proper for the present Parliament to pass on them.

I called a caucus of the Smallholders, and the debate went on for days; albeit it seemed that a majority favored setting up a republic, the final decision was doubtful. It was as if the deputies had sensed what later proved to be true, that the Communists and the Russians were behind the idea.

The caucus revealed the true democratic sentiments of the young deputies who were later accused of conspiracy. Without exception they were the ones who desired the immediate proclamation of a republic; only the most farfetched libel could seek to prove that they had plotted to overthrow the republic they helped to create, or had planned to restore the monarchy.

The mood of the conferees vacillated. We saw that a decision had to be reached. With this in mind, Béla Varga took the floor and said that he had been brought up as a monarchist and had been pro-monarchist all his life, yet, under the present circumstances, he was convinced that it was best for Hungary to become a republic.

Then I spoke up, pointing out that her neighbors had often accused Hungary of revisionism in the past, because she had retained the kingdom, while it served no practical purpose. It was as if she were threatening with the possibility of restoring the monarchy. Now that a peace treaty was soon to be signed, we should have a number of disputed points to settle with our neighbors. It was important that the suspicions of the past should not arise, and that we should give the world proof of our good faith in democratic terms. After my speech a vote was taken in which all but two of our parliamentary representatives showed themselves in favor of proclaiming a republic.

Before the caucus I had made inquiries at the American and British Legations, where I was assured that there would be no objection raised if Hungary declared itself a republic.

It was our conviction that we were expressing the will of the majority of the people in supporting the idea of the republic. We sincerely hoped that under this form of government the Hungarian people, who had so often bled for foreign interests, might at last live their own lives.

Parliament passed the law, and its vote was almost unanimous for a republic. Tremendous crowds on Parliament Square cheered my announcement of its decision.

An incident that annoyed me considerably occurred soon after Hungary became a republic. On several occasions Marshal Voroshilov had personally asked for a list of the monarchists in Hungary. Though he had received no information from me, agents of the NKVD in the spring of 1946 seized and carried off Géza Pálffy and Louis Iván, known monarchists. This act of violence strengthened me in the belief that the Soviet Union had had a hand in promoting the change.

CHAPTER 41

A President Is Chosen

EVEN BEFORE HUNGARY BECAME A REPUBLIC, THERE WERE DISCUSSIONS as to who would be the president. Rákosi came to see me on Christmas Day, 1945, to talk things over, when it already seemed certain that Parliament would vote in favor of a republic.

Rákosi said we might choose either an active politician or some distinguished personality who stood above party factions. Of the latter there were few to choose from; and so it seemed we should have to select a politician.

"It is evident," he said, "that the president will have to be a Small-holder. The choice is between you and Zoltán Tildy. You'll have to decide which one it shall be. Since either the post of premier or that of president of the Assembly becomes vacant, we ought to consider the sectarian side of the matter. If the president of the republic should also be a Protestant, it would be proper to have a Catholic in one of the other leading positions. In fact, if the chair of president of Parliament becomes vacant, we ought to give this post to another party. It would seem rather one-sided for the president, the premier, and the head of Parliament to come from the same party."

I did not see what Rákosi was driving at, and answered cautiously:

"I am sure we shall be able to agree on who should be president of the republic, but I cannot consent to our party's releasing any of the posts it now holds."

Rákosi, however, wanted to know more. He continued:

"Tildy would be a suitable man for president, because he is the leader of your party and did much to further interparty collaboration. On the other hand, if the choice fell on you, it would mean that the president had been recruited from the largest democratic group in the country—the peasantry."

Avoiding a direct response, I began pointing out that it would be well for the Communists to curb their despotic party secretaries, whose violent acts were provoking the anger of our deputies in Parliament and might easily lead to disorders.

Rákosi, not inclined to discuss this, quickly left. He was rejoined in my anteroom by his two detectives, who by now never let him out of sight.

The question of who should be president was in the foreground of political activity. Though neither Tildy nor I had made any public announcements, factions were formed in support of our candidacies. Representatives came to me in throngs, demanding that I announce my availability. I did not commit myself. For definite reasons I kept silent.

First, I thought it proper that Tildy should be president, which brought up the question of who should be premier. I knew that Tildy would insist upon my taking that post, yet I abhorred the idea.

My silence was misconstrued by many members of our party, who thought I was just waiting to be coaxed and demanded that I take a stand. Béla Kovács and Béla Varga said it was evident that the people of the country would only be satisfied if I became president. Some deputies said openly that they had voted in favor of a republic on the understanding that I was to be its head.

Meanwhile, Tildy announced to a few of our left-wing representatives that he was a candidate for the presidency. The workers' parties favored Tildy, though, even if all their votes were combined with a few of our left-wing representatives, they would not have been able to influence the decision of the Smallholders' majority.

Obviously I had to think a great deal about the presidency, knowing that it was not wise to disappoint the expectations of the masses, and that it was up to us to give them every opportunity to cherish democracy. From this standpoint, it would perhaps be of advantage if I became president and the people could have the feeling that their wish had been fulfilled. But we also had to consider that it would be difficult to replace Tildy as premier. There were others of equal ability, but none whom the parties of the coalition would have accepted so willingly. And few could keep peace among the coalition parties as well.

I also felt that historical justice demanded that Tildy be president. He was older than I, leader of our party, and he had been our premier.

But this was more easily decided than accomplished. Tildy was unpopular. If I took an open stand now and tried to hoist him into the president's chair step by step, I should lose myself in petty denials of my candidacy, and my efforts would be doomed to defeat. So I bided my time, waiting for a psychological moment when I could throw my full weight behind him. For weeks I kept my silence. I said nothing, even to Tildy, for I was afraid he might mention it to someone, and members of my party might conclude that I had made a deal with him.

One evening, our deputies called a meeting by themselves with the idea that they would force me to become a candidate for the presidency. I was to be present at the meeting. But that day, as it happened, I was at a very congenial gathering at the country town of Cegléd, where I had been elected to a recently vacated place on the "Turin Deputation." The original deputation of a hundred members had been sent to Italy to offer Louis Kossuth, who was in exile, the mandate of Cegléd. The original members of the deputation had passed on long ago; but each vacancy was always filled by popular vote, and it was considered a great honor to succeed to their places. Well, the induction ceremonies lasted so long that I missed the meeting in Budapest. Before they adjourned, more than two hundred of them signed a declaration pledging their support of my candidacy.

I realized that the question of the presidency could not be postponed any longer. I called on Tildy, who was terribly worried over the uncertainty of his situation. I told him that, from the first, I had not been willing to accept the presidency, and that now I considered the time ripe for his election. That same day I would arrange to have the party back him for president, but on one condition. He was not to ask me to become Prime Minister. I wished to remain president of Parliament so that I could also concern myself with party affairs. On no account did I want to become premier.

Tildy, deeply moved, said he would respect my request though it would be extremely difficult to find someone else for the post of premier.

I called a meeting of the deputies for that evening and asked Tildy to come, too; all were present. I was in a difficult situation when I arose to speak. If I had the text of that speech here in America I think I could quote the whole of it without immodesty, but when I left Hungary I did not expect ever to need my notes abroad.

My talk came as a surprise, and the deputies were deeply moved when I said that the history of the Hungarian republic must not be allowed to start with a fight for power by its leaders over the heads of the people who were still suffering and in rags, as had so often been the case in the past. I should like to set an example for the future of our democracy, of how to exercise self-denial when the interests of the nation demanded it. My words were received with an ovation that lasted for many minutes. Tears were in the eyes of many of our deputy friends. We arrived at the desired result: Tildy was unanimously nominated to become president of the new republic.

In practice, this meant his election.

CHAPTER 42

Why I Became Premier

SOON AFTER IT WAS DECIDED THAT TILDY WAS TO BECOME PRESIDENT, I felt concerted pressure upon me to accept the premiership. While Tildy kept his promise not to insist that I succeed him in the vacated chair, the leaders of the other three coalition parties, Rákosi, Szakasits, and Veres, handed each other the doorknob of my office and entreated me to accept. They stated, individually and in concert, that they did not consider the coalition government secure unless I headed it. I refused. They returned in the evening, and the two vice premiers announced that they would not continue as such except with me, and clearly dropped the possible crisis of forming a new coalition government squarely in my lap.

Indicating valid reasons, I said that I could not accept the premiership, and recommended Desider Sulyok. Both Rákosi and Szakasits opposed him, but I stood my ground.

The next day I asked Szakasits to visit me and reminded him of the days of close cooperation between Social Democrats and Smallholders, and how enthusiastically Sulyok had supported the cooperation; I went to great lengths to impress him with Sulyok's ability and accomplishments. Finally, Szakasits allowed himself to be won over to Sulyok's candidacy.

Conferring with Sulyok, too, I told him that I trusted his capabilities and the straight line of democratic policy he would surely follow, and offered him the premiership. Sulyok emphasized the great sacrifice an individual would have to make, the unsolvable problems the next premier would have to bridge in the immediate future, and said that there was little glory in store for the man who undertook to head the government in these times. But he accepted.

Tildy agreed on Sulyok, and so did my fellow Smallholder deputies after I had convinced them that it would be best for all. With this mutual accord, Rákosi was prevailed upon to accept Sulyok. But I felt that the Marxist parties were still uneasy about him.

Deciding to give Sulyok a dramatic opportunity to dispel all leftist doubts and fears, I induced the leadership of the Smallholders to let him report the constitutional bill of the republic in Parliament. The reporter is not limited in time, and I wanted to enable Sulyok to make an address which would at once prove his statesmanship, allow him to lay down his belief in democracy and the republican form of government, serve to dispel all doubts of the Marxists, and give them assurance regarding cooperation.

We placed high expectations in Sulyok's speech, which I awaited on the assumption that it would undoubtedly be a political success, sincerely hoping that through it I might escape the premiership. Sulyok mangled his opportunity.

He delivered a long but irrelevant speech. Aside from hailing the republic, he went into a debate with himself as to whether the Hungarian Communist Red army fought the Czechs in 1919 to revise the postwar frontier or not. He presented comparisons between the reactionary terror after our first Communist interlude and some police murders of the present era, getting so deeply involved in the internal affairs of the Marxist parties that hardly had he finished when Rákosi and Szakasits unequivocally declared that they would not, under any circumstances, accept Sulyok for premier. Since he showed no ability to create harmony in political life, there was no further discussion needed, they said, because coalition could not operate under him. Naturally I was disheartened.

At the interparty conferences which followed, I presented the name of every Smallholder with political training who commanded respect; and they offered exceptions and objections to person after person. The ring was tightening, and colleagues in the cabinet frankly told me so.

I owe an explanation for my reluctance to become premier. Truly it was not a question of vanity because I had not become president, nor one of personal comfort since all of my life I had been a hard-working man, burdened with constant worries; but instinctively I felt that the premiership would destroy my popularity with the people.

This popularity I did not regard as a treasure of my own, but wanted to save because I felt that democracy would need it in the future, knowing that our strength in dealings with members of the Marxist parties could be based only on the affection and trust of the masses. It was clear that fulfillment of the Soviet demands awakened suspicion and distrust among our voters, and also that governing with the Communists demanded a great deal of yielding.

I faced it squarely that the great mass of Hungarian peasants whom I loved so dearly, and whose every thought I knew, would not understand. I came to the conclusion that, with Tildy's heritage on my hands, no government headed by a premier intent on resisting the Soviet and the Communists in these days would last more than a few weeks. I was afraid, I must admit, of losing my influence on the common man, who, instead of learning to cherish democracy and take his rightful place in it, might turn and become its enemy.

These were my personal reasons for not wishing to become premier, and obviously I could not state them publicly. My family and close friends understood.

But after Sulyok's speech was received so critically, and all the other Smallholder candidates were rejected by the left, the movement to draft me received new impetus. In Hungary, where the structure of the new democracy was still loosely knit, a hand was needed to guide it securely and balance its precarious equilibrium, to maintain the political cooperation unavoidable under the circumstances, until the two great milestones were reached: the signing of the peace treaty and the end of occupation.

My decision was precipitated by an ever present fear that in a vacillating government the influence of the Soviet would increase and the Communists would conquer more ground. In existing conditions and the feeble state of the national economy, the fear was ever present that a stumbling government would open opportunities for internal disturbances, and a slowly developing democracy would be exchanged for the destructiveness of a possible civil war.

Many a prayer preceded the decision. My thoughts wandered to my mother, who had instilled in me the conviction that the interests of the great family, the community, came before one's own.

Through introspection I concluded that Hungary could be steered through the coming difficult times only by one who was ready to sacrifice his political value, his popularity, and the people's confidence, and was ready to face possible attacks on his honor. I felt that I should be ready and, if needed, sacrifice it should be. Whatever might happen to me as a man, I would try to guide my tottering nation to the dawn of a happier morrow.

Before officially accepting, I told Rákosi and Szakasits my conditions:

1) Before the harvest there must be no strikes which would increase dissatisfaction among the already ill fed population.

2) Under no conditions must any political demonstrations be staged which would endanger peaceful governing.

3) The proportionate distribution of administrative posts should be continued and made effective throughout the police and civil service.

Since both accepted my conditions and pledged themselves to maintain them, I informed the president that I would accept the premiership.

In fact, the post was already vacant. My friend Béla Kovács, then minister of agriculture, drove to my home to get the black suit which I would wear when taking oath. When Béla told my wife that I was to become premier she cried bitterly. The poor woman would have preferred coming with me on the road to Bisse, fighting the earth, the storm, and drought, to following the road to power. Instinctively she felt that the step I had taken was not toward tranquillity and peace of mind.

Thus, in the thousand-year-old Hungary, a peasant for the first time held the reins of government. For sixteen long months I tried to steer my country on the road to self-realization; to build a new way of democratic life. In truth the young republic made great strides in the concert of nations.

But the dark powers which have caused and will continue to cause much heartache and bloodshed to humanity advanced against me. Instead of finishing my work, I find myself after sixteen months writing this book—in exile.

CHAPTER 43

The Cabinet

WANTING TO AVOID SUDDEN CHANGES, I TOOK OVER TILDY'S CABINET. Besides, it would not have been easy to find men in our party suitable to become ministers in a new coalition cabinet. It often happened that men qualified disliked the Communists, or else the Communists would not agree to having them. As for portfolios held by members of other parties, the premier did not have much latitude; he could only accept or reject candidates put forward by their respective parties. To me it seemed best to leave the cabinet as it was until I could devise means for improving it.

Let me sketch the men who, with few changes, were to govern the country with me for a period of sixteen months.

Rákosi has already been introduced. As time passed his cunning and determination increased. He was first in rank of the two vice premiers, because his party had one mandate more in Parliament than the Social Democrats.

Árpád Szakasits, leader of the Social Democratic party, was the other vice premier. Beginning his career as a stonecutter, he was a well read man with a penchant for writing, the editor of his party's newspaper, the *Népszava*. Since Rákosi's reappearance on the scene in Hungary, he had ceased to have political opinions of his own. Szakasits' every act and thought were inspired by that crafty agent of Moscow. The left wing of his party supported him, through the mediation of men of unsavory past for whom he secured leading positions. Many Social Democrats of long standing had no liking for him because of his intrigues against the former leader of the party, Charles Peyer, whom he had ousted. He often tried mediating between Smallholders and Communists to the extent Rákosi was willing.

An interesting figure in the cabinet was Ernest Gerö, minister of transportation. He could well serve as a model of the real Communist, resolute and without scruples, ready to work day and night in the interest of the party, never departing for an instant from the party line. In all his dealings he is a Communist through and through. A Muscovite, he speaks Russian fluently.

Emery Nagy was the minister of the interior in those days. Among the Communist ministers, he was most closely Hungarian; for a long time he lived in a little country town. Possessed of an ingratiating manner, he is a politician of small caliber, who blindly follows the instructions of the party chieftains.

Eric Molnár, minister of public welfare, was a lawyer of Kecskemét who, in times past, had written leftist articles and kept up a secret communication with the Communists. He is a simple, everyday sort of man, fond of the little and big comforts of life.

The minister of justice, Stephen Ries, had been the lawyer of the Social Democratic party. He was counsel for several leftist defendants in political trials and received, it is said, very high fees for these services. At first he showed an unbiased legal mind; but gradually he came more and more under the influence of Szakasits, the Communists, and Russia. Always conforming to the views of the Communist party, he was extremely biased in the course of the so-called conspiracy trials. It was a great blow to the administration of justice that he dismissed experienced, worthy judges and replaced them, for the most part, with shady Communists and left-wing Socialists.

Anthony Bán, minister of industry, is of German descent and comes from the county of Baranya. This well intentioned man was unquestionably in Communist power. Having had no experience in industrial administration, his ministry was soon overrun with corruption.

Then there was Alexander Ronai, last in the list of Marxist ministers, who had originally been a secretary of the Social Democratic party in one of the country districts. In my cabinet he was minister of trade. In the temporary government he had been minister of supply but, instead of organizing food distribution, kept issuing dismal bulletins from week to week, saying that it would not be long before the populace would die of starvation.

The Peasant party had only one minister in the cabinet; Desider Keresztury, minister of education, well known as a writer and head of a teachers' college. Under his democratic leadership there were no clashes between the churches and the ministry of education.

Among the Smallholders I should first like to mention John Gyöngyösi, minister of foreign affairs. He had held the same post in the temporary government organized in Debrecen, at a time when his portfolio's sphere of influence was extremely limited. Later, when there were tasks of greater importance, he proved himself equal to them, carrying out his duties with integrity and consistency of purpose. At first he was considered a leftist; but then, particularly after the discussions preceding the signing of the peace treaty, he became an increasingly resolute champion of democracy and a popular man in the party.

Charles Bárányos was minister of supply. His gifts for organization in agriculture and food distribution became evident before the war. Taking no part in party politics, he achieved high standards in his ministry. He skillfully solved the problems of food distribution in the winter of 1945–1946, despite the prophecies of his predecessor to the effect that the people of Budapest and the inhabitants of the industrial districts would die of starvation within three weeks.

Francis Gordon, a prominent businessman, was minister of finance. In politics he was a purposeful representative of the middle classes, energetically opposed to Soviet economic penetration.

My minister of agriculture was Béla Kovács, who did not remain in the cabinet for long, since he had to resign his portfolio when needed for important work within the party. History will tell more about this outstanding Hungarian patriot.

Joseph Antall was minister of reconstruction. He had been my undersecretary when I had been engaged in organizing this ministry. For aiding Jewish and Polish refugees he had been thrown into prison during the German occupation. He helped the churches greatly with grants to repair their ruined buildings and schools.

Eugene Tombor, minister of defense, was an outstanding authority and writer on military affairs, who had a genuinely democratic background. During the war he was not afraid to explain, in his writings and lectures, just where and how the Germans were losing the war. He had been one of the closest friends of Andrew Bajcsy-Zsilinsky, the Smallholder leader who died a martyr's death.

Anthony Balla, a newspaperman and author of significant books on history and economics, was minister of information. His post was no easy one.

Stephen Dobi was our minister without portfolio. He was a simple farm hand who at first showed no leanings toward the left, but later came under the influence of the Communists.

This was the government with which I faced the difficult problems ahead. There were four different political ideologies among the ministers, which it was no easy task to reconcile. I regarded the policy of the coalition as a policy of compromise, which I was forced to achieve in the majority of cases.

I had a series of difficult problems to solve in the very first days of my premiership. In February the United States government proposed an agreement which would have incorporated Budapest as a stop in its network of air routes to the Far East. The proposal raised a difficult problem.

Such an agreement would naturally have been in the interest of Hungary; to be linked to the world's greatest air route would of course be important to any little country. We asked the Allied Control Commission for its approval, but the Russian president would not even allow us to begin discussions in this matter. Pushkin, the Russian minister to Hungary, also intervened, saying that Hungary's air fields were under the control of the Russian commander of the occupation forces. The landing of American planes in Hungary would be regarded as the creation of air bases. If landing fields were needed, they could be provided in Russia.

We had to reply that we should be pleased to cooperate as soon as we had "regained our national sovereignty."

Russia's one-sided intervention kept us from concluding an aviation agreement with the world's greatest power, the United States.

As premier I had to devote myself first of all to the country's interests and only secondarily to my party. It was my intent to raise living standards, increase reconstruction, secure national independence, readjust Hungarian agriculture to the basis of small units of production, and work for economic and social consolidation. But I considered that my most important task was the maintainance of the continuity of productive work, in order that I might lead the country to the signing and ratification of the peace treaty, strengthened; that when occupation ended I could hand the government over to a successor who could guide the affairs of state in the way a free and independent country should be governed.

CHAPTER 44

Coalition with a Bleak Outlook

HARDLY HAD I BECOME HEAD OF THE GOVERNMENT WHEN I PERCEIVED that I was under constant surveillance of the Russian secret police, the NKVD. After conversations with American or English diplomats or military officials, the NKVD would secretly summon my interpreters and interrogate them as to what had been discussed. Experience proved that those who had once been questioned by the NKVD could no longer be used as interpreters or employed in any sort of confidential work.

It was under such conditions that the rudder of state had to be held on an even course.

As soon as the new cabinet settled down to work, the difficulties which we faced at once became evident. No matter what project was discussed, the country's great poverty was an ever present barrier.

Reparations payments lagged, although we were aware that our dependence on Russia was in exact proportion to our debt. Owing to inflation, there was practically no national income. Though six hundred thousand new owners of farms were in urgent need of assistance, we had no means of aiding agriculture.

The mint printed floods of paper notes, which barely served to keep the wheels of industry, so vital to meeting reparations payments, rolling. It was too early to think of making a budget, but it was evident that a national income comparable to that of prewar years could not be sweated out of the impoverished populace. State expenditures must be slashed.

During the war bureaucracy had increased tremendously, and even before it, there had been far too many civil servants. As a member of Parliament I had drawn up a chart showing the percentage of people engaged in various occupations in the different countries. In agricultural employment, Hungary held eleventh place among the other countries of the world. In industrial employment it held nineteenth; in commercial employment, twentieth; but in state employment it held fourth place in the world—Germany coming first, then England and Sweden, closely followed by Hungary. We were forced to conclude that the number of civil servants must be reduced. We learned that even the United States had reduced by half a million the number of those who had been in government service during the war.

It was natural, in view of the political conditions, that not only nonessential men would have to be dismissed, but all who had lent aid to fascism. We knew that the sifting process would awaken party differences.

The coalition form of government made it necessary to hold preliminary interparty conferences for threshing out every question; and one was called on this occasion. The number of civil servants we agreed to retain was 90 per cent of the number employed in 1938. There was little debate on this point. The make-up of the body charged with the dismissals was a more controversial problem. Knowing that here, too, the Communists wanted to play politics, we proposed that the government set up a three-man commission appointed by the premier, the minister of finance, and the minister of the particular department in which the commission took action.

The Communists violently opposed the plan, suggesting that the finance minister's delegate be replaced by a trade-union representative. According to my plan, there would have been a Smallholder majority on every committee; according to the Communist scheme there would have been a leftist majority in every ministry held by the workers' parties.

The Communists claimed that, if my plans were followed, reactionaries would remain in state employ. We, on the other hand, said that under the Communist plan, experts in administration would be exchanged for Communist and Socialist dilettantes.

For weeks the two camps stood face to face, neither willing to yield.

The Communists, wanting to settle matters violently, ordered workers to stage demonstrations. Rákosi found it convenient to forget our agreement outlawing demonstrations. On one occasion, a great throng broke through the gates of Parliament and surged into the offices of the premier. I promised the crowd only that the trade unions would have an advisory voice.

The tenacity of both sides precluded the reduction of the number of civil servants until, by a ruse, Rákosi won a decision later favoring the Communist-led trade unions.

There was another major issue when the Communists won—in the endeavors to prepare the world for a just peace for Hungary.

By the end of 1945 it seemed probable that a peace conference would be held the following year. Obviously men with the interests of their country at heart must prepare accordingly. It was important to define the Hungarian aims and be ready to ward off possible attacks.

Throughout the entire year it was impossible to arrive at any kind of decision with the other political parties. The Communists constantly evaded methodical discussion of the problems Hungary was certain to face at the peace conference. They loudly maintained that Hungary would gain more at the peace conference by admitting its guilt with open humility than by trying to defend the actions of past governments.

Since April, 1945, the Smallholder party experts in foreign affairs had been holding a series of deliberations to this end. We knew that the peace conference would not concern itself primarily with the people's opposition to the war, but rather with the attitude of the former official government. It was our opinion, however, that we should prepare to prove that it was not merely her weak, guilty leaders who let Hungary slide into the war, but the pressure of conditions. In the first place, there was the fact that the Allies made no effort to help Hungary retain her independence and neutrality. Then we expected that there would be an opportunity to show that Hungary was no more guilty of aiding Germany than other countries who were already, seemingly, favored by the Allies.

There is no point in my discussing here the relative guilt or merit of other European countries, and it is too late now to state emphatically that Hungary was in no position to determine how and when she should turn against Germany. In any event it was the duty of Hungary's political leaders to prepare to secure the best peace terms possible.

When the Communists learned that we were planning for the peace conference, they immediately attacked all peace aims. Anyone preparing to speak in Hungary's favor at the peace conference was a chauvinist and "revisionist," they said. Later, at the peace conference in May, when the Soviet Union opposed Hungary's claims, it became obvious why Russia had inspired these attacks.

At any rate, the Communists succeeded in tying the hands of the foreign minister, whose task it would have been to draw up an official presentation of Hungary's aims based on memoranda submitted by the coalition parties. Since the coalition could not reach an agreement on peace aims, the foreign minister had to act independently and with only the Smallholders' backing.

Hungarian public opinion was shocked by the attitude of the Communists. Everyone saw that the countries with claims against Hungary had mobilized public opinion solidly behind them. The Hungarian peace delegation's inability to present evidence freely, because of the internal dissensions and Communist influence, was an assured handicap.

It is doubtless true that the Communists did not decide for themselves and did not take this "line" of their own free will, but would have supported our aims if they had had the slightest inkling that success was in the offing. They prevented interparty consultations during all this time and attacked the peace aims, because the party line from Moscow so dictated; Moscow knew that it would not support them in Paris.

Notwithstanding, the burden of responsibility before history rests on the shoulders of the Communist party of Hungary. In sabotaging the best interests of the country, it served the pleasure of a foreign power instead of echoing the prayers of a humbled nation and betrayed the trust it had accepted when it shared the government in a democratic coalition.

Alas, at the eleventh hour, to save face before world public opinion, the Communists, again by obvious direction from Moscow, suddenly half-heartedly cooperated in the formulation of the peace aims.

In dealing with the Communists, I was never able to forget that they always had, in addition to Red army support, a mighty weapon up their sleeve: psychological warfare. They used it well.

The Communist party injected two concepts into the politics of southeastern Europe, democracy and reaction. Both quickly became slogans.

To non-Marxist parties, "democracy" meant independence and freedom of the people and the strengthening of autonomous forms of government.

The Social Democrats held the vague, fantastic notion that democracy was a transition phase between reaction and Socialism.

The Communists revealed more and more openly their belief that democracy was that state of affairs which most nearly conformed to conditions in the Soviet Union. The real democrat, they said, was he who followed most faithfully the Communist party line.

In the eyes of non-Marxists, democracy was associated with consolidation, reconciliation, and majority rule. To Communists, it meant fighting the traditions of the past, increasing police interference, more and bigger internment camps, nationalizing property, and absolute submission to the Soviet Union. They knew well enough that their "democracy" was a lie, but they lied boldly and with apparent conviction.

There were similar differences about the definition of "reaction." The Smallholders drew a distinction between Nazism and reaction, believing that Nazism, as a political form of life, had vanished forever at the close of World War II. All that remained was to punish fascists in accordance with the magnitude of their crimes, and reeducate the youth. On the other hand, we considered as reactionary anyone who hindered the political, economic, cultural, or social progress of the people; anyone who had had a share in making the peasant and the worker a slave of the large estates and capital, anyone who had helped to force Hungary into the most disastrous war of her history.

The Communists regarded anyone as reactionary who, as a simple citizen, had attended to his office during the former regime. They stigmatized as reactionary the nonpartisan official who refused to join a party, and all those whose conception of democracy differed from theirs. Whoever protested against the crimes of the Communist police was a reactionary, and whoever respected the provisions of the agrarian reform law was a reactionary. But the worst of all was he who interpreted independence of his country as independence from Russia, too. In their eyes it was also a flagrant "reactionary" sin to comment on the behavior of the Soviet army of occupation.

The Social Democratic and Peasant parties, in their definitions of "democracy" and "reaction," moved more and more in the direction of the Communists until all at once we perceived that we Smallholders stood alone in our opinions.

Not a single member of our party yearned for the past. We had no wish to see the peasant politically oppressed, economically exploited, culturally retarded, and socially ostracized; nor did we wish to see again a situation in which the worker who fought for his rights would be regarded as a common rogue. Therefore, we had taken upon ourselves the responsibility of waging a sincere and determined war against the forces of reaction.

The "fight against reaction" evolved as the hallmark of Hungarian political life. Only it soon became evident that Russia was behind the movement, and that whoever wished to engage in it on a non-Soviet basis would do better not to begin.

It was far from sincere in the Communists, knowing that organized reaction existed no longer, to harp on the slogan which came in handy to stigmatize the opposition. The former rulers of Hungary, the fascist leaders, were either in custody abroad or in prison at home. Officials who had collaborated with them had been relieved of their posts by the interparty clearing committees. The former owners of large estates were now impoverished and had no thought or dream of entering the political arena.

Together with other Smallholders I tried to create order in this intentional confusion of ideas, for, on looking into the matter, the average citizen could come to no other conclusion than that "the most active forces of reaction" were within the Communist party itself; and, through a public statement explaining our interpretation of "democracy" and "reaction," we made a deadly enemy of the Communist party and aroused the displeasure of the Russians.

The political situation was very bleak when I took office. I felt that day by day my forebodings came closer to realization; I should have a desperate struggle to carry through my determination to avoid revolution while the Russian forces occupied Hungary.

CHAPTER 45

Russian-Managed Unrest

ON THE FAITH OF THE PEOPLE AND TRANQUILLITY OF CONDITIONS RESTS the success of a democratic government.

The Hungarian people had proved their faith and were now yearning for peace. It was a most natural desire. The nation had experienced a cataclysm comparable to none, and with simple loyalty had held its ground, giving witness to its ideals and standing firmly by its traditions; but the disasters and the fight for survival gnawed on the nervous system of the people, and constructive life could exist only under conditions of domestic calm.

Soon after my accession to the premiership, I made it my major task to instill in the population the feeling of quiet. Public opinion reacted well, but my friends were watching developments filled with anxiety.

Economic conditions began to settle as well as could be expected in a raging inflation. The peasants set to their spring labors with a will, and the people in general, in the midst of all their daily difficulties, found hope. What little capital was available in the country was invested in productive enterprise, and soon foreign capital began to show interest in Hungarian economic developments. All the country needed was to be allowed to work and strive in peace.

This was exactly what the Communists and the Soviet Union did *not* want. The promotion of unrest is an essential part of Communist tactics; it is difficult to foster revolutionary tendencies in a country calm, hopeful, and confident. So the Communists began to stir up labor.

If workers complained of lack of food, the Communists blamed the Smallholder minister of supply. If prices were high, because of inflation, the Smallholder party was responsible. If one of our leaders made a speech, the Communist press would seek to ascribe antidemocratic or anti-Soviet sentiments to him. If there was unemployment, because of the lack of raw materials, the Reds at once tried to make some non-Marxist official the scapegoat.

When inflation was at its height, bringing much suffering to everyone with a fixed salary, they set up gallows in market places, from which hung effigies of straw with placards which said: "This is what happens to those who exploit the workers!" In short, they gave the people no peace of mind and tried everything to create a condition of permanent restlessness.

The Communists replaced Emery Nagy, their minister of the interior, with Leslie Rajk, assistant secretary of their party. Rajk was the very personification of the half-educated Communist; a resolute and fanatical exponent of the most violent moves precipitated by Communist ideology. If the latent evil in this gentle-seeming schoolteacher had become evident sooner, I would never have accepted him as a member of my cabinet. But, right up to the moment when he became minister of the interior, he played the role of "meek youth" well.

At the time of the Spanish Civil War, Moscow had sent Rajk to Spain. He became so impregnated with the spirit of civil strife that he regarded politics as a kind of barricade fight. I had trouble with him continually. Though a Communist, Rajk hated Jews—which probably accounted for the admiration felt for him by the large group of anti-Semitic Communists, recruited from among former members of Nazi organizations. This segment of the party liked him much better than Rákosi, Gerö, Révai, Zoltán Vas, or the other leaders, who had officially become atheists. The anti-Semitic favor may also have been meant as a tribute to Rajk's notorious Arrow Crossist family, for his two brothers had held important posts under the Szálasi government. Now Rajk, this strange Communist, as minister of the interior sought turmoil instead of equilibrium.

The opinions of the coalition parties with regard to the Smallholders did not agree—which disturbed the Communists and Russians, too. To change this, the Communists proposed that the Social Democratic and Peasant parties should join in an alliance. By what means they persuaded them to form a leftist bloc did not become apparent; the explanation probably is that it followed a direct order from Moscow.

With this step the Peasant and Social Democratic parties lost their independence completely. Henceforth their leaders and parliamentary deputies could only act in concert and in accordance with instructions issued by the leftist bloc. Even the ministers in the cabinet were, for the most part, under its control. Only the Peasant party's minister of education, Desider Keresztury, was able to steer an independent course. The three parties denied that their alliance was formed against the Smallholders, but the alliance meant this in practice.

In the first weeks of my premiership I began apportioning appointments to administrative and economic posts proportionately. Marshal Voroshilov sought to dissuade me.

"Look here, Gospodin Premier, it makes no difference what party an official belongs to, as long as he knows his business. Don't insist too much on a proportionate distribution of positions, because this causes dissatisfaction in the ranks of the workers' parties. An official has to follow the instructions of the government in any case."

"It is my aim, too, that every post should be occupied by a man who knows his business," I replied. "My reapportioning of positions will help to achieve this. It is evident, for example, that a democratic Smallholder official will make a better mayor than the bricklayer's assistant placed there by the workers' parties. And I am sure that an expert of appropriate background and training will make a far better foreign-trade conferee than the druggist's clerk who, without any training, is in charge of international trade negotiations at this moment."

"Substitutions may be advisable here and there," replied Voroshilov, "but I should like to ask you not to insist on a general redistribution of positions. It would only cause dissatisfactions."

"I can understand that this does not satisfy the minority," I answered, "but the present situation is the cause of the just dissatisfaction of the majority. I am therefore forced to insist on the proportionate distribution of posts."

This conversation made Voroshilov's opposition to my endeavors clear. Nevertheless our work of apportioning went on, and I consider it likely that the leftist bloc was formed mainly in order to combat, in closed ranks, the proportionate redistribution of government posts.

Soon the trade unions, too, were taken in, and then I saw that my first serious mistake was allowing the formation of the leftist bloc. I should not have permitted a separate alliance within the coalition, even if it had been motivated as a joint defense of the interests of the worker class. I should have stated that I would lead the coalition only on condition that each party retain its complete independence. The Soviet Union would no doubt have interfered in the dispute, but perhaps it would not so soon have ordered the Communist party to break with us openly.

But all these signs pointed to anything but calm. Naturally the political activities of the Communist party and the leftist bloc evoked strong criticism from Smallholder leaders who particularly singled out the attitude of Communist leaders and actions of the minister of the interior. But the people did not remain silent, either. They besieged the Smallholder deputies to take a firmer stand, who in turn brought pressure to bear upon me. Not only the workers' parties were uneasy; there developed again increasing restlessness among the peasantry and middle classes.

I tried to calm the excitement; but emotions on both sides were aroused, and a clash seemed inevitable. Some of our deputies favored steps that would have led unavoidably to the breakup of the coalition. But Tildy, the party's leaders, and I were of the opinion that we must avoid an upheaval and try to continue the coalition until the end of Soviet occupation.

The Communists called our protests in Parliament the "voice of reaction." They began to attack us vehemently, not only in their press but at mass meetings.

These organized denunciations were cleverly launched, always combined with demonstrations against high prices or other critical issues. Entirely new tactics came to light. In country towns they staged scenes of mass violence. Gangs would break into government offices, seize some non-Marxist official and beat him up, then announce that so-and-so had been thrown out of office by the will of the people.

On learning of these outrages, I at once protested to the minister of the interior and to the leaders of the workers' parties, calling upon them to put an immediate end to them and punish the participants. Szakasits announced emphatically that the Social Democratic party was not responsible, and immediately claimed that Social Democrats had also been beaten up and forcibly thrown out of their offices.

Rákosi at first replied hypocritically that these were spontaneous acts on the part of the people. Later, however, he confessed that they were ordered. He frankly admitted it when, before a Communist mass meeting, he said:

"Yes, there is a place in a democracy for spontaneous acts of the masses, and it is only right that the people should take justice into its own hands when it sees fit."

Had a throng tried to remove a Communist official by such methods, Rákosi, I am sure, would have immediately found an axiom proving that the people had no such prerogative.

The minister of the interior took no action. We felt that it might become necessary to mobilize our members in order to preserve stability. When this was indicated, mob action ceased in the districts with strong Smallholder peasantry. But in communities where our membership consisted mainly of meek city dwellers mob violence continued. I told the Communists that if they did not stop their violence the Smallholders would go into action; in a number of communities in the county of Szabolcs, gangs of terrorizing Communists were driven out to the last man. Thereupon the Communist party issued instructions to their gangs that violence should cease.

Attacks against the Smallholder party continued, however, aimed at forcing the men most objectionable to the Communists out of the party. Local Reds would not have been successful had not the Russians intervened.

First, Pushkin and Voroshilov protested to me about speeches made by some of our members in Parliament. Seeing that this had no effect, they resorted to more direct measures in support of the Communists.

Desider Sulyok made a forthright speech in Parliament, denouncing the activities of the Communist party. Following it, I received an official memorandum from the Allied Control Commission to the effect that Hungary was lagging in reparations payments, and hinting at stern consequences. This letter in itself would not necessarily have suggested special Soviet pressure. After all, they had a right to demand reparations payments. The following Sunday, however, there were a number of quite unmistakable free expressions of opinion at party meetings in the county districts. Whereupon, I received another letter in which the Russians recalled their food loan to the capital and demanded immediate payment in kind. It can easily be imagined that in the first days of March, 1946, no Hungarian government was in a position to repay the food loan.

A bold article in the *Kis Ujság* next day evoked another letter from the Soviet Union. This time we were reminded that Hungary was not fulfilling her obligations under the Potsdam decision and was not handing over German property in Hungary swiftly enough. Our government was warned to speed it up, and immediately!

At an interparty conference I spoke sharply in reply to a demand by Rákosi that we purge our party of "reactionary" elements. Almost immediately I received a letter from the Russians saying that the Red army was not being properly provided for and warning us that, if necessary, the army would again take requisitioning into its own hands.

After another resolute Smallholder expression of opinion, we received a letter from the Russians saying that Hungary was not fulfilling her trade agreements, and that the Soviet Union would therefore suspend its shipments of raw materials. This would have meant that our factories would be even less in position to deliver on the reparations account, and that our workers would be threatened by unemployment.

The notices contained demands that were strictly just; but their grouping and timing made it clear that they were being methodically used as political weapons. It was easy to perceive that the representatives of the Soviet Union in Hungary had abandoned the projected policy of basing friendship between the two countries on the Smallholders party, and that they were ready to back Communist violence against our party. This was the Soviet Union's first open attack against democracy in Hungary, proving unmistakably that it was ready to stand behind the Communist party through thick and thin.

Marshal Voroshilov, president of the Allied Control Commission, was leaving Hungary at this time. With his departure, the situation grew worse. Voroshilov, a leader of great prestige in the Soviet, could allow himself more freedom of action than his weak successor and "deputy," General Sviridov. Voroshilov, known at home as "Stalin's friend," was able at times to make at least some conciliatory gestures. Thus, while it was evident that Russia had dropped the idea of a common ticket at Voroshilov's suggestion, Sviridov always delayed acting on important questions, saying that he would first have to "talk it over" on the telephone with Voroshilov. Pushkin, who by his behavior had revealed his inflexible aim to aid the Communists by every means at his disposal, became master of the situation.

When, therefore, the situation had deteriorated to this point, I called on Pushkin and asked why Russia was exerting pressure on the government all at once. He denied that there was any particular reason behind it.

"These communications have absolutely no political purpose. They are simply notes to the Hungarian government reminding it of its obligations," he said.

"You also confirmed Voroshilov's pronouncement that Russia wishes to base her friendship with Hungary on the Smallholders party. If you overwhelm us with these demands at a time when there is tension between us and the leftist bloc, it is impossible not to discover the political motive," I answered.

"We have never said that we did not wish to be on good terms with other parties," said he, trying to twist the meaning of the well remembered statement. "The behavior of the Smallholder party during the past few weeks leaves much to be desired. I am afraid that its attitude is harmful to the relations between our countries and also serves to create dissatisfaction in the workers' parties. We are responsible for the internal peace of Hungary, but political tendencies must not be ascribed to communications of an economic nature."

"The attitude of the Communist party rightfully causes dissatisfaction in the Smallholders party," I replied. "Members of Parliament who comment on this are entirely justified. Not one had any thought of undermining friendly relations with the Soviet Union, but these demands by Russia do not in the least make for deepening friendship between our countries. It would be better if you were to persuade your 'Communist gentlemen' to take a more moderate stand."

"Reaction is still active in Hungary," answered Pushkin. "When it protests the speeches and articles that encourage reaction, the Communist party is only defending democracy."

"Democracy cannot be overthrown in Hungary," I countered, "and no one would dare attempt it. But Communist violence disheartens truly democratic elements, particularly when they see that the Soviet Union approves of it."

Pushkin made every effort to pretend discouragement.

"We don't wish to interfere in your internal politics. It seems as though flowers do not bloom for us in Hungary."

I saw that I should have to create tranquillity in some way, but sought to avoid concessions. I set to work to meet Russia's demands, or at least show that we were doing our best, even if our strength was not sufficient.

I told our reparations commissioner to notify all factories engaged in producing goods for reparations to speed up deliveries. I had a talk with the minister of supply, who informed me that the provisioning of the Red army was, in general, proceeding smoothly. A few counties were behind on food shipments, but he promised to see that the deficits were met. In conference with me regarding the fulfillment of our trade agreements, the minister of trade pointed out the difficulties but agreed to scrape together everything he could find in our impoverished country, in order to speed up shipments. I told Zoltán Vas to speed up the handing over of German property in Hungary. Then, in a conference with leaders in industrial production, I emphasized the importance of prompt reparations shipments. In short, I did all I could to take the wind out of Soviet sails.

In the meantime the Communists again took occasional recourse to mob action, coupled now with anti-Jewish demonstrations. It seemed that former Arrow Crossists, at home in this atmosphere, were giving voice to their own sentiments. Miners at Ózd and Sajószentpéter shouted anti-Semitic slogans and even assaulted Jewish citizens.

After a month and a half as premier, I found myself in a desperate situation, which I sought to judge calmly. The most popular step would have been to let the coalition break up; but I could not take this popular course and plunge the country into turmoil. It would have been vain to hope for help from the other great powers; the example of other occupied nations proved that the Communist party, aided by Russia, came out victorious in every internal struggle.

It had to be feared that in the event of an internal upheaval, no peace treaty would be signed with us; the only road open was to buy internal peace through concessions. Tildy continually encouraged it, and the leaders of the Smallholder party saw no other solution.

Instead of wasting the country's strength in useless battle I continued on the appointed road of trying to accomplish as much as feasible, avoiding conflicts where the Reds were strongest and maintaining a straight course wherever reason and good will could avail.

CHAPTER 46

The Smallholders Are Forced into Concessions

APPROACHING POLITICAL EVENTS CAST THEIR SHADOWS THESE WEEKS, which many consider as the beginning of the decline of democracy. Our opponents think we should not have made such sacrifices to reach agreements. But I sincerely believe that there was no alternative under the circumstances.

I could have refused, with my party, the demands of the Communists, but the consequences seemed ominous. Crowbars were distributed among the workers of Budapest as handy weapons in case of mass demonstrations; everywhere it was whispered, even among the reliable members of the police force, that old-guard Communists had received guns and pistols. Naturally the Communist police prevented us from checking the truth of the rumors. Incredible as it sounds, it is undoubtedly true that a mass of radicals equipped with crowbars and led by a group equipped with automatics could have taken over Budapest. We could not count on the Communist-commanded police, and as the Soviet permitted only a single company of Hungarian soldiers to remain in Budapest, calling out the army would have been a farce.

In view of the fact that during the two and one-half years following the defeat of the Germans we had been able to avoid spilling blood for political reasons, I personally could not permit the lives of thousands of Hungarians to be taken by their countrymen during this period. I dared not, by refusing a concession, clear the way for the Communist minority to assume power in the country.

In the Balkans, where during the last decade violence had decided political issues, leaders in my place would have chosen this road. We Hungarians, bled by others much too often in the course of our history, are hewn of different stone. We do not like to see our brethren fall uselessly in internal strife.

Another road was open to me; I could have resigned the premiership, because my conditions on accepting the post had not been fulfilled. But I simply could not run away from responsibility and leave my successor in a much worse situation.

Besides, this was the first concession made to the other political parties, and we could not know then that the agreement would be short-lived and not worth while; we honestly thought that with the sacrifices endured by the Smallholder party we should be able to reach or at least approach the time when the Soviet occupation would end and a real democracy begin.

When the Smallholder party received the communication of the leftist bloc demanding the expulsion of deputies who were against the coalition work within the government, upon the suggestion of Zoltán Tildy, we, with heavy hearts, were forced to advise twenty-two Smallholder members of Parliament to leave the party and so enable the coalition government to continue peacefully.

Following this, we began interparty negotiations about the conditions of the agreement. All coalition parties declared that they would fight reaction together, and agreed to bring the points of the election proclamation of the Independence Front to life. After the agreement, the noise of the political battles between the parties ceased; and it must be admitted that during the following months the most fruitful era of Hungarian reconstruction began.

All my life I had believed that public opinion is reflected by the mood of the people. After this agreement I awaited the signs with great interest. On the last day in March, the Smallholder party held a mass meeting at Pécs, the first since I became premier. Over a hundred thousand people assembled, and their boundless enthusiasm, coupled with the impressions gathered on the trip, where at each railroad stop large crowds hailed us, proved to me that the concessions made to the other parties had not shaken the Smallholders; the party continued in closed ranks behind its leaders and marched steadfastly on the appointed road.

CHAPTER 47

The Soviet Dictates Deportation

IN THE WAKE OF THE CONQUERING RUSSIAN ARMIES, SOVIET ADMINISTRA-tors tried to plant their ideologies in foreign soil and weed out any interfering elements. The Soviet did not promote agrarian reform for any social considerations, but to quickly eliminate the landowner class. It established the political clearance committees to pluck from public administration all who disagreed with the Russian conception of democracy. The more or less prominent leaders of the economic and financial life in the occupied countries were tolerated in the early years only because their removal would have disturbed industrial production and economic balance, thus endangering reparations payments to Russia. The expulsion of the German-speaking elements was not promoted by the Soviet to speed the transition into national states, but because Russia feared that in these circles they would be up against more anti-Sovietism than would be found among the natives of the country.

To gain their end, the Russians did not hesitate to distort the facts; for instance, construing the Potsdam agreement to the Hungarian government in such a fashion that it was "forced" to expel the German-speaking population.

When the Communist Leslie Rajk became minister of the interior, one of his very first moves was against the German-speaking population. He made his own plan, based on the decree issued during the premiership of Tildy, for the expulsion of all the Germans with the previously noted exceptions. As the actual deportations started, it was discovered what injustices lurked in the decree, and especially in the directives for its execution.

In the ministry of the interior a special section was established which dealt solely with the deportation of the German-speaking population. This office sent to the German regions "exemption commissions" with a chairman who represented the minister of the interior and members delegated by the political parties. These commissions secured from the Census Bureau the statistics on those who admitted German as their mother tongue and began compiling lists on which they marked especially those who during the last census had claimed German nationality, all who were members of the Nazi-sponsored Volksbund, and all who were members of the S.S. These lists were then exhibited publicly. Anyone who felt that he deserved exemption, by exemplary acts of loyalty to the country, could petition exclusion from the list.

The German settlements in Hungary were practically compounds, many of them over two hundred years old. Like the Pennsylvania Dutch in America, they had preserved their language and culture. Diligent people and good farmers, they had to their credit many advances in cattle breeding, particularly with two strains, the Simmenthaler and the Red-Spotted. They cooperated constantly with the agricultural societies and research laboratories of the government and operated excellent dairy cooperatives. Always maintaining friendly relations with the administrative leadership of the country, they ostensibly valued their prosperity and pleasant relationships in Hungary more highly than all the seductive promises of Hitler. A great number openly opposed all anti-Hungarian movements. The membership of the Volksbund was recruited from the poorer classes of the German-speaking population, who became its blind followers; only their concerted pressure forced an occasional well-to-do farmer to join the Pan-German movement.

The "exemption commissions," with an overwhelmingly leftist membership, did not consider the patriotic merits of the individual petitioner, but first looked into his wealth and party affiliations. If the man had become a member of the Communist, Social Democratic, or radical Peasant parties, they found an excuse for exemption, even if he had formerly been a member of the Nazi party, the Arrow Cross, or the Volksbund.

If the petitioner was a Smallholder, and in addition had wealth, a big house, land, or good farm buildings, he was not exempted even though he could prove conclusively that he actively fought National Socialism and the Volksbund.

There was naturally an appeal from the decision of the commission —alas, to the minister of the interior! The old members of the Smallholder party and the anti-Volksbund Germans sent in their appeals by the tens of thousands. Obviously the Smallholders, in their dire need, asked for help from the national leadership of the party and also from me personally. For weeks I devoted my free time to each of these appeals, and took steps on behalf of every petitioner; but soon I was swamped and discovered that I could hardly save thousands by handling individual cases. However, I saw clearly that if the government continued to place responsibility for the political crimes of the past on an entire national minority, true democracy in Hungary would be irreparably undermined. I decided to take steps to effect a fundamental change in the decree itself issued by the Tildy government.

My proposal to have the decree changed met with determined opposition from the Communist party. As a last resort against my accusations, Minister Rajk declared that he could not accede to a revision of the decree because the Soviet would never agree to it.

Unexpectedly the Americans came to my assistance; one day General Key, the American member of the Control Commission, communicated to me that the decree dealing with the expulsion of the German-speaking population was issued on a mistaken conception, for the pact of Potsdam did not "force" but "empowered" the Hungarian government to deport the Swabians. The letter also announced that the American Zone of Occupation in Germany could accept only a restricted number of such resettled people, as the military government of the zone must be guided by social and humanitarian principles in these cases.

I went to see General Sviridov, who usually represented the Soviet rather than the Allied Control Commission in his dealings with the Hungarian government, and informed him that I wanted to have the decree changed:

"Minister Rajk says you would not agree to a change."

"Why change it?" asked Sviridov. "There is a proviso in it anyway that democratic Swabians can be exempted."

"I am absolutely against collective expulsion. The decree has to be changed to deal specifically with the guilty. Any measure which compels proof of innocence must be unjust."

"Germans do not deserve consideration," exclaimed Sviridov.

"I ask you to remember that Russia claims her national minorities live under ideal conditions. We Hungarians have always treated our minorities well. The guilty must be removed, but no pressure exerted on the innocents," I answered.

"Do you know that the Americans have already interfered in the German expulsion?" interjected Sviridov.

"Naturally, as you yourself transmitted to me the letter of General Key which dealt with this question." In these days the American and British members of the Control Commission were permitted to maintain contact with me only through the Soviet chairman, and it was obvious that General Key's letter had gone through the hands of Sviridov. "The letter of General Key strengthens my point. If the American army is slowing up resettlement, we could not deport all of the Swabians anyway. From some regions we should deport the innocents, and from others be forced to leave the guilty ones in peace—a gross injustice."

On this basis the talk continued for a few hours; late at night Sviridov gave up and declared that he would accede to the change of the decree so that first the four guilty categories, as listed by me, should be deported. At the same time automatic exemption must be granted to those of German birth who, openly declaring themselves Hungarian nationals, had not taken part in any activities against their adopted country.

In agreeing, Sviridov imposed one condition: that this order of the minister of the interior must be a confidential directive to the executives and administrators, not to be made public.

This condition worked against my cause, for the minister of the interior ordered all who did not belong to the first four categories, as listed in the decree, automatically exempted. The administrators had made this public in all places, and the petitions for exemptions ceased, but—here was where the close cooperation between the minister of the interior and the Soviet bore fruit—nobody was eliminated from the original lists. And when later the expulsions were resumed and the resettlement of the Hungarians expelled from Czechoslovakia had to be undertaken, the guilty categories of Germans were to be concentrated in certain regions, to make place for the returning Hungarians; it developed that the administration tried to do it on the basis of the original lists. Again the same situation arose—thousands of innocents raised their cry for help and every well-meaning member of the government was forced to devote himself to saving the guiltless from deportation.

Undoubtedly there are still a great number of Germans in Hungary who have violated the ideals of the Hungarian state and injured its people. It would naturally be good to be rid of them, but after French Foreign Minister Bidault proposed in Moscow that the population of Germany should not be further densified but rather decreased, it is very improbable that the deportations can be resumed unless the Soviet dictates, in concert with the Hungarian Communists, to the government controlled by them, irresponsible, inhuman actions.

But the Soviet worries little about irresponsibility or inhumanity when it concerns only "people."

CHAPTER 48

Looking Across the Fence

IN THE SPRING IT BECAME CERTAIN THAT A PEACE CONFERENCE WOULD assemble during 1946 to do no more than map the treaties with the so-called satellites of Germany. The Hungarian government faced the problem of creating at least a bearable atmosphere for the time when the fate of Hungary would come before the great powers. Among many other reasons, it was desirable to establish personal contacts with the outstanding leaders of the victorious powers because the security of our ascending economy depended upon concrete support. Another reason was the painful, daily pressure by the Soviet. We felt that we should share with the other Allied powers our friendship with Russia, and so interest western aid in the preservation of our independence.

The fact that Russia occupied Hungary made it obvious that the Hungarian government must trek to Moscow to pay its respects to the government of the Soviet Union before visiting any other nation. Any going west without having first visited Moscow would have meant political suicide. Also, the Communists could not object; on the contrary, they found it advantageous to their own political aims to strengthen our ties with Moscow by a personal meeting between the Hungarian and Russian leaders. I felt that by going to Moscow we might be able to improve our relationship and avoid being victimized again by such Soviet pressure as we had had to suffer in March, when they forced us to mutilate the Smallholders' party.

When I told Pushkin of the plan, he gave no hint that he had already been informed of it, and every other word spoken at cabinet meetings, by the Communists. He said that the visit might be feasible in the very near future.

Under these circumstances the Communists could not continue refusing to discuss Hungarian peace aims. It was obvious that a government delegation could not simply vacation in Moscow, and pay homage to Stalin. Such a visit must not only improve both economic and political relations, but, more important, win friendly understanding of Hungarian aims in the peace treaty from the Soviet.

The President of the Republic appointed me to head the delegation, with Vice Premier Szakasits, Ministers Gyöngyösi and Gerö as members. When we met with President Tildy, I also invited Rákosi. I asked him to state his position regarding Hungary's peace aims, and he acerbly admitted that now *he would have to* consider the Hungarian peace treaty.

We in the Smallholder party were fully aware that the aims of a vanquished Hungary could only be very limited. We considered Yugoslavia as one of the victors and did not want to introduce any requests whatsoever against that country. From the moral point of view we certainly could not consider Czechoslovakia as one of the victorious states. While the Czechs might have had some feeble claim to such recognition, Slovakia, under Tiso, had most ardently fought for Hitler, exceeding even the Nazis in inhuman violence. With her internal strife, disunity, and petty partisan skirmishes, she could certainly not claim the title of a victor. Knowing that the great powers had before the war given certain guarantees to Czechoslovakia and would thus have to maintain her semblance of a victor, we decided not to press our claims for the purely Hungarian-populated territory across the border but only to ask that the great powers insure equal citizenship rights to the Hungarian minorities living in Czechoslovakia. In case Czechoslovakia should insist upon a purely artificial transformation from a state of nationalities into a national state, we would demand that with the transfer of population there should be a transfer of territory. The densely populated Hungary, already cut down in size, would not permit the settlement of additional hundreds of thousands.

In view of the fact that Rumania had proved to have been a more willing satellite than Hungary, and had entered the war against Russia earlier and under less duress, we proposed to announce our claim to part of Transylvania, which had belonged to the Hungarian realm for countless generations. Neither Rákosi nor Gerö could object to this plan.

Rákosi, letting us suspect that he relied on certain Soviet information, proposed that of the 103,000 square kilometers involved we should claim not more than 4,000 to 10,000 square kilometers; in which case we could hope for a certain amount of support. In the case of Transylvania, our claim was based partly on a clause in the armistice agreement which stated that the great powers would grant Transylvania "or the larger part of it" to Rumania; we assumed that the case of Transylvania was not closed although Russian occupation authorities had installed the Rumanian administration everywhere.

Foreign Minister Gyöngyösi informed me that his ministry had two solutions in preparation. One involved approximately 4,000 square kilometers, Hungary's minimal claim; the second covered a territory of less than 20,000 square kilometers, hardly one-fourth of historically Hungarian Transylvania. His plan, as against the Rákosi proposal, was finally adopted, and we decided to find out in Moscow which could enjoy Soviet support. It was also decided to ask the Soviet government to spread reparations payments over a period exceeding the six years which was fixed arbitrarily, to ask for the return of Hungarian prisoners of war, and to have a charge of fifteen million dollars canceled, which the Soviet army made for the restoration of some railroad lines, most of which were not even on Hungarian territory.

The plans for the trip to Moscow naturally remained no secret. The Ministers of the United States and Great Britain called on me to ask for information, which I was only too glad to give them in detail. After I had explained the reasons for the trip they both approved of it heartily.

I prepared with the high hopes that it would lessen my nation's burden, begin a new era in our foreign relations, and vindicate my political faith that an independent Hungary could voluntarily be a friendly neighbor to Russia.

CHAPTER 49

Moscow

DURING THE FIRST DAYS OF APRIL, MINISTER PUSHKIN CALLED FORMALLY
and informed me that the Soviet government regarded the Hungarian
delegation as its own guest. We agreed to leave on the 10th of April;
in addition to Pushkin the counselor of the legation, Grigoriev, was to
accompany us. Grigoriev was especially elated by the trip, because, as
he said, he had never met Stalin personally and now he was even going to
talk with him. Grigoriev spoke Hungarian perfectly; until the summer
of 1946, when he was unexpectedly ordered back to Moscow, he was
the constant interpreter for the Soviet officials in Hungary.

We took along our wives, and the party also included my private
secretary, Dr. Francis Kapócs, and the secretary of Minister Gerö. We
traveled straight across the Carpathian Mountains to Moscow in the
luxuriously outfitted American Douglas plane of Marshal Voroshilov.

Flying over the Carpathians is never very easy, because air currents
from north and south, and east and west, meet there, making rough
weather even for the very high-flying planes. On the day of our flight
the weather was especially rough. Pushkin tried his best to make us
forget the plane's unpleasant bounces; he soon had the table set with
the choicest foods and wines and endeavored to create a merry atmosphere among the passengers.

After four and one-half hours, we neared fog-shrouded Moscow.
Until then the weather had been clear, so that we could easily compare
the Hungarian and Russian landscapes. In Hungary the fields were
green, the fall seed had already sprouted, along the white ribbons of
highways groups of red-roofed houses marked the villages. Beyond the
Carpathians the landscape was gray, with no sign of green, budding
crops; and instead of roads there were winding paths, along which
sparse black dots indicated villages.

Because of the dense fog the pilot of the plane, a colonel and member of the Soviet parliament, apparently received orders not to land at
Moscow but at another airdrome. Pushkin, who knew that some kind
of reception had been prepared at Moscow, insisted that the plane land
there.

This was my first flight. My head was pounding, my ears were tingling, and my stomach was whirling as we landed. If the choice had been mine I would have gone to bed instantly; but this was impossible. As soon as the wheels came to a stop on the concrete runway, excitement spread among the Russians in the plane. "Molotov," they whispered to one another.

Truly, there at the head of the diplomatic corps stood Molotov, greeting us with strict observance of the protocol. With the help of Grigoriev he introduced to us the diplomatic representatives of the thirty-four nations who had come to the airfield. Later we were told that this was a Class Triple A reception.

Molotov then presented the military commandant of Moscow, who asked us to accept the presentation of arms by the honor guard of the Moscow garrison. The band played the Hungarian and Russian national anthems. I was told that the band leader had received the score only two days earlier; on the reverse side of the sheets was printed the march of the Hungarian fascists. It was fortunate that the band had not learned the wrong side.

After reviewing the guard I was led by Molotov to a group of microphones and asked whether I cared to speak on the Soviet radio to the people of Russia. Since I felt ill, I really did not want to; but I could hardly evade such an invitation and spoke for a few minutes. As was expected and desired from southeastern European politicians, I delivered flowery remarks on Soviet friendship and praised Soviet generosity.

Then we were finally taken to our lodgings. The members of the delegation and their staffs received luxurious apartments in the Hotel Moskva, while my wife and I were driven to a little boyar palace in Ostrovsky Street. This exquisitely furnished house was serviced throughout by a selected staff, under expert direction. It was said that my predecessor in the little palace was the prime minister of one of the central Asiatic countries. A large detachment of palace guardsmen, under a captain, was on constant duty, supplemented by a large number of civilians from the Russian secret service.

There was no program for the day of our arrival, but a special motion picture was shown for us that evening in the palace. So began the lavish hospitality which continued throughout our stay. Three times a day the richly decked tables reminded us of the Hedonistic despots of the East.

The next day Molotov gave us a noon dinner at which Marshal

Voroshilov appeared, already complaining of his health. During the meal both drank toasts to Hungarian democracy and us; afterwards they retired with me and Foreign Minister Gyöngyösi. Molotov inquired what subjects we wished to discuss with Stalin and declared, before we had a chance to go into details, that we might introduce any questions we chose since our negotiations would not be restricted.

Molotov's wife showered my wife with unusual attentions—once by asking her for photographs of our three children. A few days later, on a visit to a chocolate factory, they were returned to her, built into huge chocolate Easter eggs.

In the evening we were taken to the opera, to hear the famous *Prince Igor*. The Moscow Opera House makes an overwhelming impression upon the visitor. Although lacking any training in classical music, I cannot forget the performances in Moscow. During our stay we attended several historical operas or ballets; this musical institution was already world-famous during the reign of the Czars, but the Soviet government has lifted it to new heights.

One evening we witnessed a most astonishing mass emotional expression, during the performance of *Ivan Susanin,* with Russia's most famous baritone, Michailov, in the title role. The story deals with the attack of the Poles on unprepared Russia. They are storming toward Moscow when, in a small village, they try to force the nobleman Ivan Susanin to guide them. In patriotic fervor he misleads them into a large forest, where the cruel Russian winter will annihilate them. When the Poles discover the ruse they prepare for his execution, and Ivan Susanin sings a dramatic farewell to his family. This scene received a burst of applause from the audience. Next, Susanin falls on his knees, bows his head and, crossing himself, remains kneeling in silent, fervent prayer. The audience broke out in frenetic applause, continuing to hail him throughout the prayer. To us it was an incredible demonstration; even a quarter-century of Communism had failed to destroy the religious fervor of the people.

On the third day, the Foreign Ministry notified us that Stalin would receive us that evening for official discussions. The Hungarian delegation was accompanied by the Minister to the Soviet Union, Julius Szekfü, the Russian Minister to Hungary, Pushkin, and the official interpreter, Counselor Grigoriev. At the entrance to the Kremlin we were joined by a military car which led us to Stalin's quarters.

He received us, in the presence of Molotov, in his office furnished in simple, hard wood. Dressed in a marshal's tunic, he wore a single decoration on his chest; hanging from a red ribbon was the gold star of a "Hero of the Soviet Union."

Looking at us through half-closed eyes, he shook hands silently and with no sign of cordiality. He motioned us to the end of a long conference table and himself sat opposite. Between us was Grigoriev, the interpreter.

After thanking him for our gilded reception, I told him first of the progress of democracy in Hungary and the diligence and accomplishments of its people. Proceeding with the reasons for our coming to Moscow, I began with the economic aspects and drew his attention to the difficulties in the reparations payments. Stalin interrupted:

"We want to help you, so we shall extend the time for the payment of reparations from six to eight years. This will make payments easier."

Thanking him for this concession, I requested that the prisoners of war be released. Stalin again answered immediately.

"We will begin to return the prisoners of war even before signing the peace. It will proceed as transportation facilities and administrative procedure permit."

"I am very grateful for this, and would like to ask the Premier to agree that, until the release of all of the Hungarian prisoners of war has been completed, they shall be allowed to correspond with their relatives."

"It shall be," answered Stalin.

Minister Gerö then presented the request of the Hungarian government to have the $15,000,000 charge for the restoration of railroad lines canceled, especially because most of the lines enumerated in the bill of the Russian army were not on Hungarian territory but on Czechoslovakian, Rumanian, or Austrian. Gerö spoke very plainly and without the slightest diplomatic courtesy.

Stalin cut him off: "Do not pay it!"

I proceeded to present Hungary's peace aims. To the statement that Hungary had no claims on Yugoslavia Stalin nodded approvingly. Regarding our possible differences with Czechoslovakia, he listened attentively and responded immediately:

"I believe in an exchange of populations. A nation has no greater treasure than its people, and its increase is beneficial to the country. Nevertheless I acknowledge that you are just in desiring equal citizenship rights for the Hungarian population in Czechoslovakian territory, and I state herewith that the Soviet Union will support such undertakings."

In expressing my gratitude for his statement, I thought that the return of a few million Russians would pose no problem as their vast territory had still wide spaces to support them. This was not the case in Hungary: on each square kilometer lived nearly a hundred souls, and to further increase the density of the population would lead to an ultimate decline of the living standard of all of the Hungarian people.

We proceeded to discuss the territorial questions relating to Transylvania. Stalin asked whether we had brought maps with us. Gyöngyösi unfolded them and pointed out the territories Hungary desired to have returned. Stalin turned to Molotov.

"How does the section of the armistice agreement that deals with Transylvania read?"

"It says that, if Rumania fulfills her obligations enumerated in the armistice agreement, it will be granted Transylvania or the larger part of it," answered Molotov.

"Yes," Stalin said, turning to us. "This section of the armistice agreement gives you an opportunity to introduce the question of Transylvanian territory."

Gerö then brought up the idea that Hungary was willing to sell the Soviet Union our coal mines at Petrozsény in the Rumanian section of Transylvania, to lessen the load of reparations payments. Stalin answered that he would instruct the minister in charge to study its feasibility.

Stalin's manner improved appreciably as the conference proceeded; he seemed to warm up by degrees, and at the conclusion turned to us jokingly:

"It seems as if you had some trouble with the money. How does Hungarian inflation stand today?"

Taking a deep breath, I used this opening to describe the great difficulties Hungarian economy was experiencing.

As the two-hour conference ended we were inclined to believe that it had accomplished something in the economic field; as regards our peace aims we at least had received no rejection and so hoped that the Soviet might remain neutral.

In leaving, we told how the Germans and their partners, the Arrow Crossists, had ransacked and plundered Hungary. Laughing out loud, Stalin remarked:

"Say, our soldiers carried away quite a bit from there too—even if you do not talk about that now."

Descending the staircase, I thought bitterly how good it would be to settle with Stalin for what, according to his own admission, the Soviet soldiers had stolen in Hungary.

The following morning we paid our respects to Marshal Voroshilov in his offices in the Kremlin. In the afternoon Molotov gave a large reception in honor of the Hungarian delegation, where I met General Bedell Smith, the American ambassador, with whom, a few months later, I had a very interesting meeting in Paris. All the diplomats at the reception showed great interest in Hungary's affairs.

When, a few days later, I reciprocated by inviting the leading Soviet dignitaries and the diplomatic corps to be our guests in the palace on Ostrovsky Street, Molotov pulled Gyöngyösi, Pushkin, and me into a corner.

"We have studied the Hungarian aims regarding Transylvanian territory. Adjustment would be easier if you could reach an understanding with the Rumanians. I think it would be right for you to initiate negotiations with Groza's government."

"I doubt very much that we could accomplish anything if the negotiations had to originate with us," I answered, surprised by Molotov's advice. "Elections have not yet been held in Rumania. For a maze of internal political reasons, Groza can take no steps which would satisfy Hungary."

"Still, direct negotiations should be tried," insisted Molotov.

"It would be worth while to begin them only if the advisability of such negotiations is suggested to the Rumanian government," interjected Minister Gyöngyösi.

"I will state only that it would be right if you would 'initiate' the direct negotiations. The Rumanians either accept or decline, but *you* have done *your* duty." Molotov also told us that the reparations payment extension to eight years had been approved; no further time extension could be granted because the Rumanians and the Finns had received the same. The railroad repair bill would be canceled—the Soviet Council of Ministers had agreed; Minister Gerö was to discuss the details with the Soviet Minister of Transportation. Molotov also let us know that the Council was studying acquisition of the coal mines at Petrozsény.

When there were no conferences or official functions our time was nevertheless fully occupied with a "program of education for the guests of the Soviet." One day we had to inspect the exhibition of Red army war booty. On extensive grounds on the bank of the river Moskva they had assembled an impressive collection of captured guns and war material.

The next day they showed us a tool factory, called the "Red Proletar." The manager said that when the German armies neared Moscow this entire factory was transplanted to Siberia. When the Germans had been chased out of Russia half of the plant had been returned here, half stayed there, and now the production of each of the plants equaled that of the prewar unit.

"Thus," the manager added, "from each transplanted factory we created two."

We inspected the chocolate factory called "October Revolution," the tobacco plant, "Dukat," where cigarettes with paper mouthpieces are manufactured. In each of the factories one or two workers were called upon to tell, under excellent dramatic coaching, how much better their lot was than it had been under the Czar. This was undoubtedly true, for in these exhibition factories the social welfare of the workers was kept on a very high level. We saw the Kremlin museum, with its tremendous wealth and jewels amassed throughout Russian history, the historical museum and the Tretjakov collection. In the art galleries hung portraits of figures in Czarist Russia whom the Communists think of as progressives. There were many relics from the time of Ivan the Terrible and Peter the Great.

Next to these, naturally, Soviet art has a prominent place. The paintings and busts of Lenin, Stalin, Molotov, and Voroshilov stare at the visitor from every corner, niche, and wall. Because Russia had just emerged from her greatest war and greatest victory, the Soviet government publicizes Russia as a military nation; everywhere one notes the glorification of the Soviet soldier and his arms.

In the museums the paintings and the busts depict the heroism of the Russian soldier with the same conspicuous animation as the twenty-nine marble stations of the undoubtedly beautiful Moscow subway.

Two days before our departure Stalin invited us for supper. The question of dress caused great excitement both among the Russians and among our legation personnel. The invitation called for tails and white tie, and I, as a peasant, had never had a tail coat or dinner jacket. At social affairs, even as premier, I simply wore a dark suit and, if the occasion called for tails, generally wore the festive garb of the Hungarian peasant, a simply trimmed black suit with high black boots. I did not want my peasant brethren to get the impression that my changed station of life had caused me to drift, even outwardly, from my people. Alas, the rest of the Hungarian delegation had no tails or dinner jacket either.

The Chief of Protocol of the Russian Foreign Office apparently worried himself sick over this drastic deviation from the accepted mode of diplomatic garb; the members of the Hungarian Legation in Moscow were simply panic-stricken. Fortunately no tragedy developed from our sartorial simplicity; when the members of the Soviet government heard that we would not wear dress suits, they, too, appeared in ordinary business clothing. But for a while it looked very, very serious—to some.

At the supper I was seated on Stalin's right; next to me sat Grigoriev for the translations. The menu was typically Russian; there seemed to be no end to the numberless courses. Stalin ate only bits from each course, but between courses smoked a long Russian cigarette with a paper mouthpiece. Molotov, on the other hand, busied himself by delivering a toast before each course. First to Tildy, then to me, then to each of the Hungarian delegation, one by one. After he finished, I thanked him in the name of all of us. Then Stalin rose and delivered a very interesting, in fact very reassuring, message with his toast.

Many times I meditated about the divergence between Soviet political action and the high-toned speech of Stalin. One could not but admire the high ethical levels of the human spirit it conveyed, and at times I felt that the Soviet leaders do not execute the policy of Stalin because the toast of that night and all his personal statements made to me during our stay in Moscow have always been in direct contrast with the acts of the Soviet government.

"In my opinion," said Stalin, "it is easy to create friendly relations between Russia and Hungary. The Soviet Union never sinned against Hungary. Czarist Russia, speeding to the help of the Austrian armies in 1849, committed a grave assault against Hungarian interests; but we shot the last Czar in 1920, and we cannot assume responsibility for their misdeeds. Soviet Russia never wanted to be involved in a war with Hungary. The leaders of Hungary declared war on Russia, which under such circumstances had to defend herself. . . .

"In 1944 the Soviet Union was glad to receive Horthy's offer of an armistice; but Horthy was weak and could not enforce the temporary agreement signed by his emissaries. Hungary has leaders today who sincerely love the people, and this is an assurance she will stay on the correct political road, in the future. The Soviet Union does not wish to meddle in the internal affairs of Hungary; in general the peoples of small nations are frightened needlessly of Soviet oppression. If the Soviet Union would undertake to oppress or influence small nations it would betray the ideologies of Lenin and invalidate its practice in the past. The Soviet state consists of a union of many nationalities; among these are some who, under the Czar, were destined for extinction. To these we gave protection and culture, and today, advancing swiftly, they enjoy their own flourishing life. . . .

"We are conscious of the fact that each and every small nation contributes its own to the treasury of mankind; with its own culture it enriches life throughout the globe. Consequently, if we do not influence or suppress small nationalities within our borders, this should be a guarantee for the small nations beyond our borders that we have no desire to exert influence upon them or oppress them. We wish only to live with them in peace and friendship. It is our conception that there can be true friendship between a major power and a small country without endangering the independence of the latter."

I must admit that these words had a quieting effect on us, because during our stay in Moscow we had been impressed with the singular respect Stalin enjoyed and his dictatorial power. We had no reason to assume that, not long after the visit to Moscow, the policy of the Soviet government toward Hungary and the other eastern European nations would deviate so far from the ideology expressed by Stalin that evening.

In fact I felt more convinced that the actions of the Soviet authorities in the countries occupied by the Red army were mostly ungoverned, and that on the basis of Stalin's statements a firmer position could be taken against them.

Sipping his demi-tasse, Stalin turned to me:

"How is Regent Horthy?"

"The only news we have is what trickles into Hungary," I answered.

"I ask you, do not condemn Horthy," said Stalin, to the astonishment of those present. "First, Horthy is an old man; secondly, one should not be permitted to forget that he made the offer for an armistice in the fall of 1944."

The faces of the few Hungarian Communists who were present on this occasion flushed as they heard the magnanimous declaration of Stalin.

"I'll show you a peasant movie, if you like," said Stalin, and after my acceptance led us to his private motion picture theater, where we sat through two very long films depicting life on the Russian kolkhoz farms.

We were sitting in large, comfortable lounge chairs; in front of everyone stood a small table with champagne and dishes heaped with chocolates and fruits. I sat between Molotov and Stalin; Grigoriev was behind me and translated occasionally, when the picture was not self-explanatory.

During one of the beautiful shots of some grazing grounds, Szakasits, our vice premier, suddenly broke the silence:

"Generalissimo! Only a people led by a man like you is able to accomplish such miracles!"

I did not see Stalin's face, but his answer was translated to me: "Please, I am not a Frenchman." And he added, "At one time the French loved compliments, but I do not."

Stalin told me he had seen these movies several times, but always found new joy in viewing them. He explained some of the scenes with youthful enthusiasm.

After five and one half hours with Stalin, we took our leave. He had proved a most gracious host; his early coolness had thawed, and as we were leaving the Kremlin he bade us a warm farewell.

We, the members of the Hungarian government, all simple people, not burdened with the cunning of professional diplomacy, judged everything in good faith. Complacent to a certain degree, we were satisfied to have done good work in Moscow. We believed that the friendship between the two countries would be sincere; and, since Pushkin had heard all Stalin's statements and had been a party to all the conferences, we thought that the ideology expressed by Stalin would have its effect on the attitude of the Russians in Hungary.

CHAPTER 50

In Retrospect

EVERY MAN, WHEN TRAVELING IN A FOREIGN COUNTRY, IS CURIOUS TO see the sights that most interest him. During our stay in Russia I tried several times to emphasize my desire to see some of the kolkhozes, the

Communist cooperative farms. Up to the very last minute of our visit, I hoped that this wish would be granted; it would have meant a great deal to me. Having spent the greater part of my life on the soil, and being trained accordingly, I could have pierced their "milk and honey" camouflage and sized up their real worth. Frankly I hoped to observe any improvements that we in Hungary could adopt to our own advantage. But I had no success in my attempt to view the farms; most of the Soviet officials were perplexed by my suggestion and indicated that they had to refer it to the respective department—I never found out which one. Others, like the chief of Soviet protocol, just smiled and had the interpreter tell me that the farms were "too muddy."

We encountered this muddy alibi when we, not suspecting anything extraordinary, simply wanted to use a few "unscheduled" hours to leave our gilded cage and walk on the streets of Moscow. Actually we wanted to buy a souvenir for President Tildy in a near-by antique shop which Minister Gerö, an old Muscovite, had recommended. It really never entered my mind that there could be anything wrong with our strolling on the sidewalks of Moscow.

When the chief of the officials "assigned to our service" for our comfort was informed of our intention to go for a walk, he almost had a fit. The very idea seemed to upset everyone along the line. Up to now we had entered our luxurious limousines under guard and had always been driven through the city at high speed. Now, when we wanted to walk, they insisted that we should be driven wherever we wanted to go, but walk—"niet." We were finally driven three blocks, then permitted to walk the remaining block—but in such fashion!

Our little group was preceded at a distance of about fifty feet by two chief detectives; ten feet behind them marched the captain of our guard with a staff who ordered everyone off the sidewalk; they were followed by numerous NKVD men, who also cleared half the roadway of all passers-by; and finally, in a neat little vacuum, came our group, accompanied by the "gentlemen from the protocol." I do not think it is necessary to describe what followed us. The army would have been adequate to suppress a full-size South American uprising. By the time we entered the store all other customers had been pushed into a corner and surrounded by our friends from the NKVD.

When Marshal Voroshilov, or General Sviridov, or any of the Russian potentates appeared in public in Hungary, they did not need such "hospitality"; and it never entered the minds of the Hungarian officials charged with public security to provide such protection from our own people.

Two things struck me about the people I saw in Moscow. Most of the faces on the streets were haggard and tired, and their clothes, while not ragged, were depressingly uniform and ill-fitting. According to western standards, they all seemed to be stamped, in different sizes, from the same die. They seemed to be human robots, scientifically numbered and catalogued.

As a human being in a foreign country with strange customs, I was struck by another incident. While we were visiting a tool factory, one of the Hungarian Communists proposed that our itinerary should include the welfare institutions of the plant. This side trip was not premeditated; the plant was in the suburban factory district, and we had to leave the main structure and walk across a street to reach the hospital and kindergarden. As we left the building through a side door, our NKVD men suddenly stopped us. Along the street uniformed men with tommy-guns were driving about a hundred men and women. A Russian major of our entourage ran over and gave orders to the tommy-gunners. While we were kept standing, frozen with an astonishment we dared not display, the manacled mass of human misery was speedily ushered into the alleyways of the factory, and we were led in a wide circle away from it.

It will always be one of my greatest regrets that I did not meet the "common man" of Russia, had no chance to hear his conception of democracy, and was unable to observe the real conditions of the people who till the Russian soil.

Naturally my report to the Hungarian people had to be restricted to official subjects. In addition to presenting all details to the president and the cabinet, I decided to make a report in open session of Parliament, to encourage even a short debate about Soviet-Hungarian relations.

Just as the Hungarian people expressed little enthusiasm about our trip to Moscow, my report was received coldly. The behavior of the Red soldiers in Hungary and the methods of the Communists prevented the public from expecting anything pleasant from the Soviet Union; besides, it was openly suspected that we had had to make some concessions to the Russians. The only thing that brought a sigh of relief from the average citizen was the fact that I could openly state, remembering Stalin's declaration, that after our trip to Moscow we did not have to fear that Hungary would be forced to.join the Union of Soviet Socialist Republics as a member state.

The real politicians were thoroughly satisfied. I remember well how enthusiastic were our young Smallholder deputies, later charged with conspiracy by the Soviet; they envisioned a future in which Hungary's relationship to the Soviet need not be based on the Communist party. They hoped the Russians would recognize the political wisdom of accepting the friendship of the Hungarian people when, according to parliamentary laws, the Smallholders would govern the country.

The experiences with Stalin inspired me to show my good faith and my belief that the pleasant Russo-Hungarian relationship could be made lasting; thus I again took the matter of the fulfillment of our obligations to Russia into my own hands. To head the office of reparations, I appointed the strong-handed former Lord-Lieutenant of Szabolcs, John Eröss, and made it his business to visit every plant working on reparations orders and reduce as much as possible the backlog of deliveries. I asked the National Association of Manufacturers to instruct the factories to devote increased attention to the delivery of reparations goods on time, because otherwise I should be forced to recommend action against those who intentionally increased the backlog. New arrangements were made, more methodical in supplying the occupation forces, and we decided to issue "wheat bonds" to farmers from whom produce or livestock was requisitioned to feed the Red army or for deliveries on the reparations account. It would not have been honest to pay them in inflated money, for by the time it would reach them from Budapest, they would not be able to buy anything with it. We did this not only to reimburse them for requisitioned goods, but also because we did not know when requisitioning for the Red army and the reparations account would end. When the government would be forced to ask them for supplies in the future, we did not want them to refuse.

We also began to assemble the goods we were to deliver to Russia in accordance with the trade treaty. With superhuman efforts we finally assembled part of the products which we were to supply to the Soviet in exchange for raw materials, and began to ship them to Russia. Negotiations with General Sviridov began regarding the painful loan of food the Red army granted to the Communist mayor of Budapest, and an agreement was reached about what parts would be repaid before and after the harvest.

For a long time negotiations had been under way for the establishment of Russo-Hungarian corporations, in accordance with the economic agreement signed in the fall of 1945 by the two countries. I invited the two commissions to meet with me and, after endless discussions, was finally able to convince the Soviet that the rights and jurisdiction they were demanding for the general managers of these corporations, to be sent from Russia by the Soviet, would be contrary to Hungarian sovereignty. The Russians agreed that the directors' acts would be subject to Hungarian law, and we assented to the establishment of two or three such corporations.

It was my wish to reduce the differences between the two countries and, if possible, eliminate all obstacles to friendly relations with the Soviet.

CHAPTER 51

The Soviet Janus

ALL THE THEATERS OF BUDAPEST WERE GIVING SHOWS, WITH THE EXception of one which had been bombed. The painters and sculptors were having one exhibition after another. The artistic life of Hungary was again in full swing, as if the artists wanted to replace treasures lost during the war; their efforts seemed to concentrate on reawakening, through art, the people's love of beauty during the dark days of history.

On the evening of May 7, at a charity dinner at the Hungarian artists' club known as the Nest, my secretary whispered to me that earlier that day the Foreign Ministers' Conference in Paris had reached a decision on Transylvania and they would recommend to the Peace Conference that Rumania receive "all" of Transylvanian territory.

I could not believe this, and asked him to seek confirmation through the official news agency. Upon receiving it, I informed Foreign Minister Gyöngyösi by telephone that it would be best if I saw Soviet Minister Pushkin that same evening.

Pushkin knew very well why I came; I asked immediately if he had heard about the Paris decision.

"Yes, I heard something," answered Pushkin.

"This decision is overthrowing all of our calculations," I said.

"How does the Soviet government reconcile its stand during our visit in Moscow with this decision?"

"Please understand," he replied. "First of all I am not certain that the decision has been made as reported; second, if such decision has been arrived at, it was not proposed by the Soviet Union."

"Mr. Minister, you will remember that Molotov suggested in Moscow that we 'initiate' negotiations with the Rumanian government regarding Transylvania. We made the right step and sent Envoy Sebestyén to personally call on Premier Groza in Bucharest, who most decidedly refused to enter into any negotiations on the subject. When we called this possibility to the attention of your foreign minister, Mr. Molotov, he answered that Hungary can only benefit by initiating negotiations with Rumania. In your opinion, sir, where and when shall we enjoy this 'benefit' now, after the decision of the foreign ministers?"

Pushkin went into a dissertation far afield from the subject, but I pressed the issue.

"You will probably remember that Premier Stalin, when I took the liberty of bringing up the question of Transylvanian territory, acknowledged that Hungary had a right, in accordance with the armistice agreement, to raise the issue; he examined the maps of the disputed areas personally and indicated that Russia would not oppose the return of some Transylvanian territory to Hungary."

"You have learned Moscow's attitude toward Hungary, and this should satisfy you," were Pushkin's parting words.

The next day, meeting with the Minister from the United States, I could not hide my bitterness about the Paris decision, which by this time had become public not only in Hungary but throughout the world. Minister H. F. Arthur Schoenfeld clarified the situation by telling me not only that the United States was willing to examine the request of Hungary—in fact, Secretary of State Byrnes had proposed some readjustments in Hungary's favor—but that Russia insisted stubbornly that the first part of the section in the armistice treaty dealing with Transylvania be accepted as categorical, and "all of Transylvania" be granted to Rumania. Reportedly Molotov won his point by stating that Stalin had promised this to Groza.

A tremendous upheaval on the Hungarian political scene resulted. In Parliament the deputies charged the foreign minister with having failed in his duties by not dispatching the Hungarian claims in time.

In answering Gyöngyösi disclosed that on his own responsibility he had sent notes to the powers, enumerating Hungarian peace aims.

Bitter outbreaks against the Communists arose for their prevention of an earlier definition of Hungarian peace aims.

As a result political anger against the Communists increased that much more; they juggled with public statements that at the decisive meeting in Paris the chair was occupied by Secretary of State Byrnes and thus it was obvious that the United States and not the Soviet Union had made the proposal which resulted in the unfavorable decision for Hungary.

This underhanded, and unquestionably unfounded, attack on the United States by Communists was probably caused by the fact that the United States government, through Minister Schoenfeld, had just informed us that we had been granted a $10,000,000 credit to buy some of the surplus left by the United States army in Europe. This infuriated the Communists, because it was the first loan or credit Hungary had received from any nation since the end of the war. The credit was of great economic importance because it enabled us to buy desperately needed material which we could not otherwise have secured.

In general the Communists resented the increased interest the United States began to show in the condition of Hungarian economy. Members of the American mission counseled several times that we should officially submit our difficult economic situation to all the great powers. László Ecker-Rátz, the economic advisor to the American mission, proposed specifically that we should make detailed presentation, with clear-cut supporting statistics, and ask the three great powers in the Control Commission to make a unified effort to assist Hungarian economy. Minister of Finance Gordon did make a step in this direction in December, 1945, by preparing a statement on the economic situation and bringing it to Marshal Voroshilov himself; two copies were presented by members of his staff to the American and British ministers, respectively. Voroshilov, after one glance at the paper, threw it at Gordon, remarking that he was not "inclined to devote any of my time to the subject." At the very time the copies of the document were in the possession of the Americans and British; but their hands were tied because the Russians took no cognition of the presentation.

In May of 1946 the American government again intimated that it would like to be informed of economic conditions. I had to turn to the president of the Control Commission, as the Hungarian government had since received strict directives that it might communicate only through the president of the Commission—then, General Sviridov. He emphatically rejected the suggestion that we give any information to either the American or the British representative.

One night Captain Gruber, Sviridov's interpreter, telephoned to announce that he wished to speak with me urgently.

"Fine! Please come to see me early in the morning," I answered.

"Sorry," answered the captain, "General Sviridov has commanded me to ask you to take some steps in a very important matter. Because of this, I ask you to be kind enough to receive me immediately."

More annoyed than sleepy, I dressed, and soon the Russian captain arrived.

"Mr. Premier," Captain Gruber began immediately, "General Sviridov received information that the governors of the National Bank are preparing to hand some very important document to the representatives of the United States tomorrow morning. It is General Sviridov's request that you be kind enough to take instant steps to prevent this under any circumstances."

I tried to reach Emery Oltványi, president of the National Bank, but for some unknown reason my telephone was still connected to Soviet Headquarters and I was unable to get through. There was nothing to do but call in person on President Oltványi, at three o'clock in the morning. No imagination is needed to picture his astonishment when I got him out of bed at that hour.

"What kind of documents do you intend to deliver to the Americans tomorrow morning?" I asked Oltványi.

The flabbergasted president of the National Bank told me that according to his knowledge the National Bank had no such intentions. I informed him of Sviridov's message and asked him to look into the matter early in the morning. We both wondered why the Russians had dragged us out of bed.

My first caller next morning was Oltványi, who reported that the whole matter was a simple administrative procedure and no secrets were involved; the National Bank had received a letter from the American mission in which fourteen questions were asked involving nothing confidential in the answers as most of the facts had been aired in the press already. Anyway, the answer had not been delivered and if the President of the Control Commission protested, then it would not be.

In the afternoon I called on Sviridov and told him no important documents of the National Bank were involved.

"Ah, bah!" exclaimed Sviridov. "They have tried to put something over on you. I have definite proof in my hands that the National Bank did want to hand over very important information to the Americans." With this he went to his desk and pulled out a photostat of the letter showing the fourteen points of the American questions, on which a penciled remark could be read: "Approved for release. Gordon, Minister of Finance."

Sviridov considered the document as of vital importance because "the Finance Minister endorsed it."

I could have smiled at the whole affair, but the fact of the photostats being in the drawer of Sviridov's desk annoyed me considerably.

When men used to law, independence, and freedom of action ask me at times about the form of pressure applied by the Soviet to the Hungarian government, I am reminded of the hundreds of cases similar to this call at three in the morning, which no one could know who did not live in Hungary, or try to govern facing the constant smirk of the Soviet Janus.

CHAPTER 52

America

AFTER OUR RETURN FROM MOSCOW, I AWAITED ONLY AN OPPORTUNE TIME for a government delegation to visit the great western powers. Both the American and the British minister, who considered our trip to Moscow as a success, encouraged a visit for personal discussion with the western statesmen of Hungary's situation. Independently of their suggestion, and even before the Paris decision of May 7, I had thought this journey advisable, because the difference between the policy of the Hungarian government and other southeastern European countries would be emphasized by our establishing the first personal contact with the statesmen of the western powers. The Paris decision now made it urgent.

The loudest clamor for a journey to the west came from public opinion; it was as enthusiastic for a western trip as it had been cold toward the trek to Moscow. I discussed the matter with the members of the cabinet. The foreign minister and the Smallholder ministers voiced a lively support while the Communists at first dourly approved. The Social Democrats loudly opposed it, because of a report from our minister in London, himself a Social Democrat, expressing much doubt of success.

As is usual under such circumstances I questioned the diplomatic representatives at Budapest about our welcome. The United States Minister said that his government had already intimated to him, after our previous conversations, that it would be very glad to entertain a Hungarian government delegation at Washington. The British Minister told me that, while his government could not entertain us, it would be glad to receive members of the Hungarian government. Foreign Minister Bevin might not be available, as he intended to return to Paris in the near future for renewed talks.

Before going abroad we were forced again to appease the Communists in one of the most pressing problems: reduction of the number of civil servants. This problem, since our return from Moscow, had employed my best efforts to reach an interparty agreement, to adopt a method both practical and humane. The Communists stubbornly insisted that the trade unions should have the deciding voice, and would not budge from their stand. The majority of civil servants trembled with fear of losing even the meager subsistence inflation was affording them.

With much bitterness the civil servants decree finally came forth. We were forced to accept the trade union representation in the commission. In the interest of national economy it would have been inadvisable to further delay its execution; also, the subtle threats of the Communists gave us to understand that further tabling of the measure might promote strikes and mass demonstrations; these would discredit the government abroad and endanger any negotiations we might be able to conduct with the western powers. Regretfully we bowed before the threat of using the masses for anarchistic political purposes.

It was my earnest endeavor to put as many of the political controversies aside as possible, so that we might concentrate on saving Hungarian economy, which had made such strides despite being in the throes of an uncontrollable inflation. The Supreme Economic Council was holding daily sessions: one day to fix prices, the next to increase wages. The black market was a deadly threat to the entire commerce of the country. Two values were considered to be stable: the dollar, and gold. In stores and even in restaurants the cashiers had small scales for weighing the gold offered by customers in payment. It was hardly worth while for employees or laborers to carry home their pay, for by the time their wives went to market, the paper money had devaluated so far that it would hardly buy anything.

Eugene Rácz, who later became finance minister, aptly described it: people spent the greater part of their energy during the day getting rid of money received in the morning, for he who had to keep it overnight was the loser.

One cannot imagine the social upheaval caused by the collapse in value of the media of exchange, unless one plays a part in the cold drama of the nameless citizen's daily struggle for survival. Scholars were trading priceless bindings for a loaf of bread or two or three eggs; fathers bartered their overcoats for food for their children. The gold of the wedding ring bought a few days' groceries for a household. Nationally prominent professional men were hiring out as day laborers in exchange for food for their families. Yes, a bag of flour brought half a dozen Persian rugs at street corners. Values went completely "haywire," and only the black marketeers, the scavengers of misery, prospered.

To the average man, inflation means only one thing—loss of faith in the currency. In his conception of the financial economy, there can be no greater tragedy. The currency to him is an exchange medium measuring the value of his labor or services for a certain number of hours or days; it represents his toil and sweat. When this is recompensed in a worthless medium he feels cheated, robbed, because it is as if pure gold has been stolen from him by an unseen enemy.

It was easy for the Communists to watch smugly what they termed the "collapse of capitalism"; the Red army, by supplying their personal needs, helped maintain their complacency. Had it not been for the food supplies I was receiving from my wife's family and my father in Bisse, I should not have been able to support my family on the premier's salary—now amounting to less than two dollars a month.

Saving our economy meant first of all stabilizing finances. We could expect backing in this endeavor only from the West; it believed in the way of economic life we were trying to salvage. I firmly trusted that our western trip would help in executing stabilization.

While we were preparing to leave, Count Michael Károlyi arrived. After the First World War he had been, by revolutionary declaration, president of the Republic for a few days; later he had emigrated to western Europe. He came to take the seat in Parliament to which he had been elected "in absentia." We gave the old refugee an impressive reception; upon his arrival he immediately held forth with a speech in Parliament. He showed surprising ignorance and political haziness in his long but confused and weak parliamentary address.

An interparty group was finally agreed upon as personnel of the government delegation; I was asked to head it. Gyöngyösi as foreign minister, Stephen Ries, the minister of justice, as representative of the Social Democrats, and Mathias Rákosi, the vice premier, as representative of the Communist party, were the members. We took along Eugene Rácz as economic adviser and my son Ferenc, who had been attached to me because Dr. Francis Kapócs did not speak English, acting as secretary.

The president of the Republic, the members of the Cabinet, and the American and British representatives bade us farewell at the airport, when we took off in the personal plane of General Weems, American member of the Allied Control Commission. Mr. Bigelow, the counselor of the United States Legation, accompanied us to Paris, where we boarded the transatlantic plane.

Before we left I visited General Sviridov, as the head of the Allied Control Commission, officially announcing the trip. He received me in the presence of Soviet Minister Pushkin, who gave me the distinct impression that he would have advised us to stay home but, after the Paris decision of May 7, found it wiser to avoid any attitude that might show that the Soviet government intended to prevent Hungary from further asserting herself. Pushkin blandly advised Gyöngyösi not to trade Hungary's independence for a loan, upon which he received the answer that without a loan of some kind we could not stabilize our economy and as a result would not be able to meet reparation payments. Pushkin then remarked cynically, "Then you'd better get a loan."

After devastated, poverty-stricken Europe, our impressions of New York were overpowering. We gazed at the activity at the airport, with its shined and starched porters servicing the thousands of passengers. This was our introduction to the importance of speed in American life. Freedom of movement was everywhere in evidence, in sharp contrast to the difficulty of travel in Europe, where innumerable borders and laws hamstrung the individual.

A gentleman from the State Department took us for a short drive through New York until we were to resume our flight to Washington.

Few people can imagine the impression received on coming from a continent of ruins to one with buildings, bridges, and roads intact, people well groomed and brimming with health, streets jammed with the traffic of hundreds of thousands of cars, show windows full of not only the necessities of life but its luxuries—merchandise which we in Hungary remembered only from the past. The people, courteous and friendly with the gleam of happiness in their eyes. I could feel the pulse of life of the American metropolis.

The view of the city, with its sky line, its huge blocks of buildings and busy harbor, was exactly as we Europeans imagine it; but here we could sense, within and beyond the cold steel and concrete, the strength of a people whose determination to create and whose uncorroded faith in the freedom of the individual built this living monument to the democratic ideal of our age.

Our trip from New York to Washington was a trying experience. There was a terrible storm; the plane danced constantly, and at times we thought the terrific gusts of wind would tear the plane apart. Everyone, afraid, simulated calm. Rákosi pulled out a book and tried to look as if he were unconcernedly reading. Those sitting behind him reported that he did not turn a single page all the way from New York to Washington!

At the National Airport we were not received by a brass band or a guard of honor; a representative of the State Department welcomed us with warm friendliness and took us to the official guest quarters, historic Blair House—an elegant but subdued Colonial residence with rooms furnished in the styles characteristic of the different regions of the United States. I enjoyed the friendly and direct American hospitality that pervaded this historic mansion.

Interesting days followed. The frank cordiality of Washington's statesmen made me forget even its scorching heat.

Our first meeting was with Undersecretary Dean Acheson, to whom we presented the two main topics we desired to offer for consideration by the United States government. Above all we wished to win United States support for Hungary's cause at the final negotiations for the peace treaty; secondly, we asked that the United States government permit return of that part of Hungarian national wealth which had been carried away by the Germans and later by the Arrow Cross government of Szálasi and was now under the jurisdiction of the American forces in Germany and Austria. The return of any part of this would greatly help the economic reconstruction of Hungary, but the financial stabilization was practically impossible without the recapture of the more than $30,000,000 worth of gold bullion of the Hungarian national bank, which was in American custody.

Mr. Acheson showed deep interest in the problems of Hungary, informing us that, although Secretary Byrnes was preparing to leave for the Paris Conference, he would like to see us; and he asked that we present our case to Mr. Byrnes also.

At the luncheon in honor of the Hungarian delegation given by the House Foreign Affairs Committee, I experienced an irresistible cheerfulness unknown to Europeans under the same circumstances. Several of the lawmakers impressed me, in their speeches, with the depth and detail of their information about European affairs. At the end, Chairman Sol Bloom kindly asked me to make an address; and I was glad of the opportunity to plead the cause of my people before men in whose hands rested the destiny of Europe. During my short plea the faces of my audience mirrored their deep sympathy for the tragedy-ridden Hungarian nation.

In resuming the chair, Congressman Bloom jokingly asked me not to be a candidate in his district during the next elections, adding, as the interpreter conveyed this to me, because he would consider me serious competition.

A Republican Congressman, at that time senior member of the minority party on the committee, remarked on hearing Bloom's statement:

"I consider you Hungarians very decent people. That is my judgment of the voters of Hungarian descent in my district, who are very wise because they all vote for me; and you good people have certainly strengthened my opinion. Why don't you all pack up, leave that country wrapped in trouble, and come over here to America? You are just the type of people who would fit well into our community."

Frankly, I was touched by the charm and originality of their compliments.

As the delegation arrived to pay its respects to the secretary of state, Mr. Byrnes invited me to confer with him alone first. He greeted me as an old friend, and, cordially patting me on the back, asked straight away what I wanted to accomplish by the trip. After listening attentively he told me how the question of Transylvania had slipped entirely into Soviet hands, and that the decision of May 7 was entirely at their insistence. If the Soviet government would undertake to introduce the Transylvanian question again, the United States was ready and willing to support Hungary's position.

When the rest of the delegation joined us in the chambers, I officially put Hungary's pleas before the secretary of state. With a glance at Rákosi, Mr. Byrnes stated that if the Soviet Union introduced the Transylvanian question, the United States government would not abstain from supporting Hungary's claims. In answer to our pleas of economic character, he stated that the United States government would try to deliver an answer as soon as possible.

The next day we were received by President Truman, who was most cordial and expressed his satisfaction that we had been able to come to the United States. He inquired with great interest about the plight of our people and of Europe in general, seeming to be especially interested in the Danube as a political and economic factor in the life of central Europe. During our visit we were invited to meet photographers in the garden of the White House with the President. As we walked to the garden, Mr. Truman intimated that one cannot escape dictatorship even in America: and truly, whatever pose or rearrangement the photographers suggested, the President obligingly followed. He shook my hand, but that was not enough; we had to repeat our handshake at least a dozen times to enable all of the photographers to "get it from the right angle."

I left the White House impressed with the sincerity and human kindness of the President.

In the evening Undersecretary Acheson gave us a dinner at Blair House, and I was delighted to meet some of the outstanding personalities in the American capital. I enjoyed immensely the high intellectual level of the conversations and the good-humored informality of the gathering. Considering that everything had to be translated, it took me some effort to keep pace with the lively exchange of *bons mots*. Mr. Justice Felix Frankfurter, who sat on my right, in referring to my repartees, remarked in his jovial manner that he had come to the conclusion that the Hungarian people chose me for their premier because I had an answer for every question.

"No, sir," I answered jokingly. "The Hungarians, as proof of their sincere democratic feelings, wanted a man for the premiership whose cultural training did not go beyond reading and writing, who had never been abroad, and who spoke not a single foreign language. As they could not find these qualifications in anyone but me, I became the premier."

Rákosi looked at me with surprise, unable to understand how I could tell a joke on myself—as if a sense of humor would have ever injured dignity. He was even more astonished when Undersecretary Acheson, our host, began to speak: "This house has a tradition that no formal toasts are delivered. That is why I shall not rise. But by lifting my glass I greet you, the representatives of Hungary, and tell you how glad we are that you came. Success to your trip, and to your efforts to rebuild your nation!" Mr. Acheson emptied his glass, wishing good health to President Tildy and me and happiness to the people of Hungary.

I was struck with the simple warmth of the toast, and in my equally short answer thanked him for the hospitality and many gestures of good will we had already experienced from the United States.

Sitting in the garden of Blair House, we continued into the wee hours the lively interplay of ideas.

We also held a press conference in Washington, and what a throng there was! I tried to give a straight and definite answer to each one in the rapid fire of questions, but some were quite embarrassing, like one from a pert young newspaperwoman: "Mr. Premier, would you tell us who robbed more from Hungary, the Germans or the Russians?" A deathly silence followed the question: one could have heard a pin drop. I took a deep breath. Rákosi fidgeted painfully in his chair.

"A difference between the two must be recognized," I answered. "The Germans and the Nazis robbed; the Russians took it as booty."

This was received with general hilarity.

A visit to the Tennessee Valley, as one of the most recent miraculous accomplishments of American engineering, was arranged for us. Before we left Washington, Mr. Acheson handed me a note containing the answer of the United States government to the wishes presented by the Hungarian delegation. This very clear and straight statement once for all put an end to the speculation on whether the American trip would achieve success.

In the note the United States government stated that it desired to support the efforts of the people of Hungary to stabilize the economy and would unconditionally return the gold bullion of the National Bank of Hungary. It also declared that orders were being issued to deliver to the Hungarian government other national treasures carried away by the

Germans and the Nazis and now held in safe keeping by the United States Army Forces of Occupation in the European Theater of Operations. It contained further the announcement that it would return the Hungarian Danube fleet to sail for Hungary under the Hungarian flag, but wished to reserve decision regarding the ownership of the ships. Obviously it did not want to give the Russians an opportunity to take them from us. It stated, to our great surprise and elation, that the surplus credit of $10,000,000 which had been granted to us a short time earlier had been raised to $15,000,000. The political questions, the note said, would be entertained by Secretary Byrnes in Paris.

The note contained two more points. First it asked the Hungarian government not to be reticent in informing the United States about the economic conditions of Hungary from time to time. Secondly, it welcomed the idea of an agreement by the Hungarian government to begin negotiations with the United States government for an air pact.

My joy over the accomplishments was clouded by these two simple suggestions. I considered the least Hungary could do in return for the magnanimous attitude of the Americans would be to grant these without a second thought. But I knew well that the Soviet government—in fact, the chairman of the Allied Control Commission—would never permit us to do so. I was ashamed that, as the head of the government of my country, I could not repay the many splendid acts of the Americans with the fulfillment of two simple requests which were in the interests of the Hungarian people to begin with.

When I informed the delegation of the answer I had received, sincere joy and satisfaction ensued. Only one man, Rákosi, tried to hide his uneasiness and adverse reaction. He would have preferred us to return from America without accomplishments.

I remember that night well. The glad tidings had made us all very happy. We were dinner guests of a prominent Washington attorney, Wilson Wyatt. Most of the evening I conversed with Secretary of Agriculture Clinton P. Anderson, who described American life in a most interesting way. I recall well how I yearned toward his word pictures of the American farmer; surely, on that evening, it never entered my mind that a short fifteen months later I should be in Virginia, one of those very farmers.

The next morning we flew to Tennessee. During lunch in a Knoxville hotel, one of the directors of the TVA summed up the great project, which supplies electricity to a territory larger than all of Hungary, making fertile and prosperous an agricultural area which once was poverty-stricken. My thoughts wandered to my own country and what such a project could do for the peasants; suddenly I discovered that my spiritual journey to my homeland was inspired by the pianist in the dining room, who continually played Hungarian melodies: the rhapsodies of Liszt and the waltzes of Lehár. This thoughtfulness on the part of our hosts touched me deeply.

We first went to see one of the great dams; the realization of man's will to accomplish overwhelmed me, reminding me of what a country which puts the happiness and progress of its own people before all else is able to accomplish if it is not periodically exposed to the ruinous destruction of war.

We were taken for dinner to a city built especially for the workers at a power plant, and found ourselves admiring one of the typical institutions, the cafeteria. Here, every one paid a few cents for the day's menu, entered the hall, took a tray, put it on the endless band, and as it moved along, attractive waitresses heaped the different courses on it. None of us could finish all of the plentiful worker's meal, which I understood was planned in detail by dietitians. The only one who cleaned his plate was Mathias Rákosi, who summed up his philosophy of the meal in these words:

"This is the land of plenty. Why should we spare the Americans by leaving any of this food?"

Next day when we were viewing the mighty Norris Dam, one of the engineers of the power plant turned to me.

"Pardon me—what was the largest denomination of bills when you were still in Hungary?"

I told him that when we left Budapest inflation had reached the point where bills of a hundred billion pengös were common in circulation.

"Then I am way behind, because the largest bill I have is a ten-billion-pengö note." He told us that a week earlier a man just arrived from Budapest had given him this note.

"Well, I would not dare state that since we left Hungary no higher denominations have been printed; but, considering that you are so much behind, I want you to accept a hundred-billion note from me." He accepted with a smile and asked us to autograph it.

That evening we sat with David Lilienthal on a terrace beside a romantic lake, relaxed in conversation. Part of the beautiful Tennessee night we spent discussing the turns in recent history, the fate of humanity, and, naturally, conditions in Hungary.

Lilienthal posed the question of whether similar water-power plants could not be built in Hungary. We told him that the Treaty of Trianon, following the First World War, had detached all of our rivers' upper reaches; our reaches of rivers were entirely in the plains. After the Paris decision of May 7, we had scant hope for the return of any of the upper streams that would be ideally suitable. We could discuss only the middle Danube and Tisza as possibilities.

At this point Rákosi suddenly interrupted with an enigmatic attack on American imperialism, to prevent any discussion of possible American assistance in the conception of such a project.

Lilienthal told us that his mother was of Hungarian descent, and that he would love to greet her with a Hungarian word the next time they met. We taught him that one word which expresses so beautifully, as I believe no other language can in one word, "my sweet mother." It is the Hungarian "édesanyám."

We also saw farms in the Tennessee Valley. I was especially interested in farming, for that was the only thing I really knew. There is a great divergence between American and Hungarian methods of farming; but, considering the difference in conditions, I could understand the reasons.

On one of the farms a dairy worker passed by, in dungarees slightly torn at the knee. This was the first piece of torn clothing we had seen in America. Rákosi, who did not miss a thing, immediately crowed: "Look at those rags! All is not cream in America either."

It was annoying to all of us to observe the disdainful attitude of Rákosi during the entire American trip. While we were visiting the TVA he constantly raved about the power plants of the Soviet; later he went into tirades about the Hungarian farmer being more progressive than the American. One knowing him could plainly discern that he was not at all happy to have the members of the Hungarian government see accomplishments other than those of the Soviet Union. He would have loved to draw an iron curtain around the delegation, so that they would be under Soviet influence even in America.

Rákosi's criticism knew no limits, but we tried to overlook his efforts to spoil our impressions. In Tennessee he outdid himself as the *enfant terrible*. We were shown some prefabricated houses, beautifully equipped. This was a very hard one for him. I could see him peering about critically. At last he came forth with the comment, "Once the bedbugs get into these houses, they'll never get them out again." And his face relaxed in complacent self-satisfaction.

"But," said another member of our party, "there don't seem to be any bedbugs in America."

"Don't you know," snapped Rákosi, "that bedbugs originated in America, and were exported from here to Europe and Russia?"

On many occasions during our stay in the United States, I was reminded of the fact that Rákosi began to support the plans for a trip to America and England after our London envoy, Stephen Bede, had come home to Budapest and tried to induce the cabinet to drop plans for a trip to Washington and London, because, as he assured us, it would not bear any fruit.

Rákosi must have known the plans the Soviet had for us, because at dinner in New York with the members of the Hungarian Legation he made a very revealing statement.

"I better enjoy something as long as I am here. The way I see the international situation, they will never ask us to come to America again."

Before leaving for Europe we spent three days in New York—to me, the world's busiest and largest city. This short time was hardly enough to see all of the wonders; but as we no longer had an official program we could walk and see for ourselves; in observing the life I was constantly reminded of the Soviet propaganda regarding conditions supposedly existing in New York. When I left the Waldorf Astoria together with a member of the delegation for the first time without a host, he turned to me and said:

"Remember when we wanted to walk to a shop in Moscow?" Yes, in this comparison lay the difference between the two worlds.

During my stay in America I met with a great number of people, representing many different strata of a society unique in its principles and systems. Its principle, so admired throughout the civilized world, the absolute freedom of the individual, is a cornerstone of its political and economic system, free enterprise. Much striven for but never approached by nations of the world, it will remain the goal if we, the little people of the world, can live and work and are enabled to continue to believe in the social and economic order of a civilization devoted to the service of a community of all the peoples.

In America I have seen wealth comparable to none: wealth accumulated through the relatively short span of the young republic, by individuals whose freedom of movement enabled them to choose their occupations freely, in a society organized to produce commodities and services for their fellow men in free competition. This system, the envy of all the common peoples on the globe, living mostly under political or economic duress, made America the prosperous island of democracy in the world.

Most people regard the high standard of living in the United States as a particularly American phenomenon. It can spread throughout the world if people are permitted to share in the basic human privileges of the four freedoms, and allowed to vote continually on the course their freely elected leaders are to follow.

True democracy and its resulting privileges cannot come to people whose political and economic destiny is controlled by the state, when the individual and his will are submerged in the abyss of the law of force.

Two worlds or one: the individual can judge them only by their liberty, human decency, and progress.

CHAPTER 53

Disappointments in Paris

FROM AMERICA WE FLEW TO LONDON; OUR ARRIVAL WAS UNFORTUNATELY somewhat spoiled by a delay of eight hours in Newfoundland. We therefore could not enjoy the grand reception arranged for us by the British people.

Anxious to return home, we tried to shorten our stay. The British statesmen were very cooperative, and our negotiations had a distinct air of expediency.

First we met Secretary Philip Noel-Baker, a pleasant, kind gentleman who listened to our peace aims but did not give us much encouragement. Although advising us to call on Foreign Secretary Ernest Bevin in Paris, he could hardly conceive of the reintroduction of the Transylvanian issue. Regarding the minority rights of Hungarians in Czechoslovakia, he said courteously but pointedly:

"Don't you find it slightly unusual that you desire support for a defeated nation at the expense of a victorious one?"

"It is debatable, sir," I answered, "if Slovakia, bordering on Hungary, could be regarded as a victorious nation. Undoubtedly Slovakia, during its short independence, pursued the war against the Allies much harder than Hungary. But please understand that we are not seeking an advantage for Hungary at the expense of Czechoslovakia; we want only to secure human rights and liberties for the many hundreds of thousands of Hungarians living on Czechoslovakian soil."

We did not get very far with Noel-Baker.

The next day Prime Minister Clement Attlee favored us with a lecture on democracy to the effect that no country is truly democratic unless its government has an active opposition in Parliament. This was a dig at Hungary, where all political parties in Parliament were represented in the governing coalition.

It did not surprise me that, in a classically parliamentary country where a coalition had been created during the war, the necessity for a coalition in Hungary after the armistice could not be understood. I answered the Prime Minister:

"I know that opposition to a government party is the lifeblood of the democratic parliamentary system. But Hungary's problems do not permit her the luxury of a party government which would have to face and fight not only economic and political difficulties but a parliamentary opposition as well. Aside from that, I hardly think a system is any less democratic if it insures the parliamentary minority not only the right of criticism, but a part of the power and responsibility of governing in proportion to its strength."

Attlee's academic monologue on democracy came to my mind at the time of the Communist putsch in May, 1947. I was waiting for him, so sensitive to democratic forms, to administer more than just a weak rebuke to the Hungarian Communists and take a decisive stand against the terror of that parliamentary minority. But he failed to emphasize his tenets of democracy then.

Our political aims received no encouragement from the British Prime Minister during our visit; but he informed us that his government would not interfere with the return of Hungarian property taken by the Germans and found in the British zone of occupation.

Despite the fact that we were richly entertained by the cabinet and by a group in the House of Commons, we could discern the dire need

of the British people. After the abundance in America, the scarcity in
Britain was all the more dramatic. But I respect the self-denial and
sacrifices endured by the people to rebuild their war-torn country; individuals accept a lowered living standard so that the coming generation may live in a sound, reorganized economy.

After a few hurried days in London we flew to Paris and paid our
respects to Foreign Minister Bidault, who received us with sympathetic
understanding but made it clear that France was in no position to raise
her voice in major issues.

We also met Ernest Bevin, the British Foreign Secretary. When we
reached the subject of the Hungarian peace aims Bevin went into an
extensive dissertation about developments on the world political scene
and the measures to be contained in the peace treaties.

"You ask," he said among other things, "that the Czechoslovak-
Hungarian peace treaty should, in a separate section, insure the rights
of the Hungarian minority, a method tried unsuccessfully after the
First World War. Nationality complaints arose after that, too. It would
be much better to insert into every peace treaty all the basic human
rights which should be guaranteed to all men regardless of nationality.
The United Nations would exercise jurisdiction over such measures in
the peace treaties and could rush to aid those nationalities whose rights
suffered injury. Far better that the countries of the United Nations
exercise control over these rights than that a single nation be left to
keep to the letter of the treaty."

I hope that Bevin admits, now, that I was right. Since then the
Soviet Union has successively put its own interpretations on the superficial and generalized terms of the treaties, using them to further its
own political and economic expansion.

We also expressed our desires regarding Transylvania, but received
no decisive answer. Bevin said:

"Believe me, it would be more important in the future to foster an
efficient economic development than split hairs about borders. The goal
should be: enabling produce from every part of the world to reach all
peoples everywhere; thus is the well-being of humanity assured. That is
why it is important to provide free transit over the Danube."

In Paris we also called on Viacheslav Molotov, the Russian Foreign
Minister. As the Americans had indicated willingness to support Hungary's Transylvanian aims, if the Soviet Union would initiate the step,
we had to determine whether the Russians were ready to do so.

Molotov began the conversation by asking about our accomplishments in Washington and London. When we informed him in detail of the economic generosity of the United States government, he remarked that our trip had undoubtedly been successful.

I also informed him that, under certain conditions, we were to receive our Danube shipping if the Soviet command in Austria would permit them to be operated.

"Well, we won't hinder it," said Molotov. "The Americans could really have returned these things already." As a matter of fact, after delaying as long as possible, the Russians gave permission many months later.

Then came the cardinal question. We reported that America was ready to support us on Transylvania if the Soviet Union would reintroduce the issue. Molotov answered as if he had completely forgotten the encouragement he had given us in Moscow in April:

"The Union of Soviet Socialist Republics cannot change its attitude toward a question from one occasion to another. Besides, at the conference where the Foreign Ministers reached a decision to grant the whole of Transylvania to Rumania, the issue was formally introduced by the Secretary of State of the United States of America, and we acquiesced because this decision is in accordance with the respective section of the armistice agreement."

We parted, bitterly aware that all hope for Soviet support on the international scene was lost. Molotov showed no inclination to give Hungary some slight reward for accepting his Moscow advice to initiate direct negotiations regarding Transylvania. We were sorely humbled.

This Paris meeting with Molotov taught me a bitter lesson: The Soviet Union had no interest in the welfare of a people determined to live in independence, a country over which it cannot exercise unrestricted control.

CHAPTER 54

Sviridov's Surprises

WHEN OUR PLANE LANDED AT BUDAPEST WE WERE AWED BY THE ELABORATE reception accorded; the President of the Republic, accompanied by diplomats of the western powers, greeted the returning Hungarian delegation; the crowd echoed the words of welcome with rousing cheers. The scene brought tears to my eyes. As we drove into the capital, flags snapped in the breeze and the streets were lined with cheering multitudes, demonstrating their approval of the accomplishments of our western trip.

But two grave surprises awaited me. Stephen Balogh, undersecretary in the Prime Ministry, informed me on the way from the airport to my office that Szakasits, acting premier in my absence, had received a memorandum from General Sviridov: charging mismanagement of the ruble fund, he wanted President Emery Oltványi, Managing Director Louis Farago, and Director Arthur Kárász of the National Bank dismissed and prosecuted.

The second piece of news Balogh gave me was equally serious. A few days earlier Russian officers walking along the Theresian Boulevard had been shot at from an attic, and two had died. General Sviridov's speech at the funeral contained a clear threat to both the Hungarian government and the people.

Szakasits had hurried to express the regrets of the nation to Sviridov and ask that the National Bank case be tabled until my return.

It was obvious that the Communists, anxious to eliminate the three top officials who blocked their assumption of National Bank control, used the murders as a bridge to their dismissal demands.

The next day I familiarized myself with both matters. As inflation was still increasing, the National Bank issue was of tremendous importance. It seems that the Red army circulated Russian rubles in Hungary. The National Bank was later instructed to call them in, and did so, assembling the rubles in the country. Several times Russian army personnel appeared at the National Bank, asking for rubles. The management at first refused. Soon Russian tommy-gunners arrived and simply ordered the vaults opened and the rubles surrendered. Large amounts of Russian currency were carted away in this fashion. The Russian control officer attached to the National Bank ordered rubles delivered from its supply. Soviet currency was used only twice for Hungarian purposes; once Zoltán Vas, mayor of Budapest, got some to buy a few cars, and fifty thousand rubles were made available to the Hungarian delegation to Moscow.

The Soviet Union did not recognize that the rubles had been stolen by the Russian soldiers, nor that the deliveries were made on vouchers signed by its own control officer. The management was held responsible for the missing currency and, although entirely different persons were responsible for the handling of the ruble accounts, the Russians emphatically demanded that Oltványi and his two associates be removed.

Calling on Pushkin, I vigorously but unavailingly defended the three officials, and cited their democratic background and exemplary behavior during our nation's difficult times. The Soviet government insisted on their removal and succeeded; but I refused to have them indicted for something which they had not done.

The more ticklish issue was the murders on Theresian Boulevard; undoubtedly other Russian occupied countries saw more soldiers killed by the people for less reason. We knew, however, that the Russians would publicize the incident to our disadvantage and so exert more pressure on a democratic Hungary with a Smallholder majority. I believed that expression of my personal abhorrence of the affair was right; the murderer could not be punished, for he had immediately committed suicide. Investigation proved that he was a member of the Social Democratic Youth, and that it was a *crime passionnel*.

The case was complicated by the fact that just about this time attacks on Russians had occurred near Gyöngyös. A boy whose mother had been raped by seven Russian soldiers in one night secured a gun afterward and shot a few Russian soldiers.

When it was discovered that the youth had a friend named Antall in the office of the Smallholders party who used to visit Father Salés Kis, the Russians sought to give the incident the appearance of a "conspiracy." They cunningly involved a few Smallholders deputies, then arrested Father Kis and all the young men to whom he had been a spiritual mentor. Father Kis, a well educated man once pastor of a parish in America, was confined in a dark, solitary dungeon.

The case of Gyöngyös was becoming a *cause célèbre*, as Sviridov's men tried to pin the entire affair on the Smallholders party. Members of the Smallholders staff were accused of assembling a secret cache of arms for use against the occupation forces.

The facts were that, before the 1945 elections, an armed mob of Communists had stormed the Smallholders headquarters in Budapest, causing havoc and destruction. Victor Chornoky, Tildy's son-in-law and executive secretary of the Smallholders party, then ordered the headquarters to organize and arm gatekeepers, like the Communist and other party headquarters. One of the subalterns gathered some of the guns and ammunition that could still be found among the ruins and overzealously brought in a couple of hand grenades as weapons for the guard. As it had never become necessary to use these arms, Leslie Gyulai, parliamentary deputy and head of the public relations department, had ordered Joseph Antall, a clerk who lived in Gyöngyös, to remove and destroy them. Antall had taken them home. Questioned later under torture about the young man who had avenged his mother's dishonor, he admitted that he had brought the hand grenades to Gyöngyös under instructions from Gyulai. Thus the Communist police were given an opportunity to involve the entire Smallholders party.

The police, endowed with the fantastic imagination characteristic of the Communist mentality, immediately visualized the affair as an extensive armed conspiracy against the occupation forces and delivered Father Kis, Joseph Antall, and the youth who had shot the Russians to the Soviet authorities. That was the first step toward arrest *en masse* of youth in and around Gyöngyös by the Soviet secret police. Together with Father Kis and the others, they were carried off to Russia, never to be heard of again!

CHAPTER 55

Bargaining at Bayonet's Point

THIS PHANTASMAGORIA ARISING FROM THE MURDERS BY A YOUTH avenging the bestialities committed on his own mother, and the succeeding transfer of the prisoners by the Communist police into Soviet custody, gave Sviridov a loophole through which he could again inject himself into the internal affairs of Hungary. The Soviet Union knew well how to expand the rights granted to it by the armistice agreement and still remain within the pale of legality. Advice and legal backing were naturally received from the well versed Hungarian Communists.

On July 7th, General Sviridov sent word that he wished to confer with me. As usual, we met in the presence of Pushkin. Sviridov was aggressive from the start, stating that developments in Hungary were of grave concern to him and he had come to the conclusion that the Hungarian government was not energetic enough against men who imperiled the security of the Red army and, at the same time, the future of democracy in our country. He therefore was delivering to me the demands of the Russian occupation Command, which were to be executed by the Hungarian government.

At once, he produced a long letter—in Russian, so that I could not answer it immediately. However, I made the point of telling him that, although some persons would naturally take exception to the behavior of the occupation forces, their acts could not be regarded as representative of all the people. Concrete cases would be investigated, and justice would be done.

The letter, which I must reconstruct from memory, was translated as soon as I returned to my office. Its demands were cleverly worded, avoiding presentation in the name of the Allied Control Commission because that would have made the British and American members part of the action and enabled them to express opinions.

I was more than surprised by the letter's content; the demands, point by point, were remarkably similar to those made by Hungarian Communists in their press and at public meetings. Undoubtedly the Communist party had written the letter and had induced the Red commander to give it force by signing it. It reeked of Rákosi and Pushkin, who used the killing of a handful of Russians, a retaliatory outburst from an enraged population, to weaken opposition to Communist designs on the internal political structure of Hungary.

Had these demands been made openly by the Hungarian Communist party—instead of by Soviet military authorities backed by hundreds of thousands of bayonets with the dubious legality of misconstrued sections of the armistice agreement—we could have issued a flat refusal without a moment's consideration. But, especially in their present form, they could never have been made in the coalition cabinet, which included the Communists. Therefore, the Hungarian Communists, a government party, used extortion in the guns of a foreign power to gain its end.

There seemed to be no defense against demands so presented; the only course open to the Hungarian government was bargaining and appeasement in which some of the demands would be met, some compromised, and some refused.

It is easy to look back and wonder if really no other course was open. Possibly it would have been wiser to refuse all the Soviet demands and, by bringing the situation before world public opinion, turn over a new leaf in our relations with Russia. From my personal and political viewpoints this would have been both right and popular. The people would have stood behind me more firmly than ever; if necessary, I could have resigned and carried with me the accord of every Hungarian. This would have been my natural reaction, because I had detested extortion all my life.

On the other hand, the Hungarian government was kept in constant suspense by the threat against the ideological independence of the nation; obviously an open political battle with the Soviet must be avoided during the time of the peace conference.

Neither I nor, I believe, anyone else, could have shouldered the responsibility before history of opening the way for a Soviet attitude resulting in peace terms which would cripple, impoverish, and visit suffering upon generations to come.

There was still another consideration to block my natural impulse— I could not hope that Hungary, in a dispute with the Soviet, would appear as an equal opponent of mighty Russia before the court of world opinion. We could not hope to enjoy strong support from any source against the Soviet which would outlast all consequences.

My choice was simple: I had to examine the Soviet demands and decide which must be fulfilled, in the best interests of the nation, and which could be evaded.

The first part of the letter established that a series of attacks had occurred against the armed forces of the Union of Soviet Socialist Republics occupying Hungarian soil—"attacks originating with the fact that certain political personalities and Hungarian institutions were encouraging these atrocities. The commander of the occupation forces is therefore obliged to demand that the Hungarian government take certain measures."

The first demand was the immediate dissolution of the Catholic Youth Organizations and the Boy Scouts, accused of being "nests of reaction" where youth was taught to hate the Red army. I consulted with the Minister of the Interior, who indicated that he had already received orders from Soviet officials to disband these organizations.

We finally agreed to dissolve them on paper, and let them reorganize under different names and with new leaders. Alas, the Communist Minister of the Interior dissolved these youth groups but immediately afterward, undoubtedly with Soviet encouragement, created insurmountable bureaucratic difficulties to the granting of new charters. Only the Boy Scouts were permitted to reorganize.

The second demand was that the Hungarian government should

"forcefully direct" the clergy to cease attacking the institutions of democracy and inciting the people against the Red army. It was claimed that an overwhelming section of the clergy, under the leadership of Joseph, Cardinal Mindszenty, Primate of Hungary, was fostering hatred for the Red army. This demand caused no difficulty. I issued a declaration to the clergy, calling upon it to support democracy and promote cooperation with the occupying forces.

The third demand was the immediate removal of four lord-lieutenants: Daniel Andrássy, of the county of Szabolcs, Francis Vidovics of Somogy, Paul Zeöke of Esztergom, and Cornell Milasin of Heves, who as heads of their county's governments, "were responsible for the lively opposition to democracy and the Red army." This also caused little difficulty, because these lord-lieutenants sat in Parliament, too, at a time when a bill was considered prohibiting members from holding appointive government office. They would have had to resign either their deputyships or their appointive posts, and I delayed action until the bill was brought before Parliament. All resigned their county posts and kept their seats in Parliament.

The next demand was that I ask the resignation of Zoltán Pfeiffer, Undersecretary of Justice, accused of impeding the swift investigation of crimes against democracy and punishment of the guilty. I firmly refused and Pfeiffer remained in office for more than half a year.

I also refused to have two Parliamentary deputies—Leslie Gyulai, head of the public relations department of the Smallholders party, and Stephen B. Rác, president of the powerful Independent Smallholder Youth—indicted on general charges. The Communists never succeeded in bringing Rác to court; but Gyulai was arrested as a "conspirator" some months later.

Another demand, of lesser importance, was that I order a housecleaning in the directorship of the Independent Smallholder Youth and appoint new leaders. I handled this by appointing a commission of Smallholders to supervise the organization, and left it to the youth to reorganize its leadership.

I seem to recall that the communication also asked me to lower the voice of the Smallholder press and warn it to support democracy and the coalition more emphatically.

Naturally, such part-satisfaction of their demands did not please the Soviet; and it pleased the Hungarian Communists even less. I believe that my acts indicated to Russia that she could not regard me as her tool, nor use me for the dissemination of Communist power propaganda.

The Soviet-Communist-party collusion had reached the point of grabbing every opportunity to weaken the western idea of democracy and promote the spread of Communism. It appears that they now first conceived the hellish plan to prevent, by unlawful and immoral methods, my remaining at the helm of my country.

The fact that I dared refuse some of Sviridov's demands, and the failure of the trick of using the commander of the occupation forces, brought the anger of the Communists to red heat. Tactics changed; the slogan, "Fight against reaction," reappeared, but naturally this fight became concentrated against the Smallholders party. Mass terror again ran rampant through the country.

A mob of Communists attacked the county offices at Szolnok and, using physical violence, forced Lord-Lieutenant Andrew Baráth to resign. Breaking into his office, they tried the same method at Szabolcs with Daniel Andrássy, but he escaped uninjured through the timely intervention of a Cossack major with whom he was friendly. The police did nothing to curb or counteract these outrages of mob violence, and at times these "guardians of the law" actually encouraged the mob.

Facing the renewed terrorism of the Communists, and sensing that the comparatively peaceful equilibrium of the country was endangered again, we tried a new tactical move.

Béla Kovács published a series of editorials in the Smallholders papers pointing out the Communist acts and serving notice of a forceful Smallholders resistance. In these editorials the Smallholders party made new demands, that responsible, trustworthy men be placed in the administration offices to remedy the condition prevalent since the "liberation." The Communist ministers and police administrators continually substituted their stooges for non-Marxists. Our demand for a housecleaning of the police was rooted in the fact that Communist police chiefs abandoned the law to side with the terroristic mob. Under such conditions Hungary could hardly expect to maintain her peace and tranquillity.

Another demand was that elections be held in all corporate towns and cities whose autonomy was guaranteed by law. The people of these communities found it inexplicable that, although elections in Budapest had been held before the national ballot, six months later they had not yet had an opportunity to make their own choice of local government.

The last and most important demand was directed at Parliament:

The Smallholders party wanted a law enabling the peasantry to form an organization to represent its interests and enable it to exert influence on the government's economic policy—something of an agricultural chamber. The peasants did not want to stand idle and voiceless while taxes were determined, prices were fixed, or measures were passed forcing them to deliver produce to the government, and on to Russia as reparations. The peasant wanted only a chance to break the economic stranglehold of the Communists. These demands, natural in a true democracy, infuriated the Communists all the more.

While political wisdom would have dictated that, in the interests of satisfactory foreign relations, we keep internal peace at any price, it would have been unjust to turn a deaf ear to the protests of the majority, disregard their will, and allow their livelihood to be further endangered by the collusive actions of Hungarian Communists, as the vanguard of an alien ideology, and the armed forces of the Soviet Union.

CHAPTER 56

The Communist-Staged Pogroms

WHILE THE NON-MARXIST MEMBERS OF THE CABINET WERE CONSTANTLY trying, in the face of terrific odds, to preserve peace and tranquillity, the Communists devised new means to upset the delicate balance of public emotion.

We were faced with a new issue when racial hatred was suddenly fostered by the Communists. A typical example of their unscrupulousness in inciting men against their brothers occurred when they marched the workers from the factory of Diósgyör into the city of Miskolc, ostensibly to demonstrate against high prices and the black market. The mob was led to the Jewish-owned mill, where a few henchmen broke into the offices, abducted the two Jewish owners, and dragged them by their feet along the pavements of the city. One of them died as a result; the other, seriously injured, barely escaped with his life. A sizable pogrom developed.

The demonstration had hardly ended when I was notified. I instantly instructed the Minister of the Interior to make a thorough investigation; in view of the fact that he assumed the murderers were not Communists, a few were quickly arrested. When the workers of Diósgyör learned of the arrests the next day, they told the Communist workers of the district to assemble *en masse* in Miskolc the following afternoon. They came—a bigger crowd than ever—and demanded immediate freedom for the murderers. When the Minister of the Interior asked my advice, I said, "The law must be enforced."

When the local administrator refused the demand of the mob, it broke into the prison and freed the killers, who complained that during their examination a Jewish police officer had dealt harshly with them. That was enough. The mob stormed the building, found and lynched the officer, and proceeded to the internment camp. Breaking in, it released all the Nazis and Fascists.

The Communist-controlled police, watching impassively while their own officer was killed and the Nazis and Fascists released, did not take a single step to halt the terrorism. This made it clear that the police force was under Communist influence and did not disagree with the anti-Semitism of the Communist mob.

In response to great public indignation, the Minister of the Interior finally assembled several groups of police from different parts of the country and had the murderers rearrested. A few of the police officials were dismissed, and some transferred; but, alas, Justice Minister Ries eventually ordered the murderers freed without trial.

Another typical Communist-inspired pogrom developed in Kunmadaras; but in this case the Communists, having learned their lesson in Miskolc, tried to make political capital out of it. As soon as I heard that a mob had attacked some Jews in Kunmadaras, I again directed the Minister of the Interior to bring the offenders to justice immediately. At a cabinet council that day I brought the matter up and declared that we were deeply shocked by these outbursts of anti-Semitism and strongly condemned the inhuman acts. Rákosi quickly asked that the Kunmadaras case be dealt with by a specially constituted martial court. The cabinet agreed.

The murderers were soon apprehended, despite the police officials' scandalous clumsiness. The martial court assembled, and on the first day of testimony Rákosi telephoned to complain furiously that the prisoners' dock was full of poor people while the wealthy Smallholders, who probably had incited the whole affair, were missing. I directed Zoltán Pfieffer, the Undersecretary of Justice, to investigate the case immediately in person and report on the progress of the trial. Pfieffer telephoned from Kunmadaras to report that not a single Smallholder had had anything to do with the obviously Communistic pogrom.

The next day Rákosi called to ask that I stop the proceedings of the martial court and transfer the trial to another court which could investigate the responsibility on a wider scale.

I made myself very plain. "I am deeply interested in having this outrageous affair dealt with in the most objective manner and am not willing to remove the trial from the martial court before the case, in all its aspects, is investigated in every detail. I am going to attach the chief of the security division of the Ministry of the Interior, Counselor Szebenyi, to Undersecretary Pfieffer, and if both agree that the procedure of the martial court does not afford adequate thoroughness, I shall be glad to grant your wish," I answered.

Rákosi was forced to agree because Szebenyi was an avowed Communist. Soon I received a report.

In Szolnok, the county seat, where the court sat, they called on the district attorney charged with the prosecution.

"Sir," said Pfeiffer, "you are not prosecuting the case to the fullest extent. You are charging only the actual murderers, although it is reasonable to assume that others had a hand in inciting the outrages. Information has reached me that two members of the local Smallholders party, a teacher named John Nagy and a secretary, Gregory Toth, were supposedly instrumental in inciting the masses against Jewish citizens. I would suggest that you include these two in your prosecution."

"Mr. Undersecretary," answered the Communist district attorney, "I have thoroughly investigated all aspects. On the morning of the pogrom, a number of Jewish merchants arrived from Budapest and, in view of the inflationary tendency of prices, made a higher bid for eggs than on the previous day. The local poor people, faced with this competition, became enraged and hurled imprecations against Jews in general. A moron, Esther Kabai-Toth, suddenly began to scream that the Jews had killed and made sausage of her sister's child. As a result, the crowd lost all reason. First attacking any Jews they could find in the market, they then marched to the homes of the local Jews and flailed them, until some died. A Jewish merchant from Budapest escaped from the market place and began to walk rapidly homeward along the railroad tracks. A few workers unloading a carload of bricks noticed him and accosted him. After he told them why he was escaping, the workers stoned him to death. These workers are members of the Marxist youth, and I must say, sir, that I have found not an iota of truth in the claim that Smallholders were involved in the pogrom."

Pfeiffer then turned to the Communist attorney for the Communist defendants. "Counselor, you are in a position to broaden this trial. Why don't you ask the defendants and the witnesses such questions as might incriminate the supposed inciters and possibly some Smallholders?"

"Mr. Undersecretary," answered the attorney for the defense, "I won't let anybody trick me into this. I have convinced myself that the Smallholders had no connection with the pogrom whatsoever, and I can't risk slandering them in open court."

The Communist Szebenyi agreed with Pfeiffer's report in all details, and this made it clear that the flogging and murder of the Jews in Kunmadaras was a locally organized Communist action.

I called Rákosi and said: "The report of the trial proves conclusively that the Smallholders had nothing to do with the pogrom of Kunmadaras. The chronology of the affair shows that there were no inciters; nevertheless, I want to spare the Communist party the odium of a one-sided anti-Semitic action and am therefore ordering the trial transferred to a court not bound by the speedy procedure of martial law. This should satisfy you."

What followed was a classic example of Communist perfidy. The Minister of Justice, a tool of Rákosi and his gang, ordered the formation of a special panel of justices who arrived at a most peculiar verdict. While all of the murderers received varying prison sentences, John Nagy and Gregory Toth, against whom a whispering campaign was conducted, were sentenced to death. I was horrified. As the head of a coalition government I wished to protect the Communist party from a disgraceful world scandal; and at the same time the Communist party shamelessly turned the consequences of an outrageous crime against the Smallholders.

The case was finally reviewed by the People's Court of Appeal, which declared the two groundlessly sentenced men innocent and set them free.

My attempt to shield the dastardly actions of the Communists for the sake of the coalition was a grave mistake. After learning this lesson I instructed all functionaries of the Smallholders party to keep a constant watch over the Communist tendency to incite racial hatred and foster prejudice against persons of Jewish faith, most of whom had endured soul-shattering tortures at the hands of the Nazis and Arrow Cross. While no more pogroms were openly attempted anywhere in the country during my administration, the minor Nazis and Arrow Cross followers, who had found refuge in the ranks of the Communist party, continued to promote anti-Semitism by conducting a whispering campaign to hold the Jews responsible for the disastrous economic plight of the poverty-stricken population. Naturally the Communist party was delighted; here was an opportunity to remove some of the blame for conditions brought on by the Russian occupation forces and the strangling acts of the Soviet.

CHAPTER 57

The Why of Our Policy

DURING THIS TRYING PERIOD, THE QUESTION, OFTEN ASKED AFTERWARD, arose of why the Smallholders party or I did not step before the world and call attention to the dark political clouds from the east which overshadowed Hungarian life. Why did I insist on continuing a coalition, and why did I maintain a silence which gave the Communists a chance to tighten their strangle hold on the world?

History and the world demand an answer. Some aspects of the question may be clarified by simply illuminating the conditions that existed on the world political scene.

The draft of the Hungarian peace treaty had become public. It made clear the hard battle we should have to wage during the peace conference if the people of Hungary were to be granted a bearable treaty. By this time we knew well that certain meaningless small paragraphs, which the western powers considered of negligible importance, might mean our extermination. We learned this lesson from the Soviet method of interpreting the Potsdam and armistice agreements. Still, it was to our best interest to have a peace executed with the victorious powers. Only thus might we reach a point from which the resumption of our sovereignty and the termination of the foreign occupation might be visible.

Our negotiations abroad had convinced us that the major decisions regarding our future were in the hands of the Soviet Union. At that time no one was ready to stand by and support us against Russia. The conclusion was simple: Russia's viewpoint would be decisive at the peace conference; therefore, until peace treaties were signed and ratified, it would be to our advantage to do everything to promote and insure her indulgence, if not good will.

But it was obvious also that, if the peace conference were concluded by an agreement of all the great powers, Hungary, even after regaining her sovereignty, would be dependent upon the friendship of her mighty neighbor, Soviet Russia.

On the other hand, we realized that we could not allow Russia to become anxious about our attitude, or even let the claim arise that Hungary "threatened the security of the Soviet Union."

We had to preserve cooperation and the appearance of internal peace because—this has come to my mind many times—we were given to understand that a Hungary torn apart by civil war or existing in a state of revolution would not be considered as a fit signer of a peace treaty. Postponement of international peace and extension of occupation meant catastrophe for our country.

Aside from the desire of humane statesmen and politicians to give the emotions of the population a rest, a very important consideration forced us to maintain internal peace. This was Hungary's financial condition, which had dropped to a practically unbearable low level. The value of the currency sank from minute to minute, and persons on fixed incomes were being driven to the verge of destruction. The Finance Minister announced to the cabinet that he had to reduce the number of colors in the currency so that the printing could be done in one operation, because the available mechanical equipment was inadequate. In the last weeks of inflation, he even had to eliminate numbers from the bills to save machine operations.

Stabilization had to be achieved in any case and at any price. If the political situation got out of balance with the fluctuating economy, there would be even less hope of creating a new and stable currency.

When we are asked what specific pressure the Communist party and the Soviet Union applied to gain new territory in, and increase their influence on, our country, the answer is simple: Compromises were forced upon us by general internal conditions, the fact that Hungary had to fend for herself, and the reluctance of any of the major powers, considering the numerous points of tension in world politics, to take a definite stand against the Soviet Union and for the people of Hungary.

To resist Soviet demands and pressure would have been possible only if I had been ready to face a complete upheaval, or had held the slightest hope that better conditions would result. That upheaval would have brought negation of all our incredible accomplishments, and the threat of a national collapse delivering many thousands of our citizens to all the dangers and vicissitudes of temporary anarchy.

The distinct difference maintained between Hungary and her eastern European neighbors would have disappeared before the world; she would have been added to the group of politically unstable countries not worth the trust and fellowship of democratic nations. Such would have been the result of ending the policy of compliance, and by our resistance straining the thread of coalition to the breaking point.

Many times politicians who I well knew would shy from the slightest step involving their own courage and physical safety, pained me by their encouragement to resist Soviet inroads.

That my feeling was right was proved when I was forcibly removed from office, and these men became subservient tools of the Soviet Union. They flung mud at me—they who had formerly urged me toward ever stronger resistance and criticized my middle-of-the-road policy.

CHAPTER 58

Stabilizing Finances

A GOVERNMENT BASED ON ITS PARTY STRENGTH HAS NO DIFFICULTY IN sponsoring a bill in Parliament; not so a coalition government, in which the wishes of all the member parties must be considered and an agreement reached.

The Minister of Agriculture, Stephen Dobi, had prepared a bill creating a corporate institution to represent the economic interests of the peasantry. Such a law was sought by all peasants in the land, and Béla Kovács voiced their demands in his editorials.

Dobi negotiated with the parties for weeks. The Communists objected strenuously, and persuaded the Social Democrats to oppose such a law. They would allow it to be offered as a bill of the coalition with a passage providing for a centralized employment exchange.

This would have meant that a union would control all farm labor as an employment agency. A farm hand would not be able to find work on his own; he would have to go to the union hall, which would decide what kind of labor he was to perform, where, for whom, and at what pay. A farmer could not choose his help, but must accept whomever the union hall sent. Moreover, such union employment centers would have a political aspect: under instructions, they could withhold farm help from Smallholder land owners and refuse employment to Smallholder laborers.

I was infuriated by this Communist cunning. No decent, right-thinking person could accept such personal and economic slavery; it was an outrage to democracy.

Concluding that Minister Dobi's negotiations had no hope for success, I permitted one of the Smallholder deputies in Parliament, Alexander Kis, to introduce it as his individual bill. According to parliamentary procedure the majority would decide whether it wished to consider the bill or not. Kis presented his bill.

At the same time, after lengthy negotiations, the Minister of Justice prepared a bill to grant amnesty to petty offenders. I looked to the furtherance of peace and consolidation among the different segments of the population. The persecution since the liberation of minor violators held in custody must be ended. The Minister of Justice agreed to present a bill, freeing prisoners under sentences of less than two years for political offenses and reducing by 50 per cent political sentences of two to five years.

This law was necessitated by popular desire because, during times of tension, many persons had been sentenced without much consideration. Also, the support of these unproductive persons weighed heavily on the national treasury.

The Communists naturally revolted because this popular move had not originated with them and they could claim no credit for it.

Soon the well established machinery began to operate: General Sviridov invited me to see him.

In the garb of chairman of the Allied Control Commission, the mighty patron of the Hungarian Communists declared that the bills were undesirable, and that he disapproved of having either of them debated in Parliament. The bill to protect the economic interests of the peasantry had a corporate character, unnecessary because the existing political parties were well equipped to represent every interest of the peasantry. Regarding the bill for an amnesty, he said that he would not agree because the time for clemency toward political offenders had not yet arrived.

I called to Sviridov's attention the fact that the peasantry was the largest democratic political segment in Hungary. It must feel that it had a decisive voice in the new system. It must be raised to the same level of power as organized labor. He answered that he would investigate the question further and "return to it." He never did.

As for the amnesty, I told the Soviet general that in the American and British occupied zones of Germany petty offenders had received amnesty some time ago. We must take similar steps in a less infected country which already had a functioning government and could prevent furtive organization of reactionary or Fascist groups. Sviridov tenaciously resisted, declaring that he would go so far as to let the president of the Republic exercise clemency toward individuals whose release would not endanger the republic.

Again Communist intrigue was victorious, and again the dissatisfaction of the Smallholders mounted. Furthermore, the western democracies indicated their distaste for conditions which obstructed the will of the people. But only a few members of the cabinet actually knew how the Communists had won their point.

This performance convinced me again that some agreement with the leftist bloc was absolutely necessary for easing the constant tension and achieving at least part of the Smallholders' goals. Foremost in my mind was the desire to present to the world a tranquil country, ready to receive a just peace and take its rightful place in the community of nations.

While work kept me at my desk from early morning until late at night, I always tried to maintain close personal contact with the two great men of the Smallholders party, Béla Kovács and Béla Varga. Father Varga lived in a small cell in a convent, where Béla Kovács and I often had the evening meal with him.

On one of these intimate evenings, I poured my heart out, telling them of the tremendous difficulties with the Communists and of the type of pressure exerted by the Soviet Union. No outsider could know the details. The welfare of their country was uppermost in the minds of these selfless men; they would do everything in their power to help.

I conveyed my desire for some sort of understanding with the left bloc, even temporary, in order to limit the crisis and preserve the delicate balance of our internal and external politics. Both agreed.

Thus far I had attended the interparty conferences; now I thought that if Béla Kovács would represent the Smallholders party we might induce the leftist bloc to yield to some of the wishes of the Smallholders. I asked Kovács to be the negotiator at the new interparty conferences.

"Why, Ferenc?" he asked.

"Because," I answered, "I hope that the negotiations will result in some gain for the Smallholders, and it would be desirable for you to accomplish this for the party."

"I am not an easy negotiator, and, aside from that, the Communists detest me. The negotiations may not turn out as expected, simply because I am a party to them."

"On the other hand, you are the outstanding authority on the self-government and the laws concerning autonomies; as the coming conferences between the parties will deal with elections in the autonomies, it would be well for you to be the negotiator."

Béla Kovács finally agreed, and negotiations went on for quite some time. He kept President Tildy and me daily informed of the progress and complained bitterly of the perfidious attitude of the Communists. It was practically impossible, he said, to break down the resistance of the leftist bloc and achieve an agreement which would satisfy the people. Finally, he reached an agreement with the left on four points, which he brought before the national committee of the Smallholders:

(1) From 100 to 150 Smallholder police officers would be appointed to the police force.

(2) Elections in the autonomies would be held in the fall, at which the Smallholders would refrain from pressing for proportionate distribution of offices; the voters would automatically decide, in the elections, who should be their administrators.

(3) Vacancies in the post of lord-lieutenant or mayor under the law dealing with the reduction and retirement of civil servants would be filled by nominees of the Smallholders party.

(4) The negotiators released a communication on behalf of all parties announcing that they would "fight reaction" even within the individual parties, the Smallholders not excepted.

Béla Kovács was not satisfied with the results, but the party leadership decided that the agreement must be accepted. In the party caucus, I praised his achievements.

(Later, during the witch hunt for the "conspirators," the Communists asserted that Kovács had demanded proportionate distribution of civil service posts so strenuously because the "conspirators" were egging him on. He only pressed a demand justified in any democracy.)

The Communists apparently agreed to something they had long resisted, only to attack from an entirely new direction.

After one of the cabinet councils the Minister of Defense, Eugene Tombor, called me aside: "Mr. Prime Minister, I am forced to ask you to accept my resignation."

He had called by request at the office of General Kondratov, the Soviet head of the military section of the Allied Control Commission, who had instructed him to increase the border guard from 5,000 to 10,000 men and appoint as commander a Colonel Pálfi-Oesterreicher. This man, one of the vilest Communists in the Ministry of War, headed the army political squad which dealt with confidential police matters.

"By what claim does the Soviet inject itself in the internal affairs of the army?" I asked.

"They claim," answered Tombor, "that the armistice agreement gives them an opportunity to concern themselves with army appointments. On this basis they have ordered me already to present to them every appointment made above the rank of captain."

"Did you look up the armistice agreement, to note if it contains such a proviso?"

"Yes, I did. I looked it over carefully myself and had our legal experts study it; the armistice agreement gives no opportunity for such a direct intrusion. I told that to Kondratov, but the general pointed to the paragraph which deals simply with the establishment of an army and told me that on the basis of this paragraph they have the right to take such steps."

I was shocked by this new infamy, but I weighed the pros and cons of action. For some time the Communists had been trying to infiltrate the Ministry of Defense, but the minister would not appoint Communists to important key posts. Now the Soviet rushed to aid the party, using the misinterpretation of a paragraph of the armistice agreement. I told Tombor:

"I will not accept your resignation, for I should be unable to find a man as skilled and resolute to replace you. Under the conditions we are forced to execute the Soviet orders in the hope that the peace treaty will end all these intrusions."

At this time the cabinet council dealt at length with stabilization. All our energies were concentrated on bringing a basis for economic security to the people. After long study by all factions, including the Supreme Economic Council headed by Muscovite Zoltán Vas, we set August 1 for the introduction of the new unit of currency, to be called the forint. Men with a traditional economic education shook their heads, but the government believed in its own plan for stabilization. We knew that the living standard would drop to half the peacetime level, but we also knew that a stable currency would ease the minds of the Hungarian people. Queerly enough—and it was one of the most misleading signs —the Communist ministers and experts were most eager to contribute to an early stabilization. No one knew then that they were fattening their own cow for the future.

The decision to bring about stabilization necessitated three very important steps. First, we had to express wages and salaries in terms of the new currency; the same had to be done for the prices of consumer goods. We also had to establish the value of the forint in relation to the currencies of other countries. None of these tasks was easy. Finally we agreed to fix wages and salaries at 50 per cent of the 1939 income standard, on a progressive scale so that workers in the lower income brackets would receive slightly more, and those in the higher brackets slightly less, than 50 per cent of their peacetime pay.

In the fixing of prices for consumer goods, the peasantry received a raw deal. First, prices for the agricultural products were fixed, which would have been high enough had we used a corresponding scale for manufactured goods. But by a clever maneuver, when the agricultural prices had already been determined, and we were to establish the prices for manufactured goods, lobbies produced statistics and cost estimates proving that industry would perish unless the government raised the price level of manufactured goods. When prices were finally fixed, the relative scale for agricultural products was far below the corresponding scale for industrial goods.

The most serious mistake by the government was in fixing the dollar-forint relationship. The Finance Minister and other Smallholder experts wanted to establish an exchange rate of seventeen forints to the dollar; the Communists insisted that the dollar was overvalued at such a rate and maintained that it was worth only seven forints. Stormy conferences ensued, and finally the cabinet council set the exchange rate at 11.7 forints to the dollar. When we made it clear that in our opinion this would make the establishment of trade between the United States and Hungary impossible, Rákosi declared that the Communist party would agree to a revaluation if it could be proved that that rate of exchange would have an unfavorable influence on Hungary's trade with the West. No one could imagine that, from the very first, Rákosi was scheming to make trade with the West not only difficult but impossible so that Hungary would be forced to rely on trade with countries controlled by the Soviet type of economy.

That is how the intricate methods necessary in a coalition government achieved stabilization. While much anxiety accompanied the government's steps, the internal functioning of the stabilization program undoubtedly was adequate and successful. In putting a depleted agriculture to work, rebuilding the factories from the ruins, putting commerce on a firm basis, and starting economic life on the road to normalcy, stabilization, emerging from a financial chaos, was one of the greatest achievements of the new government of postwar Hungary.

CHAPTER 59

Attempts at Consolidation

STILL, ONE CRISIS FOLLOWED ANOTHER, AND EVERY EFFORT WAS MADE to avoid becoming opposed to the Communists and the Soviet in their political chess game.

At great sacrifices, the political thermometer was kept below the boiling point. In the meantime, the harvest had taken place.

Hungary is an agricultural country; the yearly harvest is a very important event in our economic life. But none was so eagerly awaited as the harvest of 1946. Every one expected the time of subnormal rations of food, of privation and starvation, to end. An abundant crop would ease the general distress.

We had a bad year, the second successive year of all-destructive drought which broke the country's agriculture. The unfortunate climate of the Danube valley did its worst, and when the war-ravaged people most needed a rich crop the lean years came. Hungary's major crop is wheat, but in 1946 the country harvested less than agriculture required for its own use. The result was even worse in other produce. Nevertheless, the new harvest brought bread to the people, and at least the Minister of Supply, Charles Bárányos, was able to plan with what was available to feed the population during the coming year. But stabilization accomplished, and immediate worry about where the daily bread was coming from eliminated, gave the people an atmosphere of rest. I felt it was time to take some serious steps along the road to consolidation.

The fact that the Minister of the Interior was still holding in crowded internment camps thirteen thousand "unreliable persons," whom the Communist police had found dangerous to democracy, caused widespread bitterness. These people had been interned without indictment or trial, preponderantly during the early days following the liberation.

I conferred with Minister of the Interior Rajk and proposed that the cases of these persons be reexamined, since stabilization and the completed harvest had created a desire for peace among the people. Rajk, the fanatical Communist, was miraculously amenable, immediately agreeing to work out an executive order to revise the internments.

Next I called his attention to the delayed reorganization of the dissolved youth organizations. He appeared to assent, and we agreed about the details. I also discussed with him the decision of the interparty conference to hold the autonomous elections during the fall and asked him to have a bill prepared in time for interparty council approval. This he agreed to undertake, too.

Parliament being in session, I decided to encourage the people and, rising in the chamber, stated that the internments would be revised and the youth reorganized. Also, it would soon receive for consideration a bill dealing with the elections in the autonomies. Great enthusiasm and reassurance were noticeable among the deputies.

First the executive order to reexamine the internments was promulgated and, upon my approval, came into effect. Within a few weeks, 8,000 prisoners were released; the Minister of the Interior also decided to reduce the number of internment camps to two. This order, received with great satisfaction, was an important step toward pacifying the population.

Unfortunately the other two issues were not so satisfactorily resolved. Reorganization of the youth societies continued to be balked.

While it could not be proved that the Russians were pulling the strings, it became obvious that the Minister of the Interior was constantly impeding the issuance of charters to the religious groups.

I had no more luck with the elections in the autonomies; Rajk prepared a bill which I found unacceptable. His idea, and that of the Communists, was naturally that the law should be connected to certain executive measures for reorganizing the administration. In practice this would have meant that, instead of all of the officials being elected by the people, a government appointee would sit in every village and township. My conviction is that the appointment of officials within the autonomies is contrary to democracy; only autonomous governments in which every official is freely elected can be regarded as truly democratic.

Thus were elections in the autonomies delayed, causing new dissatisfaction among the people. But when autumn arrived I decided not to force the issue too much, because elections had been held in Rumania and, according to official reports, the "common government ticket," as against the Peasant party led by Maniu and the Liberals led by Bratianu, received an "overwhelming victory" at the polls. I went to great pains to secure complete information, and this proved that the official reports did not express the true will of the people. My informants, who had traveled all through Rumania, reported that Maniu's Peasant party had received at least 70 per cent of the popular vote—but the government bloc was publishing claims of a victory exceeding this percentage. I concluded that if, despite such an obvious popular showing, the Communist-dominated government bloc was able to report such a "sweeping victory" at the polls, then surely the Russians stood behind the election, managed it, and their will was expressed in the official reports. A note sent by the United States to the government of Rumania, observing that it felt the will of the people had been denied expression during elections, strengthened my belief.

I had to consider, therefore, what effect our autonomous elections might have on relations with the Soviet Union. I foresaw the election results: in at least 2,000 of the 3,400 villages and autonomous communities only a Smallholder could be elected dogcatcher, to say nothing of membership in the council. Furthermore, in a thousand or more communities, the Smallholders party would receive an absolute majority. Only in 400 communities could the leftist bloc assume the upper hand. My figures were securely based on knowledge of the strength of the parties and the mood of the population. The entire leadership of my party agreed with me on the results to be expected. The people were sick and tired of watching saloon loafers amble into city hall for a few minutes, issue orders received from Communist party headquarters, and then retire to the saloon. An election would have flung this scum out at the nearest exit.

If, after the "overwhelming victory" in Rumania, the elections in the Hungarian autonomies should result in a defeat for the leftist bloc, the Soviet Union undoubtedly would exert an unbearable pressure on Hungary. After discussing it with Smallholders in Parliament, the party leaders agreed that elections should be postponed until the Russian army had left Hungary, regardless of the desirability of an early date.

In the meantime the order for the reduction of the number of civil servants was put into effect, and the "B list" commissions began to function. The name arose from the fact that people remaining in the service were listed under classification A, while those dismissed, relieved, or retired met their fate as classification B.

The work of these commissions was as sorry as could be expected. Each commission consisted of a chairman appointed by me, one member delegated by the minister whose department was being scanned, and one member delegated by the trade unions. This composition was the result of the left bloc's earlier stubborn insistence.

The Communist and Socialist ministers had compiled in advance, lists of all civil servants they wanted to eliminate from their departments, and handed them to the respective delegates. These men, working hand in glove with the trade-union representative, consistently voted against the chairman appointed by the Prime Minister, without discussing the merits or ability of the person involved. Naturally the Smallholder ministers did the same thing; their delegates voted with my appointees against the trade-union representative. While the Smallholder commission members generally attempted, with a measure of success, to clean house by putting all useless jobholders on the "B list," the Communist-Socialist combine created havoc in certain departments of the administration by "B-listing" outstanding civil servants, reliable experts, and top executives simply because they were not members of the left-bloc parties.

The most atrocious performance took place in the Department of the Interior. Through the Communist-trade-union combine on his commission, Rajk brought about the dismissal, among others, of all the old-time village clerks, to whom the population was deeply attached. Delegations from all over the land came to voice their complaint against this action, which hurt them deeply, and demand the immediate reinstatement of the faithful, proven servants of the community.

The Communist-trade-union combine wreaked havoc through these commissions; beyond the personal tragedy of thousands, it resulted in one political disaster. For the Ministry of Defense, I appointed Albert Barta, a Smallholder deputy, chairman of the "B list" commission. Minister Tombor delegated his old friend, Colonel Daróczi, with instructions to keep reliable, well trained and tested officers in service and to "B-list" such recent appointees as lacked adequate educational training and Communist political appointees who were chiefly responsible for retarding the efficiency of our small armed force. But Colonel Daróczi was already a secret member of the Communist party. Instead of siding with my appointee he allied himself with the trade-union representative. Their two votes, against Barta's one, eliminated a long list of valuable, respected, and well trained officers from service merely because of membership in, or sympathy with, the Smallholders party.

Minister of Defense Tombor, when he was informed of the betrayal, suffered a fatal heart attack. The betrayal by his friend had killed him.

Among Hungarian democrats, dissatisfaction with the use of force by Communist party officials, the behavior of Communist civil servants, and the acts of the Communist police, gained momentum as time went by. It found expression in Parliament, where the deputies, one after another, entered interpellations on the dockets taking exception to the outrages against the people.

Of the deputies' rights in Parliament, interpellation is the most cherished. It is an act whereby ministerial policies or actions are formally questioned in the open forum of the legislature. On the days set aside for interpellations in Parliament, the mood of the people comes closest to expression; their complaints and wishes are aired at the highest level of popular expression. In times of one-party government, interpellations are no danger, for the majority party is in a position to outvote the critical opposition deputy, no matter what answer the interpellated member of the cabinet has given.

During the Hungarian coalition, the situation had to be slightly different. The individual ministers occupied their chairs by agreement of the coalition parties; and care had to be exercised with the parliamentary vote, and foresight used before interpellations were allowed on the docket. Therefore, no matter how occupied I was, I reserved the right to weigh the advisability of interpellations by Smallholder deputies. Interpellations which attacked the Communists on unimportant issues and needlessly endangered the coalition were erased. On the other hand, I made Rákosi and Szakasits, leaders of the Communists and the Socialists respectively, direct the erasure of interpellations by their party deputies against the Smallholders party which would have also jeopardized the coalition. Naturally this was a serious inroad on the parliamentary rights of the deputies, but during the transitional days of coalition government, it was unavoidable.

One could not, even with the most peaceful intentions, eliminate interpellations dealing with injuries to the interests of the large majority of the population or those uncovering injustices which could not be left unremedied.

In such cases it was neither wise nor democratic to prevent an open debate in Parliament; in fact, this would have defeated the ultimate goal of democratic government.

A typical issue was that of the youth groups disbanded at the direct insistence of the Soviet Union. The deputies revolted against Rajk's postponement of their reorganization and of the issuance of new charters. A rapid succession of interpellations was entered; first asking, then demanding, speedy action. The Minister of the Interior generally answered with curt notes, believing that he could adopt an overbearing attitude in his replies and relying on the assumption that, in the interests of cooperation with the coalition, Parliament would not dare vote him down. He experienced a mighty disappointment.

On one of the interpellation days, Rajk's answer to a previously delivered interpellation was read. When the clerk finished the curt note, the deputy who originated the action rose, objected to its arrogant tone, demanded more respect from the Minister of the Interior for Parliament, and declared that he would not accept the answer. According to parliamentary rules the question had to be put to the floor, and the presiding officer ordered a vote. The Smallholder majority supported the interpellator *en bloc,* rejecting the answer of the Minister.

Great excitement followed the tally; the Communists flew into a tantrum. Under normal conditions the Minister would have had to resign immediately; but Rajk was saved by the existence of the coalition. In retaliation for his public defeat, he bored against the Smallholders more resolutely and with greater fury.

The Smallholders could have continued in this manner in Parliament—the actions of the Communists on numerous occasions invited such treatment from the Smallholder majority in Parliament; but it would have led to a breakdown of the coalition.

An undercurrent now indicated that Communist-party-Soviet collusion was to take a new turn. It had seemed that the Communists were relying on the Soviet Union for aid in achieving their ends; but about this period one instinctively began to feel that the Soviet was encouraging the party to act according to preconceived plans.

Outwardly, the political picture did not change. The parties, aware that the autonomous elections would be held at some future date, increased their organizational activities and displayed their strength by holding mass meetings. Never in the political history of Hungary could such large crowds be moved as during this period. It was curious to see a larger crowd assembled at some Smallholder mass meetings in an outlying city than could be accounted for by the census of that community. At some of the district meetings where I was privileged to speak to the voters, the crowd reached as far as I could see. Meetings attended by more than 100,000 persons were not rare.

Political mass meetings of this type are unknown in many of the western countries. In Hungary, politicians hold them in their districts not only at election time, but throughout their term of office. The exact time and location of mass meetings are advertised in the newspapers and on posters; the attendance at the meeting indicates the popularity of the politician or his party. After reporting to his constituents, the politician spends some time with them and his party workers to estimate the mood of the people and chart his future course.

Naturally the Communists tried to outweigh the overwhelming strength of the Smallholders' mass meetings; but their relatively small following made this difficult. Therefore, whenever Rákosi was to speak at a mass meeting in the country, they arranged special trains that carried their "following" from all parts of the country to the scene. The Minister of Transportation permitted excursion rates for such trains, amounting to half the regular fare. Later, the Smallholders party used trains on two occasions, each of our members paying the reduced fare. Soon we discovered the trick behind the Communists' excursion trips: the reduced fare was not paid by the individual travelers but remitted for the entire trainloads by the Communist party treasury directly to the State Railroad Treasury. This neat little trick enabled them to get "masses of followers" to take free "excursions" every time a Communist bigwig desired an audience. One could hardly compete with such a scheme—especially since the Communists had a Fortunatus purse.

Public opinion was outspoken about the "free trains"; criticisms were aired, and it was even suggested that, not only did passengers receive free transportation, but the "enthusiastic followers" were paid by the Communist party by the day, to travel to the meetings.

The Communists did not hesitate at the most disgraceful methods of political agitation, the best example being their instigation of a campaign against the mill industry.

In Hungary the peasant does not buy his bread in stores but takes his wheat to the mill, where the miller traditionally retains a tenth of it as his fee. The peasant wife bakes bread from the flour at home.

After the harvest, the government issued a decree ordering those peasants who had their produce milled to deliver to the miller not only his 10 per cent but also an additional 20 per cent for the general relief of the poor. By Communist instigation, the peasants in some districts began to believe that the entire 30 per cent remained in the possession of the miller. We had tried to spread the truth to the farthest hamlet in the country—the additional charge was actually a relief tax to benefit their own hungry brethren and the people as a whole; but the Communists used this issue all over the country for a forceful campaign against the millers, claiming that they were practicing usury on the peasants.

"The only defense against the usury of the mills is to have the state take them over. The smaller ones would become the property of the village communities . . ."

The idea grew until it became a slogan of the leftist bloc. We determinedly resisted this attempt at Sovietization, not only defending the basic rights of individual enterprise but recognizing, in this attack on private property, the danger of the Communists' action in which the trade unions would do everything in their power to secure control of the state- or village-owned mills, put them under Communist direction and thus deliver the entire peasantry to the whims of the Communist-directed mill managers.

The resistance shown by the Smallholder party and its representatives in the cabinet naturally created new tension within the coalition, making the peaceful operation of the government all the more difficult.

CHAPTER 60

Verbal Sparring

THE MOUNTING DIFFERENCES INSPIRED THE COMMUNISTS TO START NEW actions; now they openly and shamelessly tried to break down, in fact eliminate, the Smallholder majority in Parliament. They invented that, while there were sizable masses of democratic citizens within the Smallholders party, it had a "right wing" which had become a hotbed of "reaction" and stood in the way of progress. Unfortunately the Social Democrats were persuaded to join in this game, which was possible only because the independence of the Social Democratic party had virtually ceased. It was obvious that there was only one leader on the left —Mathias Rákosi; servitude from all who desired to remain in the leftist bloc was expected.

Because of this situation, the attack was actually started by Árpád Szakasits, leader of the Socialists. Speaking publicly in a small community, he formulated one of the most peculiar theories in the history of democracy. He claimed that a majority was an "arithmetic illusion," that the composition of the Hungarian Parliament "took an unfortunate turn" during elections by giving the vote not only to the democratic masses but to reactionaries as well.

"If we notice," he said, "how many democrats voted the Smallholder ticket, we see that the Independent Smallholders party did not receive its majority from the democratic masses."

This sorry political appendage of Rákosi forgot that great numbers of Nazis and Arrow Crossists swamped the polls, voting and promoting votes for the Communist party; and the immutable opportunists found their niche in the Social Democratic party at election time.

At a popular meeting of the Smallholders party in a Budapest sport arena, I answered Szakasits' speech, rejecting his thesis and clearly describing how the Social Democrats secured most of their voters—opportunists and devoted followers of past regimes. Because, as proved, I presented the fact that during the darkest days under Nazism and the Arrow Cross the Social Democrats numbered fewer than one hundred thousand and were hardly able to meet the party's budget.

Anthony Bán, the Minister of Industry, answered me in a threatening speech saying that, as deputy secretary of the Social Democratic party, he could state to the nation that when Hungarian labor got fed up with the impertinence of "reaction" it would march through the streets and create a new order with its fists.

This speech was answered by Béla Kovács in an editorial that poked fun at the fist-shaking of the Socialists, flourishing under the political patronage of the Communists. He also called on all the Smallholder organizations to disregard any Communist or Socialist irritations; the masses must not be sucked in or allowed to set off a chain reaction of unpleasant incidents. Naturally Béla Kovács knew that nothing would develop from the verbal sparring of the Socialists; but he wanted to keep the respectable and honest Socialist masses from being misled by such slogans and bravado.

Rákosi pulled a new trick from the miraculous bag with which he was endowed by the Comintern school of Moscow. Speaking to a "free-ride" crowd at Kecskemét, he shrewdly made himself out to be the peasants' protector and declared that their unhappiness and well founded economic dissatisfaction were due to the Smallholders party.

"If the peasants complain about the low agricultural prices fixed during stabilization, why don't they consider that the Smallholders party has the parliamentary majority and is in the position to take a successful stand on behalf of the peasantry?"

Not satisfied with this eyewash, Rákosi went on to blame the Small-holders party for high retail prices, high taxes, and the "usury" prac-ticed by the mill owners.

This impertinence infuriated the Hungarian peasant, who knew well how vigorously the Smallholders party fought for his rights. The peas-ants could not be misled; their deputies and the Smallholder organizers lived among them, and contact was constant.

By chance, the Smallholders party was already planning to hold a mass meeting in Kecskemét soon after Rákosi's speech, and now I de-cided to go there myself.

In my address I made it clear that in the interest of peaceful opera-tion of the coalition the Smallholders had many times refrained from using the power of the majority, but with the encouragement received from Mathias Rákosi we would use this power. I declared that we would not agree to the socialization of the mills because this violation of the right of private property would soon be extended to the blacksmith's anvil and the cobbler's last. Let the peasant be on guard: to the party methods the Communists had employed thus far, they had now added lying.

The Communists used this speech to identify me with the "reactionary" circles of the Smallholders party; attacks appeared in the *Szabad Nép,* the yellowest of Red publications on the European continent.

The deputies who, under the leadership of Desider Sulyok, had left the Smallholders party had decided to organize under the name of the Freedom party. Because the armistice treaty had decreed that all new political parties must announce themselves to the Allied Control Commission, Sulyok turned to me for support of their announcement. I called on Sviridov and proposed that he issue a permit to Sulyok's new party. General Sviridov, following the Russian method, tried to drown the subject in words; but I gave him no peace. Finally he declared that if I could obtain the consent of the other parties he would consider the question. I immediately talked with Rákosi and Szakasits, who made no objection to the new party. Sviridov, hearing this, answered that he would not act without the consent of Marshal Voroshilov, the all-powerful president of the Allied Control Commission, on the formation of a new political party.

The next move was typical of the Soviet's political game: after many weeks' delay in the issuance of a permit, Captain Gruber brought a letter from Sviridov taking cognition of my announcement that under the leadership of Sulyok a new political party, known as the Freedom party, was to begin functioning.

Construing the letter, I informed Sulyok immediately that his party had been approved. Sulyok rose in Parliament, happily announced the birth of a new party, and immediately made a speech setting forth its platform.

As a result, Captain Gruber visited me again, with the message from General Sviridov that I had obviously misinterpreted his letter, which only took cognition of my communication about the formation of the Sulyok party: it did not authorize the formation of the party nor its beginning to function.

This typical Bolshevik equilibrism infuriated me, and I prepared to battle for Sulyok's party under all circumstances, because I thought it most important that there should be a democratic opposition party in Parliament free from the limitations imposed by membership in the coalition and able to express, with candor and courage, its opinions about developments in Hungarian political life, the malignancies, the

Soviet influence and the resulting expansion of the Communist party. It could make necessary political moves which the Smallholders, being in the coalition, could not.

In this manner, the formation of Sulyok's party was hindered for a long time; only much later and under interesting circumstances, did I secure for Sulyok the permit to operate.

CHAPTER 61

The Peasantry Demonstrates

SINCE THE END OF HOSTILITIES, THE SMALLHOLDER PEASANTRY HAD wished to hold a national meeting at the capital. In 1920 the old Peasant party under Stephen Nagyatádi-Szabó had held such an assembly at Budapest, attended by more than a hundred thousand peasants; and many remembered its great significance and political influence. In 1945 disorganized transportation made such a gathering difficult to arrange; but in 1946 it became possible. Moreover, it became timely because the Communists were trying to expand their party with frequent mass demonstrations; and the impatience of the peasantry to show its own strength was natural.

We then decided to call a national meeting of the peasantry at Budapest on St. Stephen's Day, August 20th; it was customary for the peasantry to come to the capital on the name day of the first king of Hungary. We also decided that the meeting should be held under the sponsorship of the Peasant Alliance, and that the Smallholders party should instruct its rural branches to promote attendance. We informed the two vice premiers, Rákosi and Szakasits, of our decision. The latter did not dare express an opinion until he had heard what Rákosi had to say.

Rákosi tried to talk us out of holding such a mass meeting. "There is no call for such a show," he began. "The Smallholders party has held so many impressive mass meetings in the country, which innumerable thousands attended, that there is no reason or necessity for such a demonstration in Budapest."

"The peasantry must be made aware that democracy is as much its property as anyone else's, and it must be active in this democracy. Aside from that, masses of peasants demand this meeting, and we cannot turn a deaf ear to their wishes," I answered.

"Oh, really? But such a monster assembly of the peasant masses in Budapest would appear to be directed against the unity of the workers; it would seem as if the peasantry wished to show its strength as against labor's," said Rákosi.

"No such thing," I answered. "The meeting would be held in such fashion so that no doubt of the peasant's sympathy for the aims of labor could arise. There would be no antilabor speeches; the peasantry is not prejudiced against the working class although it disapproves of methods employed on occasion by one or the other of labor's political parties."

"But, anyway, it would not be wise to hold such a meeting on St. Stephen's Day," said Rákosi stubbornly. "For one thing, the peasants of the Communist party, of the Social Democratic party, and of the Peasant party will come to Budapest, too, and tension between the Smallholder peasants and peasants in the other parties could arise."

"All that would happen is that the peasants you mention would not attend the meeting," I answered. "But I insist upon its being held."

I knew that this shrewd Communist leader would try anything to have the peasant demonstration canceled or impeded. Naturally Szakasits soon echoed everything Rákosi had said.

Since the meeting was to be representative of the whole country, I had to announce the plans to the Allied Control Commission. I did not want the peasantry to prepare for the mass meeting, and then have its plans go amiss at the last moment with an order from Sviridov.

Sviridov was ready for me; his air indicated that Rákosi had already taken steps.

"Mr. Prime Minister, I want you to know that I disapprove of holding the peasant meeting," he announced as I entered.

"Why?" I asked, simply.

"Because all indications point to a belligerent attitude toward labor by the peasants at this meeting. Nobody can guarantee that there would be no bloody consequences."

"Where did you get this information?" I asked with deference.

"I read the proclamation of the leaders of the Peasant Alliance saying that the traditional strength of the Hungarian peasantry must be displayed at the Budapest demonstrations. Under such circumstances it would not be advisable to gather large crowds of peasants at the capital."

"This gathering of the peasants of the nation," I answered, "would assemble with peaceful intentions. General, our peasants have never given you cause to infer that they ever used their own demonstrations to commit any act of force. If labor is allowed to hold mass demonstrations every month in the streets of Budapest, then, after two years, the peasantry has the right to assemble at the capital of its own country to hear its leaders and discuss its problems."

"It might interest you to know," answered Sviridov, "that I have received reports from the local heads of the Control Commission in the counties, saying that the peasants are taking large amounts of wine with them; in fact, there are signs that many of them intend to come armed. What will happen if people, befuddled by wine and in the possession of arms, gather at a monster meeting?"

I was flabbergasted by such flagrant lies and did not keep my reaction secret.

"It is an ignominious lie. If anybody states such a thing, or if your subalterns render such reports, they have been misled by the Communists. The peasants haven't enough wine to take on trips, and neither have they arms. I want you to understand, they are coming to Budapest peacefully, soberly, and unarmed."

"I beg your pardon. I fear that this peasant demonstration will cause trouble, and I will not shoulder the responsibility of permitting it to take place," said Sviridov.

Losing patience, I turned to Sviridov: "Well, General, if you so openly use two sets of standards, denying to the peasantry what you grant to labor, I cannot further head the coalition and shall tender my resignation to the President of the Republic."

Sviridov, taken aback, softened perceptibly. "You don't have to think of resignation immediately. Mr. Prime Minister, why can't this meeting be sectionalized, so that it would occur in several large cities?" he purred.

"We have frequent meetings in the cities of the rural districts; these do not represent anything extraordinary to the peasantry. To make it something special, the meeting must be nation-wide and held in the capital; I must insist upon this—unconditionally."

Sviridov began to pace the floor. "All right. I will acquiesce to the meeting, but not on August 20. It must be held at some later date."

"What is your objection to August 20?" I asked, knowing well that Rákosi had his finger on the calendar.

"Well, frankly, we received a communication from the Peasant Alliance announcing that it is arranging an agricultural exposition for the day of the meeting, and inviting the Soviet Union to take part by exhibiting the most modern agricultural machinery. We, on our part, should really like to show our agricultural equipment at this exposition; but it would be impossible to have it arrive here by August 20. As I have heard that the British and Americans have received a similar invitation, we should very much like to participate with our machinery at the same time. I thus ask you to kindly agree to the postponement of the date of the Budapest meeting by a few weeks."

I knew what the game was and could well conclude why they played it. Sviridov and Rákosi reasoned that the meeting must be postponed, because it was not probable that the peasants would again come to Budapest a few weeks after St. Stephen's Day; surely there would not be so large a crowd on any other day. The success of the mass meeting had to be undermined by any means.

I concluded that insisting on the date set by us would be futile, once General Sviridov backed up the desires of the Communist party by throwing Soviet prestige into the consideration. I also knew that we could get large masses of peasants to attend any meeting in Budapest, even one directly after St. Stephen's Day. Bowing low before the prestige of the Soviet Union, I agreed with Sviridov that the meeting should be held on September 8, a holiday.

The peace conference had assembled in Paris. Czechoslovakia suddenly came forth with a troublesome demand for Hungary, insisting that in addition to the already existing agreement to exchange native populations, it receive the right to expel an additional 200,000 Hungarians from its territory. The people of Hungary received this news with consternation; we were all dumfounded and unable to understand why the public opinion of the world was not incensed over this injustice. Simply to transfer Czechoslovakia, a country sharing the war guilt to some extent, from a country of nationalities into a national state, an additional mass of human beings would be uprooted from their ancestral soil, increasing the millions already made homeless by the war and its aftermath, by another 200,000 souls.

This demand pained me particularly because, in my conception, Hungary and Czechoslovakia of all the eastern European nations, had the firmest basis for friendship and seemed predestined for cooperation. I still believe that, once southeastern Europe is ordered according to the will of its peoples, the two countries will find a common bond and a common interest, and will live in brotherhood and friendship.

The Hungarian public anxiously awaited the Paris dispatches, with the gripping fear that Russia had turned its back on Hungary and that we had no friends among the major powers to whom we could turn for consistent support.

Foreign Minister Gyöngyösi suggested that it would be advisable under such circumstances that I go to Paris as an observer, and try to serve Hungary by conferring with the heads of the delegations of the great powers. Knowing that Hungarian public opinion would be behind me in such a step, I agreed.

With little preparation I started out by car, accompanied only by my son Ferenc. The trip began under an unfriendly star, and on the outskirts of Budapest the car presented to me by the Soviet government skidded into a tree, smashing its front. We continued in another car.

The Hungarian cause was in bad shape in Paris; there were bitter arguments about whether the Hungarian delegation should be heard at all in some questions.

Before paying my respects to Secretary Byrnes, I visited Walter Bedell Smith, the United States Ambassador to Moscow; and we discussed all questions involving Hungary, including the additional Czechoslovakian demand for seven villages on the right bank of the Danube. He took out a map and, with Aladár Szegedy-Maszák, our Minister to Washington, and Frederick Merrill, the American diplomat stationed in Hungary, considered the facts of that demand. I believe that the groundwork for the decision that Czechoslovakia should receive three instead of seven villages on the right bank of the Danube was laid at this time.

Secretary Byrnes was just preparing to leave for Stuttgart to deliver his memorable speech, but found time to listen to my pleas on behalf of Hungary, receiving me with his customary kindness and cordiality. I based our cause on political considerations.

"Mr. Secretary, undoubtedly you are familiar with the situation in southeastern Europe; Hungary is the only country in which the Prime Minister's chair is occupied by a representative of the democratic citizenry without being entirely under the thumb of the Soviet and in the power of the Communists. The enslaved masses of the other southeastern European countries watch anxiously to see how long I can remain at the helm. If I fall, all of southeastern Europe will fall to the Communists. It isn't right that we, who fought and suffered to preserve the kind of democracy the non-Communist world believes in, should be punished."

"It would be to your country's best interest," said Byrnes, "to sign a peace treaty as soon as possible. If we reintroduce the Transylvanian question, and cause difficulties regarding a settlement, peace with Hungary will be delayed. We are doing everything in our power to free you both politically and economically as soon as possible. For that reason we are expediting a peace treaty, and placing no more obstacles in its path than we can help. Don't be disheartened; once the independence of Hungary is assured, a firm economy will follow. We will assist you in this also."

As Molotov had left Paris for a few days, I visited Andrei Vishinsky, the deputy foreign minister of the Soviet Union. Our long conversation was fruitless, except that he dangled before our eyes the possibility of negotiations with Rumania about Transylvania after the peace treaty had been signed. His method followed the usual Soviet rule that what is decided at a peace conference regarding a territory of which the Soviet is master does not count. One can always change things for the benefit of one country and the detriment of another, according to which little boy behaves better toward the great Red father sitting in the Kremlin.

I had a most pleasant conference with Field Marshal Jan Christiaan Smuts, Prime Minister of the Union of South Africa. This candid, charming statesman told me: "Indeed, it is very curious that those Czechoslovakians want to uproot 200,000 persons. It would be fairer if the Czechs would give them their homes, their lands, and their churches, so they might still feel at home."

After another few days in Paris, I left with the impression that the peace conference was a fiction. The spirit of the Atlantic Charter was not realized, and the great ideals with which humanity had been encouraged during the war, were not brought forth as cornerstones for a better future. The peace conference only blessed the haphazard agreements arrived at between the great powers—agreements resulting from a conviction that further negotiations would be useless. Undoubtedly, humanity was getting a raw deal.

Hungary had to fend for herself at the conference; only the Australians endeavored to put the great ideals into practice. The Soviet

Union ardently protected the interests of all the countries already in its yoke, but Hungary, striving to gain a democratic independence, had no protector. The democratic trend in Hungary was not strengthened; if anything, it was weakened by the indifference of the West.

The Hungarian public had reacted so enthusiastically when the Americans took a determined stand against the expulsion of Hungarians from Czechoslovakia that the later indifference was a tremendous disappointment.

The Communists, not once but many times, made sarcastic remarks to those who trusted in the Americans. Occasionally they announced, "American declarations remain declarations—one does not have to be afraid of them."

My feelings were mixed, but I was forced to conclude that under these circumstances Hungary would remain under Soviet influence; our fight against the Communist onsurge, nurtured artificially by the Soviet Union in Hungary and in all the surrounding countries, would be long and hard.

I returned from Paris on September 7, the day before the scheduled great mass meeting of the peasants. The national committee of the Smallholders party met in the evening, and I reported about the trip to Paris. I implored the leaders to bear the situation patiently so that we might insure continued cooperation with the political parties of industrial labor.

The organizational staff reported to me that all arrangements had been made for a peaceful assembly of the expected two hundred thousand peasants.

President Tildy invited Béla Kovács, the leaders of the peasantry, and me to join him on the balcony of his home to view the throngs on their way to the meeting place.

It was an unforgettable sight, this orderly march of peasants, dressed in black and with shiny black boots. Their women and children, in picturesque peasant habits, transformed Andrássy Avenue, reminding us all of the flower-spotted fields of our beloved country. Thousands of the red, white, and green flags of Hungary waved in the breeze. When labor demonstrated, Red banners were everywhere; only as many national flags as were needed to substantiate their claim to be Hungarians were used.

There were many youth groups who were inspired to perform

dances instead of marching in line. Each delegation paused in salute before the balcony of the President.

As the parade was ending, we went to the meeting place. Never did such a throng assemble at Hero Square! For weeks afterward, the press was arguing as to the number of peasants who had assembled, the figures ranging between three hundred thousand and five hundred thousand. An assembly of half a million in a population of nine million is quite an accomplishment.

When we arrived the entire cabinet, the diplomatic corps, and the Allied Control Commission were already seated on the platform. Deputy Alexander Kis, the director general of the Peasant Alliance and an outstandingly competent young man, opened the meeting. When he announced that the members of the Allied Control Commission, headed by General Sviridov, were present, a deep silence followed, broken only by scattered handclaps. But when he informed the meeting that H. F. Arthur Schoenfeld, the envoy of the United States of America, was also among the guests, the frenetic ovation rose in waves from the limitless throng. As Kis introduced each of the dignitaries, the popular reaction was evident. The names of party leaders Mathias Rákosi, Peter Veres, and Anthony Bán drew a chorus of boos which thoroughly drowned out the few cheers; the crowd did not trouble to hide its disgust.

The Peasant Alliance and the Smallholders party had selected me to be speaker of the day, and for two hours I addressed the largest assembly of peasants in the history of Hungary. The peasantry, I said, would not permit itself to be annihilated; if it continued the good work started Hungarian democracy would be the kind which the peasantry desired.

During the meeting, the chairman announced that my father was also present; suddenly voices from the throng demanded that he join us on the platform. When the simple old man appeared before the crowd and was embraced by President Tildy, the peasantry paid homage to him as the personification of the peasant's life, spent in sweat and toil.

President Tildy spoke briefly, and the meeting ended with a reading of the resolutions of the peasantry.

A very unpleasant incident occurred at the conclusion: when the large mass of people, led by the army bands, sang the national anthem, every one on the platform rose. It was observed that Rákosi had one hand in his pocket and the other curled around a cigarette.

Somebody yelled, "Rákosi, throw away that cigarette!"

Thousands joined the protest; finally, fidgeting, Rákosi stepped on his cigarette.

As a result of the mass meeting, the entire country was swept by the conviction that in the hands of the Hungarian peasant rested the ideal of true democracy.

Minister of Transportation Gerö came in for a good deal of criticism for not putting enough trains at the disposal of the peasantry. It was moving to realize with what sacrifice Hungarian peasants, lacking money and living in dire need, made the costly trip to Budapest.

While the "B list" commissions were at work Minister of Education Desider Keresztury, a member of the radical Peasant party, showed himself to be a man of honesty and backbone. He directed his deputies in the commission to retain worthy Smallholders who were experts and of good standing. Thus the Communists did not achieve their goal of eliminating reliable civil servants in the field of education.

They forced Peter Veres, the leader of the Peasant party, to tell Keresztury to resign; while the Peasant party membership stood solidly behind him, the cowardly leadership instructed him to resign and immediately proposed that the editor of the Peasant party paper, Joseph Darvas, be appointed in his stead.

I refused the recommendation, knowing Darvas was absolutely subservient to Rákosi. I was afraid that he would force changes in our cultural policy—changes which were diametrically in opposition to the Hungarian soul. The entire left bloc very aggressively disapproved of my attitude toward Darvas. Rákosi tried several times to force Darvas on me, but I argued that in Hungary the portfolio of Education had always been held by a Catholic. I would not offend the Catholics, the majority of our population, by appointing a Protestant.

One day Sviridov asked me to visit him for some "economic discussions." After we had talked about several unimportant issues, he turned to me:

"Well, Mr. Prime Minister, what happens with the portfolio of Education?"

"I am waiting for the Peasant party to nominate a suitable man," I answered.

"Well, there is a nominee. I heard the Peasant party had nominated Joseph Darvas."

"Yes, but I won't accept Darvas."

"No? What's your objection to him?" asked Sviridov slyly.

"He is not suitable," I answered. "I do not see him as a man destined for leadership, and I don't trust him. He is a man of scant education and is only good for devoting himself to petty attacks against the Smallholders party. Aside from that, I don't wish to place a Protestant in the chair of the Minister of Education; the Catholics would be rightfully indignant if, besides a Protestant President and a Protestant Prime Minister, a traditionally Catholic post were filled by still another Protestant."

Now Pushkin put his two cents into the discussion. This poisoner of Hungarian public life had no interest in basing the friendship of the two countries on the entire Hungarian nation, and remained throughout a one-sided Communist agitator.

"Bah! How on earth can one pay heed to such ancient customs in democracy? One has to choose as Minister of Education a person who, from the point of view of democracy, is most suitable. Religion doesn't matter."

"Pardon me, Mr. Minister, I am the one who must deal with the difficulties of Hungarian political life, and with the intricate weave of a coalition government; I have to wrestle, not you. I don't think I should increase the difficulties of cooperation, but I must attempt to make the large masses of the people sympathetic to the coalition. Under the circumstances, it must be made as palatable as possible."

Pushkin now developed his opinion that, in the progress of the Hungarian democracy, there must always be trouble as long as the Church had any influence. Democracy must step forward, decidedly and aggressively, and then those who continually caused difficulties on behalf of the religious institutions would have to draw back.

Joseph Darvas was the director of the Hungarian-Soviet Cultural Society, formed under very peculiar conditions. Generally cultural links with foreign countries are furthered through associations or groups by people with a special interest in the cultures of the respective countries. The large masses could never take part in such societies. But the membership drives for the local Soviet-Hungarian cultural societies were unusual; the Reds tried to gain membership among the masses by all possible means.

People were forced into membership who, aside from certain vulgar expressions they could not help hearing from the Soviet troops, knew not a word of Russian, never learned any, and never found out on which tree Soviet literature and art grew. Prefects, mayors, officers of the army, and police were instructed to whip up a membership drive and get masses to join the "cultural society." Their dues supported the tremendous budget of this peculiar outgrowth of Soviet-Hungarian relationship. Darvas maintained an exceptionally servile attitude toward me to promote the cancerous growth of the society. He gave me no peace, coming time and again to ask that the Prime Minister give some money toward the development of his "culture." Several times pressure from Rákosi forced me to grant some support, but every time I expressed my objection to the fact that the society was working with a paid staff of over a hundred. Practically all were atheistic Communists; not a single Hungarian church member was included.

I did know that my refusal to give the portfolio of Education to Darvas pained the Soviet and the Communists very much; it interfered with their smuggling the intentions of the Soviet and of Communism into Hungarian education.

I thought it important that the Minister of Education, instead of serving the Soviet and Marxist culture in the cabinet, should serve the culture of the Hungarian people. The Soviet-Communist combine lent such force to the candidacy of Darvas that for months I could not fill the portfolio of Education, and for months Desider Keresztury, the resigned minister, had to continue temporarily in charge of that department.

CHAPTER 62

Ultimatums and Resignations

THE COMMUNIST PARTY HAD PREPARED ALL SUMMER LONG FOR ITS ANnual congress. In the tense political situation there were many conjectures as to its aims, some thinking the congress might lead to a putsch. Undoubtedly the workers at this time docilely followed, already, all Communist instructions.

Communist trade-union tactics had been successful. Sharing the leadership of the unions with the Social Democrats, the Communists in practice dominated. The workers, dazzled by revolutionary slogans and enticing promises, did not realize what was happening to and around them. They were not aware that gradually, without direct use of force, they were becoming slaves of the Communist party dictatorship. The majority of workers came under state control when mines were nationalized and the three greatest centers of industrial production became state enterprises for the period of reparations payments. And where workers came under state control, the Communists were always able to drive them under the Red yoke.

Naturally the workers' freedom of action ceased; they could not demonstrate against factory owners or strike for higher wages. Overwhelmed by the slogan that the factory was theirs, the workers did not realize that they now had an employer with whom it was not possible to argue. The "new boss" had political police, internment camps, and prisons. Anyone who differed with Communist leaders soon came into contact with these institutions. The former owners did not have the use of police and prisons; it was easier to reason with them. Or at least it would have been easier under a democracy than in the former reactionary era.

Thus labor fell under Communist power. To the Social Democratic party was assigned the role of appeasing those workers who, here and there, still clamored for Social Democratic rule in their affairs. It was beyond doubt that the Communist party was in a position to mobilize the workers at any moment, not only for political but also for revolutionary purposes. Communist and union discipline was so strict that it could have ordered workers to the barricades; a large segment of public opinion predicted preparations for revolution. Perhaps the Communists, annoyed by the Smallholders and me, had something like this in mind. But apparently they had not received such orders from the Soviet, and independent action without the blessings of Moscow was of course inconceivable.

The Communists, trying to make a show of sincerity and self-criticism, gave their congress another aspect. Though excoriating "reaction" and attacking the Smallholders party, they spoke chiefly of their own errors. Speakers analyzed correct and incorrect tactical moves, and indicated the advantages of a friendly and cordial approach. Then they had their press sing praises of the congress and point to it as a model of frankness and honest politics. The Smallholders party would do well, they said, to admit openly that it was a hotbed of reaction, instead of denying its right wing. Their new slogan was: "Now that the workers have come into their own, the peasantry is next."

After the Communist congress I wrote an editorial acknowledging its constructive attitude and proposed that the statement about the peasantry be realized. Let us give the peasants administrative and police posts in proportion to their numbers, I said.

The Communists quickly saw that it would not be good tactics to allow the congress to leave a conciliatory impression. So, after its adjournment, Rákosi wrote an article in which he announced that the Communist party was ever ready to crack down on reaction, if its impertinences did not cease.

To avoid misunderstanding, Rákosi called a meeting of the leftist bloc, where it was decided to concoct another ultimatum to the Smallholders party. The greater part of its demands had long been on our docket: for example, extension of credit to peasants and reduction of their land tax, dissolution of cartels, nationalization of mills, supervision of the banks, and complete freeing of democracy from the trammels of reaction. The Smallholders party replied with demands of its own which included proposals for the improvement of the peasants' lot. Not leaving out political demands, we asked for just distribution of posts, improvement of the police force, establishment of trade unions on a legal basis, definition of the sphere of factory production committees, and recognition of the Peasant Alliance as their trade union.

Rapprochement between the parties progressed slowly after the exchange of letters. Meanwhile there were also governmental affairs to attend to. I still had to appoint a new man as Minister of Education, and another in the place of Eugene Tombor, Minister of Defense, who had died. The Finance post was also vacant—Gordon had resigned to become envoy to Switzerland. But I wanted further changes, including a substitute for Stephen Dobi, Minister of Agriculture, who had proved incompetent.

My nominee for the Defense post was John Eröss, until now reparations commissioner. As Minister of Finance I wished to propose Eugene Rácz, who had accompanied me to the United States as economic adviser; and as Minister of Agriculture, a first-rate expert, Charles Bárányos. Joseph Bognár, who was secretary of our party in Budapest, would have been a good Minister of Propaganda, and I still awaited the Peasant party's proposal of a suitable candidate for the Ministry of Education.

When I proposed these names at an interparty conference, Rákosi and his clique violently opposed Bárányos and Rácz. Nevertheless I took my list to Sviridov. Sviridov's attitude was as I had supposed. First he protested sharply against my wish to appoint a civilian Minister of War; then he objected to Bárányos. I began to argue with him, pointing out that we had no high-ranking soldier capable of reorganizing the army well. For this reason a man distinguished in public affairs should head it.

Sviridov began to name a list of generals. I knew well that he wanted me to appoint General Pálfi-Oesterreicher, but he did not dare mention his name to me. Finally, he proposed Albert Barta, retired general and a Smallholder Member of Parliament. Since Eröss himself did not wish the post, I finally did nominate Barta, retaining Eröss as Minister of Supply.

Sviridov replied a few days later, saying that he approved of Rácz and Barta as Ministers of Finance and Defense, but that he would have to consult Voroshilov about the rest.

Meanwhile an interparty conference was called to confer on the reciprocal ultimatums. I asked Béla Varga, President of Parliament, to be chairman and sought to send to the conference men whom the Communists, too, had always acknowledged to be democratically minded, eliminating the possibility of personal attacks. Our delegates were Emery Oltványi, former president of the National Bank; Joseph Bognár, chief party secretary in Budapest, and myself. As an advisor I invited Eugene Rácz. Béla Varga brought parliamentary stenographers to cover the conference, and we went to the meeting thoroughly equipped. During the discussions that lasted for days we had the upper hand over the Communists, who had gambled on our unpreparedness; and the parties came to an agreement on economic issues. In the political part of the agenda the Communists refused to face the issues and kept stalling for time. In the end, we had to break off discussions. Soon afterward they saw fit to announce publicly that an agreement in political matters had not been reached.

The lack of accord precipitated one of the longest crises in our democracy.

Meanwhile, Voroshilov, through the good offices of Sviridov, had sent a message saying that he did not approve of the other ministerial appointments. I became indignant at this quibbling and flagrant illegality of procedure. After all, the armistice granted the Control Commission no right to interfere with the composition of the Hungarian cabinet. The political situation was extremely tense because of the deadlock. I pretended not to know that Rákosi was familiar with the Soviet reply and informed him and Szakasits of the message received from Sviridov.

"You see, that's what comes of insisting on Bárányos and Eröss," reproached Rákosi.

"Maybe you shouldn't have insisted so much on this Bárányos," said Szakasits cautiously.

"Since Bárányos is the best agricultural expert we have and our agriculture has desperate need of the best possible leadership to solve its problems, I must continue to insist on Bárányos," I answered. "If the Soviet Union will not allow these ministers to be appointed, I'll hand in my resignation today."

"Go ahead and resign then," said Rákosi nervously.

"We'll see," I answered, and left.

I called on Sviridov, hardly stepping into his room when Pushkin arrived. Sviridov conferred with me in the presence of Pushkin.

"I received a message from you, General, that you disapprove of my ministerial nominations," I began.

"Well, look here," said Sviridov with a show of cordiality. "Marshal Voroshilov, even in past times, didn't favor Eröss in the cabinet. And the trouble with Bárányos is that he is the best expert on food distribution and it would be a pity to remove him from the post of Minister of Supply."

"I don't agree with you," I replied. "Eröss has done a fine job as reparations commissioner and Bárányos is our best agricultural expert. Both are excellent men for the tasks to be accomplished."

"But there is Stephen Dobi," said Sviridov. "A fine, democratically minded fellow of peasant stock. It would be a pity to dismiss him from the government. He wouldn't deserve such treatment."

I was startled. Here was Russia recommending Dobi, a Smallholder of long standing and one of our former organizers. Although I knew that Dobi inclined strongly to the left, I had no idea that he enjoyed so much confidence from the Communists and the Soviet Union.

"I am sorry," I said. "No matter how fine a man Dobi may be, he is not suited now to fill the post of Agriculture. I must therefore insist on his resignation."

"All right," said Sviridov. "I'll try to get in touch with Voroshilov once more, but I don't think he'll be willing to approve these appointments."

"Look, General," I replied. "It's now four o'clock. If I receive no answer by seven o'clock, or if I receive an unfavorable answer, I shall call on the President of our republic and resign in the name of the whole cabinet. I have striven honestly to follow a policy friendly to the Soviet Union, and until now I have steered the coalition through every crisis. But if you are unwilling to take cognizance of my right to govern the country with the men I find to be most suited, then I don't wish to remain at the head of the government. I have asked the President to remain in his office, so that the new ministers can take their oath of office. Either this takes place tonight or else I shall resign. Good day!"

The ministerial appointees sat in my office, waiting to take their oath. They suspected, but did not know, what storms were raging around them. Under the circumstances I had to inform them of the state of affairs. Thereupon, each asked that I withdraw his nomination, so the crisis might be bridged.

"Now it has become a question of my political integrity," I replied. "I am therefore compelled to insist on your appointments."

At ten minutes to seven the telephone bell rang. It was Captain Gruber speaking for Sviridov. He said Marshal Voroshilov would approve the list of new ministers, provided that I ask for the resignation of Stephen B. Szabó, Smallholder Minister Without Portfolio, and appoint Stephen Dobi in his place.

I was about to decline the offer indignantly, but finally decided against settling the matter alone and telephoned Zoltán Tildy, Béla Kovács, and Stephen Balogh. All three insisted on accepting the Soviet offer—even if there was a blemish, I was the victor in this struggle. I replied to Sviridov that I would accept the condition imposed, and shortly after seven the new ministers took their oath of office.

CHAPTER 63

Striving for a Unified Peasantry

THE POLITICAL TENSION WAS APPROACHING THE BREAKING POINT. MEANwhile the peace terms had been settled; when the treaty was signed and ratified, we should regain our sovereignty. It would have been easier to continue the disputes and let the crisis go from bad to worse; but that would have been gambling with the country's peace and its future.

Varga, Kovács, and I met daily to discuss events. Kovács had a plan. He wanted us to choose, once for all, whether we should bring matters to a showdown with the Communists and the Soviet or try to achieve a settlement that would produce a solution unthreatened by further crises. We decided on the latter.

Béla Kovács came forward with a significant proposal. Let us, he said, create a Peasant Federation, make a peasant party of the Smallholders, and incorporate within it the present national Peasant party.

"We should achieve several goals," he explained. "First of all, it would become impossible to attack the party as being reactionary if members and leaders were mostly peasants. In the second place, we should neutralize the leftist bloc, and only the so-called 'Solidarity of Labor' would remain to counterbalance it: we should have a unified peasantry. Peasant party men in all government posts would join our ranks, and the Smallholders would no longer be a minority in the national committee and other organizations. We should have to expel some of our 'gentlemen opposing the coalition'—perhaps more members than the number of Peasant party representatives we should gain; but our peasant masses would consent, knowing that peasant unity was being achieved."

The Kovács plan was food for thought. I was of the opinion that if it really brought a union of the peasants into being we should be killing two birds with one stone. For one thing, a more permanent collaboration with the workers' parties could be established; and, in addition, a unified peasantry would be a dike against further Communist domination. In 1919 the peasantry had overthrown Communism in four months, despite being unorganized. A strong union of peasants would prevent even an attempt to install a Communist regime.

I first mentioned the plan confidentially to Emery Kovács and Peter Veres, leaders of the Peasant party, and they favored it because by this time they were strongly disposed to shake themselves free of the domination by the Communists in order to become more closely associated with the Smallholders party. But they thought that the idea could only be realized gradually; first, the Peasant party ought to declare that it was willing to cooperate with our party in the Peasant Alliance. A resolution to leave the leftist bloc would follow. Finally the two parties would merge, after our party had dropped representatives inacceptable to the Peasant party.

Knowing that the Communists would be against a unified peasantry and would do all they could to oppose it, I was afraid that the plan might be scuttled through Peter Veres. They were in a position to exert pressure on him because he had written articles in rightist publications in the days of National Socialism, addressed Fascist youth organizations, and carried on a flirtation with Imrédy, the Nazi Premier who had ended his career on the gallows.

When Rákosi learned what was in the offing, he protested vehemently against any such merger with the Peasant party. The plan had thrown a scare into this cunning political agent, for he knew that it would rule out all schemes of a Hungary with a Communist future. He began to argue that the merger would not mean peasant unity anyhow, because the Communists and Social Democrats also had peasant members and a struggle would begin inside the peasantry itself.

Actually, I think the Russians were most frightened of all, remembering how much trouble they had had with their own peasantry when they tried to coax them into accepting their modern type of slavery within the Soviet Union. They were strongly opposed to any form of unified peasantry, because they realized that the peasants were the largest truly democratic group in all southeastern Europe, one that could not be swayed by any form of extremism and could be depended upon to resist all dictatorships.

If Russia and the Communists had had any idea of establishing democracy in Hungary, they would have approved the plan, finding no better bulwark against the return of the former reactionary institutions than the peasantry; but, though they shouted the word from the housetops, they had not the slightest idea of permitting democracy. What they wanted was a Soviet type of absolutism of which the peasants, too, would be victims. The peasants must be prevented from forming a political entity.

As could be expected, Peter Veres backed down first. Taken in hand, presumably, by Rákosi, he called an executive meeting of the Peasant party at which he spoke for fourteen hours. Dramatic appeals alternating with sobbing and remonstrance finally achieved a decision to remain in the leftist bloc.

Thus Béla Kovács' plan was wrecked and we had to continue the struggle against three parties backed by the armed might of a Russia increasingly determined to bring southeastern Europe under its yoke.

The crisis which began in September remained unresolved and took on a permanent character. I tried everything in my power to bring it to an end because the destruction it was causing was only too evident.

The disruptive influence was noticeable first in the political arena. Mutual suspicion made constructive administration impossible. Important economic measures were blocked, because personal relations between cabinet members had deteriorated so far that, when a minister brought up the appointment of some official, his colleagues of another party would raise all sorts of objections based on suspicions. If a minister wished an expert to go abroad, the others would look for some hidden political motive. It was characteristic of the situation that the post of Minister of Education was still vacant. There was talk of appointing a Smallholder to this position and giving the Ministry of Reconstruction (left vacant by the resignation of Joseph Antall) to the Peasant party if it could not find a suitable candidate for the former post. But both remained vacant for months.

The poisoned atmosphere began to spread throughout the country; nowhere was it possible to reach satisfactory agreement on current questions. Fights between party followers, instigated by the Communists, sprang up in every community.

This picture was the more dismaying because summer and fall had been extremely productive. The end of summer saw the completion of the largest bridge spanning the Danube, the former Francis Joseph Bridge which the Germans had blown up in their retreat. Stabilization was an accomplished fact and the forint stood firm. The gold reserves of the National Bank had been returned from the American zone, and we had received favorable information indicating the early return of our Danube fleet that had been run off to Germany. The daily bread ration had been increased from 150 to 200 grams; the ration for manual laborers was higher still. Railway traffic was expanding, and the number of automobiles in service grew by leaps and bounds. We had more trucks than in peacetime. Some of our coal mines attained and passed the prewar level of production. There was lively progress in the industrial field, operating at 60 per cent of its prewar capacity. Land reform was nearly completed.

All this was proof of the healthy economic progress our democracy had made and the amazing diligence of the Hungarian people. It was a deadly sin to put a stop to further advance by the incitement of political unrest.

Rumania had suffered far less in the war than we, and her soldiers had been at hand to protect her interests when the Russian army of occupation arrived. Yet the drought of 1946 almost swept her off her feet, and inflation began now in Rumania when it already had been effectively curbed in Hungary.

I saw that political turmoil might nullify the results we had achieved so far and told my friends that it was up to us to end the crisis on the basis of "The wiser one gives way." Smallholder deputies in Parliament were rebellious. Our party had not gained strength in proportion to our accomplishments for the country. There were continual complaints that it had been cheated out of its aims. I was forced to become stern in order to quiet the party. Smallholder deputies in Parliament received a letter from me outlining the course of future action in Parliament and at mass meetings. I called on those not willing to comply to leave the party. Today I see that I should not have done this either.

Following my letter, the caucus decided unanimously to follow my advice and the directives. However, dissatisfaction remained, for the actions of the Communists were more provoking day by day. Rajk was the recipient of most of the wrath, and he was especially detested for the way he treated the German-speaking minority and for his ruthless political tactics.

I, too, saw the danger in the advance of the Communists. If I had had any doubts about the desire of the Communist party to stir up unrest and disorder, they would have been thoroughly dispelled by Rajk's speech behind closed doors at a conference of Communist leaders. He said, among other things:

"Learn from Lenin; if you have five enemies, you should ally yourselves with them; arrange to incite four of them against the fifth, then three against the fourth, and so on until you have only one enemy left in the alliance; you can then liquidate him yourselves and kick him out of the alliance."

This speech would have been enough to settle Rajk and get him out of the cabinet; but we could not name our witnesses, for the Communist police would have liquidated them once their identity became known. Rajk went even further at this meeting, saying:

"It was these Leninist tactics that the Soviet Union followed when it made an alliance with the reactionary capitalistic great powers."

There is no doubt in the minds of the signers of the sworn statement in my possession, that by "the reactionary great powers" Rajk meant the United States and England.

I made several more attempts to solve the crisis, but to no avail. The only solution acceptable to the Communist party would have been for the Smallholders party to keep on weakening itself by expelling another series of representatives. But this was a solution which I would not even permit to be discussed.

The Social Democratic party, which could boast of so fine a past, was gliding into a pitiable state. The party which had represented the economic and social interests of the workers for decades had been an unwitting accomplice during the past two years in the game played by the Communists with the destiny of Hungarian labor. As I have said before, the men of backbone, principle, and conviction who had been its leaders had been pushed aside. Árpád Szakasits, a man more influenced by the dynamics of the Communists than by the just interests of labor, ruled the party.

The workers perceived bitterly that the party had lost much of its influence. Their strongest organization had been the trade union. But experienced union leaders had been brushed aside to be replaced by new men who were willing Communist tools. Social Democratic workers became a docile herd in the hands of Communist leaders. They allowed themselves to be ordered around for political demonstrations and became resigned to the fact that, like workers in the Communist countries, they could not strike or demand higher wages.

There were often bitter complaints from the Social Democratic rank and file. Brave and determined miners and factory workers displayed stiff resistance to Communist aims, but this was generally quelled by leaders who had been put in power by the Communists. Many of the men would have preferred their party to keep to the letter of the agreement made with the Smallholders during the war in 1943. But Szakasits' clique broke the bonds that held the two camps together during the critical times.

What reward did the Social Democrats receive from the Communists for their thoughtless yielding? A doubtful form of political support and, for the most part, just condescension. The Communist party allowed the Social Democrats to grab by force all sorts of governmental positions. In the towns and country districts, mayors and lord-lieutenants were mainly Social Democrats, because the party sought to build up its ranks by guaranteeing political patronage to its members. The Communists preferred Social Democrats to Smallholders in these posts, because they could direct their actions through the leftist bloc. They knew, too, that they could remove them much more easily than Smallholders, who were growing in strength. The Communists were extremely indulgent toward Social Democrats, who became notorious for corruption as members used all possibilities to make money and amassed tremendous wealth, which then was taxed for the benefit of the party treasury.

Once when I was conferring with Sviridov about Soviet-Hungarian joint enterprises, he unexpectedly asked me:

"Tell me, Premier, when are you going to get rid of the Oil Commissioner, Zoltán Gombosi?"

"Why do you wish me to, General?" I asked, knowing very well the answer.

"Well, this Gombosi is Oil Commissioner and at the same time president of the Soviet-Hungarian Oil Corporation. He's such a terrible grafter that in my opinion he cannot be allowed to remain in his present positions."

"Gombosi is a distinguished member of the Social Democratic party," I replied. "Therefore, his removal must be accomplished through Szakasits, the leader of the party. I shall call on Szakasits to request Gombosi to resign."

"After all, it is an impossible state of affairs, for a man who holds an important government commission to run an oil business for his wife, through which he earns millions," protested Sviridov.

"I suspect, General, that it will not be because of his wife's business that we shall find it difficult to remove Gombosi."

"I know well that it is a matter of the Socialist party treasury," said Sviridov; "but this Gombosi's activities are not to be borne with in any case."

Budapest drawing rooms were full of stories that the focal point of graft was in the Ministry of Industry, which was controlled by the Social Democratic party. In one particular flagrant case of graft, Zoltán Vas, Communist head of the Supreme Economic Council, hurried to the rescue and saved the face of the ministry.

In the Ministry of Trade, another leading Social Democrat, Emery Vajda, was undersecretary. This smooth, crafty fellow could never be caught redhanded, but he was definitely accused, for example, of having accepted splits and commissions from firms interested in particular sections of an international trade agreement which he negotiated.

The Communist party winked at these irregularities, which gave it a stronger hold on the Socialists. The laboring class did not suspect that its humiliating position was due to its leaders' eager pursuit of personal gain; and that as a result it had fallen completely into the power of the Communists.

Charles Peyer, for decades the stalwart leader of the Social Democrats, on returning from deportation, looked with dismay on his party's decay. Its political and moral strength had decreased in inverse proportion to its expanding membership.

Some prominent Hungarian diplomats once met a leading Social Democrat on a diplomatic mission and expressed the belief that the Socialists shared the guilt of preventing the Hungarian delegation from introducing the question of reparations at the peace conference, because they supported Rákosi's demand that Hungary should not embarrass the Russians by discussing reparations. His answer was characteristic.

"You know, there are some old horses in a circus; if the trainer whispers one word in their ears, they stand on their hind legs; if he whispers another, they begin to dance. I am just like one of those old circus horses—I have my own opinions, but if the magic words are whispered into my ear, I get on my hind legs or dance. The magic words are: 'Unity in the ranks of labor.'"

That is the way the Socialists lied to themselves to excuse their betrayal of democratic ideals.

In the days before the autumn congress of the party, Peyer and a few of his friends decided to make an attempt to shake the workers out of their torpor and appeal to the conscience of the leaders. Peyer dispatched a powerful memorandum to the party leaders and had it published in the press; it pointed out the mistakes of the Socialist leaders, accused them of having betrayed the party principles. As a result, Peyer was branded a rebel. They would have liked to expel him from the party, but no one dared take such a step against the revered leader with an unspoiled record. Peyer has since fled from the terror and, as these lines are written, is living in exile.

News leaking out from Hungary, and all signs, indicate that the workers are beginning to see that their party has been heading for destruction. They recognize, too, that they are slowly becoming slaves of the Communists. But no one dares bring matters to an open break, for Soviet bayonets are held in readiness to quell any attempt to improve internal political conditions in Hungary. It is my conviction, however, that the masses of workers in the ranks of the Social Democratic party have not abandoned the principles of true democracy and are awaiting the moment to step forward and bring to judgment the leaders who betrayed them and the party because of cowardice, ambition, and greed.

During some of the long political crises I tried to get Szakasits to mediate between the Smallholders party and the leftist bloc. He undertook to do so several times, but without success, and it became plain that he no longer had any influence on the Communists. By then he was so well under their thumb that they could plainly disregard any proposal and wish he might express.

Instead of lessening, the tension between the parties grew as the Communists completed preparations for their Christmas attack that was to strike at the very roots of our democracy.

The Communists never weaken their hand by taking up small issues.

CHAPTER 64

Soviet-Engineered Communist Tactics

BY THE FALL OF 1946 IT BECAME CLEAR THAT IT WAS NO LONGER THE Communist party that was making use of the Soviet Union to further its aims, but the opposite. This was true of all southeastern Europe. The Rumanian and later the Polish elections had been under the absolute direction of the Soviet. The various "conspiracies" in southeastern Europe, invented by Russia, were needed to justify stronger Soviet intervention; in Hungary, because her polity was obviously differentiated from that of her neighbors. The free elections "permitted by mistake" in 1945 and the attitude of her government allowed the country far more freedom than the other states in this region enjoyed. For the Soviet Union it became essential to eliminate this difference, even if its political representatives had to turn their backs on Stalin's statements to the Hungarian delegation in Moscow.

The Soviet secret police, the NKVD, swung into deadly action, and nearly everyone in Hungary came under its observation. Men in the confidence of Smallholder leaders were forced to spy on them. Any who were reluctant suddenly found themselves in the dreaded cellars of the NKVD. Many of the younger members of the staff of the Ministry of Foreign Affairs were later declared to be "conspirators," because the information they had given the NKVD in the course of nightly interrogations turned out to be misleading and they were actually warning the personages they were supposed to spy on.

I might mention here one of the "conspirators," a young member of a Hungarian legation abroad. In 1943, when he was visiting with his parents in a little town on the Hungarian plains, a stranger came who told them in German that he was a Polish refugee and asked to be allowed to stay for the night. The family were already very active in the resistance movement and were glad to shelter him. The "Pole" remained for a day or two and, on learning that the family had a vineyard with a little hut, asked to be permitted to hide there; and they assented. Some days later, when the son, anxious for the stranger's welfare, came to bring food, he was astonished to discover that the stranger had a radio antenna set up and was busily transmitting messages. Our young man became alarmed, being afraid that the presence of the antenna might betray their guest and get the whole family into serious trouble. But a short while later the stranger disappeared, leaving no trace.

The young diplomat continued his work with the forces of resistance and maintained contact with the British and American armies himself by means of a secret radio transmitter. After the Christmas of 1944, when the Red army had surrounded Budapest, he contacted the Russians, holding daily conversations with a Russian radio operator. When the Russians captured Budapest, the radio operator called on him. The caller turned out to be the mysterious Polish guest, who now introduced himself as Counselor Ossukin, attached to the Russian diplomatic mission to Hungary.

From this time on, the young man had to report every night to the Russians. Ossukin and his men had conversations with him lasting until dawn, in the course of which they actually interrogated him on Smallholder leaders. Later, when we appointed the young diplomat to a legation, the NKVD tried to prevent him from leaving the country, because they were afraid he might tell the British and the Americans about the Russian methods. When we were finally able to spirit him out of the country and he arrived at his new station, they rented quarters next to his and kept him under constant surveillance and observation; this, in the capital city of a major western power.

The young man proved loyal to his country and of no use to the NKVD; they named him a "conspirator" so as to force him out of Hungarian government service.

The best example of Soviet attempts to secure desired confessions was the case of twenty-two-year-old Leslie Horonyi-Pálffy, assistant secretary in the Prime Ministry.

In December, 1945, two officers of the Soviet military police accosted the young man on the street, pushed him into their unregistered sedan, and drove off to NKVD headquarters. Another Hungarian prisoner, later released, testified to having overheard continuous questioning from six in the evening until three in the morning:

"You are the secretary of the Monarchist movement in Hungary. You will deliver immediately the roster of members and financial supporters. You will name all the leaders of the Smallholders party who take part in this movement. We have definite information that Ferenc Nagy, Béla Varga, Béla Kovács and twenty other Smallholder members of Parliament are active in the Monarchist movement. You will serve democracy well by naming these people, even if you lack the roster. We shall prepare a sworn statement; you will sign it. These gentlemen are undermining Hungarian democracy in many different ways. It will be to your advantage to do this speedily, because we already have statements from many other witnesses in the case, which, by the way, is directed against the Soviet Union also. Soviet jurisdiction, just and indulgent, rewards true democrats and voluntary confessions, but it punishes stubborn enemies with death."

Horonyi-Pálffy repeatedly assured the Reds that he knew nothing of an existing Monarchist movement, had never had any connection with such an organization, and was innocent of the activities of which he was accused. The only Monarchist group he had ever heard of existed during the German occupation, when he led a group of young partisans against the Nazis, blew up their transports, and cut their communication lines.

During the lengthy questioning, the examining major several times instructed some soldiers to beat the frail, pallid young man. At the end of the fifteen hours the beating became so severe that Horonyi-Pálffy fainted and remained unconscious for over half an hour.

The questioning was interrupted at three in the morning. After

Horonyi-Pálffy had regained consciousness, the examining Russian major released him with the threat that unless the demanded roster were supplied by the next evening, he would again be taken into custody—this time for good! If he was ready to sign a sworn statement to the effect indicated, he could enjoy a splendid career with the support of the Soviet administration in every respect.

Horonyi-Pálffy went directly to his desk in the Prime Ministry and wrote farewell letters to his parents and to a Smallholder deputy friend. To the latter he described the experience in detail and ashamedly admitted that he could not again bear the third degree of the NKVD; he was certain that they would exert such physical violence as to force an accusation against the people he loved—a confession contrary to his convictions. He could not swear to something he had never heard of and knew nothing about. Finishing the letters, he removed a gun from the security cabinet. The orderlies found him next morning, his brain blown to bits.

In Hungary the NKVD made one arrest after another. While I was in Washington in June, 1946, they arrested and abducted Ivan Lajos, an official in the Ministry of Education, the author of the famous "Gray Book," written just before the outbreak of war. His book, which received worldwide notice, analyzed the reasons for Germany's defeat in the event of a war, arriving very cleverly at conclusions from writings of German military experts whom he quoted. However, in the eyes of the Russians, Lajos was guilty of a greater sin than an alert mind: he was a "legitimist," believing in the restoration of the Habsburg monarchy. He recognized, of course, that it would be improbable for a long time and might never come to pass; but this did not alter his convictions. The Russians felt always that the legitimists might oppose the maintenance of the republican form of government, and were therefore anxious to get them out of the way. This explains the arrest of Count Géza Pálffy and Margrave George Pallavicini by the NKVD. Russia was preparing to transform the Hungarian political scene by systematically clearing away all possible hindrances to her designs.

The expulsion of the German minority from Hungary was also clearly developing into a political move. Russia was afraid the Germans would present a solid bloc opposed to Communism; therefore it became necessary to expel all of them, even though this meant falsifying the interpretation of the Potsdam decision. While Pushkin's pronouncement of March, "It seems as though flowers do not bloom for us in Hungary," had been somewhat consoling to Hungarian democrats, it could now be realized that the Russians were exerting every effort to make "Red bloom" possible and successful.

In countries bordering on Hungary, the resistance of the democratic elements to Soviet penetration had weakened steadily. The Soviet-dominated election in Poland resulted in Communist-directed totalitarianism, and circles in that country with which we could have maintained contact lost their strength completely. In Rumania, Groza himself became a tool of the Soviet Union, and the real leader was his undersecretary, Bodnaras, who had learned in Moscow the technique of silencing democracy in free countries. In Yugoslavia, Communist rule had become more absolute than in the Soviet itself. Tito had destroyed the last vestiges of democracy and of political independence. In Slovakia, bordering on Hungary, the Communists, who only so recently had been members of the Fascist Hlinka Guard, became absolute masters of the situation.

In this raging sea of Communism, Hungary had to hold tight to the raft of democracy. We held tight. In all humility as a human being, I am confident that future historians will find that our policies were more fruitful than those in any of the neighboring countries. I can proudly state that our policies enabled us to hold out much longer than any of our neighbors; until a time when the "violent overthrow" of democracy before the eyes of the world became impossible. If I had allowed an open political clash in 1946, the organized force of Communism would have swept us beyond the help of any western power.

To avoid this constantly threatening clash and yet clear the air, I decided to try a different—and more personal—approach, a man-to-man discussion with Pushkin in a pleasant setting.

One night at a reception I asked him,

"Wouldn't you like to go duck-hunting?"

"Gladly," replied Pushkin.

"Come with me to the Hortobágy next week. It will be just a small party."

"How many will there be in the party?" asked Pushkin.

"I am bringing Béla Kovács and my secretary. If there are too many people, we won't have a chance to talk."

"Good," answered Pushkin. "I'll bring along Captain Gruber as interpreter and a Russian colonel."

The Communists at this time were attacking Kovács with increasing vehemence. It was also my purpose to give Kovács and Pushkin a chance to exchange views at length while we were hunting. This would probably have some effect on our Communists, too.

We set out in our cars for Hungary's lovely plains of Hortobágy, where the wild geese prefer to alight. Here the cautious birds can perceive the approach of danger from afar. Since there is no cover, the only way to hunt geese here is to settle down in a pit at night and await their flight.

I rode in Pushkin's car all the way. He was proud of his knowledge of Hungarian history, and we had hardly started when he began to recite certain episodes from the past of our nation. Now, however, he had a particular purpose.

"It is amazing," he began, "how great an influence the church has had on the development of Hungarian history right up to this day."

"Now it has only an indirect effect through the faith of its followers," I answered, "which cannot be compared with its influence when it actually dominated politics."

"Look at your history," continued Pushkin. "It is interesting to observe that for centuries the policies of the church were synonymous with advance in Hungary; it represented democracy and social progress. Then, how quickly it left this road and became the hotbed of conservatism, which it is today."

"In Hungary we must recognize a distinction; here Protestantism took the place of the universal church in democratic progress and became the standard-bearer of democracy and social progress," I replied.

"That may be," said Pushkin. "But today the Protestant churches are just as opposed to radical progress."

"The churches have their traditions. It is no cause for wonder that they do not always comprehend the swift changes that take place overnight."

"But there is no sign of gradual progress, either. Mindszenty on the part of the Catholics, and Bishop Ravasz on the side of the Protestants, do all they can to obstruct progress."

He expressed at great length his views on the harmful influence of the churches.

"You know well," I replied, "that we Smallholder leaders do all we can to induce the church to join us on the road of democratic progress; but this cannot be accomplished in a day. You yourself perceive that the question of the churches must not be solved by force; in fact, you made it a point after liberation not to interfere with the work of the churches and their leaders. We will not take a different course. The Hungarian people are attached to religion and their churches. We cannot force a faster pace on the church than the natural course of progress permits." With this I closed the discussion.

That evening, arriving on the Hortobágy, we went to the pits which had been dug in advance; but we had no luck in bagging game.

At the inn on the Puszta, Pushkin and his two friends were more interested in listening to gypsy music than in talking politics. At dawn we went again to the pits, where Pushkin and I each bagged one bird. Then he proposed that we go pheasant-hunting on the grounds where he generally went.

"Who owns the hunting grounds?" I asked.

"I have no idea," he replied. "It's here near Kunhegyes. I enjoy going there; its full of pheasants."

Perhaps Pushkin and his party did not know that it is a custom in Hungary to lease hunting grounds. Strangers hunt only at the invitation of the holder of the lease. But the Russian diplomats followed the practice of their soldiers and did not bother about formalities. They went hunting wherever they pleased.

On our way to Kunhegyes we began discussing political questions. I told Pushkin that there was no reason for continuous political tension. Hungary was making such progress that changes would now be more retarding than helpful. I told him I had made many efforts to end the crisis, but the Communist party refused to cooperate and attacked Smallholder leaders with increasing violence.

"Certain members of the Smallholders party are unquestionably serving the cause of reaction," said Pushkin.

Here Béla Kovács cut in angrily: "What's all this talk about reaction? The Smallholders party is rightfully dissatisfied. Our party won the elections by a great majority. In the interest of peace and with regard for the desires of the Control Commission, we went into coalition with the minority parties. They, instead of being content with the decision of the voters, are becoming more and more unmanageable. In the end our party will have no voice whatever in the coalition."

"The President, the Premier, the Speaker of Parliament, and half the members of the cabinet are Smallholders. How can anyone talk then of Communist oppression?" asked Pushkin.

"This only aggravates our differences," I replied, "for, though I am Premier, I could not call out the armed forces in defense of our democracy at need. The police are completely Communist, and the Minister of the Interior could turn them against me in case of a conflict. And for a whole year now we have not been able to carry out the proportionate distribution in civil service which would quiet the complaints of the majority. The people bring pressure on our deputies to voice their complaints in Parliament, and as a result the Communists declare them to be the voices of reaction."

"Since the Minister of the Interior is loyal to you, you do not have to worry about his turning the police against you in support of the Communist party. And matters will not come to a conflict; after all, you have always been successful in ironing out differences. Believe me, it would only stir up unrest if you were to insist on the proportionate distribution of civil service and police jobs."

"That is very well, but democracy is democracy only when the will of the people prevails," answered Béla Kovács. "And if the people demand the proportionate rights in government we are obliged to respect their wishes."

"The Communist party provokes crises in order to secure material advantages," I said. "In the present crisis, too, it seeks to weaken the Smallholders party further and cut down the moral gains our party achieved through the elections. I want you to understand clearly that this is a game I will not stand for. I consider myself equally as good a democrat as anyone, but what the Communist party demands is the opposite of democracy."

Béla Kovács then began to explain at length and in detail the aims behind the actions of the Communist party and the underlying reasons for the crises; he finally declared flatly that its activities did not promote friendship between Russia and Hungary.

None of this was news to Pushkin, of course, for he was thoroughly informed of the situation; every Communist step was taken with his knowledge and, by this time, probably on his initiative. He abruptly changed the subject and began to attack our system of education.

"You took many steps in the direction of democracy, carried out land reform, gave an important voice to the workers, and punished war criminals. But the most important step is still delayed. You do not want to touch or deal with progressive education. Public education is not guided in a democratic direction, because the churches have an exaggerated influence on the training of youth. It is our opinion that you ought to abolish non-secular schools. Education is an affair of the state, and only the state can enforce educational reforms that guarantee democratic training of youth."

We knew Pushkin and Sviridov never gave "advice" without the official sanction of Moscow. It was evident, then, that this was the "advice," or "desire," of the Soviet government. Moscow was not content with managing our political affairs and pushing themselves slowly but surely into the control of our economic life; now it was ready to attack Hungarian life at its roots, even the churches.

"Church schools have a great past in Hungary, as every faith has had schools founded centuries ago. The famous school at Zirc is staffed by Cistercian fathers; the Jesuits maintain high standards at the Piarists, and many other institutions directed and supported by the Catholics have a notable past. The Presbyterian colleges at Sárospatak, Debrecen, and Pápa have world renown. It should never be forgotten that the elementary schools of many villages are maintained by the churches. There can be no question of abolishing church schools; it would burden the state with an impossible task and arouse universal opposition. Our people regard their schools as their very own and would insist on their continuance at all costs. In Transylvania, which was taken from Hungary after the First World War, and in those parts of the country which were incorporated into Czechoslovakia and Yugoslavia, our people, even as a minority, insisted on maintaining such schools. How, then, could we deprive them now of these educational institutions in Hungary? This would not be a democratic move and would only arouse hostility."

"It is not the task of democratic leaders to preserve antidemocratic traditions," Pushkin answered, "but to lead the people on a new road. We can't speak of democratic unity as long as youth training is even partly in the hands of the church. You ought to appoint Darvas Minister of Education; he'd see to it that young people received a democratic education."

The Russians had made it plain that democracy must be interpreted as they conceived it. Evidently there were two kinds of democracy, a Soviet and a western brand. The less democracy was related to their policies, the more they liked to use the word, and the more the suspicion, or rather the conviction, grew on the Hungarian people that the Communists wanted dictatorship.

"It is beyond doubt," said Béla Kovács, "that there are still men active in education who are not devoted to democracy. We shall gradually eliminate them, but we must be careful not to interfere with our people's innate respect for traditions. The Hungarian people will accept innovations gladly if they see that the nation will gain by them; but they will be hostile to all measures depriving them of advantages without giving them others of at least equal value. We must certainly make changes in our educational system, which is based on laws of bygone decades; but such changes cannot be directed under any circumstances against the church."

The conversation was not to Pushkin's taste; meanwhile we had arrived at Kunhegyes. At once it turned out that the leaseholder of the hunting grounds was General Leslie Sólyom, a man playing a very dubious role. In 1942–1943, he had been active in the intellectual division of the Smallholders party together with his colleague, General Pálfi-Oesterreicher. After the liberation he became a favorite of the Communists, and it was never possible to tell whether he was a Smallholder or a Communist in his sentiments.

After shooting pheasants for a few hours we set out again for Budapest; and along the way a new conversation began.

"Why doesn't the Control Commission allow Desider Sulyok's party to organize?" I asked.

"Does it mean so much to you?" asked Pushkin.

"Yes," I replied, "because it would be a proof of the sincerity of our democracy to permit freedom of action to an opposition party."

"Aren't you afraid that Sulyok's party may achieve sweeping results, if it is legally allowed to organize?" warned the Russian minister.

"If our Smallholders see that they receive just treatment within the coalition, then I don't think the coalition will be in danger. After all, the people are convinced by results and judge by them whether the government is following a proper course," I replied.

"All right. If you want it that badly I shall propose to Sviridov that the Sulyok party be allowed to function. But the responsibility is yours if its activities endanger the democracy."

"We accept the responsibility," said Kovács and I in unison.

A few days later a message from Sviridov really arrived, saying that the Control Commission had granted Desider Sulyok's Freedom party permission to organize. I conveyed the good news to Sulyok.

A few days afterward Tildy, Varga, Kovács, and I got together. The hunting trip and the conversations with Pushkin came up.

"The Russians and the Communists seem to be preparing an attack against the church," I said. "It would be good if we could think up a way to take the wind out of their sails. What step of ours would be truly progressive and democratic, yet not transgress on the domain of the church?"

In a lively debate, we discussed all aspects of the relations between church and state. At last Tildy gave his opinion:

"There is only one such step and that is the abolition of compulsory religious instruction. We are agreed that there can be no question of abolishing the church schools. We cannot touch upon church tithes either. But it seems reasonable to me to change the law by which a child must submit to religious instruction even if his parents do not desire it."

"What do you think, Béla?" I asked Varga.

"In my opinion a child knows the will of God through his parents. If it should be the express desire of the parents that their child should not receive religious instruction, this ought to be made possible."

In the end we agreed that, if it proved necessary to make some progressive move affecting the churches, we would consider the abolition of compulsory religious education. This was not to be construed as a concession to the Communists, however; if it were, the people would rise in opposition.

The Hortobágy trip had not relieved the political tension, but I felt that the talk with Pushkin had improved Béla Kovác's position, as he had of late been the continual target of Communist attacks. This brave, straightforward peasant had taken upon himself singlehandedly opposition to Communist excesses. His popularity grew from day to day. I was extremely anxious that his position in our democracy should not be weakened, and I hoped that these closer Soviet contacts would counterbalance the Communist mud-slinging.

Developments proved that my efforts were of no avail, because the political equilibrium of Europe was slowly becoming swayed by the Soviet Union. The day was approaching when we should be forced into a position parallel to that of the other countries under the Soviet yoke.

The long crisis disclosed that the Soviet Union engineered the tactics of the Communist party; but we had to keep silent before the world or risk even greater danger to our country. We hoped that the conferences of the great powers would be our salvation, bringing peace at last into the lives of all the long-suffering peoples of southeastern Europe.

CHAPTER 65

Battle Lines Are Drawn

THE INTERNAL CRISIS BECAME DESPERATE. IT WAS APPARENT THAT THE Communists would not tolerate tranquillity unless we expelled more of our members in Parliament, which we refused to do. The more determined the Communists became the less inclined we were to yield. Only an explosion could result. Meanwhile we avoided bringing up topics that could lead to an open break, because I was anxious to stall for time until the signing and ratification of the peace treaty. Every day that brought us nearer to our national sovereignty was a point for our side. After the Rumanian elections it was only too clear that the Russians would deal ruthlessly with us in the event of internal disturbances.

Trying desperately to keep the country calm, I advised moderation in every speech to our party and its representatives. During the long budget debate I personally examined speeches by our members to pluck out possible explosives. And I frequently emphasized the point that we must not seek vengeance even after the Russians had withdrawn, but strive to make the transition to democratic consolidation peaceful and serene.

I had Minister of Agriculture Báranyos arrange a hunting party to which the President of the Republic and the party leaders were invited, hoping to make peace in the course of the excursion. Rákosi and Peter Veres, leader of the Peasant party, agreed to come; but Szakasits refused, saying that he did not consider it right for democratic leaders to go on hunting trips. With this mock virtue he no doubt wished to counterbalance the scandal of his pleasure trip through Italy, Switzerland, and France the preceding fall, on which he had arranged to have a private car hooked onto the international train at terrific cost. One of the Budapest papers compared Szakasits's luxury jaunt with that of the Prime Minister on his way to the Paris peace conference in a second-class railway coach.

The presence of Szakasits was, however, quite inessential, for at this time he was merely Rákosi's echo. To talk with Rákosi was to deal with the whole of the leftist bloc.

On the train Tildy, inviting us to his compartment, outlined the difficulties of the situation and pressed for a solution of the crisis.

I proposed that, since we had agreed on economic questions in October, we should now discuss the political questions. If an agreement proved to be impossible, we could postpone the discussions. But let us announce by Christmas that the parties had made peace.

Rákosi wriggled uneasily during this discussion, in which Tildy, Kovács, Veres, and I took part.

"It's no use announcing an agreement if political questions remain unsolved," he said. "The Smallholders refuse to admit that a great proportion of their representatives in Parliament are reactionaries. Unless it gets rid of its right wing, there can be no peace."

"The proportion of so-called reactionaries in our party is no greater than that in other parties. There is, of course, a reaction to the present situation, which each party interprets differently," said Tildy.

"The dissatisfaction of the Communist party is quite different from that of the Smallholders. What we want is a sincere, energetic democracy; the right wing of your party wants to turn back the clock. I must say that the Soviet Union isn't happy about this," said Rákosi, playing his first card.

"The Smallholders have no nostalgia for the past," said Béla Kovács. "No one suffered more persecution in the past than they did. They simply want justice and order. If Communists exaggerate the trend to the left, you will drive the people into the arms of real reaction, against the best interests of the country."

"That's what you always say," retorted Rákosi. "But the mailed fist is the only way of dealing with reaction. Otherwise the country will suffer the consequences. There is the persecution of Hungarians in Czechoslovakia, for example. I have resolved to go to Prague as soon as I have put an end to the crisis, in order to point out to Czech political leaders the antidemocratic nature of their actions and so end these persecutions. You may be sure that I know how to talk turkey to the Czechoslovak leaders, with whom I spent years in Russia. But there is no sense in my going there while the crisis still lasts. They would point out that Hungary is a hotbed of reaction and refuse to confer with me. But if we can polish off reaction, then we shall have Soviet support in our talks with Czechoslovakia."

Rákosi had now played his trump. Russia, he said in effect, would assist us in bringing relief to Hungarians in Czechoslovakia only on condition that we expel from our party our bravest and most outspoken members in Parliament.

The debate grew sharp, and it seemed best to discontinue it. Again I proposed that we make peace by Christmas; but Rákosi kept insisting that this would be possible only if the Smallholders party purged itself of a number of its deputies in Parliament.

Next morning we went into the woods. Tildy, disheartened, agreed that Rákosi was deliberate in his refusal.

Even while hunting, the behavior of Rákosi and his entourage was characteristic. The secret police, who shadowed him everywhere in Budapest, were with him now. They scurried around, collecting pheasants Tildy, Jr., and I brought down. These they laid at the feet of Rákosi, lest he fall too far behind in his score.

As we returned to the capital I tried to conceal my bitterness at the failure to induce Rákosi to sacrifice party interest to that of the nation.

The stubborn purpose of the Soviet was concealed behind the organized disturbances the Communists were creating; now, as before every important attack, the Communists began with mass demonstrations. They wished these actions to seem spontaneous and colored them accordingly.

A typical incident occurred after vegetables had disappeared from the markets of Budapest because prices had been set so low that they could only be shipped at a loss, and the Minister of Supply accordingly had raised the prices. This delighted the Communists, who immediately began to demonstrate for lower prices and demand the resignation of John Eröss, Minister of Supply, Joseph Varga of the Bureau of Prices and Materials, and Zoltán Pfeiffer, undersecretary in the Ministry of Justice. It was easy to recognize that these political demonstrations were directed by "headquarters."

Several times I went out to quiet the demonstrators, promising that prices would be reduced, for this had already been settled. I declined to consider resignations. The Reds sought to use the demonstrations to try my nerves; I was in my office from eight in the morning until late at night, barely able to cope with my work, and now they sent five or six delegations to me daily to rob me of energy. It was just as well that I felt ill and had to stay home for a few days. They staged a great women's demonstration in my absence. The fevered members of the throng pressed into the Parliament building, demanding lower prices and the resignations. Rákosi, head of the cabinet in my absence, even allowed a committee of the demonstrators to crash the cabinet meeting. They were forced to conclude that I was still healthy and able to cope with these "spontaneous outbursts of the masses," and so the demon-strations were called off, their purpose unaccomplished.

Rákosi visited me to convince himself that I was really ill. Since we had privacy and were able to talk, up popped the question of the political crisis.

"Look," I said, "I'll grant you that representatives of our party, in giving vent to their just dissatisfaction, at times use stronger language than members of a coalition should. But the same is true of your Com-munists. Minister of the Interior Rajk is himself the very essence of agitation." I quoted Rajk's Szentimre speech.

"It's quite impossible that Rajk should have made such a speech!" protested Rákosi.

"The affidavit in my possession was made by men who heard it from beginning to end. There's no room for doubt."

"Give me the affidavit," barked Rákosi.

"Not a chance. Your Communist police would hound to death the men who signed it. Look," I continued. "We could vote Rajk down any day in Parliament. We could expel him from the cabinet, which would be a great service to internal peace. But we don't wish to do that, mainly because we hope you'll be indulgent, too, about our outspoken representatives. There is also another side to the matter. If we were to make a martyr out of Rajk through his expulsion, the anti-Semitic Communists would at once side with Rajk, weakening your own posi-tion in the party."

"Nonsense!" protested Rákosi. "What makes you think we are such opponents? Huh, my popularity in the party is unassailable."

"I know something about the situation, too," I answered. "I know perfectly well that anti-Semitic Communist elements regard Rajk as their leader, rather than you. So I'd like you to stop these attacks against Smallholder members of Parliament and show as much patience as we do."

It was my feeling that Rákosi would have been willing, at this point, to cooperate in establishing a peaceful atmosphere. Never did I feel so distinctly the Soviet compulsion behind his actions. He was not in a position to discuss the question, because it seems he had received orders to increase the tension. Moscow had already grasped the strings with which she was to maneuver her puppets in the formidable coup soon to be executed. The Communist party was not to be allowed to conciliate; it would play quite a different role because this time it was not the Communists calling for Russian support, but the Soviet Union using the Hungarian Communists to achieve far-reaching aims. Russia kept her eyes on the clock; before peace could be signed and ratified, she was anxious to add Hungary to her string of satellites.

Just as the Hungarian Communists were subordinate to the Soviet Union, our labor unions had slipped completely under the thumb of the Hungarian Communist leaders.

The trade unions were completely dominated by the Communists; their dictator, Stephen Kossa, was able to command the workers for any and all purposes. When the number of civil servants was reduced, he used his power to ruin honest, experienced officials of non-Communist leanings; he used it at every step to back Communist policies; he even used it to tie the hands of the workers themselves, for when a plant went under state control the freedom of the workers automatically ceased.

From the Soviet Union local Communists had learned that every violent act must have the appearance of legality; and they had tantrums if anyone branded their procedures as illegal or antidemocratic. They had not dared to hold union elections since the liberation, because they feared that free elections would shove the Communists into the background and bring to the front Social Democratic and Smallholder leaders. Any paper that dared to criticize the despotic organization of the unions immediately drew upon itself a flood of vitriolic attacks.

Desider Sulyok, leader of the Freedom party, secured permission from the Control Commission to publish a daily, *Tomorrow*. The paper was not particularly noteworthy for its achievement in journalism, but throngs dissatisfied with the coalition pounced on it avidly. There was such an extraordinary demand for the first issue of 40,000 copies that people were willing to pay fifty to a hundred times the set price. If lack of newsprint had not limited the issues, they probably would have attained an all-time high in sale.

The Communists, terribly annoyed by the popularity of *Tomorrow*, thought out a devilish plan to silence the only opposition paper, which had had the cheek to criticize the trade unions. Incidentally, the article on the trade unions was relatively mild and did not come near to telling the whole truth; it merely called attention to arbitrary actions and took exception to the fact that they had still held no elections.

The Communists ordered the unions to retaliate, which forbade the printers to work on the paper. Public opinion was aghast. What sort of democracy was this, where the opposition was silenced by gagging its press? The printers confidentially informed Sulyok that they themselves were willing to turn out the paper, because every line published was the truth, but they did not dare oppose the trade-union council.

Sulyok turned to me, and I instructed Minister of Information Ernest Mihályfi to intervene. Mihályfi, on this occasion, showed a very decent and democratic attitude and asked the leaders of the unions why they had not forbidden the printing of Fascist papers in 1944. The leaders could not answer; but they refused, all the same, to withdraw their ban on Sulyok's paper. Mihályfi initiated negotiations between Sulyok and the trade-union leaders. The latter demanded that Sulyok apologize and name his informers. Sulyok refused to do so, and that ended the publication of *Tomorrow*.

This incident occurred after the disclosure of the so-called conspiracy. I only wanted to add it as one piece in a mosaic, proving that it was already possible for the Communists to use the workers for every purpose. Held in line by a barrackslike discipline, the rank and file was forced to back such disgraceful acts, which brought our democracy a step nearer destruction and forced Hungary into a state contrary to her own interests.

In the Christmas number of *Hirlap* I wrote an editorial entitled "The Road to Peace," pointing to the significant accomplishments of our democracy and calling on the parties to hoist the white flag of truce for the benefit of all the people. My appeal was made in vain; the Communists and the Soviet Union, about to launch their most grievous assault on democracy, were unwilling to be diverted by minor negotiations.

Thus far I had been concerned with consolidating the results of the heroic efforts of the Hungarian people to grasp a life of peace and democracy.

From now on I was to be forced to the defensive. I accepted the challenge in order to conserve past accomplishments and maintain at least the outward appearance of the difference between Hungary and her iron-curtained neighbors, and save my country from civil war.

We have arrived at a phase of the struggle behind the iron curtain which began to seal the fate of Hungary and incite new tension in the political life of the world.

PART FOUR

"Conspiracy"

CHAPTER 66

Political Arrests by the Army

JUST BEFORE CHRISTMAS, PRIME MINISTRY OFFICIALS RECEIVED CONFIdential reports that the army's political squad had arrested eight or ten men, including Valentine Arany, an engineer in the employ of the Swedish Roller-Bearing Company and former campaign manager of the Smallholders in Budapest; Major Szentmiklossy, who had been imprisoned by the Nazis for active resistance; and Béla Demeter, Transylvanian expert of our peace delegation. In addition, two officials, Charles Kis and John Héder, and several officers were held. No one could offer an explanation for the arrests.

This political squad, originally established by the Debrecen government to investigate officers who had fled or had been forced by the Nazis to retreat to the west, was now headed by the very dangerous Communist, General Pálfi-Oesterreicher. At that time Minister of Defense John Vörös had no idea that it would develop into a division of political police, an organization of very ill repute rumored to torture suspects sadistically. Many compared it with the notorious Arrow-Crossist organization that had dealt so ruthlessly with political opponents. The activities of the political squad had not been conspicuous enough, however, to provoke official intervention.

Startled by the report, I called the War Minister to account:

"Are you aware that the political squad in your ministry arrested a number of prominent men?"

"General Pálfi-Oesterreicher is the head of the division. He has reported nothing," he answered. "I too learned of the arrests by accident and was just about to order a report."

"Please let me have the details immediately," I instructed.

"I shall bring General Pálfi along and we shall report together," Barta replied.

A few hours later, I was informed that the political squad had taken Dominick Szentiványi, one of the signers of the Moscow armistice

311

of 1944, and a minister plenipotentiary in the Foreign Office, and another group of officers; my source added that charges of conspiracy had been fabricated.

Calling on the President of the Republic, I told him what I had learned.

"I have heard it too," replied Tildy, and requested me to inform him of Barta's report as soon as I received it.

The Communist party was suspiciously quiet; no word of the arrests appeared in their press, and the usual introductory attacks were lacking.

In the afternoon Barta and General Pálfi-Oesterreicher called on me.

"I understand, General, that the political squad which you head has arrested a number of officers and civilians. When I asked your minister for an explanation, he informed me that you had not reported the matter to him."

"We were not able to inform the Minister, because our reports were incomplete. Now, however, I am in a position to say what happened."

Pálfi began a detailed summary of his past activities. For months his men had been watching the home of Major Szentmiklossy, the scene of frequent suspicious night gatherings. The conspiracy suspected was confirmed by a surprise raid.

His story was that former officers were conspiring to overthrow the present order and set up a new regime. Civilians who had also attended the secret gatherings and taken part in drawing up illegal plans were arrested and were being interrogated. The actions of the political squad had been justified by damaging confessions already obtained. Pálfi presented the names of more than fifteen persons already in custody.

"Tell me," I inquired. "Did you ask the suspects whom they were conspiring against, and what they wanted to replace?"

"Well, not specifically; but their answers to a number of other questions indicate that they wished to supplant the present leaders."

"Were they questioned whether they were conspiring against our constitution and the republican form of government?" I asked.

Pálfi replied with growing confusion: "Well—ahem—we didn't put to them this exact question—ahem—but if someone engages in a conspiracy, naturally it is the constitution and present form of government against which he conspires."

I turned to Barta. "Please go and question the suspects yourself, to verify the assertions of General Pálfi. Then please report to me immediately afterwards."

"Good," said Barta. After Pálfi had left he added: "There are suspicious doings in the political division. I have been informed that its assistant director, Lieutenant Colonel Kruchina, is not permitted to set foot in their house of detention."

"Send Kruchina to me," I requested.

Shortly afterwards, William Zentai, Socialist undersecretary in the War office, came to tell me what he knew of the matter. I instructed him to keep his eyes open and report anything that went on.

The following morning my secretary told me that Lieutenant Colonel Kruchina had come furtively to the Prime Ministry and wished to speak with me.

"What need is there for secrecy?" I asked as Kruchina stepped into the room.

"They are watching every move I make, ever since Pálfi gave orders not to let me into the house of detention."

Kruchina told me about the questionable activities in his department; that only Pálfi and two Communist catchpoles communicated with the prisoners; no one else was allowed at the interrogations. Eugene Szatmári, a news correspondent, had got wind of what was going on and wanted to send the news to a foreign paper he represented; but then he was arrested, too. We could not know if suspects were being tortured, because no one was allowed near the prison. Kruchina thought it might be a sadistic undertaking on the part of Pálfi, who hated non-Communists and thirsted for vengeance against a world that had barred him from the army because of his Jewish wife.

A few days later, in a dark street, Kruchina was attacked and almost abducted; wounded, he shot at his fleeing assailants. He found refuge at the British Military Mission and was finally able to leave Hungary.

I told what little I knew to Tildy, who replied:

"I think it must be a group of those superpatriots who are anxious to get more and more 100 per cent Hungarians into public life." Tildy expressed the hope that the authorities would realize that these persons held innocent, childish ambitions and so release them.

With a thousand things to attend to, I had no time to probe the problem. Besides, I was anxious to hear what Barta had learned from the suspects. Kovács and Varga, although indignant over the activities of the political squad, did not attach great significance to the affair either. We all knew that Valentine Arany had long been suspected of rightist connections; such men had often been taken into custody for a few days. We wanted to help them secure their freedom as soon as possible, but we never even guessed that this was to be part of a master plan.

CHAPTER 67

The Russian Hand Appears

NEXT DAY BARTA TOLD ME THAT HE HAD VISITED THE HOUSE OF DETENTION, as instructed, but Communist subordinates had refused to allow him to see the prisoners in the absence of Pálfi. Pálfi, arriving, stated that the prisoners had been handed over to the police because there were civilians among them, and that he could not have permitted the Minister to speak with the prisoners in any case, because it had been expressly forbidden by General Sviridov.

Then Barta went to the police, asking Gabriel Peter, chief of the political division, to let him question the men. Peter likewise regretted that it was not in his power to permit the Minister to communicate with the prisoners. This, he said, required the permission of the Minister of the Interior; besides, he had been informed that General Sviridov would not approve of it. Barta indignantly demanded that he be allowed to interrogate the prisoners, but Peter remained adamant and referred him again to Minister of the Interior Rajk.

Barta went to Rajk, protesting vigorously against the refusal of access to prisoners arrested by his department. Rajk begged him to change his mind.

"I have been instructed by the Premier to question the suspects," argued Barta.

"Even then," answered Rajk, "it isn't suitable that you should wish to communicate with the prisoners. It is not desirable that you and the Premier be mixed up in this affair; besides, I am informed that General Sviridov wishes them to be kept incommunicado."

On this Barta drove immediately to the Prime Ministry and told me how he had been blocked at every step. Although sensing a mystery, he could not uncover it.

Surprised that Sviridov had a hand in the activities of the police and political squad, I decided to see him. Pushkin must have been out of town, because he was not present at our conversation, which I caused to be noted precisely.

"Are you aware, General, that the political squad of the army and the political police have been arresting a number of men, mainly army officers, on the ground that they are involved in some sort of conspiracy?"

"I did hear something," replied Sviridov, innocently.

"Is it true, General, that you gave orders that neither the Minister of Defense nor I should be allowed to communicate with the prisoners, even for purposes of interrogation?"

"Of course not," protested Sviridov heatedly. "It is not so at all. This Pálfi-Oesterreicher was here a few days ago, and I made the mistake of receiving him. He said he had unearthed some sort of conspiracy. I didn't pay much attention to what he was saying, but told him that all such matters are the affair of the appropriate Hungarian authorities. I gave Pálfi no advice of any sort."

"Are you certain, General, that this was what took place?"

"Of course," replied Sviridov. "I recollect quite distinctly that I gave no advice to the effect that he should not allow members of the government or other persons to contact the prisoners."

"For my part I consider it a serious offense to involve the president of the Control Commission in criminal proceedings and to falsely attribute to him measures which he did not take. I shall call Pálfi to account for this," I remarked.

"Quite right," answered Sviridov.

I informed Tildy that Barta had not been able to secure further information, having been kept away from the prisoners on the ground that Sviridov did not allow it. I told him, too, of my conversation with Sviridov and his vigorous denial of any interference.

"Pálfi must be called to account," Tildy advised.

"I had the same idea and shall instruct Barta to start proceedings against Pálfi immediately," I replied.

Then we again discussed all aspects of the arrests and alleged conspiracies and agreed that they probably originated with a circle whose members were alarmed by the activities of the Communist party and had discussed means of hindering its further expansion. It seemed logical that former army officers should try to regain the posts from which they had been ousted and should consider ways of curbing Communist influence. But neither of us believed that there could be a genuine conspiracy; subsequent events proved us correct. If only we had adhered to our inner convictions and not given credence to Rajk's intrigues and the infamously extorted "confessions" of the suspects! Perhaps the break in internal affairs would have come sooner and events might have taken a different turn. Maybe this base chapter in Hungarian history entitled "conspiracy" need not have been written.

Next morning, summoning Barta and Zentai, I told them of Sviridov's statements and that Pálfi's use of the former's name was a grave act which could not remain unpunished. In my opinion disciplinary proceedings against Pálfi should be begun at once; meanwhile, he should be suspended from active service.

Both concurred, and I at once named Zentai chairman of the disciplinary commission. Barta was to delegate two respected high officers to join with Zentai on the commission.

Though I knew that the Pálfi affair would raise a storm, I was glad that at last this notorious Communist agent was caught in his own trap. At the time I did not realize the Communist party and the Russians were so deeply interested in the conspiracy that it would be impossible to touch Pálfi. I thought we could put him on the retired list and thus relieve him of command of the border guard. But I also hoped that it would be possible, once Pálfi was out of the way, to disband the military-political division of the War Office and thus dispose of another temporary agency which only served to persecute and embitter the Hungarian people.

Public excitement grew from hour to hour because of the arrests, which had not ceased. Now the political police began a new series; relatives and friends of newly confined suspects streamed to the Prime Ministry, protesting loudly against the activities of both the political police and Pálfi's squad.

I sought to calm everyone, expecting the situation to clarify itself within a few days, when the prisoners would regain their freedom.

Rajk telephoned me and said that investigations would have to be continued because they had unearthed a serious, large-scale conspiracy. I instructed him to render a detailed report at the earliest possible time; he expected to be in a position to give it within forty-eight hours.

Then Rákosi, betraying great excitement, telephoned.

"I understand you ordered an investigation against General Pálfi-Oesterreicher."

"Yes," I replied, "I was forced to because he involved the Allied Control Commission in the affairs of his division. I instructed Minister Barta to interrogate the suspects personally and report his impressions, but he was prevented by Pálfi's claim that General Sviridov had ordered that no one be permitted to communicate with the prisoners. Sviridov denied absolutely that he had ever given such an order. Under these circumstances, Pálfi's actions must be investigated, and we shall have to be strict with him."

"But how can you even think of starting an investigation against someone at the very time when, discovering the conspiracy directed against our democracy, he is rendering the greatest service to it?" protested Rákosi. "Besides, Pálfi-Oesterreicher is an exemplary democrat and doesn't deserve such shameful treatment."

"The investigation will determine whether he acted for or against the interests of the state. Should the disciplinary action committee reveal that Pálfi acted correctly and in good faith, then he will be cleared. But if he is wrong, he will be punished."

Rákosi continued his protests, which I ignored by saying that I was unwilling to suspend proceedings against Pálfi.

The disciplinary body was set up, and its hearings started. Details of procedure were determined, and Pálfi began his defense in a grandiloquent discussion of the conspiracy, in the course of which he praised the alertness of his political squad that had made it possible to nip a dangerous plot in the bud.

The Communist press was silent. Rákosi and his gang behaved as if they were as uninformed about the matter as anyone else, trying to indicate disinterest and reliance on the authorities. Rákosi, in conversation, avoided the subject and simply kept repeating himself—that there were at least "ten different conspiracies" in progress.

"Do you suppose that large landowners, whose acreage was taken from them by agrarian reform, will remain inactive? Do you think that army officers who have been dismissed from their posts will not join forces with those who are still in the west in order to regain their positions? Do you think former sheriffs and farm managers will be content to be shoved aside? Or that the churches are not organizing to hinder the progress of democracy? Don't be so naïve, because it will be too late to wake up after we have been hit on the head with a brick. Reaction is impertinent. Just because there have been no blood baths and democracy has not killed tens of thousands of men, reaction feels free to do as it pleases. I tell you, you will come to see the many dangers that threaten democracy. How can you imagine that there should have been conspiracies in Poland, Rumania, and other countries, but none here? There are at least ten different groups conspiring to overthrow democracy."

Everyone thought these diatribes of Rákosi were just propaganda. No one dreamed that it was a cunning pose concealing the first arrow of the shameful assault against the independence and democratic institutions of the Hungarian people.

The afternoon that the commission investigating Pálfi began its hearings, Captain Gruber, Sviridov's translator, telephoned that General Kondratov, head of the military division of the Allied Control Commission, wished to see me. Kondratov was an extremely ill disposed anti-Hungarian who had been chiefly responsible for bringing the Hungarian army under Communist control. He regularly threatened our Ministers of Defense, and dictated to them who should be appointed, and in what capacity, to every post. In a word, he was an absolute despot in our army affairs. American and British members of the Control Commission never called to account, or dared to interfere with, the actions of this bemedaled Communist agitator. I knew that nothing good could come of his visit in these feverish hours.

The Soviet general, arriving with Captain Gruber, immediately turned to the business at hand.

"General Sviridov heard that you have ordered proceedings against General Pálfi-Oesterreicher," began Kondratov.

"Yes," I replied. "I informed General Sviridov of this yesterday."

"The General wishes to clear up a misunderstanding," continued Kondratov. "He therefore sent me to inform you of the following: It is a fact that General Sviridov did not instruct General Pálfi not to allow anyone to communicate with the prisoners. However, owing to the bungling of an unskillful translator, General Sviridov's words were mistranslated."

"I find your explanation most interesting, particularly since I know General Sviridov is particularly careful that interpreters should translate his every word precisely. How, then, could such a mistake occur?"

"I'm sure I don't know," replied Kondratov; "but that's the situation."

I turned to Captain Gruber:

"Weren't you the translator?"

"No, sir, I had something else to do that day, and so the General had to use another interpreter," answered the captain, who hailed from Budapest and spoke Hungarian perfectly.

I was taken aback by this transparent lie, but was forced to play their game.

"Has the General any further message?" I asked Kondratov.

"Yes. He asks me to tell you that under these circumstances he considers the investigation against Pálfi unfair and asks that it be suspended."

"Please tell the General that I shall convey your information to the commission, which will undoubtedly take into consideration this change in the situation; but the investigation must, of course, be pursued to its conclusion."

"The General wishes me to inform you further," continued Kondratov, "that, as soon as he became aware of this grave error, he had the interpreter arrested."

"He certainly deserved it for causing such serious complications," I answered. "I repeat, then, please tell the General that his message will be taken into consideration by the commission investigating Pálfi."

"The General insists on having the Pálfi investigation stopped," said Kondratov in a firm tone. "In the event that you, as Premier, do not suspend the investigation, the Soviet military police will take the whole matter of the conspiracy into its own hands."

I was aghast at Kondratov's pronouncement. In my mind's eye I saw the suspects—whose numbers were constantly growing—under "questioning" in the cellars of the NKVD and later plodding in a long queue along a Siberian road in midwinter.

"Will you kindly repeat this message of General Sviridov?"

Kondratov and his interpreter repeated:

"If you, Mr. Premier, do not stop the investigation of Pálfi the Soviet military police will take over the entire proceedings in the matter of the conspiracy."

"On what basis does the General intend to take this action?" I asked.

"I can't say anything else than what General Sviridov has asked me to give you as his message; and this I have done."

I thought of Ivan Lajos, Géza Pálffi, George Pallavicini, Koloman

Kéry, and the others whom Soviet military police had seized and already carried off to Russia.

"Tell General Sviridov that I shall have the investigation suspended," I replied in dismissing the Russian "Party-General."

In the political circles there were rumors that the conspiracy charge was to be broadened so as to involve members of the Smallholders party and the Peasant Alliance. Fear had replaced nervousness, and one could hear very bitter outbursts.

When I reported the latest developments to Tildy, he said: "It seems that they want to create a bigger thing of this than we thought. We had better keep ourselves informed of all developments and take special care to avoid the slightest appearance of wishing to defend the conspiracy."

As Tildy said this, I thought of Valentine Arany, sitting in the cellars of the police. He had been introduced to me at Tildy's home as an eminent patriot, one of the most resolute leaders of the resistance movement, a man who had been of tremendous service to democracy in the face of the Germans and Fascists.

It has always been my belief that the people of a nation were at all times wiser than their leaders; in this case, too, it was dramatically proved. We leaders still thought that the "conspiracy" was an episode which could be localized, but the people felt that serious trouble was brewing. A subtle, indefinable air of terror permeated Budapest.

CHAPTER 68

The President Confers

INDEED, WITHIN FORTY-EIGHT HOURS THE MINISTER OF THE INTERIOR reported to me, as promised, bringing along a tremendous number of papers. His self-admiring prologue began:

"The work which our agencies of public security have accomplished stands alone in the history of conspiracies. Practically every conspiracy is discovered by catching someone of lower rank in the act; and from him the threads lead to the head or the directing group. Sometimes it happens that the leaders cannot be found at all. In this case there is the unusual situation that the leaders have been apprehended, and through them we are able to trace the others engaged in the conspiracy.

"For it is by now absolutely certain that this is a conspiracy of the first magnitude. Its leaders are Valentine Arany, Charles Kis, John Héder, Stephen Szentmiklossy, and Dominick Szentiványi. These men head a secret organization called Hungarian Unity. Only Hungarians of pure racial stock can be members. This organization formed the framework for the conspiracy.

"The conspiracy has two branches: one, civil; the other, military. At the moment, the military branch seems the most active and dangerous. The soldiers have organized an underground staff headed by General Louis Dálnoki-Veress. Heads of the various departments are: Major Leslie Várkonyi, Lieutenant Colonel Stephen Berko, Colonel Tihamér Sóvári, and Colonel Louis Fülöp. They also agreed to name Major Stephen Szentmiklossy adjutant to Dálnoki-Veress, while General Alexander András was appointed chief of staff."

Then the Minister of the Interior discussed the role of the civilians. Dominick Szentiványi, he said, was the foreign affairs expert; former Member of Parliament George Donáth and Valentine Arany were to be in charge of internal affairs; John Héder, of economics; while the ideological leader was an official named Charles Kis. General Louis Dálnoki-Veress had also issued an order of the day, after the general staff was organized, stating that he was taking over the military command, would not recognize army appointments made after March 19, 1944, and regarded the regular army, the forces that had fled to the west, the gendarmes, and the dissolved police forces as subject to his command.

"Let me see that order of the day," I requested.

"I am sorry, but at that time they destroyed the text. We can only re-create an approximate version from the confessions which have been obtained," said Rajk.

"Is it possible to ascertain that steps were actually taken to gain control of the army and the police, organize the soldiers in the west and reinstate the gendarmerie?" I inquired further.

"All that we could ascertain was that the general staff made a list of those officers whom it intended to appoint to district commands in various cities, and that they had contacted a few. We have not yet been able to find out whether any of them accepted their appointments. It is suspected also that a Captain Pünkösdi, who is under arrest, was commissioned to seek connections with army personnel who had fled to Austria and Germany, and even to contact British circles."

Rajk expressed his desire to report on the conspiracy to the President of the Republic and the party leaders. I agreed immediately to call the party leaders together for a conference with Tildy to discuss the whole subject.

In leaving, Rajk mentioned that some of the confessions implicated several of our party members, such as Minister Mistéth and Deputies Saláta, Jaczkó, and Alexander Kis. He, however, doubted that the references to these men could be taken seriously, for it was not likely that they knew anything of the clandestine acts. I instructed Rajk to continue reporting all developments, every day if necessary.

I called Tildy and informed him that I had agreed to confer with Rajk and the party leaders; Tildy approved and I set the conference for the next day, when Béla Varga attended for the Smallholders, Rákosi for the Communists, Szakasits for the Socialists, and Veres for the Peasant party.

Rajk's pleasure at being chief informant in the affairs of the conspiracy was obvious; he plainly attached unusual importance to his present role.

He unfolded the scheme in great detail, presenting his evidence as cleverly as he knew how, for he knew that authorization to proceed depended on this discussion. After relating what he had already told me, he gave the contents of the confessions. Tildy and I interrupted frequently, asking to see the affidavits to which he referred.

In the confessions the suspects forthwith admitted that they were members of Hungarian Unity, the aim of which was to facilitate the appointment of men of Hungarian origin to government posts. Some admitted believing that the political trend was unhealthy, and discussing how to improve conditions. Army personnel in custody admitted that some sort of general staff had been created to take over the guidance of the army after the Russian occupying forces should withdraw. The Minister of the Interior stated that the movement was headed by a committee of seven although he had been able to discover the identity only of six, and that this committee had made contacts with such Smallholder deputies as Koloman Saláta, Paul Jaczkó, Alexander Kis, Leslie Vattai, and Minister of Reconstruction Andrew Mistéth.

At this point Tildy interjected his conviction that none of these men could possibly have the remotest connection with the conspiracy; he would even be willing to put his hand into the fire for Alexander Kis.

I remarked that the majority of the suspects were known to have been valiant members of the resistance that combated both Germans and fascists. These men had given invaluable service in laying the groundwork of our democracy; it was inconceivable that they would organize to overthrow it now.

"The fact that these men took part in the resistance movement means nothing," screamed Rákosi. "Not every fascist was pro-German; members of the resistance movement are not necessarily democrats. We mustn't forget that there is a large number of Jewish fascists, too. It's perfectly easy for someone to be an enemy of democracy, even if he did take part in the resistance movement."

"But who in the world could suppose that Alexander Kis and the other young deputies were enemies of democracy? Their actions bore witness to their democratic convictions. A few of them suffered Arrow Cross tortures." And then I told what I knew of these young men.

Koloman Saláta, a highly cultured economist, as an army officer organized the forces of military resistance and established radio contact with the Allied armies. Since the armistice he had been one of the most energetic protagonists of democracy in the ranks of the Smallholders party.

Paul Jaczkó, as a young officer on Russian battlefields, had effected the most audacious anti-German attacks by aiding the Russian partisans and obstructing German army operations. After the liberation he had been appointed Lord Lieutenant of the county of Vas, contributing much to its progress.

Alexander Kis and Leslie Vattai had risen the hard way from the poorest peasant families. Vattai had become a university professor while still very young. They had both been captured by the Arrow Crossists and tortured for weeks before escaping from their German prison to continue work for the resistance movement. These men could not by the wildest stretch of the imagination be supposed to have tried to obstruct democratic progress in any way.

Rajk himself remarked that he should be sorry to hear that any antidemocratic activity should come to light in connection with these men, particularly Alexander Kis.

Tildy stated that in his opinion the affair had two aspects: military and civilian. Of the civilian side, were it not that George Donáth was involved, he would say that it was merely a circle of Hungarians troubled over the fate of their country. Possibly they had spoken a lot of nonsense, but that did not make them enemies of democracy. The military angle seemed more serious; however, most of the suspects were not known to him, and without commenting on them he considered it proper for the investigation to continue.

"Whether this be a conspiracy or the mutterings of anxious men," said I, "the fact that the investigations are conducted by exclusively Communist political police renders them repugnant to the public. I consider it desirable that the Minister of the Interior include Smallholder members of the police force in the investigation, thus making the proceedings less biased."

"No one lays a hand on the suspects," shouted Rajk. "Questioning is not like it was in the past. I can bring up the case of Dominick Szentiványi by way of illustration. He, on one occasion, said he wasn't feeling well and refused to testify. A political suspect couldn't have done this in the past."

"I should say not," chimed in Rákosi. "In the past, when police caught a Communist, they gave him a healthy beating even before they began to question him. But, after all, we are democrats and avoid such methods."

Opinions differed; Communists insisted that a "conspiracy" existed. We were of the opinion that these were, at the most, gatherings of dissatisfied citizens. As for the army personnel, they might have made some stupid moves, such as they had occasionally made in earlier years.

The conference ended; Béla Varga and I, staying with Tildy, opined that no conspiracy existed. Tildy insisted that the investigation must be permitted to run its course. The Smallholders party must by no means deny the existence of a conspiracy; after all, it seemed some witless steps had been taken by military men. All three of us agreed, however, that we would defend Alexander Kis and his colleagues in case criminal proceedings should evolve.

Not one of us connected the supposed "conspiracy" with the political crisis; the underlying thought behind our decisions was that, with the investigation proceeding at the pace set by the Communists, the charges would prove to be made of whole cloth and the balloon of the conspiracy would burst.

CHAPTER 69

The "Conspiracy" Is Made Public

FOR WEEKS FOLLOWING THE FIRST ARRESTS, THE HUNGARIAN PRESS ignored the "conspiracy." However, after our conference with the President of the Republic, Rajk came to me asserting that he had to issue an official communiqué because the "requests" of the press for information could no longer be resisted; reports had appeared in the foreign press which were susceptible of misinterpretation.

I told Rajk that I shared his disinclination to keep the public in the dark, and requested that he show me the communiqué before he released it to the press. The wisdom of my precaution was shown when he presented a communiqué implicating the Smallholders party to an extent which could not be permitted. I made him delete these parts and consented to the phrase, "The conspirators sought to bore their way into the Smallholders party and into the other parties as well." Rajk tricked me by leaving out the second part of the sentence.

Publication of the official report on the conspiracy removed all restraint from the leftist press. Thereafter, the Communist and Social Democratic newspapers devoted large front-page spreads to the conspiracy, which became their sole theme. The leftist papers openly accused the young Smallholder members of Parliament: "We have often emphasized that the Smallholders party is filled with reactionaries. We have often pointed to the antidemocratic activity of Koloman Saláta and his friends. Now it develops that these suspicions were not unfounded. These young members of Parliament at least belong to the conspiratorial coterie."

Among the Smallholder members in Parliament, a small group of worth-while young men stood out. Others in the group were Tibor Hám, a young doctor, who was the Lord-Lieutenant of Sopron County for a year, and John Horváth, one of the party's experts on cooperatives. Because of their youth, people referred to them as "Holy Innocents." They cheerfully did more than their share of the work and fully discharged assignments made to numerous parliamentary committees. Alexander Kis had become the director of the Peasants' Alliance; and John Horváth, his deputy. Several would have become members of the government if we had not feared that the older members would resent their youth. Each and every one of them took part in the anti-fascist and anti-German resistance, and most of them risked their lives daily for democracy. Each had been a member of the Smallholders party since 1943, when the intellectual elements in the party began to organize.

This active and intelligent group initiated numerous useful activities, and its high moral standards were buttressed by deep religious convictions. Despite my preoccupation I often took time to meet with the young men in it, considering them the statesmen of the future in our democracy, and continually advising them.

The public was shocked to read the accusations in the leftist press against these three young members of Parliament. The "conspiracy" now began to serve as the basis for occasional attacks on the Smallholders party and on the people's democracy.

It became generally known that I personally was somewhat wary of the whole affair of the "conspiracy," and in retaliation the Communists tried early to bring its repercussions as near my person as possible. They began a whispering campaign to implicate my daughter Juliette, who was studying in Switzerland, and my son Ferenc, who had been appointed junior secretary to the legation in Washington. I did not think it worth while to take exception to the whispering because this would only have provoked further accusations.

The Communist press cast some aspersions on other young Hungarian diplomats abroad, too. It established that a few of these were friendly with the young intellectual group of the Smallholders party, and it proceeded to jump to conclusions.

The Minister of the Interior kept me informed of the new arrests. On the occasion of one of his reports I took him to task for the behavior of the leftist press, and he assured me that he would curb it.

Needless to say, as the head of the government I had a continuous row of problems and was unable to follow the alleged conspiracy with undivided attention. The plan of the exposure, however, became very clear to me. It was to cripple the Smallholders party, to an extent impossible through the successive political crises.

Béla Varga, Béla Kovács, and I met frequently at the home of the President of the Republic, whose family had also become the object of a whispering campaign. President Tildy was of the opinion that it would be better to let the excesses of the police become apparent through the legal procedure than to interfere with the established process of the law. I interviewed the implicated young representatives one by one, and in friendly talks attempted to find out what they knew of the "conspiracy," warning them that it would not be right to keep facts from me. One after another stated in no uncertain terms that he had never known of any sort of conspiracy. They had heard of a group which occasionally met for discussion of Hungarian problems, which naturally touched upon political issues.

The declarations of these young men eased my mind. I knew that they were upright and honest and would have admitted to me if they had had any part in the affair.

Béla Kovács followed the same course. He too was convinced that the young representatives were innocent, because one among them would certainly have dropped a hint if he had had a part in the "conspiracy."

When we met in Béla Varga's little cell for an hour, now and then, we often questioned each other: Was it possible that some sort of conspiracy was actually in preparation? It was always our conclusion that some of these men probably discussed questions which they might have discussed in public, too; but the circumstances were such that their private talks attracted attention and provided grounds for the invention of the conspiracy charge. None of us thought that the persecution would go so far as to smear innocent men and rob them of their liberty.

Today the whole world knows about the conspiracies in the countries under Soviet control. Today it is clear to the intelligent observers of the civilized world that, when a "conspiracy" begins, it precedes a new onsurge of the Communists, wherever it may be; and the idea of conspiracy has become a much overworked recipe of the Soviet.

The so-called conspiracy in Hungary was nowhere preceded by a claim of conspirative action of such magnitude that it would have aimed at control of a government. International political leadership was as inexperienced as was the Hungarian government in counteracting this new Soviet tactic.

CHAPTER 70

Dumfounding Accusations

THE NEXT STEP CAME WHEN THE MINISTER OF THE INTERIOR TOLD ME, on the occasion of one of his reports: "It appears that our Minister colleague, Andrew Mistéth, is party to the conspiracy. I request you, Mr. Prime Minister, to investigate the affair and remove him from the cabinet."

I asked him what evidence there was against the Minister.

He replied that Major Stephen Szentmiklossy had confessed that before his arrest he was summoned by Minister Mistéth, informed that he would be arrested and advised to disappear. When Szentmiklossy told him that he had no funds, Mistéth replied that the hundred forints on his person was at Szentmiklossy's disposal, and Szentmiklossy accepted the money. The Minister of the Interior added that other confessions implicated Mistéth as a directing member of the Hungarian Unity organization; that at the very beginning of his tenure as Minister he had established contact with the Hungarian Unity members in the Ministry and had played a leading part in the reorganization of this society.

I was shocked by Rajk's report. If Szentmiklossy had confessed that Mistéth had encouraged him to flee, and if it developed that Mistéth was a member of the society, there would be no way of avoiding his resignation.

I told Rajk that, inasmuch as his report on Mistéth closely affected the Smallholders party, he should come next day to the President of the Republic and present the new conspiracy developments to the Smallholder leadership.

I summoned Mistéth, who readily admitted that he had been a member of the Hungarian Unity and offered his resignation. I decided to take the case to the meeting of Smallholders leaders scheduled at the home of President Tildy and meanwhile to make no announcement of the resignation.

Despite the promises of the Minister of the Interior, the Communist press embarked on unrestrained denunciations. It had become common, after the Communist papers attacked politicians, for the police to direct interrogation against the same individuals and then arrest them. The Communist press, with increasing frequency, accused the young Smallholders in Parliament of conspiracy. They took pot shots at Béla Kovács, too, for failing to detect that the Smallholders party was "participating" in the conspiracy. The young representatives were annoyed, but Béla Kovács did not take the attacks seriously. During his long political career he had become hardened.

Rákosi, after one of the cabinet councils, said to me: "Well, how many times did I tell you that there was a conspiracy in Hungary? You wouldn't believe me. You thought I was only talking hot air. You are unable to be as jealous of the democracy as it deserves. Personally, I am surprised at the extent of this conspiracy, which a few weeks ago appeared to be only a minor affair. If we want to protect the democracy we must be ever on guard. We must have no mercy on the conspirators. If we handle these fellows with kid gloves, the rest will be emboldened. Don't think that this is the only conspiracy group. As I've already told you, many here are toying with the idea of upsetting the democracy."

"The investigation is in process," I answered, "and I hope it will be sufficiently objective to establish the facts. I cling to my view that this democracy cannot be upset, and that those accused of conspiracy thought of changes in the present system and not of upsetting the democracy by force. My political party is also of the opinion that legal procedure must be completed. However, the whole procedure has one basic fault: it is being conducted exclusively by the political police, who, so to speak, consist entirely of Communists. This fact does not reassure the people, and I shall demand of the Minister of the Interior that Smallholder policemen also participate in the investigation."

Rákosi was not too pleased. Béla Varga, Béla Kovács, and I discussed ways and means of confining the affair. We were, however, confronted with the Soviet Union. We knew the intercession by General Kondratov in the Pálfi-Oesterreicher incident meant that it was following the conspiracy affair with active interest, and that any interference in the judicial process would provoke further intercession.

Next day I invited the leaders of the Smallholders party to the office of President Tildy, so that they might hear Rajk's report on the Mistéth affair. In addition to Zoltán Tildy and myself, Béla Varga, Béla Kovács, Stephen Balogh, and Emery Oltványi were present.

Minister of the Interior Rajk produced his notes and the minutes which he had brought along, and began to report on the conspiracy.

When he talked about the Hungarian Unity organization and the underground leadership, he directed some remarks against the Smallholders party. He said that the conspirators doubtless wanted to win the Smallholders party to their aims, and for that reason penetrated the party in large numbers and sought to secure leading positions in it. However, the leadership of the Smallholders party was not yet held responsible for permitting the conspirators to penetrate the party in such large numbers. He confined himself to asserting that the conspirators were in contact with a number of the party's representatives in Parliament, whom they "sought" to gain for their own objectives.

The Minister of the Interior said that they had discovered a study prepared by George Donáth, one of the Committee of Seven, which must be regarded as the "conspiracy program." This stated that it was necessary to reestablish legal continuity in Hungarian political life. Since the ability of the old regime to act had ceased on March 19, 1944, the day of German occupation, and to date had not been regained, it was necessary to continue Hungarian political life where it had left off on that day.

The Minister of the Interior and the Communists concluded from this document that Donáth sought to reestablish the Horthy regime and wished to place Nicholas Kállay again at the head of the government. There was no evidence in the otherwise confused document, nor did the other defendants claim, that they wished to reestablish the Horthy regime. On the contrary, they confessed that if it were possible to bring about some change, it would be desirable to place some liberal democrat at the head of the government.

The Minister of the Interior said also that the conspirators tried to nullify the great accomplishments of the democracy—for example, the agrarian reform. This allegation seemed impossible to me from the start. The men arrested had no economic interest in the agrarian reform. None of them had lost land, and none of them had received any. The political theorists among them, I knew, were friends of the agrarian reform. In any case, they were sensible men and knew the obvious, that the completed agrarian reform could not be undone. It was impossible to reassemble the subdivided lands, glue them together, and turn them over to their former owners. I knew of only two instances where the agrarian reform had been undone. The first had occurred in 1919, when the short-lived Communist government of Hungary had prevented the completion of agrarian reform; and the other in Russia when the

Soviet government took away the land of some ten million Russian peasants and created the large-estate system, the kolkhoz.

Rajk then produced the confessions of those who had already been arrested, and in these pointed to the confessions of the underground leaders, to the initiation of the army organization, and to the admissions that they wanted to upset the democracy and the Republic. They were waiting only for the appropriate moment, which they believed would come when the Soviet armies left Hungary. At this point he turned to Béla Kovács:

"Needless to say, I have no desire to suspect you, but must admit that some of the statements seem to implicate you."

"What are these statements?" asked Béla Kovács.

"Some of the individuals have admitted that they had close contact with you and that you often met."

"That is true," Kovács replied. "I knew Dominick Szentiványi from Debrecen and talked with him a few times. As for Valentine Arany, I met him at the headquarters of the Smallholders party as the leader of the Budapest organization; and, since I believed him to be a worthy man, I made no effort to avoid contact with him."

"To be sure, this is not sufficient evidence for reaching any conclusions," said Rajk. "I merely mention that in their confessions some mention having contact with you."

During this exchange, Béla Kovács asked vehemently that his testimony should be taken by the police, because he would not tolerate suspicions of any kind.

Since Rajk often referred in his reports, to the Smallholders party, we surmised an inclination to incriminate it. The rightness of our suspicion was soon proved, when Rajk expressed his views on this matter:

"The arrested conspirators claim that the Hungarian Unity organization included some Smallholders. They have dropped hints about Koloman Saláta and mentioned also the names of deputies Paul Jaczkó, Tibor Hám, John Horváth, Alexander Kis, and Leslie Vattai. I am of the opinion that, of these, Koloman Saláta may actually have taken some part in the conversations of the conspirators."

Almost every one of us commented on the report of the Minister of the Interior. We expressed the view that none of the deputies mentioned could possibly have participated in the conspiracy, and separately described the careers and democratic virtues of each.

Then the Minister of the Interior turned to the Mistéth affair. Those participating in the meeting were much surprised to hear the charges against Mistéth and passed from hand to hand the minutes of Szentmiklossy's confession, admitting that Mistéth urged him to escape, gave him money for that purpose, and was an active member of the Hungarian Unity organization.

I said to the Minister of the Interior: "Whether a conspiracy exists or not, the public is suspicious because only the Communist members of the political police are participating in the investigations. For this reason I request that you immediately assign Smallholder police personnel to the investigations. This will serve to quiet the Smallholders party as well as general Hungarian public opinion. I cannot permit this far-reaching affair to be handled exclusively by Communist police."

The Minister of the Interior replied: "Representatives of the other political parties will also participate in the investigations. I have already issued instructions to the effect that the Smallholder deputy director of the political police shall always be present at the interrogations."

"I shall request a report on this," I ended.

After the departure of the Minister of the Interior, the Smallholders party leaders remained with the President and discussed the situation. This was the first occasion on which they had had an opportunity to see the transcript of the interrogations, and, although they were puzzled by sane men's entertaining such notions of "upsetting" the democracy, they recognized that it would be absolutely necessary to continue the proceedings against those who joined secret societies, making antidemocratic plans against the Republic. This would be true even if they did no more than talk. The conference decided that it would be necessary to accept Mistéth's resignation and, further, to localize the conspiracy lest it be exploited so as to split the Smallholders party and compromise its representation.

I conferred with the Minister of the Interior and agreed to accept Mistéth's resignation on condition that he remain free from arrest. This condition was necessary because he was not a member of Parliament and, having no parliamentary immunity, was subject to police action. The Minister of the Interior declared that the police had no intention of arresting Mistéth. He added that, if needful, they would complete proceedings against him; but under such conditions he could not remain a member of the government anyway.

CHAPTER 71

The Peasant Alliance a Target

THE DAY FOLLOWING OUR DISCUSSIONS WITH THE PRESIDENT, THE COM-
munist newspapers blared forth new sensationalism. Now they insisted
that the leaders of the Peasant Alliance also had participated in the
conspiracy. They had previously pointed fingers at the Peasant Alliance
because the arrested John Héder was employed there. Now, however,
they began to cast aspersions on a large group of its employees.

I asked the Minister of the Interior what kind of new program was
now being initiated under the cloak of the "conspiracy."

Rajk declared that John Horváth, a deputy, Stephen Oláh, Dennis
Barsi, Aladár Fáy, John Héder, Alexander Bálint, William Fitos,
Stephen Tóth, and others employed by the Peasant Alliance were
members of the Hungarian Unity organization—some of them had
definitely participated in the conspiracy, and the others were seriously
implicated.

With the exception of Horváth, those enumerated were not elected to
office in the Peasant Alliance; they were employees and worked in its
various branches as low-salaried clerks. For that reason it was an error
to call them leaders of the alliance. I was the president of the alliance,
and Béla Kovács its executive vice president; Stephen Szabó and
Stephen Dobi were the other vice presidents. The directorate consisted
exclusively of Smallholder deputies in Parliament, and none of the
clerks named was on it.

It was clear, however, that the Minister of the Interior's attack was
directed against the Peasant Alliance, and called for prompt action lest
the alliance itself be charged with conspiracy.

The same afternoon I conferred with the directors of the alliance and
proposed that we immediately serve notice on all the clerks, without
exception, keeping them in temporary status; in addition, we should
immediately dismiss all who were members of the Hungarian Unity
organization or had any connection with the so-called conspiracy. I
proposed further that the various branches of the alliance be placed
under the management of peasants among the Smallholders party

deputies in Parliament, who were also members of the alliance's directorate.

My motion was approved. The newly appointed managers assumed their duties the next day, and thus, from one day to the next, the management of the alliance was completely shifted. This decision proved to be correct because it prevented large-scale attacks on the alliance.

Naturally both the Soviet Union and the Communist party would have liked to destroy the Peasant Alliance, whose network extended over the whole country, with local offices in more than a thousand villages and towns. However, the Peasant Alliance had significance not only as an economic and cultural body, but as a strong cooperative movement; under its sponsorship more and more provincial cooperatives were organized, indicating that the peasants wanted to keep their own cooperative organizations beyond the reach of the centrally directed cooperatives.

The Peasant Alliance also had important political significance. Under its educational programs the peasants received ideological training: courses were purposefully designed to teach the facts of democracy and to enlighten the peasants on international questions. Just as in the time of National Socialism the Peasant Alliance had kept them from participating in the Nazi party movement, so now it protected them against the influence of Marxism. In addition, it slowly became the guardian of the peasants' interests, standing back of the agricultural laws and representing the peasants in wage and price negotiations. It seemed necessary to the Communists to destroy the powerful and popular organization which was such a bulwark against their influence among the peasantry.

With the help of the radical Peasant party, the Communists had reactivated two peasant organizations: the Association of Agricultural Workers and Small Landowners, and the Association of New Land Holders. Needless to say, both were Communist-dominated, and both followed radical leftist lines. The management of both associations was put into the hands of determined Communists who carried out Rákosi's orders explicitly. Through these organizations, they initiated a cooperative movement to utilize farm installations left behind after the division of large estates.

The Soviet Union also supported both organizations actively. To one of them it gave a large headquarters building on Maria Valeria Street. For the other, it vacated a large building on Szabadság Square. Obviously the Soviet policy aimed to convert the peasants to Communism; and for that reason, while it sought to suppress the Smallholders and the Peasant Alliance, it supported the Communist-sponsored bodies.

The clerks of the Peasant Alliance who have been named—except John Horváth, who enjoyed parliamentary immunity—were soon arrested by Rajk's cohorts. They searched the premises of the alliance and used harmless documents to drum up charges against other men still at liberty.

Step by step the Communist press continued its denunciation tactics. Now it began to publicly accuse Smallholders party deputies of participation in the "conspiracy."

It became standard procedure for the press to attack individuals, against whom the Minister of the Interior would then produce written confessions, demanding their arrest.

I again summoned an interparty council at the President's office. At this meeting the Minister of the Interior told us that deputy Koloman Saláta was the secret seventh member of the Committee of Seven. He declared further that Paul Jaczkó had secretly organized an armed force and, for the purpose of establishing contact with Arrow Cross officers in Austria, had personally facilitated the escape of these men from the country. Therefore, Saláta and Jaczkó had principal roles in the conspiracy. John Horváth was not only a member of the Hungarian Unity but also one of its organizers and directors. Deputy Tibor Hám was not a member of the Hungarian Unity, but was one of the most enthusiastic supporters of the conspiracy, several depositions making it clear that he carried out all the instructions of the Committee of Seven. Rajk further claimed that Leslie Gyulai participated in the "Gyöngyös conspiracy"; and in the current conspiracy it developed that, on behalf of the Committee of Seven, he had also been in communication with the Arrow Cross officers and foreign agents who had fled to Austria. Finally Rajk established—as he said, "with regret"—that in September, 1946, Alexander Kis and Leslie Vattai had become members of the Hungarian Unity organization, had taken its oath, and had been initiated.

We examined the minutes which implicated the deputies named. We were stunned to find that those making the confessions had signed them in their own hand.

Rákosi was first to speak: "Since the elections we have repeatedly stated that the right wing of the Smallholders party is an enemy of our democracy and supports the attacks on our democracy. The leadership of the Smallholders party has always rejected these allegations. Now, when the roof over our heads is aflame, it develops that we were right all along. If the Smallholders party does not accept the merciless fight against reaction and the conspiracy, then democracy will fail and the responsibility will belong to the Smallholders party. We are not prepared to wait until the conspirators behead us one by one. On the contrary, we demand an immediate liquidation of the conspiracy."

The case against Koloman Saláta appeared to be very serious indeed. If the confessions implicating Jaczkó were also true, then he also was beyond protection. The trial of Gyulai had been demanded by the Russians as long ago as August in connection with the Gyöngyös case. They proved that, despite being a member of Parliament, John Horváth was an organizer of an illegal secret society.

We had difficulties in defending these men at the conference. However, we took strong exception to the attacks on Kis, Vattai, and Hám.

Béla Varga stated that, since several members of Parliament were under suspicion, he was not satisfied to have the investigation in the hands of the police alone, but considered the appointment of a parliamentary investigating committee necessary. Rákosi, Szakasits, Peter Veres, and Zoltán Tildy unanimously opposed the idea. When I saw that the conference was not receptive to such a committee, I brought up the matter of the composition of the investigators of the political police.

I again urged the Minister of the Interior, for purposes of the conspiracy, to supplement the investigating police with representatives of the other political parties—first of all, the Smallholders: although Communist, Social Democrat, and Peasant party members were implicated in the conspiracy, it appeared that this unhappy affair touched the Smallholders party most closely; and for that reason stressed Smallholder participation with the police.

The Minister of the Interior had promised to carry out my instructions; but the promise was unfilled. Actually, the Smallholders deputy director of the political police participated in the investigation only to the extent of being summoned to witness the signing of the confessions. No political party representatives other than Communists participated either in the investigations or in the interrogations. I could not accept public responsibility for this one-sided procedure.

Szakasits rushed to the defense of the Minister of the Interior: "Your statement does not accord with the facts. Social Democratic police also participate in the investigation, and they report to me regularly on developments; and I am obliged to tell you that they state with most serious conviction that a dangerous conspiracy is in preparation, and that they consider it necessary to take political action against the conspirators."

"I do not know what the Social Democratic police tell you," I replied: "but I do not receive first-hand police reports, and for that reason I insist that Smallholders party police participate in the investigation. Otherwise I too shall be compelled to insist upon the motion advanced by Béla Varga."

It was apparent that Rajk waited for an indication of Rákosi's viewpoint. When Rákosi said that he thought it proper that representatives of other parties participate in the police investigations, Rajk reaffirmed his previously made promise.

After the departure of the members of the interparty council, Béla Varga and I asked the President what should be done if the suspension of the parliamentary immunities of the accused representatives was requested. The President replied that the surrender of the deputies could not be denied, because the evidence appeared to be fairly complete. However, it was necessary to speed the trial of the case in court, because it was quite certain that discussion in open court would cast light on the situation, and it was evident that the accused deputies would be vindicated.

That evening the political committee of the Smallholders party met to discuss the conspiracy. We summarized the report of the Minister of the Interior and stated that fellow deputies were also being accused. The report shocked the committee, and it decided to formulate its policy on a case-by-case basis, whenever the suspension of the parliamentary immunity of any of our fellow deputies might be requested. Some members of the committee voiced doubt of the existence of a conspiracy; but the majority thought it necessary to meet with the Minister of the Interior, in order that they might hear the accusations made against the deputies.

The party was most concerned over the accusation of Alexander Kis. He was an esteemed member of both peasant and parliamentary circles, who respected his knowledge, his political acumen, his puritanical philosophy and enormous capacity for work. Several of us knew also that the Communists on several previous occasions had tried to enroll both Kis and Vattai. The acquisition of these two outstanding men would have been a feather in their caps: Kis with his peasant origin and vast popularity, and Vattai with his knowledge of philosophy. Both rejected Communist approaches with decision and publicly upheld the traditions of Hungary and Christianity, making plain their belief that Marxism was a thing of the past. It was obvious that there was a close connection between the rebuffs received by the Communists and their decision to eliminate these two young heroes of the anti-Nazi struggles from public life.

Until now I had been able to carry the load of my public office without noticeable effect on my nerves, but from this time on I became depressed. I felt that superhuman strength would be required to realize our aims and to preserve the coalition government until our country regained its independence.

CHAPTER 72

The Communist Technique of Inquisition

THE TIMETABLE OF THE "CONSPIRACY" TECHNIQUE HAS BECOME COMMON knowledge.

It begins with an attack by the Communist press, which, despite the firm promise of the Minister of the Interior, receives special reports on all minute details of the developments. Then the police take the accused into custody. Finally they produce confessions incriminating other men still at liberty.

In a day or two Parliament received the petition of the prosecutor, requesting suspension of the Parliamentary immunity of Koloman Saláta and Paul Jaczkó. The indictment stated that Saláta was a member of the Committee of Seven, the top echelon of the conspiracy, and participated in its meetings; that, on the instruction of the Committee of Seven, he had undertaken to influence the Smallholders party; that he had knowledge of the existence of the underground directorate and the military organization, and that he accepted George Donáth's pamphlets and maintained contact with "conspirator circles" abroad.

The indictment against Jaczkó stated that, although his ancestry was not purely Hungarian and therefore he could not have been a member of the Hungarian Unity organization, he had accepted the Committee of Seven's assignment to create an armed organization and had personally facilitated the flight of persons who, on the instructions of the directorate of the conspiracy, sought to establish contact with fascist groups abroad.

I decided that I would never again, singly, take any steps in the conspiracy problem; that I would not accept responsibility for instructing the Committee on Immunities but would convene the party leadership for the examination of each and every issue. I invited Béla Kovács, Béla Varga, Stephen Balogh, and Emery Oltványi to a meeting in my office and had Saláta and Jaczkó brought there, too.

At the meeting I apprised Saláta and Jaczkó of the accusations against them; and both denied the charges. Saláta declared that the whole conspiracy was nothing more than after-dinner table talk. Jaczkó, on the other hand, stated that his enlisting activities were confined to the organization of the Smallholders party guard; that he had had nothing to do with any type of armed or military organization. I asked both of them to voluntarily surrender their parliamentary immunity and spare the Smallholder members of the Committee of Immunities from embarrassment, because, if the accusations were unfounded, they would in any event be vindicated by the courts.

Koloman Saláta, broken in spirit and tired, answered: "If arrested, I will sign whatever they wish. This public abuse has so undermined my nerves that they can probably squeeze out of me any confession they want." Jaczkó was unwilling to surrender his immunity because, while he felt himself entirely innocent, he was convinced that with torture any confession could be dragged out of him.

We questioned the two at length about the various accusations. I reproached Saláta because, while he was much with me, he had not told me about all the conversations he was conducting. He replied nervously:

"Nothing happened that you don't know about; but it is likely that I will tell them about things that never happened, too, if they torture me long enough."

That day Andrew Mistéth, the former Minister of Reconstruction, was arrested by order of the Minister of the Interior, who alleged that it was necessary because he was planning to escape. In the evening, Béla Kovács and Béla Varga had another talk with Saláta and Jaczkó, urging them to surrender their immunity under the conditions that the court should judge them on the basis of facts and not of police confessions.

After the talk Saláta disappeared, and next day his brother came to me crying, saying that his brother had not returned home.

The Committee on Immunities considered the case of the two deputies and, on the evidence presented, suspended their parliamentary immunities. Jaczkó was arrested. Later, it came out that Saláta had escaped abroad.

Béla Varga asked for a meeting early next morning. I looked him up in his office as president of the Parliament, where he produced a letter scribbled in pencil with a familiar signature. It had been smuggled out of the jail and informed us about the interrogation methods employed by the Communist police. The writer had had to stand in one spot facing a row of spotlights for five days and nights while he was interrogated, without being allowed either to sit or to lie down. He told us that under such inquisition people could be made to confess anything, and that all persons arrested were being closely questioned about Béla Kovács, Béla Varga, and myself. Some were questioned about Tildy, too.

Because the letter referred, among others accused of conspiracy, to people introduced to me by Tildy, I showed it to him. Tildy advised caution because, in his own words, if we brought the police to account on the basis of this letter, its writer might be exposed to even worse punishment; but it might be a plant—or it might have been written under compulsion with a view to provoking a controversy which would serve to clear the interrogation procedure of the police.

I told Tildy that, this danger notwithstanding, we could not permit use of the methods described in the letter for inciting a conspiracy and possibly implicating still other innocent persons.

Tildy again replied that public trials must be expedited in order that they might cast light on the whole affair.

I lacked his confidence in the objectivity of the courts, and was convinced that they would be under just as much compulsion as the police and would be just as anxious to convict innocent men as at the time of the Kunmadaras trial. I felt that, at the very most, a trial would have the advantage of enabling the defendants to retract confessions exacted from them by the police. Their attorneys were also of the opinion that, if they retracted their confessions, the whole conspiracy charge would collapse, because there was no other evidence against them. The party leadership thought that, so long as the confessions were not retracted, we must proceed on the assumption that a conspiracy existed, especially since the Russians had a hand in the pie. We discovered that members of the Russian secret police were frequenting the political police premises at 60 Andrássy Avenue, and interrogating the defendants either there or at their own offices.

These were the circumstances which confronted me when, as the head of the government, I stepped before the microphone to describe the conspiracy affair and to demand a trial at the earliest possible moment.

Sviridov sent for me, as usual under the pretext of discussing some economic question. After discussing some minor matters, he asked, "When do you gentlemen want to fill the Ministry of Education vacancy?"

I told him that I wished to fill this post as soon as possible, but the Peasant party had not yet designated a suitable nominee. They named the popular authors Julius Illyés, Aron Tamási, and Zoltán Szabó—anyone of whom I should have been glad to see as Minister of Education; but the Communist party objected to them all.

Pushkin, who had arrived in the meantime, interjected, "Believe me, Joseph Darvas is the most appropriate candidate."

I answered: "Please drop the idea, because under no circumstances will I accept the thought of Darvas being Minister of Education. You are familiar with my reasons, and there is no point in discussing it further."

I knew full well that the Russians were pressing Darvas's appointment because they wanted to prepare some sort of attack on the churches.

The popular subject of the day then came up. "Well, what is new on the conspiracy front?" asked Pushkin with a self-satisfied smirk.

"You are obviously as well informed as I am," I replied. He doubtless was better informed than I, because he had participated in its conception.

"Does the Prime Minister still remember the letter sent him by the Red Army Command after the incident on the Theresian Boulevard?"

"Of course I remember it. But what has that to do with the conspiracy affair?"

"It is true, is it not, that in that letter the Red Army Command requested among other things the prosecution of Representative Leslie Gyulai? This Gyulai is in the conspiracy, too. He is a sworn enemy of the Soviet Union and tries to damage it however he can."

"I consider Gyulai to be an honest democrat. He is a penniless fellow and a champion of the poor. Appearances are against him; actually, he is probably innocent."

Pushkin did not yield.

"Believe me, there is trouble with Béla Kovács, too. I do not claim that Kovács is a conspirator. It is nevertheless our suspicion that he tolerated men around himself who are leaders in the conspiracy. This at least testifies to his inability to see political issues clearly."

I felt as though the Communist press were speaking through Pushkin's lips, and could hardly suppress my anger.

"I ask you not to mix Kovács in the conspiracy, because Kovács is above suspicion. You know full well that Kovács has no personal need for any conspiracy. He has been a member of the government and can have a cabinet post at will. He is dissatisfied with the conduct of the Communists, and so am I. You know Kovács well, and know that his straightforwardness makes him inept for any conspiracy."

After this interchange Pushkin stopped criticizing Kovács and lectured on the theme that Hungarian party politics served to encourage conspirators.

"Democratic developments are not proceeding in as healthy a direction as they did a year and a half ago. The Soviet Union views Hungarian political developments with constant concern."

"I do not know what reason the Soviet Union can have for this view. The whole government and all the political parties are forever voicing the need for friendship with the Soviet Union. Whenever anyone mentions the 'great powers,' he always begins with the 'powerful and victorious Soviet Union.' Our efforts to win the Hungarian people, estranged by the Russian army, to Soviet-Hungarian friendship are unceasing, and the security of the Soviet Union is not threatened by Hungary. By the way, from the viewpoint of the security of the Soviet Union, the situation here is more fortunate than in any other southeastern European country, because all the leading political parties in Hungary have entered the coalition and therefore have no reason to revolt. In the other countries, the majorities are suppressed and deprived of authority, and it is always possible that the people will revolt not only against their own governments, but against friendship with the Soviet Union as well."

Pushkin appeared to be surprised by my interpretation of the southeastern European situation, and would not admit its validity.

"The development of democracy in those countries is entirely different. The conduct of their governments is reassuring for the Soviet Union. Hungary's democratic actions, and its ties with the Soviet Union, are the least firm."

Pushkin confirmed my belief that, from the viewpoint of its own independence, Hungary was pursuing the proper course. What alarmed me was his open acknowledgment that the Soviet Union was satisfied only with the severance of all relations with other countries and single-minded devotion to the Soviet Union.

As I left Sviridov and Pushkin, I hoped and silently prayed for the early completion and the ratification of the peace treaty.

CHAPTER 73

Kovács Attacked

THE COMMUNIST PRESS ATTACK ON BÉLA KOVÁCS ROSE TO A NEW PITCH. In addition to exaggerating some of his statements and misinterpreting them, the press began to hold him publicly responsible for the fact that men surrounding him were implicated in the "conspiracy."

The small landowners in one of the Békés country villages had been inviting me to go hunting for some time. I accepted and asked Kovács to join me. We needed a week end out of doors, and I utilized the motor trip for a serious talk with Béla.

I asked him, "Tell me, what is your present opinion of Hungarian-Russian friendship?"

"You have been familiar all along with my views. We must continue to seize every opportunity to cultivate friendly relations with the Soviet Union—not only because it is momentarily occupying Hungary, but also because, regardless of how the European situation develops, the two countries will remain neighbors and, with so powerful a nation, one can live in peace only if one carefully lays the foundation for friendship."

"I see that your viewpoint remains unchanged. Are you aware, however, that under present circumstances the condition of friendship with the Soviet Union is the maintenance of good relations with the

Communist party? It still has no confidence in any other party, and therefore identifies itself with every Communist party undertaking."

"That, precisely, is the regretful mistake of the Soviet Union," answered Kovács. "It could serve its own security and its influence in Hungarian political life more effectively if it did not lean one-sidedly on the Communist party and give the impression that it is engaging in party politics. If the Soviet Union had lived up to the declaration made by Voroshilov after the election, that it wanted to build the friendship of the two countries around the Smallholders party, then it would be very much easier to sell a policy of Hungarian-Soviet friendship to the public. It wouldn't even be necessary for the Soviet to neglect the Communist party, if it refrained from making it obvious that it is the only party in which it has confidence."

"This situation," I said, "must be recognized because, the poorer our relations with the Communist party, the less our ability to strengthen our ties with the West without appearing to be anti-Russian. It makes it necessary to avoid open conflict with the Communist party."

"I am not anti-Russian," declared Kovács.

"That I know," I replied; "but you have made some remarks which led them to the conclusion that you are their deadly enemy. Do you remember when you jokingly told Rákosi that, if they did not discontinue their aggressiveness, you would have the reactionaries demonstrate against them? Or do you remember when, on the occasion of a Russian reception, you told the Communists around you that, if they did not stop threatening you with street demonstrations, you would reciprocate by bringing the peasants out on the street? You made the remarks in a jovial mood; but the Communists are not well intentioned, and they have noted your statements. One can talk with these fellows only seriously and quietly. Remember that each of the Communist leaders has spent long years in prison, and lives in constant fear that a change in conditions will again put him behind bars. We must strive to quiet their fears."

"Needless to say," answered Kovács, "these declarations were made in an atmosphere of friendship, and it never occurred to me that they would be used against me. I see I made a further mistake in pointing out the opposite aims of our two political parties; while they are striving to realize Marxism, we must block them and advance the cause of all citizens in a democracy."

I tried to quiet him by saying: "You were right in all your declarations. However, from the Communist viewpoint every statement of fact is an attack on them if it is not accompanied by assurance of our desire to collaborate. We must continue to give evidence of flexibility and a desire to collaborate and must avoid conflicts—in which they, with Soviet support, are stronger than we are. You know that we must drag things out until ratification and the withdrawal of the occupation forces without turmoil, in order that we may then consolidate our strength for the true democracy."

Kovács was never at a loss for a reply, and, as usual, hastened to answer:

"I have always agreed with all your views and agree with your policies. If at times I have taken exception to less important decisions, that does not mean that I was out of sympathy with your broad political objectives. I will go further and say that there can be no thought of hitting back and settling accounts with the Communists even when the Soviet army has left Hungary. This transition must be accomplished peacefully in order that thereafter the Hungarian people may live without fear. It is none the less necessary to put an end to the present one-sided Communist aggressiveness."

I agreed and asked him to be cautious in his future remarks in order not to provoke the Communists to further personal attacks on him.

"You are right," Kovács said. "I will watch my utterances; but even my earlier statement can be misconstrued only with malintent, such as the Communists have. You know well how strongly I am opposed to any type of reaction: that I would never be willing to clasp hands with the past, in which the local prefects and the police persecuted the peasants. Politically they were suppressed by the government; economically, by concentrated capital. I am devoted to the new era and, believing in true democracy, the thought of suppressing those in the extreme left, the Communists, never entered my mind."

I guided the conversation into other channels.

"Tell me, Béla, has it ever occurred to you that those men, some of whom have already been arrested, might have planned a separate program, a kind of conspiracy or putsch, with a view to upsetting existing authority?"

"Look, Ferenc," answered Kovács, "if I even suspected that these men had stupid things in their heads, I would have boxed their ears, one by one. I never would have believed for a moment that they could actually upset the democracy. They would nevertheless have deserved to be punished for their childish behavior. Believe me, however, I didn't even dream that they entertained such thoughts. You, too, know Valentine Arany since Tildy has pushed him into the limelight. He likes to be secretive and gladly listens to fantastic plans, but is an unsophisticated, honest fellow incapable of conspiracy. Besides, he is realistic and would know that an attempt of this sort cannot succeed. Dominick Szentiványi is sound, and I value his foreign political views. His remarks to me were limited to emphasizing the need for solidifyng Soviet confidence in the Hungarian government. Koloman Saláta came to me as often as to you; I often listened to him and often sent him away. He's a worth-while, well trained fellow who can be very useful, and I can never believe that he participated in any type of conspiracy. I hardly had any contact with the others, but do not believe that they could have influenced Arany, Szentiványi, or Saláta. I repeat that I didn't see the slightest evidence that these men might be involved in a conspiracy."

During our long friendship, I always found Kovács sincere, and very outspoken. I knew that he spoke bluntly, even with opponents and strangers. I was fully convinced that he had no secrets from me, and I knew too that on this occasion, as always, he spoke only the absolute truth.

"Look, Béla, I cannot endure the burden of government much longer. In these times the work destroys one's strength and wears out one's nerves. Having already sacrificed much by accepting the Prime Ministership with its cares and responsibilities, I wanted to carry the burden only during the difficult period; and I hope that I can soon surrender the office to a successor who will be confronted with a lighter task. In that event, you alone can succeed me. At this moment you are the most popular man in the party; our deputies in Parliament like you; besides, you are a peasant and the peasantry has full confidence in you. I beg you, take care not to expose yourself to premature destruction, for that would be an immeasurable loss to the country and the peasantry."

"You have hinted this sort of thing before," answered Kovács. "I can only repeat what I have always said: I would under no conditions accept the Prime Ministership. I am unsuited to it. My unpolitical nature disqualifies me. You will recall that I opposed your accepting the Prime Ministership, and I have seen it turn out to the advantage of the country. You must gather your strength to lead the nation further. The task should become lighter as we get away from war. You signify the stability of the Hungarian government and are skillful in coalition. The country must not be exposed to uncertainty. It would be a loss to drop the standard of public administration you have established. I ask you, give up forever the idea of my being Prime Minister. None the less, I will respect the advice you have just given me, particularly as it would create quite a stir in the party if, for some reason or other, I were kicked out of politics."

Kovács's words quieted me, and I felt an even deeper affection for this solid, loyal good friend.

We grasped hands, smiling, and opened the windows of the moving automobile.

The wide Hungarian plains were under a heavy blanket of snow. Peace and quiet lay over the entire region. Rabbits chased along the road, and pheasants flew overhead. The police escort following us could barely retrieve all the game.

It was nightfall when we reached Békés, the home of Stephen Szabó, former Minister of State. A long and gay conversation followed in which our small-landowner friends tried to make us forget the frightful worries of the political world.

Next day our friends arranged an unforgettable hunt. Simple peasants were our hosts—they provided the hunters and the beaters. Demonstrating the hospitality of the village, the local Presbyterian minister and the notary trudged through the day with the beaters. My shooting blind adjoined Kovács's throughout the day. He was an old hunter; I had begun to hunt seriously only the preceding winter, never having had the opportunity for this fascinating sport. Béla watched my shooting with interest, and in the evening, when my bag proved to be larger than his, this giant of a man lifted me high and congratulated me.

The day's end was beautiful; the local people had arranged an elaborate supper in our honor, and we were treated to a variety of most excellent peasant dishes. In the after-dinner speeches they boasted that the different political parties got along well in the village. They attacked with unity the task of educational instruction for those who acquired land under the agrarian reform, and they had a farm appliance cooperative which insured that their soil would be well cultivated and seeded. One wished that there could be as much understanding in national politics as there was in their small villages; and it would be well if the country's living standard progressed as quietly and reassuringly as theirs.

I felt more at peace after that beautiful day. New hope sprang in me which in a sense took the place of my terrible worries and fears for the future of my country and its people.

CHAPTER 74

The Communists Bargain

IF I REMEMBER CORRECTLY, IT WAS ON JANUARY 20 THAT RÁKOSI AND Szakasits called at my office, after we returned from the Békés hunt. Rákosi began the conversation:

"When the conspiracy was discovered and it was established that a number in the Smallholders party were in contact with the conspirators, we immediately raised the question of political responsibility. The conspirators, boring their way into the Smallholders party, had influenced its leadership and, in fact, used it to advance their objectives. Arany, Saláta, Jaczkó, and others, for example, continually surrounded Béla Kovács and could persuade him to do anything they wished. On the recommendation of the conspirators, Béla Kovács appointed men to important posts. When the 'B' lists were set up, Béla Kovács prevented the dismissal of officials who participated in the conspiracy. Béla Kovács insisted that, in revising the 'B' lists, we reappoint officials who were closely associated with the conspiracy. For example, he insisted upon the reappointment of a judge who in the old regime had been a member of the most reactionary council, and imposed severe sentences upon leftist men. When I reminded Kovács of this he replied: 'I know; but he must none the less be reappointed because I need a man of mine in the Justice Ministry.' Now it turns out that Béla Kovács's anticoalition articles were inspired by the conspirators. I do not claim that he is in the conspiracy; but he must at least bear political responsibility and suffer the consequences for permitting it to develop around him so openly and being influenced by the conspiracy, however innocently."

"What do you want of Béla Kovács?" I asked coolly.

Rákosi replied, "That he resign as Executive Secretary of the Smallholders party and retire to his place in the country."

I asked Szakasits if this was his desire.

He replied haltingly: "Well, Béla Kovács ought to do something. I believe that he wouldn't have to resign immediately but simply to go on leave."

I answered in no uncertain terms: "I consider Béla Kovács to be one of the best Hungarian democrats. It is my sacred conviction that he has nothing to do with the alleged conspiracy. It is possible that he unwittingly assisted men who have been arrested; but I believe that I did that, too. A few weeks ago I recommended to the Minister of Justice the promotion of a justice to the high court, and soon thereafter it developed that he was a member of the Hungarian Unity organization and a friend of the arrested men, with the result that he, too, was arrested. If Kovács is guilty because he supported the alleged conspirators, then I too am guilty. In 1945, when I was Minister of Reconstruction, I employed high-ranking officials who, it now seems, are members of the Hungarian Unity. But I do not consider myself guilty on this account, and I do not consider Béla Kovács guilty either. I am unwilling to be party to your request."

"Look," said Rákosi, turning to me. "I don't care how you dress up Béla Kovács's withdrawal from the management of the Smallholders party; but he should leave it at least for a time, in order that the people may see that political consequences do operate. After all, we are in a coalition and the working people have a right to see who is at the head of the political party with which they are in a coalition."

"It is precisely for this reason that I will not let Béla Kovács go," I answered. "I am unprepared to contribute to putting all of the Smallholders party on trial. It is possible that there are misled men; these men are now being investigated, and the courts will clarify their actions, but I am not ready to admit that the Smallholders party is in the conspiracy. I am even less ready to sacrifice Béla Kovács to the wolves; he is a clean, honest democrat, and a believer in the coalition and in collaboration with the Soviets."

"Look," Rákosi's loyal echo, Szakasits said, in an effort to pacify, "I consider Béla Kovács to be a completely clean, honest man and a good democrat. He was with us in the struggle against fascism. Since then he has done much on behalf of Hungarian democracy. There are indications, however, that he has been careless or at least insufficiently vigilant; and for that reason I too ask you to facilitate Kovács's departure on leave. After some time has elapsed, he can return to politics."

"I will under no circumstances contribute to besmirching Kovács or in any way suggesting that he is mixed up in the affair. I ask you earnestly not to press this request, because, instead of bringing about a solution, it will only create differences between us."

Rákosi became rather downcast. "Well, if that is your view, I cannot help it; but believe me, there will be serious difficulty about Kovács if he remains in politics."

After their departure, I visited the President and told him the news. Associating Rákosi's request with the attack that day in the Communist press, I predicted that Béla Kovács's removal would be pressed with increased energy; and I said that, under no circumstances, would I help pull down one of the principle pillars of our policy.

Tildy thought for a while. "Rákosi's group has made some hints about Béla Kovács to me, too, and I gave them a similar reply. I should be very much in favor of Béla Kovács's going on leave. It would be necessary to insure, simultaneously with his departure on vacation, that so far as public opinion is concerned, he is not looked upon as a discarded man. If I were you, however, I would not hinder his going on leave."

I replied: "For Béla Kovács to go on leave would be regarded as an acknowledgment of his responsibility, no matter how it may be announced. I have the feeling that in permitting it we may be opening a dam to a flood the waves of which will carry away the whole Smallholders party. There is already talk in the party that, if Béla Kovács is dropped, it will be my turn next; and then Béla Varga, and finally you. I doubt that the Communists would be satisfied with Kovács's going merely on leave. If we acknowledge his responsibility by sending him on leave, we shall open the way for further attacks and we may not be able to save him. Therefore, don't take offense, but I am most definitely opposed to giving leave to Béla Kovács."

"I am not sure that we're doing Béla a service by this," observed the President.

Then the conversation turned to the fate of the accused deputies. "I fear," I said, "that after the surrender of Saláta and Jaczkó they will request the suspension of the immunity of Alexander Kis and his associates. This, however, will cause terrific turmoil in the Smallholder ranks. Everybody knows that Kis, Vattai, Hám, and Horváth are not conspirators, so that if the Communists want to go after these fellows, too, the situation will become critical."

"This is the fault of Arany's and Saláta's group," said the President. "Although, I do not consider Kis and Vattai to be conspirators they've been dragged into this Hungarian Unity organization, where they presumably took a pledge, and now can be held responsible; but their affair is so clean that we can surrender their immunity without hesitation. They may not even be arrested."

"I doubt that the Communists would handle them with consideration, even though they know full well that Kis is not a conspirator. They would abuse them, if for no other reason than that Kis is one of the strong men of the party to whom the peasantry looks for guidance. For this very reason, they would probably try to compromise him."

"The party must be organized strongly now," said the President, "to prevent the bad atmosphere from causing disintegration. Primarily, however, we must see to it that the behavior of our deputies is so exemplary as to give no cause for new attacks and further crises."

I knew that this was the biggest assignment, for I had been trying uninterruptedly to make my fellow deputies act in keeping with the coalition. They, however, seeing the intolerable aggressivenss of the Communists, had become increasingly dissatisfied.

In the meantime, Rajk, the Minister of the Interior, appeared at the meeting of the Smallholders deputies and gave a detailed account of the "conspiracy." When he listed the charges and, to support them, read the signed confessions of those arrested, the group reached the conclusion that they had done damage to democracy and more particularly to the Smallholders party, though without premeditation or being guilty of secret activities.

When the prosecution requested Parliament, one or two days later, to suspend the immunity of Alexander Kis, Leslie Vattai, Tibor Hám, Leslie Gyulai, John Horváth, and Vincent Vörös, the turmoil was not nearly so great as one might have expected. The Parliament, however, did not have to take a position on the immunity of the six deputies because at the next meeting Vincent Vörös took the floor and announced that, in full knowledge of their innocence, all six would surrender their immunity and would take their stand before the police. The courageous action of the deputies made a good impression. This, however, did not influence the sadistic Minister of the Interior and the political police, because, with the exception of Vörös, all the accused were shortly arrested.

We were approaching the last days of January and the end of the hunting season. An invitation arrived from near the Yugoslav border for an end-of-the-season hunt. Snow was everywhere, and the landscape was beautiful. I decided to include Kovács, and our wives. When we left, our company included also my little son Lacika whom our host was anxious to see.

We went by car and had our first hunt while it was snowing. We did not get a very large bag, but felt wonderful as the quiet of our host's home and the peace of the snow-covered region had a soothing effect on our nerves. However, after the first day the snow began to fall heavily, and when we awakened Sunday morning it was so deep that we could neither hunt nor start back. Toward noon we went out and got a few pheasants, but had to return to the house, where we talked, played cards, and read. We hoped that by Monday morning the weather would clear and the snow on the roads would be packed down so that we could begin the return trip.

That morning, my secretary telephoned. He told me that since our departure, in response to the attacks on Béla Kovács, a communiqué had been prepared by someone close to the President's office for publication in the Monday issue of the Smallholders party newspaper, *Reggel*, stating: "An authorized source announces that the Smallholders party directorate agrees that Kovács should go on vacation." Béla Varga, executive vice president of the party, who was in Budapest, had got wind of the communiqué and forbade it, saying that in an important matter of this sort, a public announcement of such importance could not be made in the absence of the Prime Minister. This caused turmoil in political circles, because the Communists and Social Democrats already knew that the communiqué had been prepared.

I instructed my secretary to send a train for us immediately in order that we might return to Budapest at once. Then I told Béla Kovács the substance of the telephone conversation.

"It would have been better to permit publication," he said quietly. "The attacks upon me go on ceaselessly, and the Communists will not keep quiet so long as I am in Budapest."

Kovács's dejection scared me.

"Béla, I will not tolerate their casting any smears on your political integrity. Thus far, the attacks probably have enhanced your popularity, because the Hungarian people love you more now than they did before the attacks began. So long as there is a possibility of protecting your political integrity, we will strive to insure that they do you no harm beyond tongue-lashing."

"They will not give me any peace. Today they only want me to go on vacation; tomorrow they probably will declare that I am a conspirator; the day after, they will request suspension of my parliamentary immunity," he answered bitterly.

During a sleepless night I had had similar doubts; but I determined to use every means possible to prevent procedure against Béla Kovács.

"We will not permit it. The party is behind you, and the people of the country will rally behind you the moment they try to persecute you."

Béla Kovács was comforted, but he remained depressed throughout the day.

That evening the three of us had supper in Béla Varga's cell. He told us that during our absence the office of the President had wanted to authorize and give publicity to a vacation for Béla Kovács. Varga was very much upset by this interference, and had been able to prevent publication in time.

When Kovács heard the report, he said: "You should not have interfered with the publication. I believe the attacks will grow in intensity, and in the end the Communists' wishes will become political demands."

"Let them demand," said Béla Varga. "We will not permit any proceedings against you. The party is already aroused—and how will they feel if they find that we are dropping you? Be calm and strong: we will stand by you because we know that you are innocent. It would be a disgrace to let you go."

Béla Varga told us that the person who had taken the communiqué to the editorial offices and later, on his instructions, had stopped its publication, had been questioned by the political police in detail. He admitted to them that the dispatch had been prepared in the presidential office, and that its withdrawal had been arranged by Béla Varga.

Varga explained, also, that the Communist party was very much excited over the withdrawal of the communiqué and that the situation in the Smallholders party also had crystallized because the deputies were now openly declaring that this game pointed to the destruction of the Smallholders party. The reason they wanted to remove Béla Kovács was that he might be followed by Béla Varga and Ferenc Nagy. The representatives were prepared for a determined fight.

We were gravely troubled that evening.

"Perhaps it would be proper if I resigned and were left free to take up the fight against Communist ambitions without the handicap of heading the government," I suggested.

"Heaven forbid," was Béla Kovács's prompt reply. "If you surrender the reins, no one would protect either the party or those innocent men who will hereafter be dragged into the conspiracy."

"I have often had the feeling that it would be better if you left the government," said Varga; "but you must under no circumstances resign now, because the Communists and the Soviet would create a situation, using the change in government that could result only in the destruction of the majority in Parliament. It is not unlikely that they would attack you publicly as soon as you ceased to be Prime Minister."

"Well, that would be very difficult after the policies of coalition and cooperation I have pursued," I answered.

"You must assume nothing good about this crowd," said Béla Varga.

We parted with the feeling that serious danger was approaching, not only for the Smallholders but for the entire country as well.

Béla Varga proved right: the anger of the Communists had been further aroused by the withdrawal of the communiqué. They decided to force their demands and ordered the unions to arrange for appropriately directed demonstrations.

Next day a huge crowd appeared before the Parliament and demanded angrily the suspension of Béla Kovács's immunity; shouted demands were even heard that Kovács be hung. The demonstrations, however, did not end well because the unions had not selected the proper demonstrators but had ordered out the janitors and janitors' helpers, who had strong Smallholders party sympathies. To be sure, they yielded to compulsion, marched, and added some volume to the shouts of the leaders.

The crowd reached the entrance to the Prime Minister's office as I arrived at the gate on my way to the President. Hearing that the janitors were there, I decided to say a few words to them. When the crowd saw me they stopped abusing Kovács and began to demand an increase in janitors' fees. I told them that the conspiracy affair would be clarified by the appropriate judicial process, and any conspirators would certainly be punished; but they should not drag into disrepute men about whose guilt they were not in the least convinced. The crowd cheered, and cleared a way for my car. As I passed among them they waved their hats, and here and there rose a shout, "Long live Béla Kovács!"

The Communists, dissatisfied with this unsuccessful demonstration, ordered new groups out on the streets who marched on the Prime Ministry, the Justice Ministry, and the Ministry of the Interior, voiced their own economic complaints, and demonstrated against Béla Kovács and the "conspirators." Some groups marched in front of the President's Palace and demanded death for the "conspirators."

The demonstrations embittered Béla Kovács; for a popular man accustomed to debate, these recriminations were depressing. He wrote me a letter saying that his physical condition made it desirable for him to go away for several weeks' vacation.

Béla Varga, Béla Kovács, and I discussed the matter of the vacation; we all felt that in yielding so far to the clamor we might avoid greater difficulties for Kovács. We trusted that a rest in a quiet village surrounded by the affection of the peasants would bring peace to Béla Kovács's overtired nerves and restless soul. It would have been particularly difficult to restrain him as he announced that, after all the happenings, he would be unable to do good work in Budapest.

"Look, we are pursuing a coalition policy. In a coalition only those men are useful who can collaborate uninterruptedly. At the moment, I am not able to do so. Every step and every word of mine is followed by new attacks which I cannot leave without reply; and thus I only add to the trouble. I will go on leave now, and we will see in a few weeks how things shape up."

I summoned the Political Committee of the party and announced a letter from Béla Kovács in which he requested leave. Some openly voiced the dissatisfaction of the whole party, and only those rejoiced who were flirting with the Communists and were closer to them in thought than to us. Yes, there were a few such committee members, as the Communists had planted their sympathizers in every party. In the Social Democratic party, the leadership of Szakasits played into the hands of the Communists. In the Peasant party, Peter Veres, Erdei, and Darvas served the Communists in every way. In the Smallholders party, Ortutay, Mihályfi, Dobi, and their associates stood close to the Communists; and they were genuinely glad when the stony-fisted Béla Kovács requested leave.

Minister of the Interior Rajk, on the other hand, pursued his merciless game on Soviet-Communist instructions. During the preceding days we had been demanding uninterruptedly that the courts put the case of the first group of "conspirators" on their calendar as soon as possible.

The People's Court for the trial of the conspiracy was finally appointed, and a trial date set. However, those accused of conspiracy still remained in the hands of the police; we continually demanded their transfer into the custody of the court and the public prosecutor. Rajk made every effort to hinder this, with the excuse that the police had not "completed their interrogation." In the course of the trial it later developed that the reason that the police held the accused incommunicado was to prevent them from recuperating before the trial and from retracting the confessions extorted from them.

Rajk is a remarkable complex of characteristics. He is the wildest and most determined Communist, despite the fact that he stems from a well known Nazi family. Two of his brothers were prominent during the Nazi terrors. One was in charge of evacuations and mercilessly drove Hungarian families and students by the tens of thousands to Germany, and is said to have returned home and to be living quietly somewhere under Rajk's protection. The other brother is still in Austria, under American military arrest. This is the brother who interceded with the Nazi judges when the present Minister of the Interior was under arrest, and persuaded them to parole him on his promise never again to engage in Communist politics.

This same Rajk, burdened with Nazi relatives, and with anti-Semitic thirst, tries to demonstrate with sadistic activities that, despite all his political handicaps, he is a good Communist and an obedient servant of the party and the Kremlin.

Béla Kovács sat in an automobile on the very day he wrote his letter, and went to Mecsekalja, his village. My personal guard accompanied him, lest he meet with unpleasantness on the trip.

CHAPTER 75

The Soviet Suggests Espionage

THE DAY FOLLLOWING BÉLA KOVACS'S DEPARTURE, I HAD A MEETING with General Sviridov. Pushkin was of course present; his significance in Hungary had increased since the "conspiracy." There had been indications in the last few weeks that since Legation Counselor Ossukin, the political secret agent of the Soviet, had left Budapest, Pushkin had become a "bigger boy." While it is probable that some officer in the Budapest headquarters of the NKVD still directed Pushkin, it appeared as if he had become top man in Soviet politics in Hungary.

This Kremlin agent, who hated the western concept of democracy with fervor, very quickly turned the conversation to Béla Kovács.

"You did well to send Kovács on a vacation," he said. "He had a much bigger role in the conspiracy than you people believe."

"Pardon me, Mr. Minister," I answered. "You can make such assertions to those who do not know Béla Kovács; however, you can never make me believe them. I have known Béla Kovács for twenty years, as a sincere, upright democrat."

"I know that Béla Kovács is the Prime Minister's good friend," Pushkin answered. "Therefore I am sorry to have to accuse him in the Prime Minister's presence. Nevertheless, we have evidence in our hands which removes all possible doubt that Béla Kovács had a role in the conspiracy."

"You people have seen ghosts earlier without reason. I would be more ready to believe the charge of being an enemy of democracy against almost anybody else than Béla Kovács." I considered the whole sequence of attacks on Béla Kovács quite ridiculous. None the less, Pushkin's few declarations shocked me. Pushkin had learned in China the technique of trial with circumstantial evidence, and even if there were no truth in them they would result in serious charges.

"I am now free to tell the Prime Minister that the Soviet authorities are also investigating the conspiracy. They harm none of the accused, merely questioning those who confess their guilt. We know from these interrogations that Kovács is in the conspiracy up to his neck," said Pushkin.

"What do these confessions allege in regard to Béla Kovács?" I asked.

"I will tell you right away," answered Pushkin. "Do you know Leslie Gyulai?"

"I know him well, and do not consider him a conspirator, either."

"Well, that is exactly the trouble," observed Pushkin. "The Prime Minister doubts the guilt of even those against whom there is irrefutable evidence. Gyulai confessed that, on behalf of Béla Kovács, a fellow called Raffai spied on the Soviet occupation forces for the benefit of a foreign power."

Now I began to see the light and recognized the opportunity for a charge against Kovács. Sometime in November Representative Gyulai had appeared in my office and had related that in the fall of 1945 they sent a man called Raffai on a membership drive in the southwestern part of the country. He, as the director of public relations, had recommended the man to Béla Kovács. Raffai escaped to Austria and wrote a letter which was brought to Gyulai by a woman said to have been General Pálfi-Oesterreicher's girl friend. Raffai's letter stated that he had established contact with the British and French secret services and requested that Gyulai advise Béla Kovács to this effect. Gyulai believed the letter was intended to be a provocation, and he asked me what to do. To my request for the letter he replied that, as he considered it damaging, he had destroyed it immediately. I criticized him for having done so and told him that the letter should have been delivered to the political police instantly with a demand for a prompt investigation, which should have defeated the purpose of the *agent provocateur*.

Now I recognized that Gyulai's "confession" about the Raffai letter might form the basis for a charge of espionage against Béla Kovács; but the letter could not be adequate proof.

Pushkin continued: "We are not concerned with the conspiracy so long as we feel that the Hungarian police has it well in hand. However, when someone commits a crime against the occupation forces, it is our responsibility to proceed against him. Raffai was sent to Austria by Kovács. This is indicated by the evidence; in addition, the other conspirators were in close touch with him. Béla Kovács is therefore not innocent in the conspiracy."

"I am unwilling to accept this interpretation," I declared. "I know Kovács better than anyone else; I've always been fully informed about every step he took, every discussion he had, and I will vouch with my right hand for his innocence. Béla Kovács is no conspirator and no spy, any suspicions you may have and any incriminating evidence notwithstanding."

"Well, you believe, do you not, that Béla Kovács instructed Paul Jaczkó to proceed with the organization of armed groups?"

"No, I do not believe this either," I answered. "Here is another case of appearances, which you would not consider unnatural if they involved the Communists, but which you immediately turn into an accusation when the Smallholders party is involved. Every other political party has a so-called guard supposed to insure order and discipline at meetings, which the Communists and Social Democrats also frequently use for public demonstrations. The Smallholders party is the only one without such an organization. Last year we discussed several times the need for organizing such a guard. Béla Kovács probably gave Jaczkó instructions to this effect, but there was never any thought of organizing an armed group. The country is filled with allegations that the Communists have armed this type of guard, which does not seem to bother you. You, however, immediately begin to talk of armed danger from the Smallholders' organizing a peaceful group to maintain order. This is the type of injustice that we talked about when we were on the Hortobágy in the fall and I referred to discrimination between the several political parties. The lack of confidence and the accusations will soon make government impossible, and it is for that reason that I ask you to look carefully at appearances before you use them to make accusations," I ended.

Pushkin was very dissatisfied when we parted. I was full of trepidation but firmly resolved not to release Kovács to the police, no matter what followed.

The Communist press continued to elaborate sensationally on Kovács's participation in the conspiracy. I had been right not to want to rclase Kovács for a vacation because, now that he was on leave, the Communist press increased its attacks and Rajk publicly accused him of participation.

We seized every occasion to refute the accusations, but Rákosi's group began to demand that Béla Kovács submit to police investigation. I replied that he had offered to appear for a police interrogation when Rajk first hinted, at the home of the President, that he was implicated. Why had they not questioned him then? "I will under no circumstances consent now to Kovács's falling into the hands of the police," I told Pushkin.

I convened the cabinet to discuss the "conspiracy." The Communists demanded that Béla Kovács surrender his immunity and give himself up to the authorities. I refused in no uncertain terms. We agreed, however, that Minister of the Interior Rajk should appear at a meeting of the Smallholder representatives and present his evidence. At the same time I telephoned Béla Kovács to come to Budapest and speak to the convened deputies.

Rajk came to the meeting, where he bitterly abused Béla Kovács and sought to prove his guilt with a photostatic copy of the Raffai letter. He supplemented the accusations with the assertion that, through Raf-

fai, Kovács had sough contact not only with the British but also with
the Nazis who had fled to the west. The deputies heard Rajk through
with discipline, but when Béla Kovács stepped into the room they
demonstrated by applauding him enthusiastically.

Kovács began to speak in a low voice, but it gradually rose. He
frankly admitted that appearances were against him, and then refuted
the accusations one by one. He related that he had been on friendly
terms with Valentine Arany and had had supper with him a few times,
without suspecting that those with whom he dined were members of a
secret society. He knew that they had a "friends' circle" but never at-
tributed a political role to it. He had sent Raffai to the southwestern
part of the country to organize the party's membership but had withdrawn the commission as soon as he heard that Raffai had left for Austria. It was possible that Raffai had carried off letters authorizing him
to perform commissions abroad, because he, Kovács, while Minister of
Agriculture, had signed the party's correspondence, frequently signing
hundreds of letters presented for signature without reading them, since
he had confidence in his staff who prepared them. Thus it was possible
that he had signed a letter giving Raffai a commission abroad.

Béla Kovács's talk made a strong impression at the meeting. The
deputies became more determined not to release him to the police under
any circumstances, regardless of how many false charges might be
drummed up against him.

Kovács remained in Budapest because he wanted personally to follow the events affecting him. He was shocked to read the more and more
insulting accusations in the Communist daily press. There were times
when he believed that the Communists actually believed him guilty.
When, however, he ran across impossible charges, now and then, he
was convinced that the accusations were being deliberately manufactured by the Communists.

Béla Kovács's person now became the central issue of Hungarian
political life. The people took the view that he was so important a
bastion of Hungarian democracy that if he were permitted to fall, no
one would be able to resist Communist expansion any more; and this
issue threw Hungarian political life into its greatest crisis. The Communists made every effort to undermine this popular spirit; we, on the
other hand, were determined not to yield.

CHAPTER 76

Storms over Parliamentary Immunity

THE PETITION OF THE COURT TO THE PARLIAMENT REQUESTING THE suspension of Béla Kovács's immunity arrived next day, and the public prosecutor supported his request with far-reaching accusations. Everyone being familiar with them, it was not difficult for the lawyer members of Parliament to analyze his brief.

The petition had to be considered first by the standing Committee on Immunities. In this, as in all the parliamentary committees, the Smallholders party had a majority. It would have been simple for the majority to reject the request of the court out of hand, but our lawyers prepared a detailed defense. Béla Varga postponed convening the committee for several days, and this afforded time for an exhaustive study of the petition and the supporting documents.

The public prosecutor's charges seemed to have originated with Stephen Ries, the Social Democratic Minister of Justice. For long periods this man had represented himself as a hard-working, honest Social Democrat; but it became increasingly evident that he too was under Communist influence. The Minister of Justice had the right to direct the public prosecutor to issue indictments or suspend charges. In this instance Ries could have instructed the prosecutor not to prefer charges against Béla Kovács.

The Smallholders party had had no undersecretary in the Ministry of Justice since Zoltán Pfeiffer's resignation after the Soviet demand six months earlier. Feeling that we had urgent need for the protective services of a Justice undersecretary, I appointed a lawyer deputy, Michael Hompola, and commissioned him to supervise very carefully the activities of the public prosecutor and the proceedings in the matter of the conspiracy. Hompola took a firm hand in the conspiracy affair, and on the day he assumed office demanded that the accused be transferred to the custody of the public prosecutor, in order that after their interrogation by the police they might come to trial rested and with a sense of freedom. Ries, the Minister of Justice, obstructed the undersecretary all along the way, and a struggle developed in that Ministry in which the Smallholders stood behind the undersecretary and the

Communists behind the Minister. Ries openly reported Hompola's activities to the Communists, who a few days later accused him publicly of having maintained close associations with the Germans during the German occupation of Hungary. To prove the charges the Communists published a photograph showing Hompola with a German officer, at a suburban railway station. Although he proved that the officer was a close friend and frequent house guest of one of the present county Communist leaders, and that he, Hompola, had been photographed with the officer only accidentally, he became so discouraged that he resigned within a few days.

Immediately I appointed in his stead Aladár Pongrác, former Lord Lieutenant, who took a firm but more careful hand in the conspiracy affair. He personally studied the Kovács indictment and reported to me that there was no reason in the evidence produced for depriving Béla Kovács of his immunity.

I summoned the Minister of Justice to the President's office and tried to convince him, first, that the indictment against Béla Kovács must be dropped, and, secondly, that those accused in the "conspiracy" must be turned over immediately to the public prosecutor. Ries replied that the indictment provided sufficient basis for placing Kovács on trial, although the court might acquit him. He made me a firm promise that, that very same day, the accused would be surrendered to the public prosecutor. Needless to say, he did not keep his promise, and the struggle continued.

One morning the Smallholders party members of Parliament held a meeting. They informed me of it with the request that I take no official notice. The Committee on Immunities was considering the question of Béla Kovács's immunity that very same day, and after long and bitter controversy decided not to suspend his immunity, but return the indictment to the public prosecutor.

It happened that the Parliament was discussing the budget. During the afternoon session, Stephen Kovács, a Peasant deputy of the Smallholders party, in an excellent speech moved that the Parliament appoint a committee to investigate the conspiracy charges against Béla Kovács and the other accused deputies. This was the result of the secret meeting of the deputies, of which I was notified in the morning.

The speech had a terrific effect on the leftist groups. They began to attack Stephen Kovács with fury, accused him of reactionary leanings and made the same charges against the Smallholders' peasant representatives whom hitherto they had acknowledged to be good democrats. Rákosi immediately summoned the leftist bloc and forced a decision that the three leftist parties would under no circumstances take part in the parliamentary committee, and that Stephen Kovács was an agent of the clerical reactionaries who wanted to block the prosecution of those "conspiring against democracy."

I had a conference that very same day with Zoltán Tildy. The President disapproved of Stephen Kovács's motion and thought it inadvisable to appoint a parliamentary committee without Communist, Social Democratic, and Peasant participations. He mentioned also that our insistence on the appointment of a parliamentary committee might bring about Russian interference.

At this time Hungarian politics took the critical turn which doubtless will be much debated in the future. What would have been the correct thing to do? To send out a parliamentary committee, even if it consisted only of Smallholder members, or to table the creation of such a committee? Such a committee could have clarified the whole conspiracy affair, examined the documents, and interrogated the accused. To be sure, it could have only given an opinion; it could not have handed down a verdict. Its opinion, however, would have established the falseness of the conspiracy charges and might have benefited the accused. Perhaps a statement by it might also have invited the attention of the foreign countries to the manipulations of the Communists. But what would have come next?

The leftist bloc had announced that it would consider the creation of an investigating committee as dissolving the coalition. Under the Soviet occupation, a change in government could naturally not have been accomplished as it was accomplished in France or Italy, by the simple removal of the Communists from the government. Our "Allied Control Commission" would never have consented to a government without the Communists. If, on the other hand, it became necessary to negotiate with the Communists, their primary condition would obviously be the abandonment of a parliamentary investigating committee. But let us assume that the Smallholders party finally decided to make the break, and was not concerned with the threat of a political upheaval because it believed that the intervention of the great powers would prevent bloodshed and the execution of those accused of conspiracy. The question is, Would this type of intervention by the great powers have followed, and have prevented complete disintegration and civil war? It could hardly have been expected under the circumstances. Although at the moment it was still not possible to tell how much of a hand the Soviets would take in the conspiracy affair, the threats by Kondratov in the Pálfi-Oesterreicher affair suggested what the Soviet Union might do if a parliamentary committee attempted to interfere in the "conspiracy prosecutions."

In any case, we were unwilling to withdraw the motion of Stephen Kovács for the creation of an investigating committee, because we knew that we could put this motion on the parliamentary calendar any time we wished to. We decided, however, that we could not immediately begin to debate the question in Parliament but should open negotiations with the leftist bloc.

I summoned an interparty council at which the leftist leaders violently attacked the idea of a parliamentary investigating committee and demanded withdrawal of the motion. I declared that we would not withdraw it but were prepared to postpone consideration if we could otherwise secure an objective attitude in the matter. After long debate the council decided that the accused should be taken over to the public prosecutor's prison in order that they might be placed before the court without further intimidation by the police. It also decided that the new undersecretary in the Ministry of Justice should interrogate the prisoners and report his findings to me. Inasmuch as the Committee on Immunities declined to terminate Béla Kovács's immunity, his case did not even come up for discussion. There is no doubt, however, that this refusal angered the Communists; in fact, before the discussion of the immunity a large labor-union representation under the leadership of Stephen Kossa noisily demanded that I direct the Committee to suspend the immunity of Béla Kovács. I warned Kossa and the crowd not to interfere in these affairs because I was unwilling to influence the Committee but would leave them to make their decision in accordance with their own conscience. On that occasion the workers left me angrily and threatened me; now I was surprised to find that at the interparty council it was possible to limit the discussion of the Béla Kovács affair to so few words.

Béla Kovács meanwhile, in a new letter, advised me that he was resigning as Executive Secretary of the party and editor-in-chief of the *Kis Ujsag,* and requested that I submit the motions to the political committee of the party. By that time, the political committee assumed that he would be unable to hold his post because he would be in no position to do freely the kind of work that was required for the organization of the party. Personally, I was much grieved to notice these developments.

In the meanwhile we reached another stage in foreign policy on February 10, when the Hungarian peace treaty was finally signed, in Paris. This was the symbol of the coming dawn which some day would have to be followed by ratification and the ending of the military occupation.

Hungarian political structure must be protected at all sacrifices until the country regained complete independence. The deluge was approaching its end, and, no matter how strong the tide, we must not be drowned before reaching our goal. This thought was uppermost in my mind and gave me strength to overcome the many domestic obstacles.

When my fellow deputies were inclined to be impatient, I said to them: "Take a look at the situation in the countries surrounding us. From Yugoslavia men are fleeing by the tens of thousands. Rumania, Poland, and Bulgaria are existing on the wreckage of an independence. We, on the other hand, are still here with a large democratic majority, just on the eve of winning our point. Men, we must survive until the end of occupation."

CHAPTER 77

The Soviet Abducts Béla Kovács

TO CELEBRATE SOME RUSSIAN ANNIVERSARY, THE SOVIET-HUNGARIAN CULtural society had arranged a reception at the Opera House. The speaker for the evening was Count Michael Károlyi, the former exile. He spoke at length about Lenin, scandalously badly, so that one could hardly hear his words. Without knowing that Károlyi had irrevocably committed himself to the Soviet, one would have thought that he was making an anti-Lenin speech; and the audience listened to his naïve and childish chatter with mixed feelings. The Communist leaders were red with anger, while others turned away to hide their laughter.

During the intermission the President called me to his box; Rákosi and Szakasits were already there. The criticism of the speech was unanimous; President Tildy expressed no opinion but skillfully intimated its stupidity. Szakasits decided that it was impossible to use "the senile old man." Rákosi gnashed his teeth and said, "If he only belonged to my party, I would soon attend to his troubles."

It soon became obvious that the President had not called us to discuss Károlyi's speech. Minister Leslie Jékely, his Chief of Cabinet, had had a conversation the previous evening with Rákosi and Szakasits; it was suggested that it would be advisable for Béla Kovács, while retaining his parliamentary immunity, to appear at police headquarters and make a deposition. Rákosi and Szakasits indicated that they would welcome a conference with me on the subject, and we agreed to discuss the matter the next day in the office of the President.

Early next day I called Béla Kovács and Béla Varga to my office and told them about the proposal. Kovács was willing to make a statement to the police as long as they respected his parliamentary immunity. He had already offered to do so on a previous occasion, at the interparty council where Rajk had first hinted at his being implicated in the conspiracy; however, he declared now that his only purpose in making a deposition was to clarify the "conspiracy affair," and that he would, under no condition, permit himself to be regarded as accused.

We decided that I would inform Kovács of the result of the conference. I went to the President earlier than Rákosi and the others; Tildy was of the opinion that Béla Kovács should at all events go to the police and state his own case.

"The conspiracy trial has begun," said Tildy. "On the basis of the confessions heard at the trial, the court will taint Béla Kovács unless his defense is there. They will actually pass judgment on him, and if the leftist parties succeed through some technicality in dissolving the Parliament, so that Kovács's immunity ceases, they will immediately arrest him."

I had serious doubts as to Béla Kovács's interrogation by the police because I feared that they would confront him with the accused people whose confessions incriminated him, and that these, in his presence, would stand by their confessions, knowing that they must return to their cells where they would be exposed to the tortures of the Communist police. But I remembered my talk with Béla Kovács and entered into the discussions.

In addition to Rákosi and Szakasits, Ries, Minister of Justice, was invited to the conference. The President posed the issue, and Rákosi produced a written proposal from his pocket, having profited from his experience at the October interparty conference, where I drafted a proposal for a settlement of the issues up for discussion and they were compelled to bargain for changes in the draft. Rákosi's proposal was that Béla Kovács place himself at the disposal of the police for three days and of the public prosecutor for an additional three days, to make a deposition. When the interrogation was completed, the public prosecutor would state his opinion and issue the indictment against Béla Kovács. The public prosecutor's indictment would be sent to the Prime Minister and the two deputy prime ministers, Rákosi and Szakasits, who together would decide whether to agree to the indictment or not.

Refusing to accept the draft, I expressed readiness to consent to Béla Kovács devoting three consecutive days to the police and three to the public prosecutor for the purpose of making a deposition. The interrogation, however, must not last longer than six hours per day, and after each day's interrogation he must be free to return to his home. The opinion that the public prosecutor would send to the Prime Minister and the two deputy prime ministers, and his recommendations, could be accepted only by unanimous decisions. I knew that, by this motion, I accepted a full responsibility for Béla Kovács's fate. I had long ago made up my mind, however, that I would under no circumstances be party to abandoning him; hence, the worst consequence of my accepting this responsibility would be that the Communists could hold me personally responsible for interfering with the prosecution.

After bitter bargaining, the others accepted this proposal. First, they tried to increase the time that Béla Kovács should spend with the police to twelve hours daily; then they wanted the decision to be by majority vote. Finally they consented to my proposal.

I immediately informed Béla Kovács and Béla Varga, who were waiting for my return to my office. Kovács considered the agreement satisfactory but expressed the opinion that I was assuming too much responsibility under its terms; however, when I declared that I accepted this responsibility knowingly, he approved. In the meanwhile, Zoltán Pfeiffer joined us to act as Kovács's legal advisor while he was being interrogated; he came to discuss with him the subjects of the interrogation and to arrange the details both with the police and with the public prosecutor.

Thereafter Pfeiffer agreed with Gabriel Peter, the chief of the political police, that Béla Kovács would appear at police headquarters at eight o'clock the next morning. He accompanied Kovács and left police headquarters only when his presence at the interrogations was refused.

At the noon intermission for lunch, Kovács dropped in at my office on his way home and complained that the police officers were discourteous and, in the midst of their questions, tossed accusations at him. One officer, among other things, called him the leader of the conspiracy. He observed to me that this type of interrogation would not have the result of safeguarding him against further incrimination at the trial of the "conspirators," but added that, having agreed, he would nevertheless go through with the interrogation.

I saw only later, from reading the so-called "white book," how honestly and frankly Kovács talked to the police: he admitted that appearances pointed against him; he denied nothing.

After a short conversation, Kovács left me and I was never again to see this real man, stanch as a rock, my best friend.

In the course of the day Smallholders deputies, particularly peasants, came to me and asked, "What is to become of Béla Kovács?" Not knowing the purpose of his presence at police headquarters, they thought that proceedings had already been started against him. I told them that, even if on the basis of these interrogations the prosecution should propose that we consent to the trial of Kovács, I would refuse.

On the morning of February 26, Zoltán Pfeiffer reported that Kovács had again gone to the police to continue the interrogation. I summoned Aladár Pongrác, Undersecretary of Justice, and asked him whether those accused of conspiracy had all been transferred to the public prosecutor's custody. Pongrác reported that the larger part of them was already there but a few were still beyond reach; in his opinion, these were being interrogated by the Soviet.

The day passed with various discussions. By this time the administration of government had become very difficult because the "conspiracy" continued to create so many problems that for practical purposes no time remained. Frequently I had to turn over the chair at cabinet councils and Council of State meetings to an alternate because events moved so rapidly that political decisions had to be made from minute to minute. Groups of demonstrators would come to see me, and if I could manage I would receive them personally. Generally they came incited by the Communists, but went away feeling peaceful and satisfied. The thing that infuriated the Communists most was my telling the demonstrators that I was glad to see them and that they should come back any time, because I considered it important in a democracy for the masses to have direct contact with the country's leaders.

Usually I went to my office at eight in the morning, lunched at my desk, and returned home only late at night. This pace fatigued me but I promised myself that, so long as my physical strength held out, I would not yield.

Evening affairs preoccupied me as during the winter there was much social activity. The foreign diplomats gave dinners and receptions, one after another, which we had to reciprocate, and so in one week I had to take part in six official dinners or receptions.

On the evening of February 26, I gave a dinner in honor of the chief of the UNRRA mission to Hungary, Stanley Sommers; his deputy, Mr. Curtis, and a number of cabinet ministers were present. The foreign guests generally had a good time at my house for, although we gave only simple suppers, I tried to make the atmosphere unstrained and friendly. That evening, however, a good mood seemed unattainable: we were all preoccupied.

We had hardly finished dinner when my secretary, Francis Kapocs, came. "I bring you very bad news, Mr. Prime Minister. The Russians have arrested Kovács."

I lost my calm, jumped up from my chair, and asked my secretary to repeat what he had said.

"Béla Kovács went to police headquarters again today, to continue the interrogation. Towards evening Soviet soldiers appeared at the headquarters of the political police on Andrássy Avenue, assumed custody of Béla Kovács from the Hungarian police, took him to his own home and there informed him of his arrest. They ransacked his documents and carried most of them away."

Social talk came to an end. It was not possible to keep the news from my guests. A few minutes later Béla Kovács's chauffeur appeared and reported that in the afternoon, according to prearrangement, he drove to 60 Andrássy Avenue and waited at the main entrance a long while, until a stranger came and told him not to wait any longer because his employer had been taken away through another gate. He then drove to Váci Street, where the entire section including Béla Kovács's residence was blocked off, virtually occupied by Russian soldiers who had established road blocks at the two ends of the street. Under the command of a Russian general in civilian clothes, Red soldiers entered the house, occupied the corridors and Béla Kovács's apartment, and within this setting took him home to his family.

In his own house they read to him the Military Commander's order for his arrest; they searched the house, confiscated his files and took him away. They did not permit him to speak with his wife, but when he kissed her goodbye he was able to whisper, "Feri." My poor dear friend had mentioned my name in the hope that, with my power as Prime Minister, I might be able to help him.

Within an hour Béla Varga came, and my foreign guests, seeing that the atmosphere was not conducive to social amenities, departed. It was clear now to us both that the Soviet Union would undoubtedly make a show to prove the propriety of its action.

The statement made by Pushkin a few days earlier explained this tragic development, but we both had believed that if Béla Kovács's interrogation by the police took place there would be no occasion for such a step. Béla Varga and I felt physical pain from the shock and from our helplessness. We were tortured by the same thoughts: at one time there had been four of us, pledged to stand together for life or death—Zoltán Tildy, Béla Kovács, Béla Varga, and I. Tildy left us when he became President. The remaining three held together so much the stronger. Now they had snatched Béla Kovács away from us; only two remained. I wondered where this road would lead. I had the feeling that Béla Varga was no more troubled about himself than I about my own person, but that his thoughts turned rather on what the two of us together could do: whether we should have strength enough to maintain the structure of Hungarian political life until the country regained her independence. Could we protect any of Hungary's interests, any of the features of the pure democracy? Through the many long and sleepless nights to come, these questions tormented me.

The shadows across my country were deepening; only the prayed-for sunlight of complete independence could pierce the gathering dark.

CHAPTER 78

Resignation?

AFTER A NIGHT OF MUCH THOUGHT AND NO SLEEP, I INVITED THE SMALL-holder members of the cabinet to my office. They had all been informed about Béla Kovács's fate, and were depressed and sad; they immediately turned to the substance of my call.

"Béla Kovács's affair is not a personal matter but concerns the entire nation, especially the Smallholders party. So long as it was the Hungarian police that dealt with the affair, I was calm because my determination was firm that we would under no condition release him to the police. Now, however, with the Soviet army's prestige opposing us, we are helpless. I believe, my friends, the time has come for the cabinet to resign."

Some of my cabinet colleagues approved; some disagreed. A long, worried discussion followed, in the course of which we examined our situation with reference to domestic and foreign policy.

"If the government resigns, the Communists have gained their objective. It is not unlikely that the Soviet interference was for this purpose," observed one of them.

"If the government remains in its place, our actions will be interpreted as indicating that we will tolerate anything," said another.

"The peace treaty has been signed; ratification will be followed shortly. Is it proper for the government to resign a few days before that happens?" was a new question raised.

"Will Béla Kovács benefit by the resignation of the government? The government's resignation as a result of the Béla Kovács affair will be so clear a demonstration against the Soviet that the country will reap its penalty," some one else added.

"Would it be possible on this occasion to obtain some western intervention?"

"No," replied several simultaneously.

Somebody thought that it might be well to turn to the Soviet and ask it to set Kovács free. I replied that this would have no purpose, and told them of my conversation with Pushkin.

"What kind of government would follow us, if we resigned?" asked some one. "The Allied Control Commission would not consent to a government without Communists, and this would give them the pretext for making all sorts of conditions to the establishment of a new government," observed one of the ministers.

Somebody proposed that we talk with the President before making a final decision: "Every one of us would probably cheerfully step out of the cabinet. But are we warranted in provoking the upheaval that would follow a change in government?"

We finally decided to call in a body on the President.

Tildy opposed the resignation of the government in no uncertain terms. "This would be a provocation," said he, "which would have unbearable consequences. The loss of Béla Kovács even for a short time is a severe one, but even this does not permit acceptance of the responsibility for creating turmoil. It is absolutely necessary to continue the struggle to avoid an upheaval."

After leaving the President, the ministers held a long and difficult conference at which they decided that the cabinet should remain in its place and attempt to continue on the course until after the completed ratification of the peace treaty. The Smallholder deputies were also bitter, but were of the opinion that we must not surrender our place because it was obvious that a change in the government would be fully exploited by the Communists to their own advantage.

Next evening, Victor Chornoky and I dined with Mr. Schoenfeld, the American minister, who discussed Kovács's arrest with much indignation and expressed the opinion:

"I do not believe that Béla Kovács is a conspirator, or that he spied against the Russian army. There is no doubt, however, that if the Russians develop real suspicion of espionage against the occupation forces, they can themselves arrest the suspect."

Undoubtedly this period of the Hungarian democracy is open for debate. Our decision that the government should remain in its place gives occasion for many accusations; I have heard some of them: "They sacrificed their friends that they might retain their positions." "They lay down before the Soviet and did not think that there are other powers which also have a voice in world developments." "Their concessions have given the Communists courage for still further demands." "It would have been better to carry the thing to a breaking point with the Soviet Union and the Communists, than to tolerate the arrest of Béla Kovács."

One can, of course, meditate over and debate these thoughts. No doubt many forums will yet debate the questions. Did Mikolajczyk, Maniu, and Petkov take the proper course when they abandoned their rightful place in their country's history as early as 1946, or I, who as late as 1947 was still able to keep a citizens' democracy alive in Hungary's government? Whether those pursued the right policy who by open defiance, and in defense of their principles, fell victims to the uneven battle, or I who wanted at all costs to achieve practical results—to recapture my country's independence?

No one can deny that Hungary was in a favorable position among the southeastern European countries. Hungary was able to safeguard for a longer time that little independence guaranteed by the armistice, and Hungary was best able to comply with the conditions of the Yalta agreement. We too could have failed a year earlier if instead of playing politics we had been virtuous. Being virtuous would have been more popular; but being political was more profitable to the nation. The process aiming at the complete destruction of the Hungarian people would have begun a year earlier, and the Communists and the Soviet Union would have had a year's jump in their penetration timetable.

The notes sent by the Western powers helped neither the Rumanian, nor the Bulgarian, nor the Polish "democracy." We had the feeling that we must reach our independence and our true liberation entirely on our own strength and by our own wisdom. In a small defeated country, in one abandoned to the Soviet, political vanity has less scope than tactics and care. And that this type of policy was the most dangerous and the most uncomfortable from the viewpoint of the Communists and the Soviet was substantiated in a few months by the events which were to surround my own person.

But it is possible, too, that I erred; I shall not call my politics infallible solely for the sake of prestige. I was determined to keep inviolate the person of Béla Kovács, a lawmaker of our country; having had the power to do so, I prevented his arrest by the Hungarian police. If the collusive hand of the Communists and the Soviet Union, determined to eliminate Béla Kovács from the political scene of Hungary, was thus forced, it could not be foreseen by anyone that the government of the Soviet Union would, to gain its ends, infringe upon the basic and accepted laws of democracy, violate by armed force Hungary's constitutional guarantees, and unilaterally transgress agreements and break international law.

CHAPTER 79

American and British Notes

THE FIRST RAY OF SUNSHINE FOR HUNGARIAN DEMOCRACY APPEARED ON the morning of March 5. The United States minister, Mr. Schoenfeld, called on me at the Prime Ministry and handed me a note. He brought his own interpreter, because when I used a Hungarian clerk he was mysteriously cross-examined the same evening by the NKVD and it was never again possible to speak in confidence in his presence. Mr. Schoenfeld communicated to me the substance of the note through the interpreter.

The United States government considered the arrest of Béla Kovács, the Executive Secretary of the Smallholders party, to be interference in Hungarian internal affairs and protested the procedure. It proposed that the representatives of the three powers on the Control Commission, together with the Hungarian Prime Minister, the President of Parliament, the Ministers of Justice, Interior, and Defense constitute a commission to investigate the Béla Kovács affair and the whole conspiracy as well. The note took cognizance of the efforts of the Communist minority to seize power by force, and the one-sided procedures of the Communist police.

Mr. Schoenfeld explained that the note was directed to the government of the Soviet Union, and that a copy was made available to us only for informative purposes.

From the viewpoint of the country I was pleased with the American note—the first concrete evidence that the United States had not abandoned us politically. I had been convinced a few weeks earlier of its efforts to assist us economically when Mr. Schoenfeld informed me that an additional $15,000,000 credit had been extended to us for the purchase of surplus material, and that, for the purpose of enabling us to make the best use of the funds, they would open to us the warehouses and stock piles in Germany. At that same time, he told me that the matter of the American cotton loan could be considered as settled.

The present note, however, had very important significance from the point of view of the political protection of Hungary. I must add, however, that from the viewpoint of Béla Kovács's personal situation it gave me serious concern. I recognized that the Soviet would now stop at nothing to produce evidence that he had committed a crime.

The evaluation of the United States note by the left began very quickly. Szakasits was in the greatest hurry to pass judgment; at one of the provincial public meetings, he criticized it and declared that the Social Democrats would intercede with the Labor party in England to persuade the British government against associating itself with the note. Szakasits was very late, because a note from that government had been handed to me the preceding day by Mr. Helm, its political representative in Budapest.

The two notes soon became known to the Hungarian public, because both Great Britain and the United States broadcast their contents on short-wave in the Hungarian language. And now, Hungarian public opinion coolly anticipated publication of the news in Hungary. Two days passed, and then it became common knowledge that General Sviridov prohibited publication of the notes in the Hungarian press before the Soviet reply was completed. This required several days.

Under the terms of the armistice, the chairman of the Allied Control Commission reserved for himself the right of censorship over the press and radio. Ending precensorship, he retained his right to mix in the affairs of the press in case of necessity. We were very much ashamed *vis-à-vis* the American and British legations on account of these restrictions on the freedom of our press, but the two legations knew why the Hungarian press was silent.

In a few days the Russian reply was ready, rejecting the American and British notes. Then the Hungarian newspapers were finally permitted to publish the contents.

In a little while the second American and British notes arrived, criticizing the Soviet procedure more sharply and expressing dissatisfaction with the Soviet reply. The substance of the second Washington note was released by the American legation at a press conference. In this way every Hungarian newspaper had knowledge of it almost at the moment that it was delivered. Since no Soviet steps were taken in the course of the afternoon, I decided that the newspapers should be permitted to publish the note.

That evening I was at the President's for a conference. Mihályfi, the new Minister of Information, telephoned. He reported that he had had a telephone call from Captain Gruber, who instructed him on behalf of Sviridov that the Hungarian press must again refrain from publishing the American and British notes until the Soviet reply was ready. I instructed the Minister:

"Request it from him in writing."

In a few minutes I was again called to the President's telephone: it was Captain Gruber himself.

"Mr. Prime Minister, General Sviridov's instructions are that the Hungarian papers shall not publish the American and British governments' notes until the Soviet reply is ready," said Captain Gruber.

I answered, "Please tell the General to give me these instructions in writing."

"I will communicate your request to the Lieutenant General." In a few minutes, Captain Gruber was again on the telephone:

"Mr. Prime Minister, the General's reply is that, by the time the instructions could be ready in writing, the papers will have been printed. Therefore, will you kindly take note of his instructions by telephone."

"Very well," I said. "I am willing to take note of the telephone instructions; but first I will give the other receiver to the President, and I will ask you to repeat the General's instructions so that the President can hear them, too."

Gruber repeated Sviridov's instructions, and I called the Minister of Information and told him to notify the press, in accordance with the instructions, that the American and British notes were not to be published until the Soviet reply was ready. Minister Mihályfi replied.

"The newspapers have already been told that Sviridov has interceded, and they have not even set the type on the two notes."

On this occasion, it finally became concrete knowledge that Sviridov prohibited publication of the notes from the two Anglo-Saxon powers.

One morning Rákosi telephoned that he and Szakasits wanted to see me. They arrived at my office a little later and brought along Peter Veres, the Peasant party leader. Rákosi explained the visit.

"We came," he said, "because we feel that we can no longer keep silent regarding the American and British notes, and we are compelled to deal with them."

"What do you propose to do?" I asked.

"The notes have to be rejected," he replied.

"Rejected?" I asked. "Have you thought this over?"

"Well," interjected Szakasits, "we don't think that an insulting reply is called for; but, on the other hand, we cannot remain silent in the face of diplomatic measures which involve us."

Rákosi added: "We must not offend the Americans—after all, we do not have the strength to enter into sharp debate with the United States; but it is nevertheless necessary to remind the United States and England that we do not look kindly on their mixing in our internal affairs."

"Well, does not the arrest of Béla Kovács involve mixing in internal political affairs?" I asked.

"You are the cause of that," said Rákosi, "because, if you had given the Hungarian police free hand in the proceedings against him, there would have been no occasion for Soviet interference. In that case Béla Kovács would have received a mild sentence from which something could have been canceled. Now, who knows what will become of him?"

"What are your views?" I replied. "Who do you think should reject the American and British notes?"

"We thought that you, as Prime Minister and the leader of the largest party, should make a statement; and with this the situation would be settled."

His answer aroused me. "How can you imagine that I would reject the American and British notes?"

"Yes, I think you should," said Rákosi. "Because in this case there would be no need for separate statements by the government and the Smallholders party."

"Understand," I said, "that as long as I hold this office, the government will under no circumstances reject the notes of the two Anglo-Saxon powers. The notes do not hurt Hungary, do not insult the government, and there is no occasion for their rejection. Let those worry themselves with the notes, who feel hurt by them. Rejection of the notes by the Smallholders party is absurd. It would be the same as if the government had done so, because, after all, the Smallholders party is the country's majority party. In any event the Smallholders party has no reason for rejecting the notes."

Rákosi became red in the face with anger.

It was clear that the Soviet Union had instructed Rákosi to take this step, and that he had dragged Szakasits and Veres into helping him carry out his assignment. It would be very uncomfortable to report to Pushkin that he had been unable to satisfy the Soviet wish. It was also certain that my opposition would substantially add to the score the Soviet had chalked up against me.

"Well, could not the Smallholders party papers deal with the two notes?" Rákosi tried a new tune.

"In my view, the most that the Smallholders party can do is to keep quiet in regard to the notes, which it should really praise; it can in no event attack or even question them."

They began to bargain. Szakasits and Rákosi both tried to persuade

me that at least some sort of Smallholder press reply to the two notes
should be prepared.

"Curious," I said to them, "on occasions like this you fellows don't
bother to consider the country's economic situation. You don't think
of the fact that it is barely a month since we received from the United
States an additional credit of $15,000,000 and a new cotton loan. You
do not think of the fact that England, in a difficult economic condition herself, offered us a half-million-pound credit. You wouldn't care
if the Western powers did not make these credits available to us.
Think it over, and decide what you really want," I answered.

"Obviously, we do not want to lose economic support," said Rákosi,
"although there is no doubt that little will come of it. This is the reason
why we would be satisfied to let the Smallholder papers pass some
slight judgment on the notes."

"The most that the Smallholder papers might write is a matter
which already in 1945 gave me concern, and to which I gave expression in my campaign speeches; namely, that it would be regrettable if
Hungary, instead of contributing in some small way to an understanding among the great powers, became an object of conflict among
them," I told the group.

At this point Peter Veres interceded. Until now he had been quiet,
and privately agreed with me; but he was in no position to forget that
he was under Rákosi's rule.

"The Peasant party is considering the two notes, but naturally we
will not attack America or England violently."

I was surprised that Veres, from whom words usually pour, had
kept quiet for such a long time. After Rákosi left, the Smallholder ministers and deputies virtually swarmed into my office, suspecting that he
wanted me to reject the Anglo-Saxon notes. They asked fearfully
whether I had consented, and I quieted them by saying that under no
circumstances would I consent to rejection of the notes, and that I
had refused, out of hand, the request of the leftist bloc to that effect.

Confidence in America was so deep among Smallholders party
politicians that I could have done nothing more sinful in their eyes
than reject the notes, which were the first evidence that the Western
powers followed our political trend with interest and sympathy.

CHAPTER 80

The First "Conspiracy" Trial

THE TRIAL OF THE FIRST GROUP OF ALLEGED CONSPIRATORS HAD BEGUN, and the composition of the court indicated the degree to which the Minister of Justice was a Communist tool.

He appointed to head the court a weak drunkard who knew he was being used by the Communists and resented having to play this role, but was so deeply in their toils that he was unable to withdraw. The prosecuting attorney was equally unsatisfactory.

Under these auspices, the trial accorded with the requirements of justice only to the extent the Communists considered it necessary to give a semblance of legality.

It began with the accused being held by the political police even after the prosecution had presented its charge and the trial date had been made public. This type of treatment had not even been accorded to the Communists placed on trial by the reactionary government during the interwar period.

The accused, so to speak, did not even have a chance to escape from the tortures of the political police before they appeared in the court. They were called upon to defend themselves against the accusations, broken in body and spirit and with shattered nerves.

The second disadvantage under which these men went to trial was that they were unable to obtain lawyers of their own choice to defend them. Most members of the Budapest bar dreaded defending the "conspirators": who would protect the lawyers from the political police or from the possible attacks of the mob?

Only the truly brave Jewish lawyers who were alumni of concentration camps and survivors of the most inhumane persecution dared to appear for the defense; and they were handicapped by being permitted to speak with their clients only ten minutes before the trial, in the presence of police officers. They were accorded two hours for "study" of the large mass of documents produced as evidence. Thus they had little chance of impressing the court with their legal skill.

For five days the public expressed intense interest in the trial. The court saw to it that the audience consisted very largely of Communists, but it provided some space for the foreign press.

The behavior of the accused was shocking; they testified against themselves virtually to the point of self-persecution. The democratic public had anticipated that they would stand up, one after another, and explain how they had been persecuted by the police and the political squad of the army. This however, did not come forth.

General Louis Dálnoki-Veress, leader of the alleged military conspiracy, made some hints that his confession was involuntary, but did not go into the details of how the confession was extracted from him.

Szentmiklossy's conduct was even more surprising. He "confessed" more about his guilt and that of his associates than he was asked to. It was the prevailing opinion that he had been bribed with the promise of a mild sentence if he incriminated himself and his associates.

The conduct of Valentine Arany was most indicative. He began his testimony with the statement that he retracted his confession supposedly made to the interrogating police, because he had not made it nor signed it of his own accord. Just as he was ending this statement, Peter Janko, presiding over the court, adjourned the proceedings and ordered him returned to his cell.

Next day the trial of Arany was not continued, and another accused man was substituted. It soon developed that during the night Arany had been carried off by the Soviet NKVD from the public prosecutor's jail. When he was returned a few days later and appeared before the court, he made no defense but instead fully acknowledged all the accusations.

Judge Janko continued to conduct the trials in accordance with political instructions. He asked the accused principally what they knew against Béla Kovács and did not refrain from questions directed toward implicating Béla Varga or me.

On one occasion, in the midst of a drinking spree, Peter Janko declared, "When we finish with this group, it will be Ferenc Nagy's turn."

The verdict of the court was decided in the Communist party. Its decision was that the court must produce three death sentences, two of which would be commuted to life imprisonment by the Supreme Judiciary Council. The third death penalty would be sustained. It was absolutely essential for one man to die in order that the existence of a "conspiracy" be confirmed.

Tildy was proven wrong in thinking that the court would serve justice and find the accused innocent.

CHAPTER 81

The Failure of the Moscow Conference

THE MOSCOW CONFERENCE HAD BEGUN, AND, WHILE THE ENTIRE WORLD followed it with interest, it was natural that the outcome should be most eagerly awaited by countries still under Soviet occupation.

We Hungarians were particularly concerned with the Austrian issue. Under the peace treaty Soviet troops could remain in Hungary after the ratification as long as the Austrian occupation continued. Although their purpose was merely to "protect lines of communication" with Austria, their presence would doubtless be tantamount to a continued occupation of Hungary. We considered it a grave mistake that the Austrian peace had not been negotiated in Paris.

It soon became plain that the Moscow Conference would not be conclusive in its solution of concrete problems. Neither the German nor the Austrian problem would be solved. Still we should have preferred that the conference end in an atmosphere which would not be foreboding to the Soviet-occupied countries. It was with grave concern that I realized that if the Moscow Conference were not successful new Soviet pressures would follow which might perhaps sap our last remaining strength.

The influence of global politics on the internal affairs of the small countries was interesting. If an issue developed between the great powers, its impact was immediately felt by every country in southeastern Europe. Under such conditions, sudden new strains developed between political parties in the smallest Hungarian, Rumanian, Polish, or Bulgarian cities, and disturbances began. This strain always caused damage and handicapped the efforts of the small countries to proceed with reconstruction, and interfered with the realization of previously laid plans, produced disturbing demonstrations, or perhaps, in combination with police proceedings, cost the life of some individual.

It was my view that, if the Soviet Union remained in uncertainty after the Moscow Conference, then internal political battles would blaze up, on central instruction, in all Soviet-occupied countries. The Soviet Union, striving to insure its own security in southeastern Europe, and, having no confidence in any organization outside the Communist party, would use every means to strengthen the Communist party in each of these countries.

These activities generally begin on a very wide front. The Communist party starts the campaign for further socialization and nationalization, demands more public offices, demands more power for the labor unions, makes personal attacks on democratic leaders, tries to create some crisis in the government, initiates public demonstrations using the slogan of some labor demands, renews the slogan to struggle against reaction, and has an unlimited score of such devices. Each Moscow instruction shakes the internal political structure of every occupied small country to its very foundations.

I frequently warned my political friends that if the Moscow Conference failed, we must be prepared for a new, concentrated Communist attack.

The Smallholders party's house had to be put in order. The "conspiracy," and more particularly the arrest of Béla Kovács, hamstrung the organization activities of the party and I had to concern myself with finding men for key posts who would carry out their instructions successfully. Nights were spent mulling over how we might prepare for the anticipated Communist attack, and how all segments of the party might be pulled together.

I made two decisions. I would put the most active man, Stephen Balogh, undersecretary in the Prime Ministry, into Béla Kovács's place. Then I would turn immediately to the termination of the long-lasting crisis. It would be well if I could arrange the party's affairs and find some answer for the political crisis by the time the aftereffects of the failure of the Moscow Conference hit Hungary.

I called on Balogh, the wise Catholic priest-politician, late at night. Balogh was an interesting phenomenon in Hungarian political life. For a long time he had been the parish priest in an extensive ranch county on the Nagyalföld near Szeged. He developed a thriving agriculture on the sand dunes surrounding his parish and made an excellent farm. Sundays, after mass, he would call on his parishioners on the small ranches and explain the political news which had appeared that week in the press; and the peasants liked him because he so occupied himself with them. He has been a jovial, robust man all his life and, despite his medium height, weighs nearly 270 pounds. After saying his first mass at the new parish, he turned to the farmers who gathered around the church and said:

"My friends, take a good look at me lest you say later that I grew fat on your substance."

Before I became Prime Minister, Balogh was largely concerned with his own personal politics. He showed similar tendencies at the beginning of my Prime Ministership; but he became more closely connected with me as time went on, and once said to me:

"We are having government in Hungary for the first time since liberation, and I recognize only one assignment: that is to support your government with all my ability."

Stephen Balogh received me with much surprise when I dropped in on him late at night and said, "I came to you because I should like you to take over Béla Kovács's duties and become the temporary Executive Secretary of the Smallholders party."

Balogh was obviously pleased. "If that is your order, I will begin work tomorrow," he answered.

"I will summon the party council tomorrow and ask for their approval," I told Balogh.

We parted in the early hours after a long discussion of the difficult situation and the big task before us.

Stephen Balogh could never fill the place of Béla Kovács, but his peculiar characteristics gave him an advantage in dealing with the underhanded political game of the Hungarian Communists.

PART FIVE

Frontal Attack on Democracy

CHAPTER 82

Tension Eases

ONE OF THE SADDEST PERIODS IN MODERN HUNGARIAN HISTORY, THE FIRST chapter of the conspiracy, came to an end. The popular democracy had suffered a frightful beating. In a sense, it would not have been possible to survive this defeat in any sort of half-equal fight. However, the Hungarian democracy was not defeated by the Communist minority, by Rákosi, but by the greatest power on two continents—by the Soviet Union—and this was no more to the credit of the Soviet than to the disgrace of the Hungarian democracy.

After the dreadful attack, in the course of which we lost Béla Kovács, eight deputies, and several hundred good citizens, Hungarian democracy was still standing and awaited the further developments with determination. We were bloody and trampled, but we turned our faces toward our goal, the regaining of the independence of our country. We counted the days till England would ratify the peace treaty, till the United States and the Soviet Union would ratify it. We allowed for the additional ninety days required until the end of the military occupation and made innumerable calculations of the time when we should finally be free of the dreadful foreign burden and might turn to lasting internal consolidation.

The pending crisis had to be terminated! That was our most important current problem, to secure internal peace for as long a time as possible in order that we might await with preparedness the consequences of the failure of the Moscow Conference. It was necessary to fill the vacancies in the government in order that the lack of governmental machinery might not interfere with our progress.

I had been Prime Minister for more than a year—a year crowded with worries and bitterness. In mortal suffering, I had endured more during this period than from the time of my childhood poverty until I was imprisoned or went into hiding. I had to struggle daily against the aggression of the Communists and the Soviet, and had to explain

387

daily to my followers the reasons for my political actions. Physically and mentally tired, I became thin and weak in body. Still everyone encouraged me and said that I could look back with pride on my year of governing.

During its thousand years' history, Hungary has had several misfortunes similar to the loss of the Second World War. However, in that history there is not another year that could show as much improvement as 1946, the second year following the war. With allowances for the unparalleled energy, the remarkable ambition, the will to live, and the unheard-of sacrifices of the Hungarian people, the improvement is attributable first of all to the fact that throughout the year artificial crises could be overcome and a certain degree of the internal peace could be assured which was prerequisite for creative work. Those men were gravely lacking in a sense of responsibility who hindered the attainment of the Hungarian aims with perpetual artificial crises.

I did not want to permit the results of that year to be lost in the last months of the struggle, for the examples of the other countries of southeastern Europe were before me. None of them had achieved as satisfactory results as had Hungary. Rumania, which suffered less, was virtually ruined by a year's drought. Victorious Czechoslovakia could barely wrestle with the deficit of nationalization. In Yugoslavia tens of thousands were fleeing from terror, political persecution, and economic misery. On the other hand, in Hungary the situation improved daily. This was remarkable after the German and Russian looting.

Now it was imperative to find a solution to the crisis. To be sure, the Smallholders party had to be kept from making further sacrifices, and in fact had to produce some steps to indicate its further progressiveness in political life.

The interparty council met in an atmosphere of mutual distrust, of indignation resulting from the events of the past weeks and months. The old seesawing began. The Communists immediately demanded that the Smallholders party be "futher purged" of reactionaries, and that a few changes be made in cabinet appointments.

There was hope for settlement because we knew that the Communists wanted to reach an agreemnt on a "three-year plan," as they would have liked to use their own plan for further economic and political penetration; our plan was to develop the country's agricultural potential.

One other issue, the teaching of religious subjects in schools, created a public storm. The Soviet Union had no sympathy for the Hungarian churches and their influence on public education. I had discussed the question with Zoltán Tildy and Béla Varga, and later with the priest-politician Stephen Balogh; and we had decided, if the Soviet insisted, to yield on the teaching of religious subjects in order to protect the churches along more important lines. We knew that the time devoted by the school children to religious teachings would not be reduced even if we permitted freedom of religious teaching, because even the members of the Marxist parties could not compel their own children to stay away from religious instruction, while the public would become increasingly insistent on it if it was no longer mandatory. People of all classes flocked to the churches. The popular trend was obvious.

In any case, the reform we planned would provide that those who did not want religious teaching should make a declaration to that effect.

The Hungarian public felt that the surrender of every traditional institution meant further Communist conquest, and therefore took a strong stand against making religious teaching optional. Heated debates developed over the issue, and delegations continually arrived to oppose the discontinuance of mandatory religious instruction. At first, the churches encouraged me to think that they would accept some appropriate form of voluntary religious teaching; later, however, they joined in a sharp attack on the new system.

I followed my own conviction when I resolutely supported freedom in religious education. I believe that there is no place in a true democracy for compulsory religious education; that no law in our modern age should compel a child to undergo religious teaching. It is up to the parents to imbue their children with the desire to know more about the faith of their fathers.

While these political attacks pained me deeply, I never felt it necessary to state that in taking this stand I was not motivated by an anti-church feeling. It was hardly possible—I was trustee of Baranya Presbytery, embracing pulpits in more than sixty cities and villages, was the ruling elder of the Calvin Square Church in Budapest, and held the highest lay office, as a member of the lawmaking body, the General Synod of the Presbyterian Church in Hungary.

In my human frailty I believed myself to be a religious man. Always, to the end of my days, I shall serve and love my church, which by its purity and spiritual strength has victoriously outlasted many trials through the centuries. But my belief in progress and in the absolute political and spiritual liberty of the individual inspired my stand on compulsory religious education. Under these circumstances it hurt me deeply to find the churches in opposition.

At the end of the negotiations in March we convened for a last meeting in order to codify the interparty agreements. We had learned that it was better to draft each point of the agreement and force the Communists to bargain with us, than to bargain for departures from a Communist draft. For the March 11 meeting, I personally prepared the drafts of two agreements. One summarized the general agreement and specified the necessity of a three-year plan for the further rehabilitation of the country's economy. The political parties agreed to prepare a further plan for the reform of the educational system, in the course of which they would introduce voluntary religious training and uniform government textbooks. The government should strive, however, to solve the two problems in harmony with the churches. Finally, the agreement provided that anyone who interfered with the realization of this program would not be tolerated by the coalition political parties; and on this very point the Smallholders party made a separate announcement.

The second draft summarized the demands of the Smallholders party. The parties agreed that mandatory participation by workers in political parties would be discontinued. No one should be forced, on the basis of his employment, to leave one party and join another. This paragraph was directed against Communist aggression.

Secondly, the parties agreed that in sectors of public administration and economic life where the Smallholders did not have their *pro rata* share of the positions, the parties would assist in bringing this about. Furthermore, the parties assumed responsibility for appointing into the ranks of police officers Smallholders party peasants, and further undertook to compel the Minister of the Interior to approve the by-laws of the Peasant Alliance. Finally, the parties agreed to take a united stand against the enemies of the coalition.

When I read this plan of cooperation at the interparty meeting, the Marxist group was much taken aback. Szakasits, the leader of the Social Democrats, declared:

"I am struck over the head and speechless. It appears that Ferenc Nagy wants to put the leftist bloc on the stand with the accused, as if the conspiracy had not originated with the Smallholders party but with the leftist parties. We shall not accept this draft."

Rákosi shouted: "We are deceived! Has anyone ever heard the like of it? We sit down to discuss with the Smallholders party an agreement to assist democratic development, and the Smallholders party wants to have a moral victory over the leftist bloc. I object to the creation of such a situation and do not accept the draft."

I listened quietly to the outbursts of the left, then pointed out that the draft was satisfactory from everybody's point of view and that the Smallholders party could not resign from its valid objectives. A long, bitter debate followed, but I was unwilling to yield. They finally accepted my draft with the condition that we would publish the first agreement in the press but would only call the second to the attention of the leaders of the political parties.

Thus, on March 11, we finally brought to a conclusion the crisis which had lasted for six months. Three members of the cabinet—Albert Barta, Eugene Rácz, and Joseph Bognár—resigned. I appointed Louis Dinnyés Minister of Defense and Ernest Mihályfi Minister of Information. We traded Education and Reconstruction portfolios with the Peasant party. Julius Ortutay, of the Smallholders left wing, became Minister of Education and Peter Veres, leader of the Peasant party, became Minister of Reconstruction.

At this time I was unable to fill the post of Finance Minister because the Smallholders party's nominee, Nicholas Nyárádi, who had been the Commissioner for Looted Hungarian Property, was temporarily in the United States. He was appointed on his return.

After this "March agreement" eighteen deputies also left the Smallholders party. A few of these were excluded by the party caucus; the others, accepting its advice, stepped out.

Louis Dinnyés became Minister of Defense by an odd coincidence. When the cabinet vacancies were being discussed by the political council of the party, the Defense portfolio presented a difficult problem. We had no trustworthy, ranking soldier, nor were suitable civilians in abundance. Emery Oltványi finally said facetiously, "Dinnyés will do." Nobody considered him suitable, but a few said, "He'll do." At that point I regarded neither the post nor the man as a serious matter, and Dinnyés became a minister.

The crises which occurred frequently in Hungarian political life had taught us that the Smallholders party grew strong only in periods of political calm and internal peace. After the March agreement, party life got off to a good start. Stephen Balogh achieved impressive results in a few weeks. He reorganized and beautifully reequipped party head-quarters, put to work the section chiefs I had designated, consolidated the party's material position, and initiated a series of large public meetings. These political meetings are indispensable in Hungary and exercise the rivalry between the various parties to attract the largest crowd in each locality, and prove their popularity.

We made an interesting test after the March agreement. We mobil-ized the approximately two hundred parliamentary deputies of the Smallholders and staged a public meeting in every village of the county Nográd. The Nográd test was an enormous success. I drafted the texts of the addresses, and every deputy made substantially the same speech. It was a good feeling to know that in more than a hundred villages and cities in the same county the public was receiving the same guidance.

It was our feeling, however, that with such thorough propaganda we should very shortly incite the wrath of the Communists. For that reason we changed our tactics. The next Sunday, we held sixty public meet-ings in different parts of the country; a week later there were a hun-dred meetings, and the fourth Sunday the Smallholder deputies spoke at two hundred meetings.

We consolidated the forty-odd daily and weekly newspapers of the Smallholders party, supplied them with editors, guaranteed their news-print supply and put their publishing affairs in order. I took part in the weekly meetings of the deputies and kept them fully informed of political developments.

Thus party life took on a new impetus, and in a few months we should have gone into an election calmly in the knowledge that the party would have been strengthened rather than weakened. This was neces-sary because, during the last months of the crisis, the leftist bloc con-stantly threatened an election. They demanded announcement of new elections at public meetings, and oddly enough they also demanded restriction of the franchise.

Suspecting a ruse by the Communists, during my frequent calls on the President I asked that he should under no condition consent to the dissolution of the Parliament; and Tildy promised.

With respect to the restriction of the franchise, I told the leftist bloc that I would consent to the reduction of the number of the voters by disfranchising all those who had been members of the National So-cialist and Arrow Cross party. Since, on the one hand, it was difficult to avoid this demand and, on the other, this would disfranchise about half the Communist voters, we knew that they would no longer demand disfranchisement. After the March agreement, I plainly brought the question to Parliament; in a speech I stated that there was no need for a new election in Hungary, and the leftist bloc dared voice no objection.

Rákosi, knowing of my constant anxiety about the fate of Béla Kovács, one day proposed that we suspend his parliamentary immunity, saying that the Soviet Union might then be willing to hand him over to the Hungarian authorities. I neither rejected his thought nor accepted his advice. At the time there was a feeling that Béla Kovács might be better off in the Soviet's Budapest prison than in the hands of the Hungarian police. However, since time was passing, I took occasion to refer to him while I was conferring with Sviridov and Pushkin on another matter.

I posed the question: "What would be the attitude of the Soviet authorities if the government requested that Béla Kovács be turned over to the Hungarian authorities?"

Sviridov and Pushkin looked at each other and began to confer at length in Russian. The question obviously caught them by surprise. Finally Pushkin answered:

"We cannot answer the Prime Minister's question, since the Hungarian government has not raised the question officially."

"I did not raise the question officially because I do not wish to be exposed to a refusal," I answered.

"If the Hungarian government officially raises the question, the Soviet authorities will reply," said Pushkin, and from his voice it was impossible to infer what kind of reply might be expected.

Soon thereafter I was informed by American and British circles that Béla Kovács's life was in danger; and I immediately decided that it would be well, regardless of the sacrifice involved, to have him transferred to the hands of the Hungarian authorities. This warning was effective, and since I never for a moment suspected that Rákosi's advice was intended as a vile trap for me, I undertook the steps necessary to secure Kovács's return.

I first presented the problem to the political commitee of the Smallholders party, when Béla Varga advised that we should obtain Kovács from the Soviet authorities even if it necessitated the suspension of his parliamentary immunity. Although the Smallholders party leadership had reconciled itself to the suspension of his immunity, I put off this step in the interest of caution and instead asked Pushkin to come to see me. I had decided that Kovács's parliamentary immunity should be suspended only if I received an irrevocable promise that he would be delivered to the Hungarian authorities.

Pushkin came to my office, and I asked that he communicate to his government the request of the Hungarian government for Kovács's return in order that the Hungarian authorities might proceed against him.

Pushkin took "cognizance" of the official request and agreed to obtain his government's reply at an early date.

Now more than ever I worried about the fate of Béla Kovács.

CHAPTER 83

Soviet Interpretation of Potsdam

THE PERIODICAL DICTATES OF THE SOVIET HAVE ALREADY INDICATED how damaging were those agreements among the great powers which, under Moscow's unilateral interpretation, exposed southeastern Europe to Communism. Of all these, the Potsdam agreement was probably the most damaging.

The Soviet Union stretched the substance of the Potsdam agreement day by day. It began to take possession of the German-owned real estate, plants, homes, and businesses as early as 1945.

One nice day it declared that, by the terms of the Russian version of the Potsdam agreement, it was entitled to the assets of every German interest and that it had no concern with the liabilities. It would take title and possession of the factories, the buildings, and the stores, but would not assume the liabilities. Still later it declared that it was entitled not only to the German assets but also to the German claims agains the Hungarian government and Hungarian citizens. This meant that if any Hungarian citizen or firm was indebted to Germany he now had to pay that debt to the Soviet Union. If the obligation was in terms of German reichsmarks, then the Soviet would decide the Hungarian forint or United States dollar equivalent.

When we began to total the Soviet claims, it developed that the Hungarian government's additional debt to Russia on the basis of the Potsdam agreement exceeded by far the actual amount of reparations.

We met with Sviridov and his economic advisers early in January to reach some agreement or at least clarify the questions. I explained that the Hungarian government was unable to comply with the Soviet demands, because they would completely upset the budget and undermine stabilization. I explained that the budget was already in bad shape and, if we divided it between internal administrative expenses and international obligations, the picture was already distressing. While, during the first five months of the fiscal year, it was possible to reduce expenditures for domestic administration by sixteen million forint, our expenditures for reparations, provisioning of the Red army, and maintenance of the Allied Control Commission had increased at such a pace that the 640,000,000 forint deficit indicated in the budget would reach 1,400,-000,000 forint by the end of the year. In view of these circumstances we could under no conditions undertake to meet additional Soviet claims.

Sviridov replied: "The Soviet Union has no desire to ruin the Hungarian economy; but the Hungarian government should try to economize in other fields rather than on Soviet claims. You are paying, for example, excessive prices for the goods which the factories manufacture for reparations account."

Anthony Bán, Minister of Industry, interjected: "These goods cannot be produced less expensively in Hungary. Raw materials are expensive, power is expensive, and wages cannot be reduced, either."

As was generally the case, our conference with the Russians was the beginning of endless arguments. A Russian colonel read an extensive document to the effect that the Hungarian government was able but not willing to satisfy the Soviet demands.

I rejected this declaration of the Russian colonel with such emphasis that Sviridov was at last compelled to doubt the colonel's findings. We could reach no agreement and sent a joint committee to examine the problem.

At about this time, the Soviet Union made still another demand. The Soviet Minister of Foreign Trade concluded that the joint Soviet-Hungarian firms created in 1946 were not yielding enough profit to the Soviet. Sviridov began to make two demands: first, that we reduce the taxes of these enterprises and give them tax equality with the nationalized enterprises; and, second, that we raise the prices of the goods produced by the joint companies and permit the proceeds of the sales to be transferred to the Soviet.

It was typical of the fact that the Soviet speaks differently when it is concerned with its own interests and when, for example, it is discussing the profitability of American-owned enterprises in Hungary. Soviet occupation forces supervised the production of oil in the American-owned Lispe oil fields. When, at the time of stabilization, we fixed the price of oil, we felt that we were making it possible for the American-owned interests to operate profitably.

This was offensive to the Soviets, and they utilized every opportunity to squeeze the American firms. When, in response to United States pressure, the Soviets decided to evacuate the American properties, they requested the Hungarian government to continue supervision. We accepted the suggestion cheerfully, in order to stop the damage already wrought by Soviet soldiers to the oil fields. That, however, did not put an end to the demands for lower oil prices, although they were simultaneously demanding an increase in the price of goods produced under their auspices.

An instructive example of trading with the Soviet Union was the agreement relating to the sale of the Petrozsény coal mines. It bought the property, worth between thirty and forty million dollars, for $12,500,000 after consenting, even before the conclusion of the sale, to credit $3,500,000 of the price to the 1946 reparations account. This transaction taught us that agreements between the Soviet Union and any small country can benefit only the Soviet.

Now the Russians reopened the question of the Potsdam claims, and their vastness became a political issue. We decided to question their legal basis, and the peace treaty undoubtedly made this possible. One of its clauses provided that only those Potsdam claims are valid which are declared by the Allied Control Commission in Berlin to represent German assets; it also canceled Hungary's claims against Germany.

When Russian suggestions provided an auspicious moment for commencing negotiations, the Smallholders ministers took the view that we could not depart from Hungary's legal rights. If the Soviet Union presented its Potsdam claims without regard for the provisions of the peace treaty, then we should be entitled to ignore the treaty provisions regarding the cancellation of Hungarian claims against Germany. If, on the other hand, it considered the peace treaty provisions regarding Hungarian claims to be valid, then we would insist on a review of the Soviet claims by the Allied Control Commission in Berlin.

The Soviet insisted that we organize, as promptly as possible, a delegation to go to Moscow and negotiate a settlement of Soviet claims under the Potsdam agreement. We appointed Finance Minister Nyárádi to lead the delegation. I insisted, however, that each party be represented in the delegation by one of its leading members. The Finance Minister, on the other hand, insisted that the delegation be headed either by the Prime Minister or by one of the deputy prime ministers, because the issues to be settled had important political implications. I had decided that I would under no circumstances go to Moscow, and urged Rákosi to lead the delegation. Rákosi also considered this inconvenient and proposed that we confine the delegation's authority to negotiations and retain for the government the right to make a settlement which would enable the Finance Minister to head the delegation.

Finally it was agreed that in the Moscow negotiations he should not surrender our right to examine the legal issues involved, but should be prepared to reach an agreement, with appropriate legal reservations, to settle the Soviet's more than $200,000,000 claim for $10,000,000.

CHAPTER 84

The Communists Attack Gyöngyösi

NEEDLESS TO SAY, IN REACHING THE MARCH AGREEMENT, THE COMmunists did not abandon their intention to cause disturbances. Now they began to concentrate their attacks on Foreign Minister John Gyöngyösi who as a member of the Smallholders party leadership, they somehow found out, had urged a firm stand against them.

Curiously enough, Gyöngyösi had long been unpopular within the party because he was thought to have pursued a pro-Soviet foreign policy and neglected the relations with the Western powers. Some accused him of being obligated to the Communists, and hinted that he had held a Communist party membership card at the time of the Debrecen government. Furthermore, his popularity was not enhanced by the agreement for exchange of populations which he had concluded with Czechoslovakia, and he unknowingly became the scapegoat for certain concessions made in that agreemnt.

These accusations were unjust. He was an honorable and persevering member of the Smallholders party, who, as Foreign Minister, was obliged to face up to his times. However, he interpreted literally the Soviet declarations in regard to Hungary's independence, and when the time arrived for reestablishing intercourse with the Western powers he sought to advance that objective, too.

Gyöngyösi urged a firmer domestic policy because he believed that it would strengthen the country's foreign policy. When it became apparent, however, that his demeanor was advancing his popularity, the Communists suddenly turned against him and began to smear him. The atmosphere became so strained that even his proposals in the cabinet council were attacked. Thus, when he proposed the elevation of Stephen Borsody, the able press counselor of the Washington legation, to the post of consul-general in New York, they opposed him bitterly and compelled him to withdraw his motion. Later he was subjected to a similar attack when he designated Alexander Szász, a director of the National Bank of Hungary on leave, serving as economic counselor of our Washington legation, to the office of legation counselor.

Some members of the party misinterpreted Gyöngyösi's situation. They alleged that he was aiming for the Premiership in the event of my resignation. This was probably untrue, though I, in fact, had thought of him as a possibility in that event.

Although the attacks did not indicate a concentrated Soviet-Communist campaign, they were disconcerting and embittered Gyöngyösi; and he hinted on several occasions that he would like to resign. I dissuaded him every time.

The year-long struggle in the Prime Ministry had exhausted me physically. I attempted to hide the exhaustion and often assured my friends that my nerves were still holding up. However, I did develop a keen and very natural craving for a rest, and decided to go abroad for a few weeks. My predecessors, Count Stephen Bethlen and Nicholas Kállay, could have shut themselves away from everyone on a domestic holiday; but I, the people's man, could hardly do such a thing in my own land. After decades of personal friendship every peasant claimed ready entry to me, and, no matter where I might go in Hungary I should be exposed to constant instrusion.

For a rest abroad, Switzerland alone could be considered. I did not want to go to Russia under any conditions; under the circumstances, it had to be a neutral country, and Switzerland was the logical answer. Two other considerations brought Switzerland to the front. One was that my daughter was there at school and my wife and I wanted very

much to visit her; the other, that I had long wished to become familiar
with Swiss agriculture, in which I had had an interest since my peasant
boyhood.

I therefore prepared my vacation plans and hinted about them
several times to the President and the deputy prime ministers. The
President, who after ten weeks as Prime Minister had openly declared
that he was completely exhausted and unable to continue, was in no
position to question my wish for a rest. The deputy prime ministers
did not oppose it either, and I scheduled my departure for May 14.

In the meantime we had received a visit from Peter Groza, Rumanian Prime Minister. At the suggestion of the President, the cabinet
had decided on the establishment of a Hungarian-Rumanian institute,
and Groza thought its dedication appropriate for a visit to Hungary.

We were familiar with the personality, political viewpoint, and
official situation of the Prime Minister of Rumania, but I awaited him
with much curiosity and the desire to become more familiar with the
condition in one of the more suppressed countries of southeastern
Europe.

Groza arrived in Budapest with an enormous entourage including
the President of the Rumanian Parliament, the Minister of Education,
the Minister of Justice, and, most important, Undersecretary Emil Bodnaras. The Hungarians drew interesting conclusions from the Groza-
Bodnaras relationship. They said that Groza was the only beneficiary
of power, a capitalist ever increasing in wealth, but that actual power
was in the hands of Bodnaras, the undersecretary in the Prime Ministry.

We received the Rumanian Prime Minister festively and with great
honor. He came to familiar territory, for he had studied law in Budapest after eight years in the Hungarian Protestant Preparatory School,
of Szászváros. He spoke Hungarian fluently and had many boyhood
friends in the Hungarian capital. I spent much time with him during
his stay, both officially and socially, and was shocked by his conduct
and not less by his political views. It was evident that his statements in
regard to Rumanian conditions and the southeastern Europe political
situation had been thoroughly discussed and approved before he left.
He said such things as:

"When President Truman sent his special envoy to me, in order to
become familiar with my foreign policies, I said to this American
gentleman: 'My dear friend, tell President Truman that if the Ameri-

cans, who have enriched the world with their wonderful technical discoveries including the atomic bomb, should discover how Rumania might be made a neighbor of the United States, then I will have no further use for these Bolsheviks' "—pointing his finger at Bodnaras— " 'and I will pursue a policy appropriate to my background and my wealth. But, so long as Rumania adjoins Russia, I will remain the most loyal ally of the Soviet Union.' "

On another occasion he said to me: "I am a rich man and the son of fortune in whose hands everything turns to gold. My policy is not Marxism, but I must permit it because the European situation requires it."

"The public is behind me," said Groza. "For months before the first of May, we were unable to give the people of Bucharest even corn flour. They nevertheless turned out cheerfully on May 1 to celebrate the Socialist holiday."

He himself related that when his Minister of the Interior persuaded him to use a bodyguard he staffed it with four police officers who would help him amuse himself. Of the four, one was an excellent singer who would begin to sing as soon as Groza woke up; another was a tennis trainer who played with him in good weather; the third was a champion track athlete with whom he raced at times; and the fourth was a boxer with whom he sparred when the weather was bad.

Groza impressed me as a very charming man who had abandoned himself to the Communists and had only one concern: that the little vessel filled with his personal treasures should not capsize on the sea of world politics.

CHAPTER 85

Leaving Becomes Difficult

AFTER GROZA'S DEPARTURE, I INVITED RÁKOSI AND SZAKASITS TO DINNER for a discussion of current political questions in order to eliminate all possibility of disturbances during my three weeks' absence. Both of them promised to cooperate.

Furthermore, I called a meeting of Smallholders deputies at party headquarters and told them that I was leaving for a three weeks' vacation to refresh my nerves and spirits, and asked them to do their part toward keeping the political peace in my absence. In addition, I commended to their consideration the need for designating Smallholders representatives to the directorate of the three large nationalized enterprises, since I had succeeded in securing these important posts for the Smallholders party.

My friends took my decision calmly and wished me well on my holiday. At noon of the day preceding my departure, Finance Minister Nyárádi called on me, saying, "I am afraid you will not be able to leave."

"Why?"

"Sviridov summoned me this morning, and asked me why I wanted to take international law experts with me to Moscow. I told him, because some legal questions were involved in the negotiations. He replied that this was out of the question, that the function of the Hungarian delegation in Moscow would not be to debate issues on legal grounds but only to agree and sign. When I said that the Hungarian government's resolution was not to this effect, he declared that at the Moscow negotiations there could be talk only of agreeing and signing. Under these circumstances, I can under no conditions go to Moscow."

General Sviridov's behavior aroused me, and I went to him immediately.

"I envy you, going on your vacation," he began.

"I note with regret that the General actively envies my vacation, because he is trying to stop it."

"I? How?"

"Before noon today you summoned the Finance Minister and prescribed the scope of the Moscow negotiations. If this is true, I will of course not leave, because the government will have entirely different functions to perform."

Sviridov began to deny in his usual manner. "I beg you, how could the Finance Minister have said such a thing? In all likelihood he misunderstood my words. There can be no question of my wanting to restrict the scope of the Hungarian delegation to Moscow. The Hungarian government's delegation negotiates as it wishes. It can be in constant telephone communication with the government in Budapest and reach an agreement or not as it wishes. I told the Finance Minister only that it would be well if he took along an authorization to sign in order that an agreement might be formalized."

I asked, "May I take this as an official statement?"

"Naturally," answered Sviridov. "It pains me to think that one would even suppose that I want to curb the Hungarian delegation's freedom to negotiate."

Towards nightfall I summoned the Smallholders ministers, told them about my conversation with Sviridov, and announced that I would be leaving the next day.

However, one question remained unsettled. Rákosi, who a few days earlier had promised that the Marxist parties would raise no new political issues until I returned from my vacation, stated at a public meeting on the Nagyalföld that the Communists were demanding the nationalization of the three biggest banks. At the beginning of the long crisis in October they had talked only about supervising the banks; and nationalization of the three big banks was a very important matter, politically, economically, and socially. It would restrict private property to even narrower limits, and advance the Communists' economic goals. Moreover, it would put the entire credit system of the country completely under government control; and, since more than half of Hungarian heavy industry was in the sphere of interest of those banks, it would bring nationalization of a large part of industry and the conversion of the workers into government employees. This, in turn, would mean slavery for the workers.

In private employment in Hungary labor could demand wage increases and could strike. In government employment it enjoys neither of these rights. It could not strike particularly since Communists would doubtless be placed at the head of the nationalized concerns, who would—using high-sounding slogans—actually suppress all of labor's rights. In other words, Rákosi was tossing an extremely dangerous and important issue into Hungarian political life.

Needless to say, Rákosi had acted on the basis of agreement with the Soviet. Under his clever plan, the enterprises already nationalized and the joint companies half owned by the Soviet Union would collaborate with the enterprises newly nationalized so that the entire Hungarian industrial output would fall under Soviet control. This would be a more than complete Soviet exploitation of the misinterpreted Potsdam agreement.

If this was the way we were to progress, it was folly to think that, after ratification and the cessation of occupation, Hungary could recapture her independence, because penetration would have become so extensive as to cast serious doubt on the value of independence. For this reason, I expressed the strongest possible opposition to Rákosi's new plan. Although it was not popular to fight for the principle of private property or the country's economic independence, especially when it involved making an issue of the big banks, I told the Smallholder deputies and ministers that I would not under any circumstances consent to further nationalization.

CHAPTER 86

My Last Meeting with President Tildy

EARLY IN THE MORNING OF MAY 14, I WENT TO MY OFFICE TO SIGN urgent documents, and to perform some other last official acts.

Among the documents submitted for signature was a most interesting one proposing some two hundred "political, economic, literary, artistic, and social leaders" for decorations. To date, the Hungarian democracy had created two types of decoration: the Order of Liberty, to which participants in the struggle against German and Hungarian Nazis were eligible; and, more important, the Order of Merit of the Republic, which had several classes. The document called for the decoration of some two hundred persons with different classes of this order. Undoubtedly someone was trying to take advantage of my haste before departure because, when I read the list, I found it to contain the names of prominent grafters, leaders and organizers of the Soviet-Hungarian Cultural Society, and politically suspect persons who, mostly in secret but none the less effectively, served the Communists in public life and in the judiciary. The list was sprinkled with an occasional truly worthy democratic writer, artist, or intellectual. I tossed it aside, declaring that at most twenty deserved decorations; that, if they would select these, I would submit their names to the President.

Thereafter I took leave of my Secretariat and the staff and drove to President Tildy. First of all, I told him about Sviridov's behavior during the preceding day: his effort to curb the activities of the Hungarian delegation leaving for Moscow, and his denial of everything he had said to the Finance Minister. Then I told the President that Rákosi and Szakasits had promised not to raise political issues in my absence which might give cause for debate, and that, his promise notwithstanding, Rákosi just before my departure had raised the issue of the nationalization of the banks.

"Look, Zoltán, here and now, I declare that I will under no condition be party to any further extension of nationalization. I am not willing to reduce private property entirely to an illusion. Please do not allow the nationalization issue to be settled during my absence, under any conditions, because I would not consent to further inroads on private enterprise.

"What is more, it seems to me that we are no longer obliged to grant Communist demands because our foreign political situation is different from what it was. The Western powers are showing a more active interest, and I believe that we are not as much delivered to the whims of the Communists as we have been for the past two years."

The Truman Doctrine began to be familiar to the masses about this time. The growing firmness of American policy aroused hope, not only in me and the Hungarian people but in all the oppressed peoples of eastern Europe, as well. Everyone expected, especially after the official interpretations, that a more positive interest in all eastern Europe would follow.

Zoltán Tildy replied that he would ask a group of economic experts to analyze Rákosi's proposal, but would not permit the question to come up for discussion until I returned.

I then reported on my arrangement with reference to the party: that I left Béla Varga in charge of the Political Committee and intrusted the leadership of the Smallholders ministers and undersecretaries to John Gyöngyösi. I left negotiations with the other political parties in the hands of Emery Oltványi, and the management of the Smallholders party's headquarters and organizational affairs in the hands of Stephen Balogh. I asked Tildy especially to see that the leftist bloc did not introduce issues which would lead to disturbances, and to keep the Smallholders deputies well in hand, lest they give an excuse for an incident.

Tildy agreed and assured me that he would watch over the tranquillity of Hungarian political life. Then he said that I would surely have the quiet rest which he wished for me heartily.

I knew that, without telling me, the left-wing deputies of the Smallholders party frequently visited Zoltán Tildy. They enjoyed Rákosi's confidence to a certain extent and frequently advised Tildy to make concessions which in turn emboldened the Communists and weakened the chances of resistance for the Smallholders party as a whole. Ortutay and his group would even unfavorably exaggerate to the President the conduct of upright and patriotic Smallholders politicians. It was precisely for this reason that I asked Tildy to maintain contact in Smallholders party affairs with those whom I designated and act through them in case of need.

Zoltán Tildy's wife was at this time in the United States, where she lectured on the social conditions in Hungary and sought relief for the Hungarian poor. At our last meeting, Tildy referred to her American activities and expressed real pleasure over her welcome in the United States, even in official circles. I remarked that Rákosi was enraged about her American trip, and Tildy replied that he did not understand, for when the question of her trip to America was raised Rákosi himself had approved it. To this I replied that Moscow apparently was displeased with this American appearance, and Rákosi was merely echoing Moscow.

We chatted awhile, and then I took my leave. I did not know that this would be my last meeting with the man with whom I associated twenty years of friendship and the memory of battles fought together. Even less did I imagine that Zoltán Tildy would, before long, deny me, who had supported him and assisted him uninterruptedly through two decades, right up to the Presidency.

Since "liberation," I several times had had occasion to disagree with Tildy's policies. From my point of view, the bitterest aspect of it all was the need for my taking over from him the heritage of the Prime Ministry, established as it was on concessions and compromises. And when, hamstrung by this heritage, in the effort to govern, I was compelled to take unpopular steps, I never gave those wanting to pass judgment an opportunity to pass it not on me but on him, who was responsible, and who amassed during his short term the encumbrances of the heritage.

CHAPTER 87

The Fateful Trip

THE HOURS REMAINING BEFORE OUR DEPARTURE WERE DEVOTED TO readying our luggage. We took very few things with us as it was not my plan to loaf in fashionable resorts, but rather to go to different places every day, familiarizing myself with Swiss methods of making land productive. Earlier I had had dinner with the Swiss envoy in Budapest, Ernest Feisst, himself an expert in agriculture, who scheduled for me a program of study that included famous livestock breeding establishments, fruit-growing sections, agricultural schools, wine-producing areas, and poultry experimental stations. He promised to alert the appropriate agricultural circles in order that they might place guides and experts at my disposal. I decided to avoid all political activity and confine my official acts to courtesy calls on the President of the Republic and the Foreign Minister. Minister Feisst explained the program in detail to Dr. Henry Hives, the Chief of Cabinet in the Prime Ministry, who accompanied me, to assist with his familiarity with the language and the country.

My loyal secretary, Francis Kapocs, shared our last hours in Budapest. He would have liked to go along, not only because he was always unhappy away from me, but also because he had developed a warm friendship with our daughter Juliette. I was, however, unable to take him because he did not know enough German nor French to serve as my interpreter. Had I known what was to be his fate within three weeks, I would not have left him behind. If I had had any intimation of the outcome of my trip, a lot of things would have been differently arranged.

Stephen Balogh came up then with the revised list of nominees for decorations for me to sign. I warned him once more to heed my instructions carefully.

"You can rest at ease, there will be no trouble," he said. "We will return the country to you in one piece when you return."

As he was returning the papers to his brief case, one fell to the floor. When I picked it up and handed it to him he said rather unhappily: "If I had been here alone my bulk would have made it necessary for me to kneel, then lie down. Only then could I have picked the paper off the rug." This was to be my last memory of the brainy political priest with whom I had worked daily in the government.

In order to carry through my planned study of agriculture, I had decided to go to Switzerland by car. The question had arisen whether we should take along our little boy, Lacika, who was not yet five, but in view of previous experiences we decided to leave him at home. He had accepted the decision; however, at the hour for departure, he tied his red miniature automobile to the rear of our large car, in order that he might follow us, and he wept bitter tears when I untied his little red car and he had to remain behind.

In spite of this last moment sadness my wife, Henry Hives, and I drove away in a lighthearted mood, like vacation-minded college students. I was on my first planned holiday. Aside from our passports, we took not a single sheet of paper, much less a document. I wanted to rest, not to make politics. I was happy to escape for three weeks from constant strife and struggle; the battlefield of many, many unpopular compromises. I was happy to escape from the atmosphere of constant intrigue and looked forward to contact with men in a foreign land who, like myself, had grown up and sweated on the soil—peasants. I believed that I should return invigorated in body and soul, and able to master the struggle and survive the foggy night of Hungarian life until the dawn of Hungarian independence, and the people's freedom.

Between wheatfields on the Vienna road, the optimistic Hives would point to a green stretch here and there; but with my peasant training I had to disappoint him, saying, "The Hungarian harvest will not be good this year." Truly, in this unfortunate country, only intrigue had a good harvest in 1947.

There were two Hungarian flags on the front of my car, and after we crossed the Austrian border the customs guards and police everywhere extended friendly courtesies. We reached Vienna at night. Minister Leslie Bartók informed me confidentially that Chancellor Figl would like to have a few minutes with me. I sent my friendly greetings to Chancellor Figl with the request to be excused after my announcement at home of my determination not to let politics intrude on this trip.

We did not rush through Austria. We admired its cloisters, its old castles towering over the valleys, the beautiful farms of the Austrian peasants, and hamlets in Salzburg for a rest. The American authorities kindly placed excellent accommodations at our disposal. On the 16th, we crossed the Arlberg in thick fog, and toward nightfall arrived in Zurich. We were happy to find Juliette waiting for us. We spent the day sight-seeing in this charming city and then started in the direction of Vevey, to inspect the first wine-producing area. A representative of the agricultural cooperatives accompanying us, we enjoyed in the next few days invitations to taste wines in different wine cellars.

Then came Simmenthal, where we admired the breeding grounds of the world's most beautiful cattle. In Erlenbach, we saw a stud bull owned by one of the small peasant cooperatives, which was famous in all Switzerland. Any breeder was happy who could boast of blood relationship between his stock and the famous Erlenbach bull. We climbed the high pastures, then went through the rich orchards of the Rhone valley, went to Sion, another famous vineyard region, visited beautiful agricultural schools, and I felt that I had learned a great deal on this trip.

After the agrarian reform, Hungary became agriculturally a peasant state. We were confronted with a large task in providing agricultural training for all those who had acquired land for the first time under the agrarian reform, and giving proper orientation to the new system of small landownership. I formulated some plans for adapting Swiss experience to Hungarian agriculture and decided to send our agronomists to Switzerland later in order to study Swiss methods and exploit their observations for the benefit of Hungarian agriculture.

At the end of my first week's stay in Switzerland, my secretary told me by telephone that, aside from minor matters, the political scene was calm. I telephoned to President Tildy, who stated that there were a few personal attacks, mostly against Gyöngyösi, but by and large the situation remained unchanged; and he suggested that I continue my vacation in Switzerland without much concern. In the nationalization of the banks, he said, he was following the plan we had discussed, but would definitely postpone final decision until my return.

I turned once more toward Swiss agriculture, with ease of mind and experiencing real pleasure from my absorption in the subject.

My son Ferenc, in Washington, would have liked to join us in Switzerland. I knew, however, that both the Communist party and the Soviet Union viewed with suspicion the activities of our Washington legation and I did not want to give further ground for political interpretation. In any event, I did not have enough money to cover the expenses of his trip to Switzerland, and I knew full well that his own savings as the junior member of the legation staff were inadequate for the trip.

As I tramped through the sun and air and saw the fine work the Swiss were doing with their small farms, my strength and spirit revived. All would yet come right in Hungary. The international skies would clear. The Russians would relax as the war receded. We Hungarians, under free institutions at last, would develop our country into another such garden spot as Switzerland. I would make my own little farm at

Bisse into a model. So it all seemed to me in the high, bright mountain air.

After our two weeks' study of agriculture, we thought of spending a day or two in Italy on the seashore, since my wife had never seen the ocean. We started for Locarno in a cheerful mood, passed through the beautiful Furka Pass, where violets were still in bloom. We marveled at the beautiful Swiss roads, and at night, after some trouble with the car, arrived at Locarno, on the edge of the warm-weather belt.

CHAPTER 88

"Budapest Calling"

THE TELEPHONE RANG IN MY HOTEL ROOM AT SEVEN O'CLOCK IN THE evening. My secretary was on the line and, in an excited, trembling voice, requested that I return at once to Budapest.

"What has happened, son?" I asked him.

"I can say only this—the Prime Minister's honor is at stake," he said.

When I pressed for an explanation, a new voice came over the line. "For Heaven's sake, come home and clear yourself," requested one of my fellow Smallholder ministers.

"Tell me—what is this all about?" I asked.

"We have just been convened for a cabinet meeting, and you will be the topic of discussion," came the anwser.

"I cannot imagine what you are talking about," I answered.

My secretary, Kapocs, took the telephone again.

"Tell everyone that I am starting back tomorrow morning. What does the President say?" I asked.

"He would also advise you to come home."

"I hear that there will be a cabinet meeting," I said. "Surely it will be over by eight. I will call you then and you can tell me what's up."

"Yes," answered my secretary.

I became very restless. Although in Hungary one is not surprised to find that the Communists break their word and stir up storms from time to time, the short telephone conversation made me very uneasy. I sent for Henry Hives, informed him of the conversation, and instructed him to have our car ready for an early departure. He answered that necessary repairs would make it impossible to leave before ten in the morning.

Through my mind flashed every phase of Hungarian political life since the liberation and my relationship to it. I considered, one after another, my declarations and agreements. I never took a single step which I could not justify anywhere, any time. I sacrified myself to the Prime Ministry for the sake of my country's peace and quiet, until it should regain its sovereignty. I never deceived either the Soviet or my domestic political opponents but played the gentleman toward them.

After all, it was I who had obtained Soviet permission for the operation of the opposition parties. What could it be that was now threatening my honor?

An hour later I called my secretary. "The cabinet has drafted a communiqué stating that General Sviridov has now replied to the request of the Prime Minister for the release of Béla Kovács to the Hungarian authorities. General Sviridov declares that he cannot comply with the request because the Kovács investigation has not yet been completed, but he attaches for possible use a transcript of Kovács's confession. The cabinet has decided to request the Prime Minister to terminate his vacation and return to Budapest. Foreign Minister Gyöngyösi is at my side, and I will hand him the receiver." Thus Kapocs completed his report.

"The situation is as Kapocs has described it. I will add only that, according to the transcript, Kovács claims that you knew about the conspiracy," said Gyöngyösi.

"Nonsense!" I answered. "In the first place Béla Kovács could not have said such a thing, and in the second place it isn't true."

"Yes, but that's of no moment now. You must return, without fail, to clarify the situation," said Gyöngyösi.

At this point Stephen Balogh took the telephone. "I too ask you to return, because you are the only one who can clarify this affair."

"I can tell you only what I have already told Gyöngyösi and my secretary. I'm starting home tomorrow morning," was my answer.

I alternated between shock and anger. What kind of disgraceful intrigue was this? What game was the Soviet starting? Béla Kovács himself knew nothing about the "conspiracy." Therefore how could he have claimed that I knew something about it?

To what torture must this fine man have been exposed that brought a confession contrary to his conviction with which they were trying to compromise me, too? I did not for a moment think that either the Soviet Union or the Communists believed this allegation. They were deliberately lying, and probably had forced my best friend to lie, too.

The Moscow Conference came to my mind; I knew that if it failed the Soviet would start a campaign to isolate southeastern Europe. So I was the victim, I thought bitterly. I knew that it was hopeless to try to prove a case against the Soviet but decided to refute under any circumstances this disgraceful incident. The last remaining, unshakable pillar of Hungarian democracy, Béla Varga, came to my mind. I telephoned him.

"Can you tell me anything about the events?"

"I only know about the happenings at the cabinet meeting. Early this afternoon I was with General Weems, who gave a farewell reception in honor of Minister Schoenfeld. The deputy prime ministers were there, but there was no hint that anything was in preparation."

"Did you speak with the President?"

"The President hasn't called me since you left the country," answered Béla Varga.

I was surprised. Tildy hadn't considered it necessary to speak with Béla Varga for over two weeks? I wondered with whom he was maintaining contact.

The telephone rang after I hung up, and an unfamiliar voice was on the other end.

"Mr. Prime Minister, Francis Kapocs was arrested by the political police this evening at nine, hustled to prison, and then they proceeded to crack your safe and rifle it of private and official documents."

This disgraceful audacity disturbed me even more. They would not even wait until I could return and refute their allegations, but arrest and drag off my secretary. What is it that they want?

Before I went to bed that evening, a Hungarian living in Switzerland, uninformed about the developments of the last few hours, called unexpectedly to caution me about one circumstance.

"Immediately after you arrived in Switzerland, I was visited by a Hungarian leftist official. He asked me to watch you daily, try to find out whom you met, possibly also what you talked about, and make daily reports to a third party who would meet me for the purpose of receiving them. I gave him the impression that I would accept the assignment. They then promised me all sorts of things and held out the prospect of granting me requests which hitherto they had flatly refused. I am convinced that the secretive third person who was trying to engage me for this assignment is Joseph Száll, the Communist secretary of the Hungarian legation in Bern."

"It is now unnecessary for you to accept this role because I am returning home tomorrow morning," I answered. And I told him the news received in the last few hours.

Early in the morning I telephoned Zoltán Tildy and began: "Look, Zoltán, I received some shocking telephone reports from Budapest last night. I would like your opinion of the situation."

"Sviridov has now replied to your request that they turn Béla Kovács over to the Hungarian authorities. He attaches to his reply a transcript of Kovács's confession stating that you knew about the conspiracy."

"There is no other insinuation against me?" I asked.

"No, there is none."

"Zoltán, you know that this charge is false. I did not take a single step or make a single declaration which might serve as the basis of a charge against me. They asked me to return, and in an hour or two I shall be on my way home."

"Very well. I approve of your coming home as soon as possible. I hope there is still a chance to save the situation. It would be well, however, if you telephoned Rákosi before your departure," Tildy said nervously.

"Are you of the opinion that this situation can be settled through negotiations?" I asked the President.

"Yes, I believe that the question can be settled somehow."

I debated for a while whether I should follow the President's advice; Francis Kapocs came to my mind, and I decided to speak with Rákosi.

"They reported Sviridov's letter to me by telephone last night, also the accusing transcript, and the decision of the cabinet," I said when we were connected. "I consider the accusation a filthy concoction, and when I get home you'll be surprised at the way I'll refute it."

"Don't take the situation so lightly," threatened Rákosi, "because there is a very serious matter at issue. I do not know with whom you conferred or what you did abroad, but with the Russians you kicked out the bottom of your barrel."

"I know that merely coming in contact with the Soviet is a very serious matter. That is the reason why I consider it necessary to disprove immediately this impossible allegation. Besides, you may tell the Russians I did not confer with anyone, had no intentions, either—as I stated at home before my departure."

"I wish you would see how your own party is aroused," said the Communist leader.

"I will see to that, too; I'll be home soon."

"What road are you taking?" asked Rákosi cagily.

Although I had planned to return through St. Gotthard and the British zone, I now decided that there was no need for avoiding the Russian zone, since I was innocent, and therefore told Rákosi that I would return through Vienna.

"Shall I send a car to meet you?" chirped Rákosi.

I answered: "My car is under repair right now. It might be well if a car came to meet me in Vienna in order that I may continue my trip even if this car breaks down again. But tell me why the police arrested my secretary."

"Because it developed that Kapocs is the leader of a new conspiracy," came the bland, cynical reply.

"What! How far do you fellows want to stretch this conspiracy affair?" I asked. "Until everyone is accused? Francis Kapocs has never had his hand in politics, and I consider that the police made a most serious mistake in daring to touch him. In any case, it was disloyal to arrest my secretary just prior to my return."

I denounced him for what had happened, and particularly for the outrageous arrest of Kapocs, a faithful official who passed practically every waking hour in my anteroom, whose every thought I knew, and who could have had neither the time nor the impulse to conspire with anyone.

I was very angry when I put down the receiver. The car had in the meantime arrived; however, my wife and daughter were still in town shopping for a present for little Lacika. As it later developed, the few minutes' delay became significant.

Our luggage was already in the car, and my wife and daughter, when I lit a cigarette before getting in. Just then the hotel porter came running. Francis Gordon, Hungarian envoy in Bern, was on the telephone.

"Thank Heaven I was able to reach you," Gordon began his conversation. "Foreign Minister Gyöngyösi called a few minutes ago and personally instructed me to find you anywhere and tell you that you must under no circumstances leave Swiss territory."

"What kind of request is this?" I asked. "Last night everybody wanted me to return to Budapest as soon as possible."

"I do not know the reason for this instruction, but the Foreign Minister personally requested that you remain on Swiss territory until Minister of Information Mihályfi arrives for the purpose of bringing you up to date."

"I have decided to return home," I answered Gordon. "I came to Switzerland to rest, and not to stay. I do not wish to change this position. None the less, please call up President Tildy at once, and ask his opinion of the Foreign Minister's advice. In the meantime, I will drive to Bern and you can give me Tildy's answer there. Find out all you can."

"Very well. I shall do so, call the President at once, and await your arrival."

We departed. On the long, winding drive to Bern my mind searched over and over the whole sequence of events. Now it was clear that my trip to Switzerland had been a serious blunder. It seemed to me that, if I had stayed in Budapest, they would not have dared to launch this attack. Now they had had time to get the entire apparatus of propaganda and terror in full blast before my return. The voices of my friends told me more clearly than words how deeply fear had already struck.

There was no danger of my arrest by the Hungarian police on my return. I was doubly protected by my immunity as Prime Minister and as a member of Parliament. But there was no protection or appeal against arrest by the Russians. They had done it to Kovács, and not even the protests of America and Britain had saved him. The crucial question was now whether the Russians would dare to go a step further and arrest the Prime Minister. I did not believe they would, and yet I had underestimated the ruthlessness of the Russians before. As I passed through the Russian zone of occupied Austria or through rural Hungary, they would have a chance to arrest me in secrecy or to arrange a fatal "accident."

I had thought the interest of America and Britain would at least save Béla Kovács from torture. His "confession" made this doubtful. It could be a complete fabrication; more likely that the horrible skills of the NKVD, in three long months, had broken even his great valor and ground down his strong peasant nervous system to shuddering help-lessness, ready to sign what was put before him.

I really did not know where I was bound, whether to Budapest to struggle further until they ran me over, or into exile. My heart ached at the thought that I might become a refugee. I, a plain son of the Hun-garian soil, who could not speak a single foreign language, so singu-larly Hungarian that it never had occurred to me that I might leave my home. It is harder to tempt a peasant from his home than almost anyone else. An industrial worker stands a chance of finding himself again in a foreign country through the international organizations; an educated person, through his international cultural ties; but the Hungarian peasant can leave his home only if dragged off as a prisoner of war or if he is unable to provide his family with food in his own country.

Why should I become a refugee? I, who always had sacrificed for my country, who never had entertained a single thought against the Hungarian people and had suffered through the Gestapo jails, who had fought through many silent battles for the independence and freedom of my country behind the iron curtain. I should leave my country? Peculiar are the onrushing thoughts under such emotional conditions. Why had I ever left it?

My wife suddenly called out: "Lacika! If only we had brought my little angel with us!"

I also thought of Lacika and recalled his every motion when he was tying his little car to our automobile, and his weeping face when we left him behind. Then I visioned my father: the broken old peasant whose happy moments were perhaps confined to those when he heard of my successes in public life; my wife's mother, who shared her lone-liness with my father. I saw my little house in Bisse, the vineyards, the border, the Baranya hills and the woods. Should I lose all this because I had served my country and my people honorably? Should I be ex-cluded from everything Hungarian and everything close to my soul, because I happened to be in the path of a shameless imperialism which, without regard for the happiness and peace of peoples or countries, strove only for its own primitive aims with its barbaric, primitive tools?

I thought that even slavery at home would be better than being an exile. But should I be a slave at home? I did not fear slavery; after all, the other tyrant had also imprisoned me. But I wondered what would be the political consequences of my possible subjugation.

While I tossed in a Siberian prison, what type of statements would appear in my name? I wondered what type of confessions they would attribute to my pen, to incriminate other Hungarian leaders. Death would be preferable to being a tool in the hands of those against whom I conducted the silent struggle for two years and the much misunderstood battle for my country's·independence and my people's freedom; a tool in the hands of those with whom I had grappled for the sake of cooperation, whom I never wanted to suppress but only to confine to the limits granted them by the will of the Hungarian people.

I could neither dismiss the matter nor make a decision. To go home, to go home—the sound came breaking through to my soul.

We arrived in Bern at Minister Gordon's in the evening. He told us "I spoke with the President and asked him whether he knew about Gyöngyösi's instructions. Tildy declared that Gyöngyösi called with his knowledge and consent, and that you should under no circumstances return to Hungary."

I fell to thinking. I could regard Tildy's and Gyöngyösi's message only as friendly advice intended to protect me from the greater danger. What had happened at home? Perhaps a decent self-defense was impossible.

I turned to my wife and said, "My dear, we must remain here until Mihályfi arrives."

The mother, with a fearful heart, replied, "What will happen to Lacika?"

Gordon said: "Stephen Balogh also telephoned me. He would very much like to speak with you and therefore asks that you make yourself available here tomorrow before two P.M."

"Doesn't Balogh expect me home either?"

"He seems to know about the advice you received from Gyöngyösi and Tildy."

Then Gordon tried to cheer us up: "Believe me, in this tragedy, these warnings mean good luck. Just imagine how much worse it could be if you returned in good faith and were then dragged off, like Béla Kovács. It seems to me that there is neither law nor good intent left there."

During the long night, while I listened to my wife's weeping, I went over the situation again and again. I wondered whether, and with what instrument of decent politics, it would be possible to stop the tragic trend in Hungarian developments; whether it would be possible to prevent world condemnation of Hungary; whether it would be possible to save some of the wonderful results which our people produced for the economic and spiritual rehabilitation of Hungary.

No, nothing could be done. Collaboration with the Communists made it impossible to use classical politics in any of its forms. It was impossible to obtain any results with good intentions and lofty political thoughts, either against the Communists or against the Soviet Union. We were confronted with merciless imperialists, and those who bowed their heads into slavery, who supported these politics, were used to assist further suppression in turn.

One of the greatest movements in world history was under way to try to change the ways of life of all mankind. Béla Kovács and I, two humble peasants, chanced to be in the way of the Soviet onslaught for world domination. It was an irresistible force; we—unfortunately— were not immovable bodies.

CHAPTER 89

Communist Demands for My Resignation

AFTER A SLEEPLESS NIGHT, THE DAWN OF MAY 30 BROKE. MINISTER Gordon was at my hotel by nine o'clock to report that Stephen Balogh had telephoned from Budapest at five that unbearable pressure was being exerted for my resignation. He had told Balogh that I insisted upon returning to Budapest at all costs, and asked whether I could reach Budapest unmolested. After a long silence, Balogh had answered stammeringly:

"It is possible that the Prime Minister could reach Budapest, but it is also possible that some misfortune might happen en route."

It was clear what type of misfortune Balogh had in mind. From the Enns Bridge in Austria through Vienna all the way to the Hungarian border, the road passed through the Soviet-occupied zone, and Soviet occupation of Hungary began at the Hungarian border. This was even worse than the Austrian occupation because the occupying Soviet military was supplemented by the Hungarian Communist border guard commanded by Pálfi-Oesterreicher. Various misfortunes could be arranged: the car might be involved in an "accident," or it could simply disappear, its passengers reappearing later somewhere in Russia. Or the Russians might arrest me, just as they had arrested Béla Kovács, knowing that this would have no serious consequences for them. Finally, Pálfi-Oesterreicher's Communist police might arrest me as a "dangerous conspirator," disregarding my immunities as Prime Minister and deputy.

Soon afterward, other messages from friends I could trust indicated that the situation was out of hand, and that the Russians would arrest me before I reached Budapest.

At two in the afternoon, I received a telephone call at the legation from Balogh. He said things had reached a point where my return could do no good; it would be better for me to remain in Swiss territory and resign from there, at the same time emphasizing my innocence.

"Your resignation from abroad would facilitate a quick solution of the problems the government and the Smallholders are facing, and you would spare the Hungarian people added suffering," said Balogh.

"But why do they want me to resign? Why should I? What is the charge against me?"

"You remember that you requested that Béla Kovács be placed in the hands of the Hungarian authorities," Balogh stammered. "General Sviridov now answers that they cannot surrender Kovács because their investigation is still in progress, but transmit Kovács's confession alleging that you were aware of the conspiracy; as a result, you were under serious attack in the cabinet meeting."

"But this accusation is false, and of all people Kovács knows it best of all. How can I be charged on the basis of this kind of confession?"

"Please understand, that is not the issue. There is no point in discussing it at this time. The general opinion here is that you would help the Hungarian people greatly if you would send your resignation from abroad."

I replied to Balogh: "I believe that all my life I have only wanted to serve the Hungarian people; I want to serve them now too, and if my resignation can help them I am prepared to consider the matter. The present situation is not of my making, and I have little control over it. I have been told that my little boy would be in danger if I did not act promptly. Very well, you can tell them that I will sign and deliver my resignation here under certain conditions: first, that they immediately send my little boy to Switzerland; second, that they release my secretary, Francis Kapocs, and enable him to join me; third, that Henry Hives, the chief of my cabinet, suffer no harm on his return to Hungary just because he happened to accompany me on this trip; fourth, that the news, as published in Hungary, cast no reflection on my integrity; further, that my son, on duty with the Washington legation, immediately be given leave; and finally, that there be no confiscation of my few possessions at home as if I were a traitor. I specify no political conditions because at the moment that would appear to make little sense."

"I can promise immediately that your little boy will be sent. I will communicate your other conditions to the 'authorities,' " Balogh replied.

"Tell me," I asked, "does the Hungarian public believe any of this disgusting affair?"

"You know your people. As to that, you can sleep peacefully."

Thus ended my last conversation with Budapest. Now the extortion with my child began. I maintained relations with the Hungarian government only through our envoy in Bern, Francis Gordon. My contact with the people stopped—with the country where alone I felt at home, and whose worries and cares I had accepted sixteen months earlier in order to lead it out of the most dreadful sufferings in its history. In spite of my innocence there could no longer be any question of my returning home. I knew that possible future Hungarian developments made it dangerous to let myself be tossed into prison. History made my decision and made me an exile.

The world press began to deal with the latest installment of Soviet territorial conquest. The hotel lobby was constantly filled with newspapermen who wanted to talk with me or just see me. I retired from public view, not wanting to add to the tragic sensationalism.

As I sat at the window looking over the friendly Swiss landscape, the past flitted before my mind's eye. My life appeared to have been very short. I could virtually measure time with the span of my hand or in days. Only the day before yesterday I was still a simple Hungarian peasant—one among many millions—unknown to the world; yesterday I was languishing in a German prison because I, with other men of conviction, had dared to oppose a tyrant and fight for my country's independence. Then I was chosen to head the government of my tattered country and lead the struggle to rehabilitate my people and preserve them from further oppression. Today, the helm of my country was forced from my hand and I was demoted—a refugee who could only collect his children from the different parts of the globe and seek a country where he might build a nest for them.

I wondered what the future held for me.

CHAPTER 90

The Letter Delivered

THE WORLD PRESS MADE MORE AND MORE OF OUR SITUATION; WHILE OUR anxiety turned in the direction of an insignificant small dot, so far as the world was concerned—our little boy Lacika, not quite five, whom we had left at home. My wife's suffering virtually became unbearable. Every thought of every moment of the day revolved about Lacika. Disquieting news from Budapest indicated that the authorities had made no move to send the child on his way.

They would refuse to send Lacika! They would hold him as a hostage in order that I might refrain from telling the truth! They would kill the child and claim he had died naturally of an illness! The thought which tortured my wife and me most was that they might drag Lacika off to Russia and make an anonymous Communist out of him.

From time to time Minister Gordon came and informed us of the news from Budapest; he did his best to quiet us about Lacika. Once he told us that he had heard that they were bringing Lacika by plane. At another time he said:

"Mihályfi is not coming to Switzerland, but I am sure that they will send the little boy."

"Lacika is with his grandparents, but they have already sent a car for him in order that his nurse may bring him."

"Lacika is to start tomorrow and will be here shortly."

Our restlessness multiplied.

My son telephoned to me from Washington that under the leadership of my friend the Hungarian Minister in Washington, Aladár Szegedy-Maszák, they would probably withdraw in protest; and they urged that I not resign the Prime Ministership under any circumstances. I answered that I had promised to resign if they delivered Lacika and set my secretary free.

Minister Gordon came from the legation to say that Budapest had instructed him to request me to communicate my resignation to him as the Hungarian Minister to Switzerland.

"If they satisfy my conditions," I replied.

Budapest wanted my resignation very urgently. Joseph Száll, the Communist secretary of the Bern legation, then called on me and said that Rákosi had instructed him directly to obtain my resignation and take it to Budapest; only then would the child be released.

I rejected this extortion in anger and told him I would give my letter of resignation only on Swiss territory in exchange for my child.

Minister Gordon informed me by telephone that an official communiqué had been issued by the M.T.I., the Hungarian government news agency, to the effect that I had appeared at the Hungarian legation in Bern and had resigned as Prime Minister.

"You know that is not true," I told Gordon. "I will not accept this premature announcement of my resignation, because in the end they will refuse to return my child."

Minister Gordon telephoned the President of the Republic and complained that every word of the official news agency release was false, and I had not resigned.

President Tildy said curtly that he did not interfere in practical governmental matters but had taken official cognizance of the Hungarian news agency's report that I had resigned.

"I warn you, Mr. President, that this is not true," Minister Gordon said.

Much to his surprise, Zoltán Tildy replied:

"I consider the reports of the news agency to be official and will act accordingly."

I was astounded. "Is it a fact that Tildy accepts a false report for purposes of an official act even when the accredited envoy labels that report a lie? What can have happened to Tildy? Is he being terrorized, or is he voluntarily participating in this disgraceful plot of the Communists?"

Gordon reported later a telephone call from Rákosi, instructing him to telegraph Budapest immediately to the effect that Ferenc Nagy had appeared at the legation and resigned his Prime Ministership. He had answered that he was not in a position to send such a message because Ferenc Nagy had not appeared at the legation and had not resigned.

Thereupon Rákosi, beside himself, shouted to Gordon that he must consider the instruction as a command and send the telegram at once. Gordon refused, declaring that he would not telegraph a lie; but Rákosi had his ways: the telegram was sent by a member of the staff.

Thus the new Hungarian regime was built entirely on lies. The Soviet Union lied that Kovács was a conspirator and voluntarily incriminated me, and lied about my knowledge of the conspiracy. The Communists lied in the news agency communiqué and then compelled the legation in Bern to lie.

However, the sequence of lies was not yet ended; and it was interesting to learn how the new Hungarian government was created.

The Smallholders party, being misled by the lies and now almost entirely under Communist terror, none the less tried to put in my place a man who would have some semblance of indepedence. For this reason they proposed Emery Oltványi, formerly Minister of Finance and president of the National Bank. Rákosi replied that Oltványi was not acceptable to the Soviet. The leaders of the party then designated three men, Julius Ortutay, Stephen Balogh, and Leslie Jékely, to call on Sviridov and persuade him to accept Oltványi's appointment. Ortutay had been invited to dinner by Rákosi and therefore could not go. Balogh and Jékely called on Sviridov.

"Well, who will be the new Prime Minister?" asked Sviridov cheerfully.

The conferees replied, "The Smallholders party would like to propose Emery Oltványi."

"Oltványi? A hopeless wish. You gentlemen know that Marshal Voroshilov does not like him. He removed him from the Finance Ministry, and it was on his request that Oltványi had to leave the presidency of the National Bank. How can you imagine him consenting to Oltványi's appointment?"

"The Smallholders party has no other suitable man," the conferees replied.

"Come now! Why is it necessary to go outside the cabinet for a Prime Minister? Why don't you offer it to one of the members of the cabinet?"

"Because none is suitable for the Prime Ministership."

"Not at all," said Sviridov. "Let us see, what are the names of the Smallholder ministers?"

Both Jékely and Balogh knew that the Soviet Union would like to see the spineless Dinnyés as Prime Minister and in enumerating the Smallholder ministers, deliberately forgot to mention him.

"There is still another there," said Sviridov, and pretended to rack his brain for the name. It was obvious, however, that he did not want to speak the name of Dinnyés lest he give proof of the Soviet desire that he be raised to the Prime Ministership.

"There is no one else," the conferees answered with innocent faces. Sviridov was unable to further delay revealing Soviet intentions.

"Oh, come now, there certainly is the Minister of Defense, Dinnyés."

"The Smallholders party would not accept him because it does not consider him suitable," was the reply of the Hungarians.

"Well, I will in any event communicate your desires to Marshal Voroshilov, although I am fully convinced that he will not accept Oltványi as Prime Minister. You in turn can be thinking about selecting Dinnyés."

The emissaries communicated the results to Tildy.

Next morning, two and one half days before my resignation, President Tildy agreed with Louis Dinnyés to make him Prime Minister.

Captain Gruber, Sviridov's interpreter, called on the President three hours later, and communicated the Soviet desire that Louis Dinnyés be appointed. It was a curious situation, that Sviridov, this one time, should not know that President Tildy had already agreed to appoint the person whom the Soviets had chosen. But the Communists, who wanted a semblance of legality for their coup, still needed my signed resignation, which was my one weapon left for the recovery of Lacika.

On the evening of that same day, May 31, we received word that my son Lacika had finally reached Vienna, was spending the night at the legation, and would continue on to Switzerland next day. He was accompanied by his nurse and a Communist employee of the Foreign Ministry, instructed to deliver the child in exchange for my resignation.

On the morning of June 1, I composed my letter of resignation, to be ready if my child should arrive unexpectedly and they satisfied my conditions.

That night Henry Hives, my chief of cabinet, received a friendly warning not to return to Hungary. As a result, my condition that no harm befall him after his return became superfluous. Since my son Ferenc, with his chief, the Minister in Washington, had decided to deny recognition to the new government, my condition involving him also ended. In other words, there remained but one important demand, aside from the return of Lacika: that Francis Kapocs be set free. With breaking hearts we awaited news of the arrival of my little boy, who so innocently had become an important political factor.

Late at night we received a telephone message that Lacika would reach the Swiss border the afternoon of the 2nd. By that time we were already at Versoix, in a rather simple hostelry, because we could not have borne the cost of the elegant Bern hotel for even a few days. We thus started from the shores of Lake Geneva to meet Lacika on the northeastern border of Switzerland. My resignation was ready, but I decided to surrender it only if they also satisfied my demand for the liberation of my secretary.

The big Packard car made naught of the Swiss mountains and approached Buchs at a high, even speed, as though it were traversing a plain. My wife and I had left my daughter Juliette near Lake Geneva to find an inexpensive lodging before our return, and we made the trip with Henry Hives and, from Bern on, the Communist legation secretary, Joseph Száll, who was to meet the emissary and return with him to Budapest. As we approached Buchs, my wife became increasingly nervous.

When she caught a glimpse of Lacika, just across the border, my dear wife, strong and steadfast through so many troubles, fainted; and it was some time before the kind Swiss border officials could revive her. I went forward to speak with the Communist employee from the Foreign Ministry who had brought the child. He requested my letter of resignation. I asked the man, whose name was Florian:

"Did you bring me any letter or message?"

"No, they intrusted me with nothing other than your child."

"Have they or have they not set my secretary, Francis Kapocs, free?" I asked.

"I can't answer that question. The Budapest papers did not mention it, but there have been some rumors that Kapocs has been freed." He said that his only orders were to obtain my resignation before giving me the boy.

"I conclude that my condition that they free my secretary has not been satisfied, and I therefore do not surrender my letter of resignation. However, I will give you the opportunity to call Budapest and inform them that I insist that this condition be met."

"But please, sir, that is impossible. I am required to take back the letter of resignation in exchange for the child."

"I will not discuss the matter further. You will either communicate with Budapest, or you will not receive my letter of resignation."

At this point Joseph Száll, the dwarf Communist secretary of the legation, interjected, "But that is not the agreement."

"I did not negotiate with you and therefore will not discuss the matter with you," was my answer to him.

Nervous telephoning from the booth of the border police began. Lacika began to cry in the locked automobile, which he was not allowed to leave so long as the affair was unsettled. His mother finally entered the car and sat alongside him, and I held his hand through the window—both of us trying to quiet him.

I was called to the telephone. The Bern legation was on the line. "Secretary Száll reports that you are unwilling to surrender your letter of resignation in exchange for the child, but insist upon the liberation of Kapocs. As you know, I had to discuss your staying in Switzerland with Swiss authorities, and I am obliged to tell you that from their viewpoint it is extremely inconvenient that this affair of world political significance is taking place in this small neutral country. I know that the Swiss government would not view it in a good light if you refused to deliver your resignation and defaulted while you were on Swiss territory," said Minister Gordon.

With this sentence my last weapon fell from my hands. I was unable to free Kapocs, a boy of whom I was very fond. I thought of his every word and every step. I saw before me his face, troubled or cheerful depending upon my mood and the political situation. I visualized him with his childlike attachment, correct and gentlemanly point of view, and unswerving loyalty. I told Gordon that I would respect the considerations of the Swiss government and would surrender my letter of resignation.

The Communist emissary reported that he had talked with Budapest and was told to inform me that Francis Kapocs would not be freed because he was a "dangerous conspirator."

"I will dictate an affidavit to the effect that your principals have not met my condition with reference to my secretary, which you will sign, and I will then deliver to you my letter of resignation."

The affidavit was written on the fender of the car. He signed it, and I acknowledged it.

At last, holding my child in my arms, I handed the Communist emissary my letter of resignation, the document they wanted so badly, to make their *coup d'état* "legal."

But they did not take the civilized world into account. While the Communists could extort the letter of resignation from me, world public opinion, aroused by their connivance and their methods, turned on them. In judging, present-day history ironically enough has never regarded as valid their claim to the legality of the coup, but concertedly regarded it as a stage in the Communist penetration of the world.

CHAPTER 91

Into Exile

WE DROVE OFF INTO THE FRIENDLY SWISS COUNTRYSIDE AS DUSK FELL.
Lacika was bubbling with excitement about American "yeeps." It seems that the soldiers in the American zone of Austria had somehow learned of his journey to his father. When his car stopped they surrounded him with candy and sympathy, and they gave him watchful protective escort in their jeeps all the way through the zone.

As we stopped before the small village of Wallenstadt alongside the Walensee, the proprietor of the hotel and his family greeted us like old acquaintances and offered us lodging; the Swiss army officers dining on the terrace stood up and saluted when they saw us.

Making our way to Geneva, we were greeted by simple Swiss folk everywhere. The Swiss papers had carried our photographs, and, wherever we stopped, everybody knew us and treated us like guests of Switzerland.

Luckily, from the very first moment a well-to-do Hungarian living in Switzerland came to my rescue and rented a small house for us in Geneva. It was here that we read the newspapers and listened to the radio. Good and bad news alternated.

The world press and radio reports had more meaning for me than for others. I saw the reason and purpose of every Hungarian and southeastern European event.

The most significant news was President Truman's pronouncement referring to the Hungarian government coup as an outrage. Then came the United States note to the Soviet Union, which loudly condemned the Soviet action. But there was bad news, too.

One day we were informed that Béla Kovács had died in a Soviet prison; but this report was not confirmed. Béla Kovács may be destroyed; his confessions implicating Béla Varga and me either were produced by merciless torture or were simply forgeries. If the Soviet is forced to face an international investigation, it may become necessary to destroy the principal witness to one of the most disgraceful treacheries in history, lest he repudiate the lies.

If Béla Kovács, that virile, splendid Hungarian, one of the political hopes of his country, died, then history has witnessed one of its most disgraceful murders, whether he was executed or died of suffering in prison. The Soviet is just as conscious of Béla Kovács's innocence as I, and his long detention in prison would be tantamount to murder.

The radio blared: Béla Varga, the President of the Parliament, has fled from Hungary to Austria. The report made me happy. Then came the report that Béla Varga was shot on the border trying to escape, but finally a reliable message that Béla Varga was safe in Austria.

News followed news: John Gyöngyösi was removed from the Foreign Ministership; Stephen Balogh was compelled to resign. I considered these developments natural after the preceding events. I later received confirmation that Gyöngyösi was compelled to issue a declaration against me in exchange for the promise of another post. Balogh was visited in the hospital and offered the choice between organizing a political party in opposition to the Smallholders and the Cardinal, and being arrested. He organized the required political party.

There was some encouraging news, too. First the report reached me that Aladár Szegedy-Maszák, the Hungarian Minister in Washington, with the majority of his colleagues had decided not to recognize the new government. Next day our minister in Bern, Francis Gordon, informed me that he considered the appointment of the new government illegal and was resigning. Then Béla Andaházi-Kasnya, the Minister in Ankara, with his entire staff; Paul Auer, the Minister in Paris, with most of his staff; Leslie Bartók, the Minister in Vienna; Andrew Perlaky-Kassa, the chargé d'affaires in Brussels, and Francis Rosthy-Forgách, the Minister in Prague, reported that they were dissidents and would not recognize or serve the new government. Stephen Kertész also went on leave and shortly thereafter went into exile. Only those of our diplomats who belonged to the Marxist bloc held on to their foreign service posts.

It no doubt would have been embarrassing for neutral little Switzerland for me to participate in political activities which, in view of the circumstances, would have been anti-Soviet. For that reason I decided to seek a home in the land of traditional political freedom, the United States.

The American government graciously granted the visa, and when my friends advanced the sum required to cover travel expenses we flew to the United States in order that we might settle down in exile with our three children.

I was already in Washington when news reached me that Leslie Jékely, the President's chief of cabinet, had left Hungary, supposedly to become an envoy abroad, but upon arrival in Switzerland had advised the Budapest government of his resignation. I received news also that members of the Hungarian Parliament were fleeing to Austria.

Now, Communist-oppressed Hungary was free of its last democratic government. The last obstacle to complete Communist influence was removed, and the country lost its independence before it could regain it through the peace treaty. The Hungarian people had been placed at the disposal of the Soviet and Communism. Within the span of a few days the area of Soviet totalitarian influence increased by a whole country. But this head of the predatory red hydra was already within countries to the west of Hungary, and it is only a question of time before the other countries will have their turn unless the Red monster is beheaded first. By its own resources Hungary, a small nation despite its valiant people, will never again be able to remove its neck from the Soviet yoke.

On the free soil of America, my thoughts turned to the fate of my country. The difference which separated Hungary from the other southeastern European countries, over which I watched so carefully, no longer exists. Yesterday Hungary was an involuntary satellite of National Socialist Germany; and with this coup it was forced to become a satellite of Communist Russia.

I wondered when the Hungarian nation would be allowed to live its own life; I wondered when the people would be free again to enrich the culture of mankind with its rich traditions and abilities.

The thousand-year-old tragedy continues. Hungary has always fallen into the path of some aggressor and been forced to shed its blood and dissipate its strength on behalf of foreign despots. In the fifteenth century there were just as many Hungarians living in the world as Englishmen. Today the population of the two countries can bear no comparison, and this decline was not caused by any lack of will to live but rather by the uninterrupted destruction of the storms of history.

The history of the Hungarian people has always been a struggle to survive, being crushed on the threshold of east and west. I wonder if peace will ever come, which will insure quietude for my people and end the continuous shedding of Hungarian blood and the dissipation of Hungarian resources.

The purpose of my humble efforts was to contribute to the realization of a democracy in which, after so much suppressive government, the Hungarian people would be the masters in their own land.

I have always regarded the Hungarian people as wiser than their leaders.

The Hungarian people sought to avoid the destructive wars; it was their leaders who always dragged them into danger.

In keeping with its origins, the new regime began at once with its indecencies. At the start, it pretended that my departure meant only a change of personnel in Hungary. Step by step, it became evident what was happening in Hungary. The Communist-controlled regime surrendered the country's independence and was abolishing the freedom of the Hungarian people. It converted Hungary into a satellite of the Soviet, dissolved the only freely elected Parliament in southeastern Europe, and adopted a reactionary election law along the pattern of the past century.

It prevented the meeting of the national leaders of the Smallholders party lest they defeat the election laws or wage war for the Hungarian people's freedom; it destroyed by force the only opposition political party, for which, after bitter struggle, I had obtained the Russians' permission to function. It prevented Hungarian participation in the Paris conference, where cooperation might have been established with the helpful Americans. It extended the nationalization program and compressed private property into very narrow limits, enslaved the working class, and stopped all resistance to Communist expansion.

Hungary was becoming equal to the other Soviet-dominated eastern European countries and now may be freely exploited for the further penetration of western Europe and the countries beyond the seas.

How does the Hungarian people react to all this? With the fine instinct of the patriot, it recognizes the traitors within its midst. The individual retires and, in seclusion prays for a new miracle which will deliver him from unbearable servitude, restore his country's independence and his own freedom.

And the Hungarians think wisely. If this liberation is not realized in time, then the world will suffer the attack of the new totalitarianism which puts to the test, in all aspects, the existing social order—the democratic way of life.

With their expectation of delivery from the yoke, the Hungarian people look not only to their own liberation but pray that the free peoples of the world may rescue their established way of life from the onslaught of anarchy and godlessness, and, in concert with the community of nations, lay the lasting foundation for every country's independence and every people's freedom.

PART SIX

The Iron Curtain Descends

CHAPTER 92

The Soviet Steamroller Advances

THE STRUGGLE BEHIND THE IRON CURTAIN HAS COME TO AN END. THE patriots who had struggled have died or ended in prison.

The first to flee Hungary was Béla Varga, the President of the Parliament and much beloved Catholic prelate. He was to have been arrested or carried off by the Russians.

Members of Parliament who dared to give the faintest voice to the desires of their constituents have either fled or been imprisoned.

Countless are the thousands of the poor and wealthy, the prominent and nameless, who, leaving behind their homes, their land, their social roots, took the hard trek to the safety of the west, to lands where freedom is realized, to await—sometimes in dire privation—the coming of a brighter dawn and the liberation of the Hungarian people from Soviet dictatorship.

Hungary is engulfed in the silence of death. Only the caw of the raven, the Communist political police, can be heard as it strikes another victim.

My country, sinking into the mire of destruction and decline, is not alone: all the long-suffering peoples of eastern Europe cry for peace, quiet, and the chance to live their lives undisturbed.

The struggle has come to an end in Poland, too. The leader of the peasants, the voice of the God-fearing and patriotic Polish people, former Prime Minister Stanislav Mikolajczyk, is in exile, and there is no other Polish statesman to take up the banner. Reymont's peasants are deep in the apathy of hopelessness and political impotence. Is it for this that the freedom-loving Poles bled and suffered?

There is little living strength left in the prolific, unassuming people of Rumania. Their gray-haired leader, Juliu Maniu, and his compatriots are locked in deep dungeons. Peter Groza swims happily in the tears of his people, the patriots who must dance to the tunes of Moscow as called by the resident managers of the Comintern, Emil Bodnaras and Anna Pauker.

The gay Bulgarians, who, overcoming natural hardships, developed such a promising agriculture, have no spokesman for their cause. Their exiled leader Dimitrov's worthy successor, Petkov, was put to the gallows.

The blood of the silent Serbs and Croats waters the grave of their dead liberty. Yugoslav Communism is more dreaded than Russian. Tito won from the Kremlin the honor of directing the suppressed countries of southeastern Europe as a reward for introducing the most efficient, inconceivable terror in his own land.

Czechoslovakian democracy has been dealt its death blow; President Beneš and more particularly the Czech people are paying for the secret treaty they signed with the Soviet while still enjoying the fruits of American and British support. Jan Masaryk, bearer of one of the greatest names in the history of liberty, took his own life; Eduard Beneš is a living wraith.

Finland is shrouded in the iron curtain. All the world knows is that the song of Kaleva's democratic countrymen has been silenced. One can imagine how Communist boots are trampling the freedom of this modern, cultured country; one fears that soon Scandinavia will be ground to complete subjugation.

The great strength, the ambition, the distinctive cultures and rich histories of these nations slumber under the aggression of the dark power that heeds not justice, nor morality, nor the laws of God in its mad pursuit of social and spiritual conquest. Eventually there must arise a power that will secure independence, freedom, undisturbed domestic development and happiness for all the little peoples, the world over.

In Hungary, the Soviet Union was forced to sound every note in the discordant symphony composed by the Comintern. With the removal of the stalwart guards of Hungarian self-determination, the last stage of penetration has now been reached; it is enlightening to observe the methods Moscow employs.

The government *coup d'état* in Hungary created the possibility of completely liquidating the democratic political institutions.

The better elements of the Smallholders party leadership are terrorized, while its leftists cheerfully endorse the liquidation. It was natural that the Communist-dominated Social Democrats and the radicals in the

National Peasant party should offer no obstacle to Communist plans. It became urgent for the Soviet to remove any difference between Hungary and the other eastern European countries, and it instructed the local agents of the Kremlin, the Hungarian Communist leaders, to take prompt action to complete the penetration, but preserve the semblance of democracy. The immediate Soviet assignment was changing the composition of Parliament. A Parliament in which popular democrats had the majority, and in which the Smallholders had equal representation with the other parties in the coalition, was intolerable to the Comintern.

The readjustment within the Parliament had to be preceded, however, by arrangements which would facilitate removal of any unexpected obstacles. The first of these steps was the dissolution of any organized opposition. They called upon Desider Sulyok, the leader of the opposition "Freedom party," to dissolve his party with the threat that, failing to do so, all the deputies of his group would be arrested after the dissolution of Parliament. Then they would not be protected by their parliamentary immunity.

While he was still opposing the more reactionary provisions of the new electoral law, Sulyok dissolved his party, wanting to protect the members from threatened sanctions. Thus ended the existence of the only organized opposition party immediately preceding the new elections, when there was not enough time to organize a new party. Sulyok and his deputies were forced to flee abroad.

With this step accomplished, the intimidated Parliament voted the Communist-prepared new electoral law which, in regard to civil rights, represented substantial retrogression; it provided that parties which had not been active in the 1945 elections must submit petitions bearing thousands of signatures of certified voters in order to appear on the ballot. In this way, the opposition voters were compelled to reveal their colors publicly at a time when opposition to the Communists meant imprisonment or danger of death. The new law provides further that the political parties might nominate for Parliament only persons approved by a Communist-dominated national commission; thus men with backbone could no longer be candidates.

The Communist Minister of the Interior was authorized to prepare a new list of voters. Needless to say, the opportunity was fully utilized for antidemocratic purposes. As the initial act, more than half a million voters who had supported the Smallholders party in 1945 were removed from the rolls.

The Communist provision in the new election law which afforded the greatest opportunity for falsification was the provision for "floaters"—individuals were not required to vote in the district of their residence, but could vote wherever they happened to be. In view of this, for the Communist party it was only the available transportation that limited the number of men who could vote and the number of times they repeated.

The 600-member national committee of the Smallholders party was determined to protest against this reactionary election law, but Zoltán Tildy forbade it to meet and threatened to invoke the police if it convened in spite of his prohibition.

As soon as Parliament passed the new election law, President Tildy signed the dissolution.

Tildy had been a party organizer all his life. He therefore knew that the truly democratic parties had no chance, in the face of this law, to achieve results even comparable to what they had achieved in 1945. I cannot conceive what considerations or compulsions prompted him to dissolve the lawmaking body. I well remember that earlier, when the leftist bloc hinted at dissolution, Tildy had promised me on several occasions that he would never dissolve Parliament. At all events, the dissolution of the Parliament resulted in the definitive loss of the influence of the democratic masses on the political framework of Hungary.

The election campaign was a veritable tragi-comedy. In the first place the Communists, securing themselves doubly against any unexpected show of the will of the people, and acting on the old Comintern principle of "divide and conquer," deliberately promoted the splitting up of the democratic masses. They permitted five or six different types of new citizens' parties to sponsor candidates. After the dissolution of Sulyok's party, there was not enough time to organize a new opposition party. This notwithstanding, Zoltán Pfeiffer embarked with a group on an opposition program. They could not secure local campaigners, hardly held any meetings, and spoke in only a few cities.

Stephen Barankovics was also allowed to start a political party with strong Roman Catholic aspects. Stephen Balogh, my former undersecretary, was permitted to escape imprisonment after my resignation only by promising to assist in the splitting up of the popular democracy, and he headed another group. A number of other small parties were created, but they only contributed to complete confusion.

The Minister of the Interior distributed hundreds of thousands of "floaters' ballots" to Communists who sped through the country on election day in special cars and voted in as many different communities as time and distance permitted. Zoltán Pfeiffer, the leader of the only opposition party, was so badly manhandled after a campaign address in one of the provincial towns that he was bedridden for several weeks.

All precautions had been taken to insure that Moscow's orders in regard to the readjustment of the Hungarian Parliament were carried out. The more conspicuous opposition voters were visited by Communist political policemen and warned of the probable results of their political behavior. Communists were permitted to do anything; other parties were permitted to do virtually nothing. The Communists, none the less, made abundant preparations for the falsification of the election results, in the event that these turned out to be unsatisfactory in spite of their arrangements.

The Communists, on Soviet advice, decided also that in this election they would not produce an absolute Communist majority, but instead would play the comedy of gradual growth to foreign observers; and their only aim was, as insured by the splitting technique exercised on the non-Communist parties, that the election leave the Communist party the largest single unit in the new Parliament. This was a very primitive method of blindfolding the world, so to speak, because the gradual development of the Russian Communist party, no less than the German National Socialist party, had familiarized everyone with the election management technique of dictatorships.

Characteristic of the sentiments and stamina of the Hungarian people, all these arrangements and further cheating and falsification notwithstanding, the political comedy referred to as an election still gave a majority to the bourgeoisie. The Communist party made a hurried official announcement that it received 20 per cent of the votes, compared with 17 per cent in 1945. To those familiar with the circumstances, it is clear that the Communist party actually received no more than 8 per cent of the votes, while the remaining 12 per cent was the result of multiple voting, cheating, and simple falsification.

In an unfettered election, the Communists would have suffered so complete a defeat that it would have been difficult for Russia to prove to the world its right to lean on Hungary.

All political parties which hitherto had a right to expect growth, failed in the election. The Smallholders party, which, in comparison with the 58 per cent majority, polled in 1945, received only 15 per cent of the votes, failed. The Social Democratic party also failed and received a smaller number of seats in Parliament.

Alas, the new split parties came to the front very unexpectedly. Barankovics' Roman Catholic party received most of the new votes; Pfeiffer's party represented substantial opposition strength. Even Balogh's party produced a noteworthy result, with the assistance of Emery Kovács, George Parragi, and a few other popular candidates. If Desider Sulyok had not been compelled to dissolve his already well known party, he might have gained a majority in the election. The parties of the coalition could receive a large majority only with the help of the "premium seats" they received in Parliament.

The aggressiveness of the Communists produced much dissatisfaction among the weakened parties of the coalition, and the coalition wobbled. Sviridov, official voice of Moscow, had a difficult job indeed, now, in maintaining order in the Hungarian hornets' nest. The loudest revolt occurred in the Social Democratic party, where Minister of Industry Anthony Bán and Minister of Justice Stephen Ries resigned. The Socialist-minded workers, embittered by their failure in the election, wanted to remove Szakasits, whom they regarded as a traitor, from the leadership of the party. Scandal broke out in the Smallholders party, too. The embittered leaders from the provinces broke in on a meeting of the party leaders and thrashed Prime Minister Louis Dinnyés.

Sviridov was compelled to call the leadership of the Socialist and Smallholders parties to his office daily in order to quiet the political revolt. Needless to say, on direct orders from Moscow the dissatisfied groups in both parties had to quiet down. Tildy issued a statement to the effect that he considered the results of the election "reassuring"; and this reminded me of the 1945 election when Tildy was literally frightened by the majority of the Smallholders party. In 1947 there was certainly no need for him to be alarmed by any Smallholders majority.

After the election, the cabinet was newly constituted. The Communists continued their tactics in accordance with the good book of the Comintern. They did not put a Communist at the head of the government, and let Louis Dinnyés remain as a figurehead Prime Minister; true, Dinnyés served them well and made every effort to gain Soviet confidence. It is reported that he secured the good will of Moscow, after the political parties had finally acquiesced to Hungary's taking part in the Paris discussions on the Marshall Plan, by calling on General Sviridov and complaining that even the Communist party was trying to inveigle him into a Paris trip when he was definitely opposed to it. No wonder that such far-reaching servitude produced momentary Soviet reciprocation.

The Smallholders' 50 per cent share in the government ended; it received four seats in the cabinet instead of nine. The Foreign Office portfolio was grabbed by the Communists, and they put Erik Molnár, one of their Comintern graduates, in the Foreign Ministry.

To completely terrorize the public, they decided on the creation of special courts with jurisdiction over economic matters, assigning, alongside the Communist judge appointed by the Minister of Justice, industrial workers to pass judgment in economic disputes and even invoke the death penalty. It can be readily imagined that sooner or later everyone of property may be found guilty of an economic crime.

In order that the new regime may not be disturbed even by the working class, they have taken steps necessary to curb workers who are dissatisfied. In the first place, they have abolished the worker's right of complaint. Hereafter, if the worker has any grievance, he can voice it to the Communist or, more rarely, Socialist trustee; but he cannot take his case directly to the union or the authorities.

The next step was to decree that unauthorized strikes should be punishable by imprisonment for as long as five years. A worker is permitted to strike in capitalist countries; in fact, in France, Italy, or the United States, some are obliged to strike if orders arrive from Moscow. But strikes and complaints are not permitted under Communist-dominated governments, because they disturb the economic plans of the regime, or perhaps the timetable of the Politburo in Moscow.

To be sure, before taking these steps they attempt to solicit the good will of labor by distinguishing between workers and bourgeois in the distribution of food ration coupons. The bourgeois have to pay substantially more for the rationed foods than the workers. In the distribution of the cheap food ration coupons, it is not so much a matter of occupation as political party membership.

Even more effective political steps were behind the unrestrained persecutions. First, they attacked all the Pfeiffer party's mandates in Parliament in order to eliminate the only possible opposition party. Their excuse was that the voters did not sign the party petitions in their own hand. Five hundred members of the political police were assigned to interrogate all petitioners of the Pfeiffer party, and it can be visualized what terror and threats they employed. The Communist political police are never prevented now from entering the homes of innocent citizens at any time.

Then they suddenly discovered that Pfeiffer was also a "conspirator" and began a move to suspend his parliamentary immunity. The Pfeiffer party replied with a counterpetition. The Communist political police entered his home, and confiscated all the collected documents implicating the Communists. Zoltan Pfeiffer and Leslie Acsay were compelled to flee. Immediately thereafter the mandates of the forty-nine deputies of his party were nullified and some of the deputies deprived of their parliamentary immunity by this move were arrested. Some found refuge abroad. With Pfeiffer's departure the last vestige of a parliamentary opposition ended definitely.

Charles Peyer, the venerable leader of the Social Democrats, also fled his country in dark of night—broken-hearted, after growing old with honor in championship of the laboring class, to see his party completely harnessed to the Communist yoke. The Communists had to overshadow his refusal to become a tool of Moscow; they charged him, too, with "conspiracy" and even with "espionage."

The Hungarian Communist regime sought to carry out Moscow's instructions in foreign policy as well. First, Hungary rejected the invitation to participate in the Marshall Plan discussions. Then Hungarian Communists participated in the organization of the Comintern. Next they concluded the Hungarian-Yugoslav alliance, followed by similar treaties with the other countries in the Soviet orbit.

It has become known that, on Soviet instructions, the eastern European countries are being instructed by Moscow to prepare for police collaboration. It can be well imagined what the result will be if, for example, the Yugoslav police should have the right to arrest people in other countries, interrogate and torture them. The very thought sends a chill down one's spine.

The fight of democratic labor to assert its rights ended, too, in March of this year. A Social Democratic party congress was called, but invitations were issued only to persons who could be counted upon to support unequivocally the now completely Communist-controlled party leadership. At this congress all officers who had been true and loyal to the cause of labor were removed from office, and hundreds of influential, proven party members were expelled because they showed backbone and adhered to their conviction as they tried to stem the crimson deluge from Moscow. In full observance of the Comintern's unbelievable ukase, the congress concluded by voting to end the independent existence of the Social Democratic party and become absorbed into a new Communist-led United Labor party. Thus the Social Democratic party with a record many decades old of honest standing for the Hungarian worker, respected by even its keenest opponents, ended its existence. Árpád Szakasits and his fellow traitors to labor sold the cause of Hungarian labor to the agents of Moscow and delivered the working class in the deal; as a result, the Socialist masses, in terror of persecution and the loss of their subsistence, rushed to join the ranks of the Communist party.

But the ideals of the Hungarian worker by no means accord with the Communist ideology. The Hungarian Socialists stood on the firm platform of democratic Marxism, and their banner was the creed of freedom and democracy. The forced dissolution of their party has not changed their convictions; they await the hour to chase the traitors from their ranks and restore true social democracy, with its spotless past, in their land.

The fate of the completely mutilated Smallholders party is that of a pitiable minority subsisting within the now misnamed coalition. The camp, which three years ago represented the overwhelming majority of the country, has dwindled to nonentity. The present leadership, out of contact with the people, obediently executes the bidding of Moscow and the Communists. It is characteristic of the situation that the remaining Smallholder leadership, meeting on the shore of Lake Balaton in March, decided that it would no longer await the demands of Moscow but would anticipate them by following a "progressive" political policy befitting the "developing eastern democracy." The declaration also stated that the leadership would initiate regulations for cooperative farming throughout the land to insure efficiency in agriculture, and the state would "support these cooperatives to help the individual farmers overcome the difficulties of production and disposal."

This decision actually means that the present Smallholders party is laying the groundwork for the introduction of the Soviet type of agricultural production, the kolkhoz. This scheme, which emanated a long time ago from Moscow, if put into execution would mean that soon not only the independence of the small farmers who received land through the agrarian reform will cease, but individual farming in old-time peasant patches will end. Actually, the large estate system will be revived, on which, under Communist farm management, serfdom will be the fate of the Hungarian peasant who always prided himself on his self-sufficiency and independence. The Smallholders party, the great, inspired organ of the peasantry of Hungary, will be in a more pitiable and more shameful situation than when, in 1944, the Nazis suppressed its activities.

The Hungarian peasant is retiring helplessly to the side lines; he does not support those who dissipate his freedom, but, in the peace of his villages and pastures, awaits the hour when he will be able to step forward again and direct Hungary along the correct road with his sober ideals and ingrained common sense.

The national independence of Hungary and her people's freedom are in the throes of death; the agony is the same as that of all the nations on which the Soviet has seared its brand.

Present-day Hungary has no political program because it has become an integral part of the imperialistic political program of the Soviet. There has never before been such a deep chasm between those in power and the common man.

Never could the Hungarian people be forced to tolerate so voicelessly the terror and subjugation that it bears today. But God is my witness: never in its history did the Hungarian people so resolutely prepare to shake off the dark enslavers of the nation and emerge into the light of freedom. When the day of reckoning dawns, and the life of the peoples of the world is rearranged, no people of the world will stand guard more vigilantly over liberty and true democracy than the men and women who suffered with invincible fortitude the full measure of cruel oppression from both Nazi Germany and Communist Russia— the valiant people of Hungary.

CONCLUSION

Tomorrow Bears a Better World

The cause of freedom is identified with the destinies of humanity, and in whatever part of the world it gains ground, by and by it will be a common gain to all who desire it. —Louis Kossuth

I

I FELT IT MY DUTY TO CONTRIBUTE WITH THESE PAGES TO HISTORY, FOR the edification of men far removed from the cold war, the bloodless conquests of the Union of Soviet Socialist Republics. My task will not be finished until I know that the wounds of the courageous multitudes, devoted to the cause of humanity, have been healed; not until the uncounted heroes whose fortitude and uprightness have caused them impoverishment and exile have returned to their homes, and are permitted to live in peace, shall I rest. Sincere humility is an ever-present part of a man whose recognition in public life depended on the suffering and sacrifice of the people who have chosen him their leader. It is with this thought that I end these pages. Throughout, I have avoided generalizations because the moves of the Soviet Union, and the acts themselves—their character, timing, and circumspect manner—offer facts and proofs that are writing history. But these chapters of political history, it should never be forgotten, are written with the lifeblood and self-sacrifice of the thousands of nameless who perish while building a better tomorrow.

The intelligent public of our age reads books with due criticism, a fact of which anyone who writes political history must be aware—particularly one who selects as his subject a period during which he occupied an office of responsibility.

The world is in labor; a new era is being born. Day after day, decisions are being made which dramatically influence the future of human society. The honest statesman is compelled to shoulder responsibility for his acts before the bar of world public opinion.

As a political paper, this book reflects the fight for democracy; but democracy itself depends on self-restraint—of the individual, the people, and the nation as a whole. And history can judge whether we taught the right way to democracy; for a statesman may be catapulted into high office by his momentary popularity, but his place in history is granted to him only by the unbiased tomorrow.

Questions must have arisen in the mind of the reader who has progressed this far, questions which I must not evade if I am to serve democracy well. The tragic fate of the countries and peoples of eastern Europe can only serve as an example. But constructive deductions are possible only if the questions of all who are geographically far removed from the tragic happenings and untouched by the drama, do not remain unanswered.

The citizen who has never seen his country chained and oppressed would first ask how a country could be led with the credulity which seemed to characterize Hungarian political life for two years after the last war. Did not the democratic Hungarian politicians recognize that the Soviet Union and the Communist party strove, from the very first moment, to gain absolute power?

This willingness to believe was undoubtedly a fault; one should not have believed the declarations of the Communists and the Soviet Union that they wanted to see Hungary flourish as an independent nation and the Hungarians as a free people. One should not have believed Stalin's declaration that the Soviet Union would make Hungary a shining example to prove that the great power and the small nation could live in friendship without danger to the small nation's independence. One should not have believed that the Soviet armies came to liberate Hungary, but should have realized that Stalin's oppression simply replaced Hitler's. Only through lack of knowledge about the conquering methods of the Soviet Union, and lack of experience in dealing with the dynamic force of a major world power, could one assume that Russia would tolerate the independence of small nations beyond its borders; that the Communist party would conform to our laws and respect our constitution. We believed because we saw that the American and British governments trusted the Soviet.

Standing before the bar of history, and facing judgment by current public opinion, I am ready and eager to admit my own credulity if all those leaders and statesmen will join me who had more to resist with, and who had to chance less danger to their countries and peoples.

Nearly all of us, the "inexperienced" and "credulous" leaders of the small nations of Europe, were misled.

If we believed for a moment that the Soviet Union would pursue a just policy, or that the Communist party would accept the will of the people as expressed in the popular vote, it was because the Soviet first appeared before us as a member of that great alliance of nations bound together to defeat Nazism and Fascism. It had signed agreements to reorganize the world and insure the independence of small peoples; it had determined policies for the reconstruction and control of defeated countries. One wonders if, when the Atlantic Charter was established and signed, the great Western powers believed that the Soviet Union would serve the great ideals of freedom and justice as well as would its allies. Or would the Yalta agreement have been signed had the United States and Great Britain known that the Soviet Union was bent on suppression, rather than independence, of the small nations? Would the Western democracies have signed the armistice agreements with the Russians and the defeated countries had they known that the Soviet Union would trespass on them, interpret them according to its own wishes, and disregard them at its own pleasure?

We knew well that, despite bilateral agreements about treatment of the defeated nations, the armed occupying power would have a stronger influence on the life of the occupied country than the powers geographically far removed. We were prepared for the occupying power to assert a closer interest in the daily internal affairs of the country than the other powers. But we thought that guarantees of the independence of Hungary and its people's liberty were securely vested in the solemn treaties signed by the great powers themselves.

If political timidity when facing an overwhelming power (like the timidity of the individual confronted by a brigand's gun) is laid against me, I am ready to plead, *Nolo contendere*.

The great Western powers did not call Soviet Russia to account for her transgressions on international treaties. Obviously, then, we could not be expected to draw attention to the infringements upon our constitution by Voroshilov, Sviridov, or Pushkin. Diminutive Hungary could not afford to defy the mighty USSR.

Frankly, our trust lay in the international agreements to safeguard the future of small peoples, where for a long time we saw our own security guaranteed—a fact well known to everyone. We lived in the hope that Soviet intrusion into our daily life would end with the termination of military occupation. The realization of the social and political freedoms prescribed by the international agreements would follow, we thought; once full national sovereignty was regained, we could cope with the Communist minority intent on retarding our freedom.

If the leaders of Hungarian political life believed during the first postwar months in the great international agreements, then they must have discovered soon that both the Soviet Union and the Communist party were pursuing a policy contrary to these agreements. Why, then, did they not take a firm stand on resistance directly these indications were recognized? But here again we must establish the parallel. True, the Smallholders party and its leaders continued cooperation after they found resistance of no avail; but it is also true that the subjugation and oppression of the peoples and countries of eastern Europe, and the brazen violation of the international treaties, had begun years earlier—and the Western democracies had taken no firm stand against these transgressions until March of this year! The Smallholders party was forced to continue the policy of cooperation after the first illegal steps of the Communists. The Western democracies signed the treaty with the Soviet Union in Potsdam in July of 1945, despite the fact that observers of international relations had ample opportunity to realize that the Soviet was busily breaking the previously signed treaties. The necessity for overlooking the illegalities and maintaining cooperation was stronger in Hungary than among the great powers.

But why did the Smallholders grant concessions to the Communist party, and why dared it not observe a sharp distinction between enforced patience and the policy of concession? This question is answered by the fact that two long difficult years of Hungarian political life were characterized by compulsion rather than concession. Until May of 1947, in the face of severe handicaps and brazen Soviet aggression, Hungary remained more independent than any other country occupied by the Soviet Union or in its sphere of influence. The difference between Hungary and the other defeated nations has been significantly obvious; concessions became more frequent as our trust in the guarantees of international agreements waned. We strove toward a condition in which the independence of our nation could be achieved. Our aim was the signing of a peace treaty, and we could therefore never lose sight of the necessity for remaining in a situation proper to a prospective signer. Civil war, a recurrent danger, had to be avoided. Our concessions were made under duress greater than any faced by Russia's allies, who, even at the peace table, made concessions to her without being under compulsion to do so. If one analyzes the results of the peace conference, this fact becomes clear; one can only conclude that the viewpoint of the Soviet dominated decisions pertaining to the fate of the defeated nations.

If the great Western powers meant to secure present-day world peace with ceaseless concessions to the Soviet Union, it is certainly much more understandable that a small nation like Hungary, suffering under Soviet occupation, had to grant, unwillingly, certain concessions to preserve tranquillity within her borders.

These pages reveal how the policy during the second half of my premiership was characterized by a race with time—and we could not control time. If peace could have been settled before March of 1946, before the Soviet Union's economic demands forced the Smallholders party to mutilate itself, the situation would have developed far differently. In 1945 the victorious flag of the Smallholders was not rent by political storms; we were strong enough to control consolidation after our sovereignty had been regained. But during this time the force behind the Soviet Union's eastern European program was still veiled, until the situation should become more advantageous. Between the signing of the peace treaty and its ratification, the Soviet became openly aggressive. As support from the democratic West would not increase, our resistance became increasingly difficult and, finally, impossible.

Our country, Hungary, bled by war and its aftermath, humiliated and robbed during the German occupation, and practically destroyed by battles and the conquering armies of the Soviet Union, lacked the great strength needed for a show of might against Communism. But, had Hungary received encouragement and an assurance of future security, she would have attempted even this. World politics, saturated with the spirit of consolidation, offered my people no support which might have enabled them to translate spiritual resoluteness into concrete action.

We raced against time toward the goal of regaining national sovereignty; the Smallholders hopefully, and the Communists fearfully looked to the moment when the peace treaty would become effective and Soviet military occupation cease. The Soviet Union could then support the Communists only by using secret organizations instead of an armed force stationed within the country.

The West could easily have supported us: Great Britain might have exerted her influence on the Hungarian Social Democrats to make them act as a brake on the Communist onsurge. The efforts of the great Western powers should have united toward an early signing of the peace treaty. Had the peace treaty been ratified as early as possible, world affairs might have been reorganized before the democratic elements in Hungary lost their initial strength.

The ordinary citizen, reared and educated in a free democracy, more familiar with classic and orderly political contests than with the ruthless politics of a dictatorship, may ask why, if the democratic leaders of Hungary saw the increase of terror and illegality, they did not openly seek support from world public opinion for their policies. Why did they not herald democracy's injuries to the world, and so force the great Western powers to take a decisive stand?

The armistice agreement, of course, provided for joint Allied control of the defeated countries. The American and British representatives sat next to the Russian on the Control Commission, and while the latter had undisputed control America and Britain had establishments adequate for keeping them informed. Members of the American and British control staffs traveled through the land, heard the complaints, and saw clearly the developments in Hungarian political life; but, lest the attitude or behavior of these representatives give any hint that the Hungarian government might take its grievances to the United States or Great Britain, the Soviet president of the Control Commission ordered that our government maintain contact with American and British representatives only through him. In practice, this meant that in every step the Hungarian government could reach the American and British members of the commission only through the Soviet president, and they, in turn, could speak officially to the Hungarian government only through Marshal Voroshilov or, later, Sviridov. The Hungarian government had to recognize that this condition was tolerated by the Americans and the British. Could we extricate ourselves from such an order when it was docilely tolerated by the Allied representatives?

Naturally, we circumvented this order wherever and whenever we could. An example was the survey of economic conditions prepared by Finance Minister Gordon in response to an American suggestion. We circumvented the Soviet directive by delivering copies to all three powers simultaneously. Although Voroshilov threw it back without consideration, we expected the two Western powers to put it on the agenda.

Frankly, the failure of the report to come up for consideration hardly enhanced our feeling of security.

Had we turned to the Western public for a hearing, the Soviet Union would have regarded the act as tantamount to a declaration of war. Such a step would have been precarious at best, since we had no one to whom we could look for support.

In drawing a parallel between the world political scene and the occurrences in Hungary I am not trying to lay the blame for Hungary's tragedy on world developments; but I cannot allow our political leaders to be blamed for a situation caused by factors beyond our control. We used the slightest signs of interest by the Western powers to solidify Hungarian democratic politics. When in March, 1947, during the interparty negotiations, I refused the demands of the Communists (in fact presented counterdemands) a very revered figure in the former political life of Hungary asked me if our refusal to satisfy these meant a strengthening of the political stand of the Smallholders. I replied that two notes addressed by the United States and Great Britain to the Soviet Union in connection with the abduction of Béla Kovács seemed to indicate that interest in the affairs of Hungary is on the increase, and naturally I wished to use this to strengthen the political policy of the Smallholders party.

"If a break between us and the Communists had occurred six months earlier the Western powers, after expressing their sincere regrets, would have done nothing to prevent tragic developments. I think these notes indicate possible Western aid if Soviet Communism tries to destroy us," I said.

In the light of events of the past years, it is obvious that the struggle of the Hungarian government against the rising Soviet audacity delayed the ruthless ambitions of both the Communists and the Soviet Union, in Hungary. I willingly accept the responsibility for delay because, for more than two years, the Smallholders governing in Hungary stemmed the tide of Communist conquest. The Magyar people, glorious despite defeat and humiliation, Soviet terror and lies, adhered to their innate conviction that a political idea based on godlessness can never triumph over entire nations. The Hungarians consecrated these convictions with their lives and strength; their chief ally has been hope and the determination of men and nations to resist dictatorship.

Developments in eastern Europe revealed the universality of the

Soviet master plan; every one of the countries in the Russian orbit was reduced to vassalage, by one means or another. Despite various attempts by political leaders of each of these countries to preserve their nations' independence, it became obvious that the brazen plot of the Comintern against their national life was executed according to preconceived plan and regardless of any of the policies followed by the country's leaders. The fact that some of the nations were not defeated enemies, but allies, did not save them from subjugation. And if the "allies," safe from Russian military occupation, could not resist Soviet conquest, then certainly Hungary, defeated and occupied, made a respectable show of moral strength.

Responsibility for the events in Europe and the policies pursued throughout the world after the defeat of the Axis powers cannot be determined until the present situation is resolved and world affairs have been rearranged. The coming great drama on the stage of world politics arises from the failure to finish the last act of the Second World War; and the performance of the individual nation and its statesman will be judged in the light of the entire world crisis.

I know well that the responsibility issue embraces not only the question of the country's independence, but also the internal political and economic reforms of the years following the war. One must answer the great ideological questions as well as those involving more specific issues. The first such question is whether it was right to exchange, almost with revolutionary speed, the old regime for representatives of the oppressed classes of society, the peasantry and labor.

Undoubtedly, some excesses occurred under the radical influence of the Soviet-Communist combine. But I approve of the principle, and will firmly defend it in the future, that political leadership should have been revitalized by the peasantry and labor. Had there been a true democracy in Hungary after the First World War, had the will of the people found expression, the representatives of the peasantry and labor would have received places in the government of their country, the political and economic development would have proceeded on a healthier plane, and the country could more easily have evaded entry into the Second World War. After the second war, democracy could not begin on the declarations of the old regime but needed new men and new decisiveness. The displacement did not take place according to social position; the Smallholders opened the political ranks to aristocrats. ministers of the Gospel and old-time civil servants if their ideas met with the demands of progress and the aims of the peasantry, on whom the people have depended for their security and the security of coming generations. The great political questions melted the different strata of the Smallholders party to such an extent that the adherents of radical progress and conservative resistance emerged as much from our peasant group as from the other classes. A democratic nation would commit a grave mistake if it permitted the administration of its life, happiness, and future again to be placed in the hands of a "chosen" minority. Instead of placing the peasantry in a position where it would be responsible for the affairs of the country, this would relegate it to subservience. We believed, in 1945, that every class of society must bear part of the responsibility for government. No future event must challenge the justice of this conception.

Another major question is whether it was wise to countenance the great economic measures, such as agrarian reform and the extension of the rights of labor. It is my belief that it was wise to execute these measures, for which the Hungarian people had clamored for decades.

While there was a necessity for agrarian reform and the strengthening of the institutions of labor, there was no necessity for the excesses which accompanied these reforms; there was no necessity for taking away the last patch of land from every man who owned more than a thousand acres; there was no necessity for workers' committees to intrude into matters of factory production, just as there was no necessity for giving to the trade unions the rights and character of a political party. But it was absolutely necessary to enable the Hungarian people to gain land and end the exaggerated political influence of the large landowner class. It was necessary for its welfare that productive labor have its own organ to control and support it, and that it be able to rely on the trade unions in questions of wages and hours. Wise minds would never undo or restrict these progressive steps, once the affairs of the world should be brought into order. To the contrary, all must strive to endow the large working class with lasting security and provide the basis for continued undisturbed creative activity.

The right of man to live in peace, to strive and work for his own better future, and that of the community, must never be infringed. On the peace, security, and independence of the little peoples depends the security of the peoples of the great nations.

In general, while it would be wise to reconsider all measures taken against the will of the people, political sagacity dictates that those reforms of which the people approve should be retained. But as the policy of suppression is more prevalent today than ever before, there is a necessity for many reforms to insure civil liberties, the national independence, the democratic mode of life, and the control of the citizen over his country.

The distortions of the internal political life were also caused by Soviet-Communist influence. The Hungarian people's healthy instinct would have justly influenced the trend of internal politics had not armed might forced them off the right road.

I stand ready at all times to shoulder responsibility for extending the political and economic rights of the Hungarian people, as I gladly assume responsibility for my part in my country's policy, and I hope that all those who had a share in shaping the destiny of Hungary will be ready to shoulder their share. Nevertheless, the reincarnation of democratic political life should not be begun with finding political scapegoats.

But I must be emphatic on one point: never must those who order world affairs place blame for the history of these years on the Hungarian people. Geographically far removed from the West, the Magyar bears the standard of democracy—for generations he strove to gain and preserve his national freedom; on every occasion he has resisted subjugation. He showed his resistance in the unfettered elections of 1945, in the municipal balloting in the capital, and even dared to show it in the elections of 1947, which were governed by Communist terror. Clearly and consistently the Hungarian people adhered to democracy. A crime was committed by the subjugating terror of the Soviet Union; mistakes were made by the great democratic powers in failing to offer aid; errors were made by the country's leaders. We thus have to shoulder the practical and historical responsibility, but no one has the right to punish or hold responsible the strong-hearted people of Hungary.

II

At the time of this writing, Hungary, like all other eastern European states, has not yet been legally incorporated into the Union of Soviet Socialist Republics; but its independence has ceased completely. Louis Kossuth wrote in his letter, on the occasion of the unveiling of the monument to the martyrs of 1849, that Hungary was a nation but not a state. This definition fits the present situation well.

Since Hungary, in unison with the other eastern European countries, refused to take part in the discussions of the Marshall Plan in Paris, it has made not a single independent move. Prodigious treason is being committed in the government of the country, resulting simply from the fact that the men in control at present are spiritually closer to the Soviet Union than to Hungary. In practice the country is governed by Mathias Rákosi with a handful of Comintern trainees from Moscow, whose ideology has nothing in common with that of the Hungarian people, and in whose life such experiences as their Comintern education, the Spanish Civil War, and the undermining of the internal structure of other countries mean more than spiritual attachment to Hungarian ideology.

According to the political ethics of the Hungarian people, a patriot's love for his country must increase as he rises in public office. The example of the leader strengthens love of country and readiness to sacrifice. Every true Hungarian knows the Communist leader does not love Hungary; that if there ever was such a feeling in his heart, it has been supplanted by the idea of the world revolution. How could the Hungarian expect him to lead the fight for the country's independence and the freedom of its people? The cynicism and hypocrisy of the Communist leaders increasingly embitters the Hungarian people; they observe powerlessly while a small minority tightens its stranglehold on the nation as the minority grows further away from it spiritually. The Hungarian, dedicated to democracy and a Christian world concept, seeing himself abandoned by the great powers and left to suffer as a helpless prey in the net of tyranny, watches discouragedly while these same great democracies commit themselves now to save democratic institutions in countries in which Communism has a much larger camp.

In the eastern European countries, in general, the proportion of Communists has never been more than 15 per cent, including the merely opportunist following. How much more expedient to save those nations for world democracy, than expend so much more effort on western European countries where elections made the Communist party the strongest unit in their respective political lives! If Hungary and the eastern European countries had received even a tiny share of the support which is now granted by the people of the United States to western Europe, then popular democracy could have victoriously resisted the Communist efforts at subjugation. Present results could have been accomplished by the Soviet Union only through overt acts of armed intervention.

With the subjugation of eastern Europe the last illusions about the aims of Moscow have been dispelled. The struggle against the Communist onsurge has assumed a world-wide character; it has become a political problem of the entire world.

Had the small nations of eastern Europe been saved, with negligible economic sacrifice but political firmness, with the international agreements, the bastions defending the democracy of the world would not be in western Europe but would still be on the frontiers of Soviet Russia's immediate neighbors. Under these conditions the program of the Comintern for the conquest of the world would still be forced to conform to Soviet Russia's role of loyal ally. The Soviet Union needed eastern Europe, not for its own security, but as an advance base for its assault on the world.

Public opinion of the world has recognized by now that eastern Europe was too easily abandoned. This issue is not raised with intent to heap reproach upon reproach, but to call attention to the dangers inherent in the repetition of tragic mistakes which involve the fate and happiness of hundreds of millions of people. The abandonment of the eastern European countries has, by its consequences, reaffirmed the eternal truth of the past—Europe is one and indivisible. A lasting partition of Europe could never become the basis, nor should it be permitted to become a condition, of the peace of the world. History has judged this issue.

As the Soviet recognizes no limits to its power, Communist conquest hovers over western Europe. Manifold are the methods of the Comintern to gain ground, methods the civilized world abhors: systematic undermining of democratic society, the constant creation of internal tension to keep the democratic citizen suspended in uncertainty. Its ultimate aim is collapse of the internal political structure amidst the turmoil of constant fear, thus making the people ripe for bloodless conquest. But there is also the ever present chance of a minority revolution in all the countries of the world—planned, fed, and fostered by the Comintern in Moscow.

No one could conceive of organizing the entire continent into an anti-Communist camp, for in the East the Soviet Union is the unequivocal master. The "Western Union" of European states, created to resist the brazenly avowed aim of the Comintern to seize power, will give new hope to the liberty-loving peoples behind the Iron Curtain. However, it is only a temporary expedient and cannot be sustained, for this would mean a division of Europe and a gradual devitalization of the continent. In reenforcing and marshaling the strength of western Europe, it must be clearly recognized that a defensive policy against the Soviet Union's dynamic thrust is destined to defeat; only a policy intent on liberation and designed to insure an ultimately united Europe could successfully confront the Soviet Union.

Communism has become a universal problem, solvable only through the creation of a new world. To hold the solution of this vast problem in abeyance jeopardizes our entire civilization and its moral, social, political, and economic accomplishments, gained by the unique capacities of free democratic society. Action is needed, or we may never regain control over our destiny. The political leadership of the world bears the heritage of past generations who strove and sacrificed to eliminate the dangers inherent in the Communist ideology of despotism and execute a program insuring the peace and tranquillity of mankind.

The evasion of issues does not promote constructive political activity. The question of the independence of the eastern European nations has been diligently avoided in all of the recent international negotiations, obviously because no one could chart a peaceful route to their liberation. At the Moscow conference, the London conference, and at the different meetings of the United Nations, every question was touched upon except those involving the peoples enslaved and nations subjugated by the Soviet Union. One deduces from this reluctance that, once the decision to create a new comity of nations has ripened, the much feared and avoided problem of the peoples of eastern Europe will have to be faced first.

Contrary to every optimistic declaration, it could hardly be expected that the threat of Communism would be removed by peaceful means. The voice of those who speak of the possibility of avoiding war wavers. It can be assumed that, aside from the Soviet, no one desires war. But certainly the free peoples would endure even an armed conflict to eliminate constant dread and secure their freedom.

The politician who announces, while freedom touches the rim of the abyss, that peace and prosperity can be secured only through further concessions, by stepping out of the way of the terror-bent Communist conquerors, and by abstaining from those preparations which are necessary to secure the freedom of the world and the tranquillity of mankind, is trusting in the ignorance and naïveté of public opinion.

This policy would lead to the loss of freedom, and to the spread of Asiatic poverty and misery over the entire earth. Such a conception, even if confined to the internal political structure of one country, could not be excused from international judgment because the expectations and hopes of all peoples of the world are bound to the decisions of that country in which such declarations have been voiced. Without creating a new world political constellation, eliminating the force intent on conquest, peace and prosperity cannot be secured in any part of the world.

Laboring citizens the world over, especially the American citizen, who up to now has been far removed from physical danger, often ask if a new war, and the subsequent rearrangement of the earth, would really bring lasting peace and mutual understanding among the long-suffering nations. The war against National Socialism also began with the purpose of eliminating tyranny forever and establishing everlasting peace. Now we face a new danger, and now we stand on the threshold of a new conflict.

The danger of German National Socialism did not unite all the free nations of the world—not even all the peoples of eastern Europe, until it was too late. However, Communism has no drawing power for any nation; its dangers, universally recognized, are creating unified viewpoints, aims, and endeavors in all the peoples of the world longing for freedom and tranquillity.

In every one of the majority parties of the eastern European countries, the decision to build a truly democratic form of life took shape. The desire to be free of Communism and establish a secure basis for liberty through majority rule, has become universal.

During my premiership, I once asked a prominent American why, in the great propaganda battle of the political ideologies, democracy did not exert force comparable to Russia's on behalf of her ideals. The countries of traditional democracy did not vie vocally with National Socialist propaganda; silently they tolerated the Communist propaganda, too. Why did not democracy emphasize, throughout the world, its own superiority with every means at its disposal? My American friend replied that democracy, by its very nature, cannot laud itself. It must develop by itself in each nation according to the specific characteristics of that very nation.

This may be right, but it must be recognized that up to now the urge for democracy has been actually fostered by the behavior of the Communists themselves. Today there is no people which does not desire to share in the democratic form of life.

Humanity's road from today's chaos to the peacefulness of a new tomorrow may lead through ruin and bloodshed, but a world democracy is just over the horizon. Therefore, plans must be drawn, not only for the strategic and tactical means of conquering the crisis, but also for the foundation of a universally free and democratic form of life.

The ideal insurance for permanent peace and security is a condition in which each independent nation lives in an essentially identical political and economic order, differentiated only by the traditions and characteristics of its people.

In my exile, people from nearly every country in the world have sought contact with me; letters reach me from the most diversified strata of society; both professional and laboring classes write. They are not officials, and their expressions of opinion are not restricted by public responsibilities. It appears that every honest working man is imbued with the same wholehearted yearning; tranquillity, freedom, and security are the core of everyone's prayer. People the world over await the settling of accounts with the peace-shattering, freedom-killing onsurge of Communism. The Canadian farmer, the Japanese student, the Australian tradesman, the Danish laborer, the German widow and the Dutch merchant have the same wish as the Hungarian peasant: that the foundation for a new world shall be laid in which men may enjoy, in freedom, the fruits of their labor.

A new world must be born, and its guiding ideals must soon be shaped. The method of rearrangement must be planned and executed as carefully and purposefully as Communism executes its own destructive program. History gives the political leaders of the democratic world powers a serious, but probably never returning, opportunity to create the greatest political structure of the ages. The political, military, and economic leaders of our age must think in world terms, because the slightest personal or national narrow-mindedness could yield no end of vengeance.

The leadership in world reconstruction is vested in the United States; international developments have created an entirely new situation for the American citizen. In the coming great crisis America will not appear as a supporting power, but as the country charged with the initiative and direction.

In the clash of the contrary doctrines of two social orders, Communism has only one great adversary—the United States. That is why the hopes of all the peoples of the world concentrate on Washington. As America eliminates Communism from human society, and as she personifies living democracy in the dreams of the peoples of the world, she must remain at the helm in traveling the difficult seas of world reconstruction. If the cause of the subjugated nations of Europe, their rehabilitation and readjustment, were left to the other powers, the ensuing partiality would be difficult to eliminate, and the required objectivity could not be assured. The United States is above petty dickering between the European nations or their relationships to nations abroad. The United States is least likely to make the small nations its dependents. It would be a grave mistake for America to abdicate, with a noble gesture, her right of rearrangement after the crisis has been overcome, and thus leave the field open for selfish, partial, or shortsighted power politics.

The primary object of world reconstruction must be the insurance of freedom and mutual respect to all nations; to achieve this, all *cordons sanitaires* must be forever abolished. No power, claiming defense of its own security, should ever have the right to force its own selfish will upon another nation. If the leading political thought in each country were respect for the freedom of all peoples, there would be no necessity for such safety zones. Men and nations must realize that love of liberty is intrinsic in the human soul; nothing that threatens liberty must be allowed to exist.

It is unfortunate that in a century of great material progress the holy vision of universal liberty has not yet become the supreme law; but, so long as there is one spot in the world where it is a crime to express an opinion, where innocent persons fill the prisons instead of criminals, where the suppressed man may not claim redress, where the socially select and political parties toss the government between them like a ball—the fight must continue.

Only that nation deserves its independence which can both secure civil liberties for its own citizens and respect the liberties of other nations. That government alone deserves support which fears not the freedom of its own people.

Progress is the most important principle in the rearrangement of affairs. There must be no opportunity for the wheel of progress to be turned backward. It would be a sin against human evolution to erect a wall against progress, preserving outdated social and political forms. One world crisis after another has cast an inconceivable load on the working classes, particularly labor and the peasantry.

Not only must they sacrifice their blood and bear increased economic and physical hardship, but the largest strata of society must rally to the defense of their own political convictions. These people awoke to their responsibilities when their country's structure broke down; they have met the challenge and are no longer willing to let a chosen class arrange their destiny. They refuse to resign their right to influence the affairs of the nation.

Historical classes emerged strong from the crisis: peasantry, labor, and the white-collar citizenry. The majority, sensible, freethinking, and uncompromised, is ambitious to begin building a happy and contented nation, with the opportunity for creative accomplishments, a high standard of living, and increased popular education. These classes, entering the political life of the world fresh and unspoiled, would never yield their nation's independence but wish to reconcile tradition and progress so that the comity of nations may be enriched by the treasures which history, culture, and ingenuity can produce.

The great sacrifices of the present generation will bear fruit only if true democracy embraces the entire world.

The new world cannot be born according to the law of the swing of the pendulum; just because today it has swung too far to the left, tomorrow cannot see a shift to the extreme right. There is just as little democracy on the extreme right as there is on the extreme left. Our generation, with great sacrifice and unforgettable suffering, has broken the tyranny of the supernationalist movements of the extreme right, Fascism; and it may be able to free itself, only with comparable sacrifices, from the tyrannical Communism of the extreme left. For this reason no road toward extremism should be opened in international or national politics. Revenge cannot be the cornerstone of true social and political readjustment, and a new order cannot be built on the punishment of the masses. In most countries of the European continent both National Socialism and Communism have resulted in mass human extermination, and reconstruction cannot be begun on a policy of vengeance. After the guilty are punished, the misled masses must be depoliticized. In the new world order, the masses must have no opportunity or occasion to go astray politically.

In the plan for a new world, the great idea of a federation of the peoples of Europe must have a prominent place. A form of cooperation must be found which will not be detrimental to the character of the nations, will not lessen their patriotic fervor and consciousness of their true independence, but will give security for the peace of the peoples, enhance their economic progress, and encourage the development of social justice and culture. There can be no two European federations. Historically, economically, and culturally, Europe is one and indivisible; the old historical dividing lines must be diminished, and no new insurmountable divisions must be erected. More opportunities must be given for a fellowship of the nationalities. Conservative political thought before the great war did not consider it necessary to promote intercourse between the peoples, and in the latter years the different forced alliances prevented any such development; today Soviet oppression prevents it. If the simple people of the different nationalities learn to know, respect, and grow fond of one another, it will be easier to create a political unit that might be the cornerstone of a *United States of Europe.*

The people, driven through common danger into common action, must assert politically that duty which was shouldered by humanity two thousand years ago in the creation and defense of the Christian world order. If the democracies of the world, besides being freedom-conscious, build on the firm basis of Christianity, if the leading statesmen of the world, aside from recognizing the political laws, will pay heed to the law of God, the creation of that new world may be perfect. In a great part of the world there is a crisis in human decency and brotherly love; the biblical precept, "Bear ye one another's burdens," is ignored. We must be watchful that these ideals are not destroyed, because humanity will be poorer and bleaker if the eternal godliness is eliminated from the life of nations.

A new world must be born in which man will be free and happy; humanity has reached the last barrier which separates it from this new world.

As I walk the Virginia furrows, the glowing vision of Hungary in this new world appears. I know that soon the time will come when I shall bend my knee and kiss that sacred American soil, and thank it for having given bread to my family and respect to me. Then I shall turn my steps home, to my Hungarian people, to shoulder humbly new cares and new burdens, and build with my modest strength, on the spiritual and physical ruins—a new nation.

Index

Acheson, Dean, 226 ff.
Acsády, *History of Hungarian Serfdom*, 18
Acsay, Leslie, 440
Adam, Eugene, 167
Ágoston, *Hungarian Secular Land Ownership*, 18,
Agrarian Reform, execution of, 111 f., 198, 286, 330 f., 441; old plans for, 14 f., 107-109; Soviet-dictated decree, 110-112
Allied Control Commission, 72, 92, 101 f., 200 f., 220 f., 230, 242, 267, 269 f., 275, 281, 297, 300, 315, 317 f., 363, 371, 375, 396, 448; cost of, 105-107, 395; misuse by Russians, 102, 105-107, 113, 114, 159-194 *passim*, 252-255
American envoy, 204, 220 ff., 225, 275, 411
American Legation, 172, 220 f., 225, 375
American principles, 233 f.
American system, 233 f.
Andaházi-Kasnya, Béla, 427
Anderson, Secretary of Agriculture Clinton P., 230
András, Gen. Alexander, 321
Andrássy, Daniel, 243 f.
Antall, Minister Joseph, 47 f., 121, 164, 181
Antall, Joseph, 164, 239 f., 286
Anti-Semitism, 37, 44 f., 190, 196, 245-249
Appeasement, effects of, 170, 223, 241 f.
Arany, Valentine, 311, 314, 320, 321, 331, 346, 348, 360, 380
Arlberg, 407
Armistice agreements, 162, 249, 373; effects of, 101-103, 115, 124 f., 134 f., 204, 209, 219, 241, 255, 445; of 1944

(Moscow), 73, 92, 213; of 1945, 100-103, 115, 124, 134, 204, 209, 219, 237, 240
Arrow Cross, 36 ff., 50-56 *passim*, 62, 79 ff., 84, 87, 98, 100, 113, 145, 170, 190, 196, 199 f., 226, 246, 249, 265, 285, 311, 323, 392
Association of Agricultural Workers and Small Landowners (Communist-controlled), 334
Association of New Landholders (Communist-controlled), 334
Atheneum, publishing house, 59
Atlantic Charter, 135, 273, 445
Attlee, Prime Minister Clement, 235
Auer, Paul, 427
Austria, 33, 100, 208, 358, 360, 381, 407, 417, 426 f.

"B list" commissions, 169, 184 f., 223, 254 f., 260 f., 276, 348
Bajcsy-Zsilinszky, Andrew, 39, 41 f., 46, 49, 52, 182
Balaton, Lake, 80
Balatonboglár, 26
Bálint, Alexander, 333
Balla, Anthony, 164, 182
Balogh, Stephen, 73, 76 f., 137, 238, 283, 329, 339, 382 f., 389, 391, 404, 406, 410, 416, 417 ff., 422, 427, 436
Bán, Anthony, 60, 84, 122, 136 f., 164, 180 f., 265 f., 395, 438
Báno, Capt., 117
Barankovics, Stephen, 436, 438
Baranya, county of, 3, 25, 45 f., 55, 62, 64, 74, 93, 118, 121, 141, 180, 389, 415
Baranyai, Leopold, 46, 49
Bárányos, Charles, 164, 181, 258, 280 ff., 302

463